The Futility of Philosophical Ethics

Also available from Bloomsbury

Ethics after Wittgenstein, edited by Richard Amesbury and Hartmut von Sass
Michael Slote Encountering Chinese Philosophy, edited by Yong Huang
Nietzsche's 'Ecce Homo' and the Revaluation of All Values, by Thomas H. Brobjer
The Aesthetic in Kant, by James Kirwan
The History and Ethics of Authenticity, by Kyle Michael James Shuttleworth

The Futility of Philosophical Ethics

Metaethics and the Grounds of Moral Feeling

James Kirwan

BLOOMSBURY ACADEMIC
LONDON • NEW YORK • OXFORD • NEW DELHI • SYDNEY

BLOOMSBURY ACADEMIC
Bloomsbury Publishing Plc
50 Bedford Square, London, WC1B 3DP, UK
1385 Broadway, New York, NY 10018, USA
29 Earlsfort Terrace, Dublin 2, Ireland

BLOOMSBURY, BLOOMSBURY ACADEMIC and the Diana logo are trademarks
of Bloomsbury Publishing Plc

First published in Great Britain 2022
This paperback edition published 2023

Copyright © James Kirwan, 2022

James Kirwan has asserted his right under the Copyright, Designs and Patents Act, 1988,
to be identified as Author of this work.

For legal purposes the Acknowledgements on p. vi constitute an extension
of this copyright page.

Cover design by Charlotte Daniels
Cover image: Various colored concentric circles (© Malte Mueller / Getty Images)

All rights reserved. No part of this publication may be reproduced or transmitted in
any form or by any means, electronic or mechanical, including photocopying, recording,
or any information storage or retrieval system, without prior permission in writing
from the publishers.

Bloomsbury Publishing Plc does not have any control over, or responsibility for, any
third-party websites referred to or in this book. All internet addresses given in this
book were correct at the time of going to press. The author and publisher regret any
inconvenience caused if addresses have changed or sites have ceased to exist, but
can accept no responsibility for any such changes.

A catalogue record for this book is available from the British Library.

A catalog record for this book is available from the Library of Congress.

ISBN: HB: 978-1-3502-6064-1
PB: 978-1-3502-6068-9
ePDF: 978-1-3502-6065-8
eBook: 978-1-3502-6066-5

Typeset by Deanta Global Publishing Services, Chennai, India

To find out more about our authors and books visit www.bloomsbury.com and
sign up for our newsletters.

Contents

Acknowledgements	vi
Introduction	1

Part I Metaethical considerations

1	Moral experience	7
2	Defending subjectivism against subjectivists	41

Part II Empirical considerations

3	What do we want?	87
4	Disregarding consequences	124
5	Disregarding intentions and materialist ethics	150

Part III Conclusion

6	The origin of morals	185

Notes	207
Bibliography	253
Index	264

Acknowledgements

I would like to thank Kansai University for the sabbatical in 2015 that allowed me to write most of the following work. I would also like to thank Andy Hamilton for the opportunity to present some of the ideas developed here in a research seminar meeting at the Department of Philosophy, Durham University, and Sorin Baiasu for the same at an invited lecture in the School of Politics, Philosophy, International Relations and Environment, Keele University. I would also like to thank Chelsey Wong, who later took my postgraduate seminar in ethics at Kansai University and, to the best of my recollection, disagreed with me about everything. I am also very grateful to Simon Kirchin and two anonymous readers for Bloomsbury for the care with which they read part or all of my original manuscript and for their very helpful comments. Finally, I would like to thank Jade Grogan, commissioning editor at Bloomsbury, for making the publishing process a pleasure.

Introduction

The main aim of the present work is not to establish the futility of philosophical ethics. Its main aim is to explain why and how we have moral feeling: the feeling that certain things are right or wrong *in themselves*. (The futility of philosophical ethics is merely a corollary of that explanation.) Since nothing can have value except in relation to our interests, to account for the existence of a feeling that things have *value in themselves* we must discover what interest is actually being engaged in order to produce that feeling. However, where we feel that we are merely perceiving an object that is valuable *in itself* – as with morality and the aesthetic – then, clearly, we have no direct access to the interest the valuing expresses. (Feelings such as fear, anger, and joy may be felt as immediately/spontaneously as feelings of wrongness or beauty, but, unlike moral or aesthetic feeling, they are, in the majority of cases, easy to account for in terms of interests we know we have.) In order, then, to uncover the interest involved in moral feeling, the present work will examine the phenomenon of that feeling as a whole, setting aside, as far as possible, the moral point of view. This will involve approaching moral experience from a variety of angles: the subjective experience of the feeling (what a moral response feels like), rational reflection on that experience (analysis of what can be inferred from that feeling), philosophical ethics itself (as evidence of what reflection *wants* from moral feeling) and, finally, consideration of the range of objects that can be the object of such feeling (what people find, or have found, right and wrong).

In order to, as it were, "surprise" the interest that gives rise to moral experience, what are particularly emphasized in the following enquiry are those aspects of moral feeling in practice that appear inconsistent *from a moral point of view*: from the point of view of the way in which moral feeling is subjectively experienced. Such inconsistencies are, indeed, the usual subject of philosophical ethics, since that discipline, as we shall see, is largely a matter of the normative: an attempt to systematically deduce rules from and test rules by the feeling of rightness and wrongness. Thus, many themes familiar from ethics are rehearsed in what follows, though they are approached in rather a different way. The main business of philosophical ethics is to resolve perceived inconsistencies in moral feeling from a point of view that is itself moral: to reconcile conflicts in terms of an acknowledged moral principle or to discover a moral principle according to which such conflicts may be arbitrated. By contrast, in what follows, the same inconsistencies are rehearsed not in order to be resolved (in moral terms) but rather in order to discover a point of view from which, as expressions of an interest, they cease to be inconsistent.

The first part of the present book seeks to establish just how problematic moral experience is from every viewpoint except a moral one. To this end, Chapter 1 begins by examining the felt experience of the moral response in order to highlight the paradoxical nature of that response. It starts by focusing on two striking anomalies. The first is the way in which moral feeling is a matter of emotion that is yet posited, in the very way it is experienced, as unconnected with personal interest. The second is the way in which we both do and do not experience right and wrong as equivalent to objective properties of the world. That is, the way in which moral feeling appears to imply *beliefs*, but beliefs that are not open to rectification in the way beliefs usually are. The chapter then clears the decks for an examination of the grounds of this phenomenon by distinguishing moral responses (feelings) from moral judgements, since it is only the former that are of interest to us here. (As we shall see later, the confusion of the two separate phenomena by the promiscuous use of 'judgement' to refer to both is responsible not only for many apparently intractable problems within metaethics but for even more pseudo-solutions to those problems.) The chapter then turns to the first possible explanation of the grounds of moral experience. This is the idea that such experience is exactly what it appears to the subject to be: the perception of moral properties of the world. I there argue that such intuitionism is not so much a philosophical position as an abnegation of philosophy in favour of 'common sense'. The problem here is that common sense about morality simply does not make sense; that is precisely why morality is a perennial philosophical topic. Two other forms of moral realism – supernatural and natural – are also considered and rejected for their lack of explanatory value.

Chapter 2 looks at a range of recent professedly non-realist accounts that have, nevertheless, attempted to somehow justify our spontaneous moral realism, our sense that things are right and wrong in themselves. The first strategy (fictionalism) seeks to circumvent the untenability of moral realism by suggesting that we are not actually realists in our feelings but only talk/behave as if we were. The second strategy (which I have called *trivial realism*) seeks in a variety of ways to recoup a sufficient degree of realism to justify treating moral feeling as if it were simply a matter of perception. Neither of these strategies, I argue, is ultimately successful in any of the forms in which it has so far been presented.

Having established in Part I of the book that the moral response really is as problematic to reflection as it first appears, the second part addresses the idea of that response as an emotion. It does so by attempting to discover what common goal – what implicit but unacknowledged desire or aversion – can be discovered by considering the range of objects of that response.

This analysis begins in Chapter 3, which examines the ostensible implicit goal of moral feeling as it is subjectively experienced. In practice, this is equivalent to the traditional pursuit of a governing principle implied in either moral feeling itself or in the majority of our moral responses: a definition of 'the Good'. However, here such a "principle" is sought not, as is customary in ethics, to serve as a conscious principle for arbitrating ethical disputes, for establishing relative degrees of "wrongness" or "permissibility", but rather to discover to what extent a single goal is actually implicit in the existence of moral responses. If such a 'Good' could be discovered, it would then give us the desired object, the achievement or frustration of which is signalled by the emotional reaction that is the moral response. For, "What is the right thing to do?" is functionally equivalent to "What would have to happen for the desire implicit in my moral feeling to be satisfied?" Unsurprisingly, no such single principle is forthcoming from the facts of moral feeling in practice; the question would hardly be perennial if the case were otherwise. Two important points do, however, emerge from this initial foray into the experience of moral feeling. First is the way in which moral feeling is often not consistent with what moral feeling itself implies; people can find, upon reflection, that the principles implied by some of their own moral responses are morally counterintuitive to them. Second, the apparent implicit ends of many responses may conflict with one another without any of those responses ceasing to be experienced as moral feeling.

What the innumerable inconsistencies – from a *moral point of view* – in our actual responses suggest is that the goal (the interest) their existence signifies, rather than being revealed by the character of the moral response as we experience it, is actually somehow obscured by that character. Thus, no system that is built upon what is consistent in moral experience will ever reveal what underlies that experience. This last can only be discovered by looking at the totality of moral experience and treating the apparent inconsistencies not as the anomalies they appear to be from the point of view of any ethical system based on the way the response feels but rather as constitutive of the phenomenon to be explained.

Thus, the following two chapters take up different forms of apparent inconsistency in order to build up a picture of moral experience in practice – released from the obligation to yield a *moral* governing principle – from which an underlying goal giving rise to moral feeling might be inferred. Chapter 4 deals with the way in which the moral response's apparent deference to the consequences of actions is routinely absent both in cases where we morally condemn what merely brings harm to mind, even where no harm is possible and in cases where we morally approve phenomena despite our own negative moral feelings about their consequences. Chapter 5 examines the obverse of this phenomenon: moral responses that fix on the consequences of an action and assign culpability (or, more rarely, merit) in proportion to the undesirability (or desirability) of the consequences of the act irrespective of the intentions of the agent. It also analyses moral responses that appear to ignore both intentions and consequences to fix on the physical properties of objects themselves.

Finally, in Chapter 6, the aspects of the experience of moral feeling that have been highlighted by the preceding analysis are drawn together to more precisely delineate exactly what is to be accounted for in accounting for moral experience. The work concludes by both describing the desire that appears to be implicit in the phenomenon of moral feeling and offering an account of why this desire is experienced in the peculiar, indirect way that constitutes morality.

Part I
Metaethical considerations

1

Moral experience

The phenomenology of moral experience

We experience moral responses. It is tempting to try to expand on this 'responses' with a list of the kinds of feeling they are constituted by: anger, resentment, contempt, disgust, admiration, gratitude, approbation, disapprobation and so on. Clearly, however, such a list would illuminate nothing. Any item that could appear on it would be either a feeling (like anger or admiration) that is neither necessary nor sufficient to constitute a moral response or simply a synonym for 'moral response' itself ('approbation', 'disapprobation').

While moral responses are self-evidently a matter of emotion – in that they are motivating ascriptions of value – they cannot be reduced to any other emotions that accompany them or perhaps signal their presence. I may, for example, be shocked by some action that I feel is wrong, but that shock appears to arise from the feeling that it is wrong rather than being the cause of that feeling. Likewise, the anger I feel towards the person responsible for the action arises from my holding them to be responsible for what I feel is wrong. The feeling of wrongness precedes the anger. The moral response, then, does not appear to either be or be caused by the anger or the shock in themselves.

We might, then, attempt a more abstract characterization of the kind of response that is a moral response. We might say, for example, that a negative moral response is a strong feeling of *this should not be*. This feeling is not, of course, an implicit appeal to the limits of either rationality or likelihood; that is, it does not bear the sense in which we might use the expression if, for example, suddenly confronted with a talking elephant in pyjamas. Neither is it possible to interpret the formula as an incomplete conditional statement – "This shouldn't be if I/you/we/they want/expect…" Indeed, insofar as the expression actually does capture the feeling of the moral response, this is precisely the sense it does not bear. However, once these rational or empirical meanings are excluded, we are left only with a meaning of *should not* that makes the explanation circular: what makes the response a moral response is that it depends upon a moral response. The same holds for positive moral responses, as feelings of *this should be* or *I am glad this is*. Once we have excluded the meaning of *should* that expresses our feeling about either the possibility or likelihood of the object or its instrumental value in relation to a definite goal, only the moral meaning remains.

If we cannot, then, identify a moral response with any emotion other than a moral emotion, it is at least possible to give an account of how we distinguish moral responses from other kinds of response: to say what gives a response its identity as a moral response from the subject's point of view. For we do, in fact, have no problem in giving intuitive assent to, for example, the proposition that anger per se and moral response are not identical. We do feel immediately the inappropriateness of a statement like "That's not fair; I wanted to win".

What follows, then, is intended as purely descriptive rather than prescriptive. That is, it is not intended as an account of what conditions a moral response must fulfil to be "properly" a moral response irrespective of the subject's feeling that it is a moral response. Rather, it is an account of how we *recognize* a response as a moral response when we experience one. The question of whether or not, in any particular case, the subject is justified in identifying their response as a moral one is a separate question (as also are the questions of what 'justified' means here and whether such a notion is even meaningful in this context). Clearly, however, that question cannot precede an examination of what are experienced as moral responses since this experience is, for the moment, all we have to work on.

First, then, a moral response must be *my* response. It may be, as we shall see later, that I can be reasoned into, or reasoned out of, a response to a situation (by being made to see that situation in a certain way), but in that case we should more accurately say not that the first response to *x* was not moral but rather that my notion of what constitutes *x* has changed, or that I am now experiencing a different moral response. Unless it is ultimately *my* response to *x*, I cannot call it a moral response to *x*. An unshakeable logical demonstration of the way in which the present case is, for example, an instance of the breaking of a principle I feel should not be broken, may lead me to make a moral *judgement* that the present case is wrong, that is, to pronounce it "wrong", but unless I actually *feel* the present case is wrong, I cannot say that in making this judgement I am actually reporting a moral response. (We shall return to this distinction between responses and judgements in a moment.) Thus, for example, when Frederic equably announces to his pirate foster family that 'Individually, I love you all with affection unspeakable; but, collectively, I look upon you with a disgust that amounts to absolute detestation', we immediately feel the intended absurdity of the pronouncement.[1]

A moral response, then, is only such insofar as it is *my* feeling that *this should not be* or, in the case of 'positive' responses, either *I am relieved this is so* (where I foresaw the possibility of a negative response) or *I am glad this is so*, which is the province of the supererogatory. Moreover, it is involuntary. That is, it appears to me to be *necessarily* connected to the situation to which it is a response. I do not arrive at the response by asking myself "Is this good for . . .?" or "Is this wrong because . . .?" (though both would be possible with moral judgements). It is only a moral response insofar as *it happens to me*.

Another way of describing this feeling of the necessity of the response would be to say that it appears to me to imply a universality. We feel – as also we speak – as if rightness and wrongness were qualities of actions, and our responses had universal application ("*It* is wrong"), in the sense of being applicable to everyone perceiving the same object. Only insofar as my response feels *exemplary* do I perceive anything as "wrong" or "right".[2] This imputation of universality is, however, only something implicit in our feeling that the wrongness or rightness is a quality of the action.

A moral response, then, feels like a response to a property of the world. What distinguishes it from other qualities that we may perceive as properties of the world – such as the qualities things possess when we find them annoying, frightening, disappointing, embarrassing, boring or desirable – is that we cannot, as we can with these other cases, feel our own sensibilities at play in determining the response we feel. That is, we can acknowledge that a thing bores us *personally* without feeling that we have at all undermined our own boredom with it, but the same does not hold with moral responses. To declare that an action is wrong (in a moral sense) merely for oneself would be to deny a fundamental condition for the intelligible use of moral language. For someone to call an action "Evil for me", using it in the same way as one might say "Cheese is disgusting" or "That's inconvenient", would be equivalent to our original example of "That's not fair; I wanted to win".[3] (That is, if someone did use an expression like "evil for me", we would take it to imply – presuming that person to have a proper grasp of moral language – that they believed the object to be evil *in itself*, and to be claiming that if we could see it as it really is (i.e. as they do), we would feel as they do.)

Yet another way to describe the felt necessity, or implicit universality, of moral responses would be to say that they are disinterested. "Disinterested" in the sense that, as we experience our response as necessarily linked to the perception of the action, there appears to us to be no personal, and thus interested, reasons to account for that response. Thus, we feel that a person cannot really be reporting a moral response if they call someone "bad" for beating them in a race, while, conversely, there is nothing at all strange about so describing the actions of the Spanish Inquisition, which cannot today have the remotest connection with anyone's personal interests, in the mundane sense of "interests". In this sense, all moral responses are altruistic: they imply a concern with the benefit of others – even when, to those others, they might appear to be merely a matter of resentment.

Hume describes this condition for a response to qualify as moral when he writes that it is 'only when a character is considered in general, without reference to our particular interest, that it causes such a feeling or sentiment, as denominates it morally good or evil'.[4] However, Hume's formulation here actually sets the conditions for qualifying as a moral response too high, since it may be that there is a reference to our particular interest without us being aware of it. Rather we should say that to be a moral response, the feeling must be *experienced as if* it had no reference to our *particular* interests.

This last is an important point since the neglect of it can also lead to a distortion of the facts of moral experience. For, it is evident that self-interest does play a role in moral responses. To return to the Spanish Inquisition for a moment, it should be quite obvious that while a vivid account of the actions of Torquemada may inspire in me a lively sense of his wickedness, this feeling is not likely to be anything like so intense as the moral outrage I will feel at the action of someone who jumps a slow queue in which I myself am standing. No doubt in another context I would certainly feel that the crimes of Torquemada were worse than queue jumping, but at the moment my queue is jumped I do not.[5]

Our first instinct, on reflection, might be to disqualify our response to the queue jumper from being a purely moral response. We might say that we are confusing our own anger at a thwarted desire (to get to the front of the queue) with the seriousness of the immorality involved in queue jumping. Indeed, this is certainly how many philosophers deal with the moral responses of those whose feelings they do not sympathize with. (This tendency to disallow responses that are inconsistent with what the moral response *should* be, according to consistent ethical systems, will become familiar as we go on.)

However, what qualifies a response as a moral response is not that it should be disinterested, but that it should be *experienced as if* it were disinterested: should feel, if not impartial, then at least merely a response to properties of the world. For, at this stage we have no theory of the grounds of moral responses that would justify our disallowing a response just because we can see an interest at work in it. It may be that anger always is a part of adverse moral responses, so that the presence of anger in the response is no indication of whether it is moral or not. It may be that ultimately moral responses always are, in some sense, a matter of self-interest; at this stage we do not know. (And we are not likely to find out if we start disqualifying responses that feel like moral responses, when this feeling is the only data we have.) What is important, however, is that, to qualify as a moral response, it should appear to the one experiencing it *as if* it is not principally a matter of self-interest. My response to the queue jumper may perfectly fulfil this requirement. It does not matter if someone else, or I myself later, can see a personal interest at work in the vehemence of my response. So long as it appears to me that I am responding to the action *in itself*, irrespective of my personal interest, then I am satisfying all the conditions that anyone could satisfy in order to legitimately claim that what they were feeling was a moral response. Even my rational recognition, on reflection, that the intensity of my response was (in terms of my normal range of moral responses) apparently "adulterated" by interest is, precisely in being rational, irrelevant.[6] It is evidence only of what I feel now, not what I felt then.

In summary, then, what qualifies a response to be a moral response as such is not that it can be shown to be made independently of self-interest, but only that it should not feel as if it is dependent on self-interest. Any particular response may be, at the same time, both a matter of personal interest and the object of a moral response, providing that response does not appear, to the subject *at the moment it is felt*, as dependent on the interest involved. That is, so long as we feel we are responding to rightness and wrongness, as these appear to us to be part of the fabric of the world, we are experiencing a moral response: whatever feels like a moral response is a moral response.

However, if moral responses are experienced as disinterested in the sense that they do not appear to the subject to be a matter of that subject's self-interest, they are obviously not, at least with regard to negative moral responses, disinterested in the sense of being detached. The moral response, as a feeling of *this should not be*, is experienced as a disposition to act (to do or to undo), or at least a wish to see action taken. (This is one way in which the felt disinterest of the moral response is distinguishable from the felt disinterest of aesthetic experience.) Paradoxically, then, a moral response feels very much like a desire, though a desire that is, given its felt disinterest, not mine.[7]

To say that a moral response, or at least a negative moral response, is experienced as a disposition to act is not, of course, equivalent to saying that moral responses motivate us to act. The response and the disposition are the same thing. There is no question, then, of making behaviour a measure of the real presence of a moral response, any more than one would make behaviour the measure of the presence of any other disposition or desire. My moral response to the idea of Torquemada is no less a moral response for the fact that there is nothing now to be done about Torquemada, just as my response to the idea of Lauren Bacall is no less the kind of response it is for the fact that there is nothing now to be done about Lauren Bacall. The disposition does not defer to possibility. Moreover, even where possibility is present, it would not make sense to say that acting on a disposition was necessary to prove the presence of that disposition. All that is necessary is the feeling of disposition, and this is already part of the phenomenology of the negative moral response.

It is precisely because of this element of disposition or desire that, despite the way in which moral responses appear to imply that I experience the rightness and wrongness of things as perceptions of given properties of the world, it is, nevertheless, unsatisfactory to describe them as perceptions. Though the notion of perception implies the presence of some belief about the world, there is something counterintuitive in talk about "moral belief".[8] I have never been comfortable, and find it difficult to believe that everyone is comfortable, with the way in which many people speak of "moral beliefs", or "moral knowledge", or being "taught the difference between right and wrong". It smacks of insincerity. This is not, however, because of any abstract sceptical commitments on my part. On the contrary, such talk strikes me as artificial precisely because terms like "belief" and "knowledge" seem inadequate to the reality of moral responses.

A moral response does not *feel* like knowledge in the way that, for example, knowing I still have water in the bottle under the table feels like knowledge. When I *feel* that, *ceteris paribus*, flaying babies alive should not happen, I also feel that I cannot imagine feeling otherwise. When I know that the bottle under the table still contains water, I can easily imagine not only that I could believe otherwise but even that I might be mistaken. Moreover, I could check to find out. (I just did, and it contained less than I expected.) My feeling about flaying babies, as I experience it, is simply not open to doubt or the notion of rectification in the light of new facts in the same way. Moreover, you would not expect it to be. If I announced that I was going to flay some in order to test the hypothesis that doing so is wrong, you would presume that I did not understand what "wrong" meant. I would never say, then, that I *believed* flaying babies alive should not happen, simply because using the word "believe" would actually be understating the case. It implies that I could be wrong, and this is something inconceivable in the baby example. Somehow, then, my feeling that it should not happen carries greater *conviction* than a mere belief that it should not happen possibly could.[9]

Similarly, although moral responses seem to imply by their very phenomenology that I experience rightness or wrongness as external, as properties of the world for which I am not responsible, when the natural corollary to this is directly reflected in language it feels, to me at least, as a misrepresentation. I refer to the tendency to speak of moral responses in terms of external compulsions, as, for example, Shafer-Landau does when he asserts that moral facts 'tell us what we *ought* to do; how we *should* behave; what is *worth* pursuing.'[10] (Likewise, of course, with talk about "deciding what beliefs to accept".) I do not find this a natural way to talk about moral responses; it suggests a degree of detachment that does not reflect my own experience. I do not feel that I am being told what is right by my responses, with the corollary that I otherwise would not "know". Nor do I feel that moral responses are somehow guiding me through a world in which I would otherwise be lost. Rather, moral responses happen to me: they are my world.

This, then, will serve to identify a moral response. (I have avoided any question of the types of situations, real or ideal, that might form a delimiting category for what a moral response is a *response to*, for the very simple reason that, in practice, there do not seem to be any limits to this category.) It is involuntary: it happens to us. It feels necessary (exemplary, universal), in the sense that we feel, *up to a point*, that we are responding to properties of the world, rather than either making an evaluation or responding to a value that we recognize as personal to us. In this sense it feels disinterested, though it also has the character of a disposition to act: it feels like a desire that is not grounded in self-interest.

As I said at starting, this account of the moral response is intended to be merely descriptive. That we should end with a characterization that tends so readily towards oxymoron is only to be expected. The phenomenon of moral responses is inherently problematic. That is why it requires an explanation.

Moral judgements

There is, however, one more topic to consider before turning to the question of accounting for such responses. This is the related, but separate, topic of moral judgements. It should be clear from what has gone before that the expression "moral judgement", while it is often used as synonymous with "moral response" as I have used it earlier, is equally often used to mean something quite different. Indeed, it is a tendency to use the term in this ambiguous way that is responsible for the perpetual recurrence of many pseudo-problems in ethics, with the actual topic of the debate slipping and sliding between moral responses and what are not moral responses all unbeknownst to the participants. While moral responses, as I have described them, happen to us, many of the things that are called "moral judgements" are things that we do.

In a weak sense, all our responses, all our emotions, can be called "judgements", insofar as any feeling of aversion or desire towards certain states of affairs implies an assessment of that state of affairs. To dislike a thing is equivalent to having *judged* it as, in some sense, undesirable. Likewise, we might say that a moral response is, in the same weak sense, a *judgement*, insofar as it is a negative or positive response to what appear to be properties of the world that we must, somehow, have assessed. (However, it is a moot point, at this stage, to what extent the world actually possesses these properties independently of what appears to us to be merely our response to them.) This implied assessment is no doubt why the word "judgement" was originally used in connection with moral responses, just as it was also used in the phrase "judgements of taste", with a full acknowledgement that such "judgements" are judgements only in the same sense that pain is your burnt finger's "judgement" on the temperature it is experiencing. Where the confusion arises in ethics (and aesthetics) is where this sense of "judgement" is conflated with the more usual sense of an opinion arrived at by reasoning. For, if every moral response is also a moral judgement (in the remote sense in which pain is also a "judgement"), not everything that we call a moral judgement is a moral response.

What are commonly called "moral judgements" may indeed, as pronunciations on the right or wrong of a situation, be judgements in the more common, stronger sense of the word, that is, consciously drawn conclusions or opinions arrived at by reasoning. Many of what we call "moral judgements" take this form. They are the result of reflection on what is, at first sight, a confused situation. Instances of this kind of moral judgement might be the conclusions we come to after considering such questions as "Can there be a just war?", "Is stem cell research acceptable?", "Should pornography be banned?", or "Do animals have rights?" It may be that I feel an immediate moral response to the ideas evoked by such questions, but equally I may not. Or it may be that I do feel an immediate response to what such questions suggest ("Nothing harmless should be banned", "Cruelty to animals is horrible"), but still am not sure whether I might not be overlooking what is actually at stake in the question. That is, I cannot be sure I am not overlooking a greater wrong than the one I see: a wrong that is obscured by the complexity of the issue and that might elicit an even stronger negative response in me if I could see it. (Which is why an immediate moral response, like "Nothing harmless should be banned", is beside the point, since it simply assumes an answer to the question that is really at issue.) Hence the existence of such fields as medical ethics, business ethics, bioethics, the ethics of food, of waste, of media, of human enhancement and so on. The very existence of such fields does not indicate a general conviction that what is right and wrong in, for example, medicine is different from what is right and wrong outside medicine, but only that a certain expertise may be involved in discovering how tacitly assumed values are to be *applied* within a complicated and unfamiliar context.

In cases like the ethical questions mentioned above there may be one of two things that we are trying to do in *deciding* the right or wrong of the case. We may be trying to find a way of viewing an initially confusing situation that will allow intuition, in the form of a moral response, to emerge. (Most probably in the form of the discovery of a consequence, entailed by the situation, that in itself elicits such a response.) Conversely, we may be trying to discover something in the present instance that can be made to fall under a conscious moral principle or generalization that we do not feel is itself at issue in the present instance. As, for example, the concept of justice is not at issue in the first question ("Can there be a just war?") or the concept of rights in the last ("Do animals have rights?"). In short, whether we are analysing the situation in order to find a viewpoint that will elicit a moral response or trying to categorize the present case in terms of what is, in the context, a given moral principle, reason will evidently play a role.

An illustration of the first type – where a process of ratiocination causes us to experience an intuition – would be the biblical story of David and Bathsheba. King David impregnates Bathsheba, the wife of one of his soldiers, Uriah, who is away at war. Unable to hide the fact from Uriah, David arranges for him to be killed in battle and subsequently marries his widow.[11] The prophet Nathan then comes to David and tells him the story of a rich man who, despite having many flocks of sheep, has taken and killed the single ewe belonging to a poor man to feed a guest. David demands to know who this rich man is, declaring that he deserves to die for such an act of injustice, whereupon Nathan declares, 'Thou art the man'.[12] David then acknowledges that he has sinned.

It could be argued that the story fits the second type – the categorization type – insofar as David draws an analogy that allows him to *see* his own action as an instance of the category of injustice/oppression that he already either feels is wrong or professes to be wrong. (Previously he has been, as we might say, *blinded* by self-interest.) However, the important point is that his reaction is emotional: he feels the wrong of it (assuming, that is, that his discomfort is not simply a matter of shame at being caught out in an inconsistency). His reason, in the form of his recognition of the analogical relationship between the two instances and the soundness of the analogy, leads to a "moral judgement" that may also be a moral response.

A very similar instance of an appeal to reason that at least seems intended to evoke a moral response can be found in those messages directed against piracy at the beginning of DVDs: the ones that begin 'You wouldn't steal a car'.[13] The message being, of course, that copying a DVD is equivalent to these other actions. This is not an appeal to reason in the sense that it is relying upon your inherent desire to be consistent in your actions. Rather it is trying to make you *see* that what you are doing is something that you already feel is wrong. It is, as it were, proving something is wrong because you already feel it is wrong. What we must not lose sight of, however, is that the reasoning process is only efficacious in such instances if the feeling appealed to is already in place: only where a predisposition to a certain kind of moral response can be assumed, where one of the premisses of the argument is taken as true. If your reaction to 'You wouldn't steal a car' is "I would, if I could get away with it", then, however sound the reasoning behind the message, it is not going to lead to a moral response.

There is also the possibility that we might question the reasoning itself: judge the analogy to be false. David might say "You're mistaken; I never stole anybody's ewe" or "Well, a woman is not a sheep", or we might say "Copying something is not the same as stealing it". That is, we may not feel any moral response to acts of adultery (leaving aside, as Nathan does, the accompanying murder) or copyright infringement, even if we would feel such a response to the act of stealing either a prized possession from a poor man or a car. That is, we do not allow that the present instance falls into any category to which we normally respond emotionally. Indeed, it might be the lack of a felt moral response that leads our judgement. "It certainly does not feel wrong" we might say and then proceed to find reasons, in the face of someone's assertion that it is wrong, to account for our feeling that it is not (or, more probably, their "error" in feeling that it is).

In contrast, the second type of moral judgement involving reason does not require the eliciting of a moral response. These are judgements made within a context where a moral principle is already implicitly assumed, as "Can there be a just war?" presumes the existence of justice and "Do animals have rights?" presumes the existence of rights. The extent of the independence of those judgements from moral response, that is, their potentially entirely rational character, can be judged by a statement such as "Embryo research is equivalent to murder". This certainly looks like a moral response towards embryo research, yet I do not have to feel a moral response towards embryo research in order to make it. I can simply look at any given definition of "murder" and then see if embryo research involves any action that will fit that definition (or, given the legal aspect involved, any action that should logically fit that definition). There need be no point in my reasoning at which I experience a moral response, a feeling of "This should not be". Indeed, I do not even have to feel a moral objection to murder per se to arrive at this judgement; all that is required is that x (embryo research) is equivalent to what is essential to membership of the class y (murder). In this sense certain statements that we feel could justifiably be called "moral judgements" can take the form of verdicts: judgements of fact.

The facts involved, however, cannot be called "moral facts" (about whether something is, in itself, right or wrong) but rather facts about whether y is an adequate definition and whether x fits that definition. We would call a debate about such a question a "moral debate" because at least some of the terms in the debate are presumed to have a moral aspect (y is "wrong"), not because it can only be settled by the eliciting of a moral response. Reasoned moral debate is certainly possible, then, but only in so far as those involved can appeal to a common criterion that itself takes the form of a moral judgement that is not in question. In short, we can only argue reasonably about whether something is "bad" if we share common criteria of "badness".

Moral debate is not, of course, usually as simple as this last example. Indeed, while it is true to say that reasoned moral debate can only be about facts or the implications of facts, this does not actually exclude debates that can at least appear to be about values (as generalizations from our moral responses). It is possible to argue reasonably about the value of criteria that may appear to those involved to be values in themselves (as happens, for example, in debates over self-reliance vs. community, or patriotism vs. cosmopolitanism), but only where there is another more basic value (a predisposition to certain moral responses) that both sides in the debate share, and which can, consequently, be *treated as* a fact. In the absence of such a shared value, that is, where neither side can appeal to any moral response the other recognizes, reason is irrelevant, and any debate really is so much hot air.

The existence of "moral reasoning" depends, then, on the assumption of moral principles that are not themselves at issue in the reasoning process: on moral givens. Although it would seem natural to presume that these given givens must themselves be a matter of moral response, this is not necessarily the case. You and I may argue about whether copying a DVD is wrong in terms of whether or not it is stealing, with the assumption that if it does turn out to be stealing, then our conclusion must be that it is "wrong". Yet, it may still be that, in fact, while we have implicitly agreed that stealing is wrong, only some forms of stealing actually elicit a moral response in either of us.

Indeed, the prevalence of digital theft and the various results obtained by Kohlberg's Heinz dilemma suggest that many people, even within a community that professes to "know" stealing is wrong, feel it is more appropriate to define it as "taking unfairly" rather than simply as "taking what does not belong to you": that, in fact, stealing per se is not something we can take as a reliable elicitor of moral response at all.[14] (However, we can certainly expect lip service to the wrongness of stealing, as we find, for example, in the very defence that certain forms of stealing are "not really" stealing.) We might still feel shame at being discovered doing so, but that is only to say that we presume it will elicit a moral response in others. Take away the possibility of discovery, and this form of stealing ceases to elicit a moral response.

However, "Stealing is wrong" still obviously has the form of a moral judgement, since it contains a moral term ("wrong") and can thus be part of a train of reason, which itself may be sound or unsound, leading to another moral judgement:

x is wrong
y is an example of x
Therefore, y is wrong

This is a perfectly sound argument. The fact that the first premise may be itself a moral judgement divorced from moral response (neither of us feel x is wrong) does not detract from its reasonableness.[15]

Regarding this second type of moral judgement involving reason, although I have concentrated on the possibility of an amoral employment of moral terms, in order to emphasize the potentially purely rational nature of such a judgement, it is not, of course, necessary to suppose an amoral judge in order to posit such a judgement. It is sufficient merely to imagine a process in which one judges without reference to one's own moral responses. It may be that the situation under review (such as embryo research) is so very complicated – either because we feel that the alternatives to the wrong are themselves so wrong or because these alternatives are so profoundly contrary to fundamental self-interest – that we will never experience a moral response and must rely on a perception of the soundness of the reasoning itself to arrive at a judgement on what is evidently (since it uses, as opposed to merely mentions, moral terms) a moral question. We must judge, as it were, blind.

However, it seems unlikely that such exclusively rational moral judgements, untainted by moral response, often occur in a pure form outside of the pages of works on ethics or law. Most "moral reasoning" demonstrably tacks between the two, with feeling often used as a way of checking the soundness of the argument. It is only where feeling becomes the actual touchstone – "I don't care what you say; I know it's wrong" – that we are back in the realm of moral response, which does not defer to reasoning.

To sum up, then, it is definitely possible to reason about moral matters in at least two basic ways:

1) Laying out the facts of the case in such a way that the result is a moral response to those facts (as, potentially, in the case of David).
2) Demonstrating that this present case is one that falls under a moral principle not itself at issue in the case. This can be done in contexts where the parties either tacitly agree on the existence of moral facts (they have responses in common) or tacitly agree to reason *as if* there were moral facts.

In the first case, however, the reasoning is only pertinent if there is the possibility of eliciting a moral response. So that, for example, demonstrating how the Bible prohibits homosexuality will not evoke a moral response towards homosexuality in anyone who is indifferent to the idea of biblical prohibition per se. In the same way, we cannot get the bully to feel in the wrong by asking "How would you like it if someone did that to you?" if their response is going to be "I wouldn't, but I'm not doing it to me". How reasonable the reasoning is in such cases is entirely dependent upon the possibility of eliciting a moral response that is already, as it were, in place. If that possibility is absent, then, no matter how sound or ingenious the argument, its conclusion will be a non sequitur. Conversely, with the second type of "moral reasoning", reason works not to produce a moral response but rather to produce a moral judgement, in the sense of a verdict on the wrongness of x on the basis of its being an instance of y, where the wrongness of y is *treated as a fact*.

If all this demonstrates that reason can play a role in moral judgements, thus justifying the use of 'judgement' in that phrase, it also seems to bring into question the justice of using the other term: 'moral'. However, even in those cases where the moral fact (the principle) being appealed to is one that neither party in the debate actually experiences as a fact, in the sense that the situation being debated does not elicit a moral response from either of them, what nevertheless makes such a debate a moral one, and its outcome a moral judgement, is that it is a debate about rightness and wrongness: categories that only exist by virtue of moral responses. Moral judgements, then, depend upon our mutual agreement on the existence of *potential* moral response, even if, in any particular judgement, no actual moral response is involved. To this extent all moral judgements and all moral reasoning absolutely depend, however remotely, on the existence of moral response, even though such responses may play no immediate role in the formation of the judgement.

Clearly, then, moral judgements, in this sense – the sense that distinguishes them from moral responses – are strictly epiphenomenal to moral responses. They are *moral* judgements only insofar as they refer to (but do not, in any particular instance, necessarily depend on) categories derived from the experience of moral responses. In every other respect they are simply judgements in the usual sense of the word: conclusions to potentially entirely rational arguments. Conversely, the moral response itself, as an involuntary emotional response of a particular, and peculiar, kind, enjoys an equally independent existence, though without, of course, any dependence on the existence of moral judgements.

If we now imagine a situation in which a single expression was used to denote both of these separate and incommensurable categories of experience, we would be imagining precisely the current situation of philosophical ethics. It is, as we shall see, the indiscriminate use of "moral judgement" to refer to both moral judgements and moral responses that is responsible not only for several apparently intractable problems in metaethics but also, and more importantly, many pseudo-solutions to problems that should be intractable. For the sake of clarity, then, the expression "moral judgement" will be confined for the rest of this book to only those moral judgements that are not moral responses. Moreover, when dealing with the literature of ethics, where "moral judgement" does routinely do the work of denoting both, I will attempt to distinguish when the expression is being used in one sense or the other, as far as the original text allows.

However, since our object here is neither normative nor, if this can be considered a separate matter, the discovery of a consistent principle implicit in either the existence of the moral response per se or in the general tendency of those responses that would allow us to judge our judgements in terms of reason, but rather the nature of the moral response itself, moral judgements need take up no more of our time.

Realism: Intuitionism

Having distinguished moral judgements, which we *make*, from moral responses, which *happen to* us, and having established that moral judgements are merely derivative in relation to the existence of such responses, we must now return to the question of what exactly it is that is happening to us in these responses.

As we have seen, one of the characteristics of a moral response is its felt necessity: it feels as if we are responding to properties of the world, or at least to values of properties of the world for which we are not responsible. That is, the response does not appear to us to depend upon fear or affection, or indeed any other feeling that would suggest it sprang from self-interest.

The simplest explanation for this would seem to be that the response feels this way because what is happening is precisely what appears to be happening: we are responding to properties of the world that exist independently of that response.[16] Such properties – those that elicit moral responses – might, therefore, be called the "moral properties" of the world. It would follow from this that, when we report a moral response, we are also reporting a belief that we hold: that this situation has the moral properties that our response implies. Indeed, the very language in which we report moral responses does take the form of statements of fact ("*That's* wrong"): statements that appear truth-apt. Moreover, with regard to moral judgements, also, it is, as we have seen, only possible for them to play a part in argument, to form a discourse, insofar as, irrespective of whether those judgements are directly tied to any particular person's actual response, the participants in the discourse talk as if there are such things as moral facts.

Thus, *moral realism*, as the theory that moral responses depend upon the perception of properties of the world that exist independently of those responses, is implicit in the very way we experience moral responses. It is, as it were, the default 'explanation' of moral experience. Thus, those who have consciously advanced such realism as a philosophical theory appeal, very naturally, to the character of moral experience itself. Moral responses feel like responses to things that are right or wrong *in themselves*. We also talk of right and wrong as if they were mind-independent properties of the world, without thereby shocking anyone with our eccentricity. Unless, of course, our particular responses are themselves eccentric; in which case, we will be perceived as either mistaken or devoid of the appropriate sense: as immoral or amoral. Moreover, when we do talk about the rightness or wrongness of things, we are not surprised to discover others share the "beliefs" implicit in our responses, to discover that others *see* the objects of our responses as we do. ('Implicit', since we should not forget the qualitative difference between moral responses and beliefs already noted.) Given that this is so, we also feel that it is meaningful to engage in arguments on moral matters in the hope of getting others to respond as we do.

Indeed, the existence of moral debate is sometimes itself advanced as evidence for moral realism, even though an argument in itself proves nothing about the reality of what is asserted by either side. People are also happy to argue about who is the greatest footballer of all time, or whether the Hulk is stronger than the Thing. (It is illuminating, in this regard, to listen to debates between children: "I like strawberry the best", "*No*, I like chocolate the best", etc.) Moreover, as we have seen, the reasonableness of moral debate does not depend on moral responses themselves being truth-apt. All that is necessary for reasonable moral debate is a mutual agreement to treat certain moral responses as if they were responses to properties of the world: to argue as if there were moral facts. Thus, if it turned out that there were no moral facts, this would still not entail the meaninglessness of moral debate. (All that is needed is the experience of being convinced that there are – that is, the existence of moral responses themselves.[17]) Likewise, of course, the meaningfulness of moral debate does not entail the existence of moral facts.

Another phenomenon that moral realists often appeal to as evidence of the cognitive nature of moral responses and the concomitant existence of moral *knowledge* is the way in which moral responses converge. They point, for example, to common agreement, often over long periods of time and across wide geographical distribution, on the validity of certain moral principles and to the way in which there appears to be "moral progress", in the sense that we can look back to past customs that are now no longer acceptable.[18] Common agreement, however, only serves to demonstrate that there are common tendencies in the way we respond. While the reality of moral facts might be one possible explanation for this, it is not the only possible explanation. What may be involved here is a truth about human psychology rather than a truth about mind-independent properties of the world. The notion of "moral progress", on the other hand, even ignoring the way in which the facts to which it appeals tend to undermine the argument from common agreement, is perfectly vacuous. Change in the direction of a consensus on feeling towards the existing consensus is inevitably going to look like progress from the point of view of the existing *sensus fidei*. If it looks like progress towards truth, it is only because the measure we are using is our own set of moral responses: what we *feel* to be true. As with pointing to moral debate to establish the objectivity of our responses, so here too the phenomenon only becomes evidence if we assume that objectivity to begin with.

However, if universal consensus is not sufficient to demonstrate the existence of moral properties, and thus the cognitive nature of moral responses, neither would it be necessary. The fact that we do not all have the same moral responses is not, prima facie, particularly significant, since the existence of properties of the world does not actually depend on everybody always – or, indeed, anybody ever – recognizing them for what they are. The fact that there is variety in moral responses tells us nothing at all about whether or not any particular response is a matter of the perception of real moral properties.

The real problem with the idea of moral properties of the world lies in conceiving the nature of such properties. If we always and only ever observe them in combination with that element of desire (the wish that *this should not be*) noted when describing moral responses, perhaps it is this element that is principally responsible for the peculiar nature of the response. (We can, of course, make moral judgements in the absence of such a feeling, but these judgements, as we have seen, tell us nothing about the moral response itself.)

The idea that moral statements are not descriptions of objective features of the world, but rather expressions of how we feel about the world, is not, of course, a new one.[19] In modern times, Hobbes asserted that the words 'good' and 'evil' are 'ever used with relation to the person that useth them: there being nothing simply and absolutely so'.[20] Whatever is the object of your appetite or desire, he declares, you will call 'good', and whatever is the object of your hate and aversion, 'evil', and these terms refer to nothing other than the objects of your desires and aversions.[21] More famously, Hume, almost a century later, wrote that 'morality is determined by sentiment', so that 'when you pronounce any action or character to be vicious, you mean nothing, but that from the constitution of your nature you have a feeling or sentiment of blame from the contemplation of it'.[22] Goodness and badness, then, according to Hume, are not matters of fact: 'not qualities in objects, but perceptions in the mind'. There is no way to discover the badness of even wilful murder by looking at the act itself, no property of wrongness to be perceived; the badness can only be found when 'you turn your reflection into your own breast, and find a sentiment of disapprobation, which arises in you, towards this action'. It may be a fact that you have such a feeling, but that is a fact about you, not about the action itself.

It is in connection with this last observation that Hume famously asserts that there is no logical way to get from a statement of fact (something 'is' or 'is not') to a moral statement (one 'ought' or 'ought not').[23] Every system of morality, he says, at some point makes a transition between these two types of statement – starting with the way things are and ending by saying what we should do – but none ever explains how the transition can be made. Attention to this point, he remarks, 'would subvert all the vulgar systems of morality, and let us see that the distinction of vice and virtue is not founded merely on the relations of objects, nor is perceived by reason', but is a matter of feeling.[24] Indeed, it must be noted in passing that, as simultaneously involuntary and motivating, the moral response is clearly a matter of emotion. Though we tend to think of describing moral feeling in terms of 'affection', 'passion', or 'sentiment' as peculiar to only a certain group of eighteenth-century philosophers (most famously Shaftesbury, Hutcheson, Hume and Smith), it was, in fact, the European norm until the end of the nineteenth century, at least outside philosophical ethics, to describe the moral response as an 'emotion' or 'feeling'.[25] (Within philosophy this vocabulary gave way during the nineteenth century, for a variety of reasons, to a preference for 'moral ideas' or 'moral judgements'.[26])

Like any other emotion, the response appears to signal what we do or do not want of the world; the decisive complicating factor in the moral case being, of course, that it is also peculiarly part of that response that it is experienced as disinterested, that we should feel we are taking 'the point of view of the universe'.[27] If, then, we cannot actually point to any distinctively moral properties of the world, is there, nevertheless, another way in which we might secure this *felt* objectivity? Even if we can dismiss as circular the arguments from the existence of meaningful moral debate, convergence and progress, there is still what is perhaps the strongest argument in favour of moral realism: that it is implicit in the very way we experience (and talk about) moral responses themselves. Perhaps, then, we should simply allow that when people feel they are responding to rightness and wrongness as properties of the world, at least some of them, some of the time, are in fact perceiving the moral properties of the world. Arbitrary as such a thesis might seem, it is, nevertheless, one that has had its philosophical champions.

The position that takes moral responses to be exactly what they seem to be might be called "common sense", though within philosophy it is known as 'intuitionism', since it consists in positing that at least some of our moral responses are *intuitions* of moral facts. Ross, for example, lists several 'objective' moral facts that underpin all of our other moral convictions, though nothing can be shown to underpin those facts themselves: we simply '*know them* to be true'.[28] If anyone disagrees about one of the propositions, he adds, he certainly cannot prove that it is true; he can only ask them to 'reflect again, in the hope that they will ultimately agree that they also know it to be true'.[29]

> I should demonstrate fidelity where I have previously explicitly or implicitly promised something, and make reparation where I have previously done wrong.
> I should demonstrate gratitude.
> I should be just.
> I should be beneficent.
> I should improve myself in terms of virtue or intelligence.
> I should not be maleficent.[30]

These are all, for Ross, 'self-evident' truths.[31] Moreover, the "should" in each is categorical: it is not that I should or should not do something for any particular reason – either to serve an interest of my own or even for the sake of any consequence that my action would bring about – but rather it is simply a fact that I should. Arbitrary as such a position might seem, we should bear in mind that this is also the common-sense view. There are some things we hold to be wrong because they are, for example, cruel or unfair, and we may hold those things to be wrong on the basis of beliefs about the situation – specifically that it exemplifies cruelty or unfairness – but cruelty and unfairness we take to be *just* wrong: they possess, for us, an intrinsic should-not-be-doneness. (This is not, of course, to say that it is only abstract notions that we take to be *just* wrong; rather, it is whatever we take to genuinely exemplify cruelty or unfairness that is *just* wrong.) Intuitionism, then, as the thesis that our moral responses are responses to irreducible objective properties of the world, responses to facts, can be seen as an attempt to philosophically justify our common-sense feeling about moral responses. For, this is also precisely the point to which common sense, when pushed, must come – even if only after floundering about for a while with irrelevant appeals to no one's liking x to happen to them, everyone agreeing that x is wrong and so on.[32] Indeed, it is worth noting that, despite the apparent eccentricity of moral intuitionism in contemporary metaethics, appeals to moral intuitions as if they had evidential weight are, in fact, ubiquitous in ethics. The mere internal consistency of any abstract principle is rarely held to be sufficient to establish that principle: it is often "tested" (usually through moral dilemmas) against how we *feel* about particular cases that instantiate it – just as if there was such a thing as moral truth and our intuition was the most conclusive evidence for that truth.

Before looking in more detail at intuitionism, there is one meaning of "intuition" that we can safely dismiss from consideration. This is its informal use to mean an impression that something might be the case, accompanied by a strong conviction that one's impression is accurate. For example, I may have a strong intuition about how Beckford's novel *Vathek* (1786) would have been received by contemporary reviewers. This is based on indirect evidence: my knowledge of the work, the genre to which it belonged and, more generally, literary taste in the late eighteenth century. Significantly, however, I am only likely to continue referring to the opinion I had formed before consulting the direct evidence as an "intuition" if, after consulting contemporary reviews of the novel, it turns out that my prediction was accurate. If it turns out I was wrong, my intuition now becomes, retrospectively, an inaccurate presumption or mistaken belief, depending on the original strength of the conviction. It would probably be more accurate to call such intuitions "inferences", but it is customary to use "intuition" to refer to such inferences when we are not conscious of either what precisely is the evidence that has led to our conviction (as when we intuit who is calling us before we pick up) or where, as in the *Vathek* case, we cannot grasp precisely how what we count as evidence relates to the conviction we have formed: in short, where we do not know how we "knew". That is, the belief is called an "intuition" precisely because of our *present* inability to articulate our reasons for our provisional belief, not because it is formed on the basis of some non-inferential (magical) way of knowing. What is noteworthy about this use of "intuition" in contrast to the way it is used in connection with the intuition that is our main topic here is that it can only truly qualify as an intuition in retrospect – after I have evidence that I am right. (For the sake of brevity, we will leave aside the question of whether or not the fact actually does justify such "intuitions"; if you "just know" you are going to roll a six and you then roll a six, you do not thereby prove that you knew.) Thus, we might accept that a water diviner had the ability to intuit the presence of underground water if they *consistently* demonstrated the ability to do just that, even if they could not explain how. Moral intuitionism is, however, an entirely different matter, for here the intuition is the *only* evidence for the existence of what is intuited.[33]

There are, however, two forms of intuition that, unlike the form discussed above, we do quite commonly take to be self-guaranteeing. The first is the way in which we grasp what must be true in order for anything else to be true, such as "If x is an A, and all As are B, then x is B" or "2+2=4". Nothing can prove or disprove such analytic propositions, since their truth depends entirely on the meaning of the terms they contain. We intuit their truth from their form. The second kind of intuition is that perceptual seeming that, though in principle open to falsification by observation, we cannot see any reason to doubt at this particular moment in time. Examples of such intuitions could be "I am writing this sentence", "There is a bottle of water beneath the desk" or "All swans are white". Having an intuition of p, in this sense, is what we normally mean when we say that we "know p".

Moral intuitionism holds that, given that we do allow certain of our intuitions to be self-guaranteeing, and that it would indeed be impossible to say we "know" anything if we did not do so, we should allow that what we experience in moral responses are actually self-guaranteeing intuitions of the same kind. According to intuitionism, then, certain of our intuitions can be expressed by evaluative propositions: we can justifiably say we *know* causing gratuitous suffering is wrong, for example, because we have no reason to doubt our *perception* of the wrongness of causing gratuitous suffering.[34] Given the meaning of "wrong", this also, of course, entails that, as the realist Huemer puts it, we intuitively see 'objective reasons for action, actions that do not depend on any contingent desires or other psychological responses of ours'.[35] That is, causing gratuitous suffering is wrong (possesses should-not-be-doneness), not because of any psychological reaction of mine – in the way that funniness, sadness or scariness depend on my being amused, saddened or frightened – but rather because it is 'objectively' wrong so that mere awareness of this fact 'intrinsically provides us with reasons for action'.[36]

The most obvious objection to this parallel between knowing that something is true because I feel it and knowing something is true either because it is necessarily such ("2+2=4") or because I have, or have no reason to believe that I could not have, the evidence of my own eyes ("I am writing this sentence", "All swans are white"), would seem to be that people frequently do disagree about right and wrong in a way that they do not about the objects of these other intuitions. However, to say that we know moral facts by intuition is not to say that every moral intuition is infallible. We may just have to accept that some moral intuitions must be wrong, and, of course, that, since there is no way of arbitrating between conflicting ones, we can have no way of knowing which these are. (The problem of an intuition that must be its own guarantee of success is, of course, that it can never know it is an intuition.) However, the idea that a moral intuition is justified solely by a mental state in the subject does not, in fact, in itself serve to distinguish moral intuitions from any other form of intuition. Perceiving that I am writing this sentence is also a mental state. It may be, of course, that in the case of a moral intuition I will have to fall back on solipsism. For, I can always ask somebody else if they can see me writing the sentence and, though my hearing their reply is merely another mental state of my own, at least I can intuit that I have grounds for believing I have involved (what I take to be) others in my intuition. In contrast, where I can get no one to concur with my moral intuition, I must rest with the intuition as the only possible guarantee. For a consistent moral intuitionism, however, this ought to be sufficient.[37]

The impossibility of arbitrating between conflicting intuitions is not, then, in itself an argument against the idea that at least some of our moral responses are intuitions: perceptions of truth. Moreover, there is no very pressing need to reconcile conflicting intuitions. In practice, as was noted earlier, moral disagreement is much less frequently a matter of what we might call foundational moral intuitions (the wrongness of, for example, cruelty or injustice) than it is of whether or not a particular situation actually instantiates the "property" (cruelty or injustice) that one party to the debate claims to perceive in that situation, and this question, since it turns on non-moral beliefs about the situation, remains debatable and the disputants' conflicting claims amenable to verification and falsification after the manner of our other beliefs, even if we accept moral intuitionism.[38] However, once we have defended the intuitive nature of moral responses on the grounds that they are both self-guaranteeing and fallible, it begins to seem rather gratuitous to assert that some of them *must be* intuitions purely in order to justify the fact that (up to a point) they feel like intuitions.[39]

Moreover, this element of gratuitousness in the case of moral intuitions weakens the argument for their existence that depends on the appeal to the existence of other self-guaranteeing intuitions that are generally taken to be uncontroversial. It is true that we must rely on intuitions or fall into a general scepticism, but it does not follow from this that rejection of moral intuitions is therefore 'arbitrary'. With regard to an intuition such as "I am writing this sentence" there are, as it were, two directions I can pursue in establishing its truth and, thus, my claim to *know* it. One of these I have already described: I can ask somebody else if they can see me writing the sentence and, though my hearing their reply is merely another intuition, at least I can intuit that I have grounds for believing I have involved (what I take to be) others in my intuition. In this way the original intuition gains (or fails to gain) support from an ever-widening circle of separate intuitions that do not depend on it. This likewise holds for less immediate intuitions such as "All swans are white". If I were living in seventeenth-century Europe, the universal whiteness of swans would certainly be part of the current state of science, and every way of checking the fact (with one exception) would lead to an intuition that all swans were white. I would be compelled, therefore, either to accept that I knew all swans were white or to embrace a very broad scepticism about everything I felt I "knew" by either observation or report. (I might, of course, decide that the current state of this part of science is not competent to pronounce on the subject and, consequently, go off to look for a non-white swan, but this is a particular doubt rather than general scepticism.)

What we feel justified in saying that we "know", then, depends almost entirely on the degree to which we have reason to doubt our belief in light of the sum total of our *coherent* intuitions. I am convinced of the existence of Antarctica, for example, even in the absence of any direct evidence of a physical kind, because doubting its existence would involve me in doubting almost everything else I know (given, that is, that its existence is a tenet of that reported knowledge that does constitute the world for me beyond my own physical experience). That is, I would have to interpret my entire life as a hoax being perpetrated upon me in order to seriously entertain a doubt about Antarctica's existence. Moreover, I would have no way of verifying whether this were the case, since, if I can suppose a hoax on such a scale, there is no reason not to suppose that the same powers that have fooled me so far could not arrange for me to believe that I was experiencing "direct physical evidence" of the existence of what I had always believed was Antarctica. To this extent, then, it could be said that I know Antarctica exists because its existence is coherent with everything else that I know: I infer it from what I consider to be my knowledge of the world as a whole. None of this establishes the truth of the existence of Antarctica, but it does show why I have no serious grounds on which to doubt it – or at least none that would not also undermine the possibility of confirming those doubts.

The authority arising from the consistency of the sum of all my intuitions is, then, a much stronger authority than that of any one of them in isolation. Paradoxical as this may seem, given that what I "see with my own eyes" might seem paradigmatic of a trustworthy intuition, it follows from the fact that, if I do have any reason to doubt a particular intuition, this can only be because it fails to be consistent with that whole. Likewise, my reason for trusting that intuition is that it is consistent, or at least not inconsistent, with that whole. Obviously, this establishes nothing about what is actually true (remember the swans), nor about whether or not we actually do ever rely on immediate intuitions, but it does show that the claim that we ever *have to* rely on a particular intuition in isolation (aside from our intuition of the coherence of the totality of our intuitions), as moral intuitionism claims, is false.

Doubting that our moral responses were intuitions of facts would only involve us in general scepticism if such intuitions were necessary to the coherence of all our other intuitions. If that were so, if moral facts were needed to explain certain non-moral facts or if other facts did necessarily imply moral facts, then we could appeal to such a coherence. However, the only non-moral fact that is involved here is the existence of moral experience itself; the only observable effect of the dark matter of moral properties is a psychological one. It could very well be, then, that the phenomenon of moral experience does not require moral properties in the world. This is not, of course, to rule out the possibility of moral properties but only to point out that the burden of proof regarding moral intuitions should most reasonably rest not on disproving the existence of moral facts but rather on eliminating the possibility of any theory more coherent with the rest of what we call knowledge than is moral intuitionism. That is, we might accept moral intuitionism only if there was absolutely no other way to account for moral experience.[40]

There is, however, another kind of coherence that we might appeal to in justifying the objectivity of moral properties, which could perhaps be confused with the epistemological coherence invoked here. After all, we constantly speak of, and treat, rightness and wrongness as properties of the world. Thus, *to all intents and purposes*, they may as well be properties of the world. Although this is a position we shall return to in greater detail in the next chapter, it is worth noting here that this phenomenon does not actually establish anything about the necessity of moral properties to the coherence of the totality of our intuitions. It is quite true that we do not in fact go through any process of broad inferential justification before believing an intuition like "I am writing this sentence" or before acting on an intuition like "There is a bottle of water beneath the table". We more or less incessantly treat things as true, *for all intents and purposes*, with a bare minimum of inferential justification ("I remember putting the bottle there yesterday"). However, the point made above was not that we do inferentially justify all our other perceptions before treating them as intuitions but only that we could do so (if they are justified) or, more importantly, could fail to do so (if we are mistaken). In contrast, while we can certainly confirm or disconfirm our moral *judgements* in terms of whether they are consistent with what we are treating as moral givens, this is not the same as inferentially justifying those supposedly intuited givens themselves. Thus, while we may, in practice, treat both moral and non-moral intuitions as true, *for all intents and purposes*, with an almost equal lack of justification, there nevertheless remains the fundamental difference that in the non-moral case we could attempt (and even fail) to inferentially justify them, while in the moral case, according to intuitionism, we could not. The kind of coherence that arises from practice is not, then, sufficient in itself to establish the existence of moral properties. (Nor, indeed, does practice require that it should.)

There is, of course, an even broader sense of "coherence" invoked in the argument that life itself would not make sense if there were no such *things* as right and wrong. However, this argument so obviously appeals to an interest in the existence of moral properties that, given the exclusively psychological evidence of their existence, it would seem to count, if we allowed it to count at all, rather against than in favour of the real existence of such properties. We cannot appeal to an interest to establish the kind of coherence that underwrites objectivity. This is not, of course, to say that we do not, but only that we cannot consciously do so without throwing the objectivity of that coherence into doubt.

However, I mentioned earlier that there were two directions in which we could look for support for the objectivity of any particular perception. So far, we have only looked at one: the degree to which it coheres with, or is at least not inconsistent with, the totality of our other intuitions.[41] The other direction to take would be an examination of the extent to which the particular perception is consistent with the way in which I usually perceive this kind of object. (Just as, if I began to hear apparently disembodied voices, I would certainly attempt to exhaust every possibility of an external source for the sound before I concluded those voices were "in my head".) So, for example, one of the factors that leads to my conviction that I am writing this sentence is that the way in which I know I am writing this sentence is, if I may trust my memory up to this moment, precisely the same way in which I have known a great many other things that I have, at present, no reason to doubt. Indeed, I might conclude that if the way in which I know I am writing this sentence is not proof that I am writing this sentence, then I *know* nothing (aside, of course, from "Thinking is happening"). Could it not be argued, then, that if I have always taken cruelty or injustice to be objective properties of the world and have never had any reason to doubt that intuition, this fact, in itself, supports the objective existence of those properties?

The problem here is that, as we have seen, a moral response, according to moral intuitionism, must be an intuition of a fact, the mere awareness of which 'intrinsically provides us with reasons for action', irrespective of my interests. This, however, would make it unique among our perceptions: even the most blindingly obvious transitions from a fact to a motivation ("It's raining; I should take an umbrella") must pass through an interest ("I don't want to get wet"). Unlike the example "I am writing this sentence", or even "All swans are white", the very form of an intuition like "Wrongness is a property of the world" is, then, not consistent with the form of any other kind of intuition except another moral intuition.[42] The felt certainty of the moral response does not, then, gain any support from the fact that we often feel justified in claiming to know something on the basis of the form of our intuition in the present instance being consistent with the form of those intuitions that make up the coherent whole we call "reality", for the form of a 'moral intuition' is quite unlike the form of any other intuition.

I do not mean to suggest that there is only one kind of non-moral intuition. However, I am excluding those intuitions that must be the grounds of the beliefs implicit in, for example, the experience of love or in aesthetic and religious experience, since these are generally acknowledged to be at least *influenced* by emotion, even where it is believed (with aesthetics and religion at least) that the object itself somehow meets us halfway. In contrast, the moral intuition, at least according to intuitionism, is supposed to be the sufficient *cause* of what is felt: no distinction can be drawn between perception and feeling.

We could, of course, continue to say that we believe there are moral properties, even if this belief is epistemologically gratuitous, but in that case our conviction is a matter of faith rather than knowledge. Indeed, something like this conclusion was suggested by the way in which, as we saw in examining the phenomenology of moral experience, our moral responses imply beliefs that possess a *greater* degree of conviction than mere perceptions. For, this greater degree of conviction is actually a symptom of the way in which moral responses are exempt from the coherence that supports our convictions in non-moral instances. Thus, while it would be odd to reply to the question "When was the French Revolution?" with "1789, or so I am told", or "Is this tea?" with "To the best of my knowledge", there are, nevertheless, conceivable situations that would render such answers justifiable. Moreover, if the context did not justify them, we would probably fall back on imagining a person struggling with their grasp of the external world. In contrast, a statement like "I suspect injustice might be wrong" (though not "I suspect this is unjust") is inherently absurd.

It is worth here observing that the preceding argument against moral intuitionism could be said to have had a foregone conclusion, since, if our intuitions of moral properties were actually either supported by, or requisite to, any of the rest of our intuitions other than our moral responses, the thesis of moral intuitionism would not be necessary. However, the failure of moral intuitionism to demonstrate the existence of moral properties of the world does not, of course, establish that there are no such things as moral properties or moral truth, but only that the argument to these things on the grounds that we *feel* they exist has no weight. Indeed, we might see intuitionism not as a way of explaining moral responses but rather as the claim that there can be no explanation of moral responses. In this, too, however, it is close to common sense: to the thesis that things are right and wrong because they just are. As such, philosophical intuitionism is helpful in bringing out some of the more startling aspects of the common-sense view. For, it turns out that to argue that moral responses are just what they seem requires the overturning of certain other foundations of common sense: both the conditions governing our normal use of the word "know" and, with regard to the distinction between "is" and "ought", the way in which we normally conceive of motivation. Thus, defending moral realism by appeal to the way in which we experience moral responses leaves us in a situation rather similar to that of those eighteenth-century chemists who, in order to defend the phlogiston theory in the face of contrary evidence, found themselves obliged to posit substances possessing 'negative mass'.

Realism: Supernaturalism

There is, however, another way of interpreting moral responses as responses to moral properties of the world, another form of moral realism, that does not have to rely exclusively on their *felt* objectivity, in the manner of moral intuitionism. It also has the advantage of offering an explanation as to why I experience moral responses as dispositional, as desire, without at the same time feeling that they can be entirely accounted for in terms of my desires. This way is to posit moral responses not as responses to natural properties (properties that could be the object of observations other than moral responses) but, rather, as responses to non-natural properties. So, for example, we might see them as responses to properties of the world that some non-human entity (one or more gods) *knew* to be wrong (even if, as we have seen, we ourselves are incapable of even conceiving of such knowledge).[43] Providing, then, that the entity had somehow implanted in us an instinct to respond to these properties as what they really are, providing 'the great laws of morality are engraven on every heart', this would explain why we feel as if we are responding to a real property of the world even though, from our own human vantage point, we are unable to offer any evidence for this beyond our feeling that it is so.[44] This would also overcome the problem of getting from an "is" to an "ought", since it would make our perception of wrongness more akin to a sensation, and sensations do intrinsically provide us with motives for action. In short, it would make the moral response equivalent to a physiological response. The moral properties would be real, even if our only access to that reality was through this instinct itself.

Thus, for example, Hume, having noted that what is right 'is desirable on its own account, without fee and reward, merely for the immediate satisfaction which it conveys', concludes that it must be one of those ends that we desire simply by virtue of its 'immediate accord or agreement with human sentiment and affection': something that is, in effect, an end in itself.[45] Given this, it can only be accounted for in terms of the very possession of what counts as human sentiment and affection: the 'eternal frame and constitution of animals . . . ultimately derived from that Supreme Will, which bestowed on each being its peculiar nature'.[46] Likewise, Kant holds that the existence of the moral disposition is 'incomprehensible' without the supposition of a divine origin.[47] (The moral law, of course, requires no grounding beyond reason itself – but only because the moral disposition is, for Kant, a *given*.[48]) This follows from the very characteristics of the moral response that we have already considered: the way in which it is simultaneously both motivating and yet contrary to any interest or inclination, without, at the same time, being actually determining after the manner of a physiological response. Thus, it cannot, according to Kant, be accounted for in terms of anything else that we encounter *within* nature.[49] Indeed, he goes as far as offering moral experience as the only ground for supposing the existence of God and the nature of that experience as the only rational guide to the construction of theology.[50]

The supernatural is, historically, a common solution to the problem of grounding our moral responses in a mind-independent reality. However, since neither the existence nor the nature of such a non-human entity has itself any mind-independent guarantee, the supposition of the viewpoint of that entity, from which moral properties are real properties, does not solve the problem of grounding our intuitions; it merely postpones it.[51]

Realism: Naturalism

What, however, if we could have moral realism without the supposition of mind-independent properties of the world, if we could discover a reason for it in our 'peculiar nature' without appeal to a Divine Will? There are, indeed, some uses of the term 'moral realism' that set much lower criteria for the reality of the properties implicit in our moral responses than their mind-independent existence. Railton, for example, holds that 'moral judgments' (including expressions of moral responses) can be truth-apt, that moral properties are objective and that moral properties supervene upon natural properties, and may be reducible to them.[52] His argument begins from the observation that we have what he calls *objectified subjective interests*: that there are things we would want if we only knew that they were the things we want (as we would "want", in a slightly archaic sense, an umbrella on going out into rain, even if we did not know it was raining).[53] To offer a personal example, I was in my thirties before I learned that the peculiar discomfort I often felt after prolonged physical activity was actually thirst and could be removed simply by drinking. Fluid would have satisfied an objective interest I had, even though I was not, before a certain age, aware of this fact. Thus we could say that, when thirsty, drinking was *intrinsically non-morally good for Kirwan* since it was in his objective interest, whether Kirwan knew it or not.[54] From such instances Railton concludes that it is possible to talk of the 'objective value' of certain things, at least in relation to our needs.[55] He emphasizes this last point because, although he speaks of the 'objectivity' of the value, he means only that it exists because humans exist. However, '[although] relational, the relevant facts about humans and their world are objective in the same sense that such nonrelational entities as stones are: they do not depend for their existence or nature merely upon our conception of them'. Given this objectivity, and our lack of omniscience (witness the thirst case), it is further possible to say that 'facts exist about what individuals have reason to do . . . substantially independent of, and more normatively compelling than, an agent's occurrent conception of his reasons'.[56]

Turning to morality, Railton notes that moral 'evaluation' is centrally concerned with assessment of conduct 'where the interests of more than one individual are at stake', that it presumes 'a social point of view'.[57] A 'genuinely' moral point of view, he asserts, is 'impartial with respect to the interests of all potentially affected, and . . . not a socially bounded notion'.[58] Thus, to find what is really morally good, what is 'objectively' in the best interest of any particular society, we can consider 'what would be rationally approved of were the interests of all potentially affected individuals counted equally under circumstances of full and vivid information'.[59] This will be equivalent to 'what is rational from a social point of view with regard to the realization of intrinsic non-moral goodness', and judgements will be relatively right or wrong insofar as they approximate to this criterion. What results, according to Railton, is 'a form of moral realism' that renders moral values objective, not from a 'cosmic' point of view but, rather, from a human yet impartial one: an objectivity grounded only in 'facts about man and his environment, facts about what sorts of things matter to us, and how the ways we live affect these things'.[60]

This seems perfectly reasonable. Given that we are both seeking what is best for everyone, there is every reason to suppose that your *judgement*, as a statement about what will best lead to that goal, can possess more factual accuracy than my *judgement* that fails to take into account relevant factors. Moreover, there really are things that will be in the best interest of the majority in any given situation, whether the majority knows it or not. However, while Railton's moral realism certainly highlights the role of rationality in evaluative discourse, it does not yield any moral realism in the sense that we are seeking. Indeed, his explanation bypasses moral responses altogether. It takes one – the taking of the social view – as given and then shows how we can adjudicate between moral judgements in terms of this original one. This phenomenon we have already dealt with in discussing moral judgements. It may be that he is suggesting that morality per se is our unconsciously taking, or at least attempting to take, the point of view of society, and that all our moral responses are, in fact, predictions about the greater good (albeit that this leaves unanswered the question as to why we should feel either an interest in or an obligation towards taking such a viewpoint). However, all this touches not at all on the felt certainty of moral responses themselves, which do not, after all, seem to take the form of predictions.

What, however, if we could take an impartial interest in a fundamental objective need of humanity for granted and our moral responses as involuntary expressions of this interest? If this were so, it would yield what is "objectively valuable", if not from the point of view of the universe, as with the supposition of some forms of the divine, then at least from the human point of view. For many writers around the turn of this century, and, indeed, around the turn of the last, the theory of evolution appeared to provide justification for supposing just such an impartial interest in fundamental objective needs. This does not, of course, mean that we are conscious of the end – personal or species survival – aimed at by those responses. It is rather a matter of a suprapersonal interest acting, as it were, *through* the individual – in the manner of, for example, sexual desire. For, while sexual desire per se may aim at reproduction, it is not the thought of reproduction that arouses our sexual desire or reproduction itself that satisfies it. Thus, we might take the moral response as the expression of a concern for the welfare of the group, or even the physical self, that the individual experiences as an imperative beyond their capacity to rationalize (though one that is so familiar that no need is felt to rationalize it). Concern for the welfare of the group would, then, simply be part of human nature.[61] This would not, of course, mean that every moral response could ultimately be justified in terms of what everyone would recognize as the welfare of the group/self. Any instinct embedded in something so complex as human consciousness is bound to be expressed in tortuous ways. Thus, we might justifiably expect there to be certain moral responses that stood in the same relationship to such an instinct to promote one's own or the group's welfare as, for example, foot fetishism does to the instinct to reproduce. Such a supposition would, however, make the good of society an "interest" of the individual, even if not one that they would own or recognize as an interest. It would, moreover, account for the peculiar, categorically imperative, nature of morality, for the moral response would now be equivalent to a physiological response, a sensation.

This is the purpose of bringing evolution into ethics: to underwrite the existence of such a quasi-physiological response. Those who have evoked evolution do so in order to posit that in the moral response we are responding to a perception not of what is morally good in itself (as intuitionism holds) but, rather, what either presents itself to us or at least what once presented itself to us, as instrumentally useful to our own or our species survival. And, further, that we experience this response as if it were an intuition of the morally good or bad (a revelation of the categorically imperative) rather than as what it actually is (a perception of what is useful), because by so doing we better secure our own commitment to undertaking what is instrumentally useful to ourselves, our group or our species.

In what way would possession of moral responses convey a survival advantage? The distinguishing characteristic of a moral response is that it implies an interest in the interests of others that does not appear to depend on any self-interest. What an evolutionary account must provide, then, is some way of showing that this deference to the interests of others could either serve self-interest or be the hallmark of the "interests" of the gene group or even species bypassing self-interest.[62] This latter option, despite the analogy I drew with sexual desire earlier, seems extremely unlikely – not least, of course, because genes and species are not actually things that can possess interests. As creatures that actually do possess interests, we may see that, given a gene's or species' "desire" to survive, a certain course of action would be "in its interest", but we can only attribute that interest to the gene or species through anthropomorphism. Species evolve through the increasing prevalence of what are originally random genetic mutations that have, coincidentally, turned out to confer a reproductive advantage given the environmental conditions. Those mutations, despite the figurative language so frequently employed when talking of evolution, are not part of a "design" to produce the subsequent organism: they are not strategies based on an interest. To claim, then, that the reproductive advantage of the possession of moral responses bypasses the interests of the individual in favour of the gene group or species would be to make an odd claim. Odd because it would oblige us to imagine a tendency to moral responses arising as a random genetic mutation: basically, coming out of nowhere. This is not to say that such a thing is impossible, but if we add to this thesis of the spontaneous generation of moral responses the further observation that the mere fact of the species subsequently surviving with this trait actually demonstrates nothing about its survival value, then the appeal to evolutionary advantage begins to appear largely redundant. It renders an explanation of moral responses in terms of evolution just as arbitrary as explaining them in terms of a unique form of the intuition of otherwise unknowable real properties of the world or in terms of our possession of a spark of the divine.

However, a more plausible linking of morality to evolution is that which posits a connection between the possession of moral responses and the interests of the individual. The idea here is that the kind of behaviour that we associate with moral feeling – specifically setting aside some of our immediate interests in favour of the interests of others or feeling the interests of others as if they were our own – is, given that we are social animals, actually in our own longer-term best interests.[63] (This is, frankly, so self-evidently the case, that one can only wonder at those who feel the need to appeal to, for example, game theory or the behaviour of monkeys in order to prove it.) Acting from enlightened self-interest is not, however, the same as acting out of a feeling of moral compulsion – even if the action is the same. Moreover, what we are looking for is not a cause for behaviour that is compatible with moral responses but rather a cause for those responses themselves. The belief implicit within the moral response is neither that is politic to act in a certain way, nor even that it is politic to feel as if we must in a certain way; rather it is the belief that, irrespective of what is politic, we must act in a certain way. How, then, can evolutionary advantage account for the way in which we feel we ought or ought not to do certain things, irrespective of self-interest? The usual answer to this is that we will be more surely motivated to set aside some of our immediate interests in favour of the interests of others if we feel that we are being compelled by reality itself to do so, rather than simply because we wish to do so out of self-interest. Hence, we experience this enlightened self-interest in the form of a response implying a categorical imperative, as something we *ought* to do irrespective of our interests, simply because this is the most effective way of ensuring that we do pursue our best interests.[64] In short, nature is deceiving us into doing what is best for ourselves.

Once again, however, as with the notion examined earlier – that genetic variation has simply bypassed our interests in favour of the gene group or species – there is something rather arbitrary about the supposition that, given that moral-like behaviour has a survival advantage, the peculiar psychology that would best ensure such behaviour should also somehow emerge from genetic variation to provide reinforcement. It was, after all, not the practical value of moral-like behaviour in itself but rather the peculiar psychology of the moral response that an evolutionary account was supposed to illuminate. It now turns out that a *presumption* that this psychological phenomenon is the product of evolution is necessary in order to maintain any link between morality and evolution. It would seem, then, that the concept of evolutionary advantage is contributing no more to the explanation of that phenomenon than did the concepts of a special kind of intuition or a supernatural origin.

The gap between the practical value of moral-like behaviour and moral feeling has sometimes been bridged in evolutionary accounts, when it has been bridged at all, by the concept of empathy. There is, of course, an obvious survival advantage to being able to comprehend the contents of other consciousnesses, and the ability to do so would seem a quite natural extension, or consequence, of *understanding* itself. However, empathy per se does not entail moral feeling. We can only get from one to the other by confounding empathy (understanding what another is thinking or feeling) with sympathy (caring about what another is feeling *for the sake of that other*). This is only a "natural" transition from the viewpoint of creatures who already possess moral feeling: it presupposes moral feeling.[65]

The other principal way in which the gap has been bridged is by the idea that the moral-like behaviour arising from self-interest, or the values potentially implicit in that behaviour, becomes 'internalized', so as to produce the feeling that certain things should or should not be done, not because this serves any particular purpose, but simply because they should or should not be done.[66] There is, of course, nothing problematic about the notion of internalization itself. As the nonconscious mental acquisition of the behaviour patterns, feelings, attitudes and beliefs of those around one, with the result that these things become one's own, internalization is, indeed, the normal process by which one becomes both oneself and, simultaneously, part of the human community. However, it is unclear how this process, routine and observable though it may be within the life span of an individual, is supposed to operate in terms of genetic variation. The relationship between our contemporary selves and our ancestors is *not* equivalent to the relationship between the infant and adult forms of our current selves. The use of "internalization" in connection with the process of evolution is, then, at best a figurative extension of its use within psychology. Moreover, if the belief that moral-type action is in one's own self-interest can be internalized in such a way that it produces the belief, implicit in moral responses – that everyone *should* behave in a certain way regardless of self-interest – then there is no reason to invoke the process of evolution at all: this transformation of enlightened self-interest into moral feeling could be something that, given the right environmental cues, takes place within the lifetime of each contemporary homo sapiens.[67]

It turns out, then, that the introduction of evolutionary considerations does not help us account for the existence of moral experience. Enlightened self-interest in itself is prima facie quite adequate to give rise to that cooperative behaviour that would convey a reproductive advantage to a sociable organism, without the further supposition of moral feeling. Moreover, it would seem contrary to any organism's objective interests to develop the trait of misperceiving the nature of its environment in the way that the moral realism implicit in moral feeling, by this very account, misperceives the world (as containing moral properties). Indeed, what we have here is not an evolutionary explanation of moral experience but rather a fairly plausible account of the survival advantage of being sufficiently forward-looking to sacrifice an immediate interest for a future one, that only becomes an account of the evolutionary origins of morality through the deus ex machina of a trait that actually functions to hide the organism's interests from itself. This may, of course, be precisely what has happened. However, given that the (genetic) cause is necessarily being inferred from the (psychological) effect, that there is no way of verifying the connection, that nothing we know of the nature of such causes helps us to understand how such a cause could be the cause of such an effect (unless we allow for a form-follows-habit rather than a Darwinian model of evolution), and that, to make it plausible at all, we must appeal to a mechanism (internalization) that belongs to psychology rather than biology (thereby potentially rendering an evolutionary explanation redundant), it must be allowed that the mere supposition that moral experience is biologically selected for possesses no explanatory value.

Indeed, the appeal of the currently fashionable recourse to evolution to explain morality, to the idea that we are biologically "hardwired", "programmed", or "designed" to be moral, would seem to rest not so much upon any contribution it makes to our understanding of moral experience as upon a desire to underwrite right and wrong with science, to transfer to Nature the beneficence once attributed to God.[68] It is, therefore, worth remarking in passing that, even if evolutionary advantage were taken as an adequate explanation of the existence of moral experience, such an explanation would still not answer the ambition of moral realism to anchor moral responses to moral facts.[69] A grounding in evolutionary advantage would not confer objectivity upon moral responses per se, since it necessarily requires the supposition that in responding this way we are in the grip of a belief that is false: that our moral responses are *not* a matter of our interests.[70] We might, however, consider that such a grounding nevertheless renders the response 'objective' in the alternative sense (used by Railton) of being a response that registers the presence of an objective need. This presumes, of course, that the fact of a certain response once possessing survival value is proof that it still possesses survival value.[71] If this objection appears weak, it is because evolutionary accounts tend to *begin* from the social usefulness of moral-like behaviour and then invoke evolution to explain the appearance of a mental state that would best ensure the performance of this behaviour, so that the contemporary survival value of the response is actually a premise in the account. Nevertheless, there is always the possibility that such a mental state might frustrate the ends that it is supposed to serve. Say, for example, that in order to ground, for the sake of reason, the felt certainty of the response while simultaneously avoiding the supposedly deleterious effect of becoming aware of the true grounding in self-interest, this mental state gave rise, in turn, to belief in a beneficent supernatural source for that certainty. This now concomitant belief clearly need not have physical survival as an implicit goal in any of the behaviours that it inspires; indeed, it might even entail an ideal of "survival" entirely different from, and incompatible with, the survival that the original mental state was supposed to ensure.

In fact, more sophisticated evolutionary accounts generally acknowledge that the mere fact of a capacity for moral feeling conveying a survival advantage does not entail that every instance of a moral response is an *accurate* perception of what should, let alone will, convey such an advantage.[72] We need only consider the myriad different rights and wrongs that have existed over the course of even that small part of the history of human culture that is known to us to conclude either that the mental state of perceiving what has survival value as "right in itself" actually always does contain a nonconscious sub-reference to what has real survival value for the particular subject *at this particular moment,* or that the mere having of a moral response is no guarantee that one is responding to a humanly objective need. This is not, of course, to say that the objective interest posited in the evolutionary account could not be established another way. If a certain kind of moral-like behaviour has been demonstrated to have survival value, then it should be possible to deduce the principles implicit in that behaviour. These principles would then yield a measure of what behaviour was either conducive or detrimental to survival. (So, if the universal practice of justice turns out to be necessary to your personal survival, then, given that you desire nothing more than survival, "You should be just" becomes true in the light of the ends for which moral behaviour exists at all.) This would, then, serve to underwrite as (coincidentally) 'objective' those responses that turned out to be in line with what was conducive to survival. Given, however, that the authority of such derived principles would not depend on any of our moral responses, the question would inevitably arise as to why we *should* defer to them. Since the only way to do so would be to consciously elect to take personal survival as the goal of our behaviour, irrespective of our actual moral responses, whatever kind of *should* was involved, it could not be a moral one.[73] (Genuinely moral principles are invariably unconditional.) If, conversely, we elect to take everyone's survival *in itself* as the implicit goal of our behaviour, irrespective of whether this is conducive to our own survival, then we are already acting morally (rather than in a moral-like way), and this clearly cannot be seen as the expression of the kind of objective human need with which evolutionary theory deals.[74] For, it was only the supposition that I would gain an advantage in terms of personal survival from *behaving as if* I had an interest in everyone else's interests that brought evolution into the debate at all.

An evolutionary explanation of moral experience, then, will not help to establish the objectivity of moral responses in themselves if that objectivity is supposed to rest upon the perception of what really is, since it requires such responses to be a form of self-deception. Conversely, if such an explanation is supposed to establish that moral responses are objective in the sense that they are responses to an objective need of which I may be unaware, it both fails to show that this is so and offers no way of even employing the supposition that they are so that does not involve replacing moral experience with a principle that bears no relation to moral experience.

Nevertheless, our principal reason for turning to evolutionary accounts was to explain rather than to justify the *felt* objectivity of moral responses, that is, to account for the peculiar phenomenology of moral experience. As we have seen, however, the supposition of an evolutionary origin to this feeling adds nothing that would help to explain its existence. From the observation that cooperation has survival value, the evolutionary account deduces the development (by means unknown) of a mental state that might help to ensure this cooperation, though only at the cost of both systematically false beliefs and, as a concomitant, an inherent unreliability in achieving its end. Thus, even if it turned out that no more plausible account of the origin of moral experience was forthcoming, acquiescence in the evolutionary account would still require a leap of faith.

Conclusion

It turns out, then, that moral realism is far from being the simplest explanation for the felt necessity of the moral responses, if only because it is not at all explanatory. Indeed, it should have been clear from the beginning that we were not going to find a mind-independent moral property: objective value. For, given that "objective" refers to that which is not dependent upon how anyone feels about it, and "value" to that which renders something desirable (or which can be considered a *fair* equivalent for something else), "objective value" is a contradiction in terms. In so far, then, as the moral response implies the perception (or, at least, unconscious assumption) of such a value, it appears to be a matter of projection. Moreover, even if we did discover another property of this dark matter, *aside* from its psychological effects, so that some people's moral responses did turn out to be somehow correct, this would still not justify the felt certainty of the response. That response, as we have seen, is experienced as necessarily joined to the object of the response in a way that appears to preclude any contribution from my self-interest and thus from emotion, despite its obviously emotional character.[75]

However, before returning to the inherently problematic nature of moral experience itself, it is worth looking at how those who ostensibly reject realism have dealt with that rejection might entail. We may recall here Hume's assertion that goodness and badness are not matters of fact, not qualities of objects but, rather, qualities we attribute to objects based on our own sentiments. Despite believing that his thesis subverts 'all the vulgar systems of morality', he nevertheless also holds that it should make no difference to how we think or behave. Realization of the fact that morality is entirely a matter of sentiment may be, he says, 'a considerable advancement of the speculative sciences', but, since nothing is more urgent to us, or concerns us more, than our own feelings or sentiments, then, so long as these are 'favourable to virtue, and unfavourable to vice, no more can be requisite to the regulation of our conduct and behaviour'.[76]

This is a moot point. For one thing, our sentiments always are 'favourable to virtue' and 'unfavourable to vice', for that is, according to his thesis, what the words 'virtue' and 'vice' mean: whatever causes, respectively, approbation and disapprobation in us.[77] Thus Hume's apparently reassuring assertion that the perception of virtue and vice is safe in the care of feeling (with its suggestion that, contrary to his own thesis, virtues and vices do exist separately from our sentiments) really, then, adds nothing. That humans can always be relied upon to have *a* sense of right and wrong does nothing to validate *my* sense of right or wrong. One can see, however, why the addition is here. Many feel that the idea of right and wrong being contingent upon our feelings in some way weakens their reality and thus their authority, so that to feel morality to be contingent would indeed alter the way we think and behave. Hume's additional comment here does seem intended to reassure. The problem is that it should not be reassuring.

However, perhaps Hume is saying that, since we cannot *feel* the truth of the fact that right and wrong are a matter of sentiment, there is no point even trying to take this fact into account in everyday life. In other words, while recognition of the subjectivity of morality may be 'a considerable advancement of the speculative sciences', it is not worth thinking any more about: it is an idea for the study, not the street. In short, his point may be that the subjectivity of morals has no practical bearing on everyday life. It might also be, of course, that he believes the validity of our feelings to be secured by their divine origin.[78]

Whatever the cause of Hume's lack of any sense of urgency, or perhaps his caution, writers on ethics that followed certainly did discern a threat to the reality of right and wrong, and a concomitant threat to the hold of morality, from the trend he represented. Thus, where we do not actually find the whole question passed over in favour of a pursuit of the normative, we find an almost reflex assumption of some form of moral realism.[79] It is unsurprising, then, given the untenability of such realism, that the first half of the twentieth century should not be short of outspoken anti-realists. In a lecture in 1930, Wittgenstein asserted that there can be no such thing as a moral fact.[80] Given that this is so, he continues, there is a 'characteristic misuse' of language running through all ethical expressions, an essential 'nonsensicality' to them in so far as, in asserting the existence of what is unconditionally valuable, they seek '*to go beyond* the world and that is to say beyond significant language'.[81] Westermarck, in the same decade, declared that, despite both the assumptions of common sense and the arguments of moral philosophers and theologians, it is simply impossible to prove that 'moral judgements' (responses) could ever possess objective validity, since all such 'judgements' and all 'moral concepts' are ultimately 'based on emotions'.[82] According to Barnes, value judgements (expressions of moral responses) are, strictly speaking, not judgements at all: they are 'exclamations' reporting the occurrence of a certain feeling in the speaker, and we will only discover their origin in 'the expressions of approval, delight, and affection, which children utter when confronted with certain experiences'.[83] Moreover, such 'judgements' will only be meaningful 'in so far as the society in which they are used is agreed on what things it approves'.[84] Ayer, in the same period, more famously declared the same: to say "You acted wrongly in stealing that money", he asserts, is not, with regard to facts, to say any more than "You stole that money".[85] The former does not add a new fact about the action; it merely evinces your moral disapproval of it – as if you had said "You stole that money!" in a horrified voice. Since the use of moral terms must have this personal reference, it follows, according to Ayer, that a sentence like "Stealing money is wrong" has no factual meaning at all: in the sense that it contains nothing that can be either true or false. (It may be true or false that I have those sentiments, but that is a fact about me, not about stealing.) Sentences that express moral propositions, he concludes, 'are pure expressions of feelings and as such do not come under the category of truth and falsehood'.[86] For this reason there can be no question of discovering truths about ethics; moreover, the task of describing the feelings that ethical terms express and customarily provoke is one for psychology rather than philosophy.[87]

Stevenson puts the matter rather differently, emphasizing interest rather than emotion (though the central thesis remains the same, since emotion always registers the advancement or frustration of a desire). When we call a thing "good", he asserts, all that we are doing is expressing our interest in that thing and trying to direct other's interest towards it.[88] What distinguishes the moral use of "good" is that it expresses a 'stronger sort of approval' than mere liking: 'When a person likes something, he is pleased when it prospers, and disappointed when it doesn't. When a person morally approves of something, he experiences a rich feeling of security when it prospers, and is indignant, or "shocked" when it doesn't'.[89] To those who object that right and wrong must be a matter of fact, of truth, Stevenson says that he can only reply that he does not understand what they are looking for: 'What is this truth to be about?'[90] The idea that there can be moral facts, he says, is the result of confusion. At best, he concludes, we can try to account for this confusion, to show the 'psychological needs' that have given rise to it and 'show how these needs may be satisfied in another way'.[91]

Russell is perhaps most overtly dismissive of moral realism. When we assert that anything has value, he says, 'we are giving expression to our own emotions, not to a fact which would still be true if our personal feelings were different'.[92] Though we may seem to be making a factual statement by saying "This is good", what we really mean, according to Russell, is "I wish everybody to desire this" or "Would that everybody desired this".[93] If we disagree about values, then we are not involved in a dispute about truth but rather enmeshed in a difference of taste. If one person says "Oysters are good" and another says "I think they are bad", there is really nothing to argue about. Differences of value, he concludes, are always like this 'although we do not naturally think them so when we are dealing with matters that seem to us more exalted than oysters'.[94]

This suggestion that questions of right and wrong are on par with liking or disliking oysters is, of course, deliberately provocative. However, in contrast to Ayer or

Stevenson, Russell does directly address the question of whether the non-existence of moral facts should make any practical difference to us. Believers in objective values, he predicts, will object that the view he is advocating must lessen our moral sense. Such a fear, he says, is groundless. Moral obligation is not a matter of belief but of desire: a desire for approval, or for some general consequence (say, the happiness of mankind) that we find desirable in itself. Thus, he concludes, if such a desire is strong enough, it 'will produce its own morality', in the sense of its own motive for acting well.[95]

What precisely the effect of the widespread acceptance of subjectivism would be is an empirical matter: we would have to see.[96] However, I do not dispute that it is possible to act in a way that other people would be likely to call "moral" (e.g. apparently unselfishly) while being oneself fully aware that one was motivated by an interest (an interest, that is, other than an interest in behaving morally). That is, morality may be a sufficient condition for "acting well", but it is not a necessary one. What I would dissent from is the view that this behaviour is actually motivated by anything that one could experience as "morality", or that anyone else would continue to call it "moral" if they understood its underlying motivation. In short, I suspect that Russell's claim that a self-interested motive for acting well, if the self-interest is strong enough, will 'produce its own morality' is a misuse of the word "morality": having a motive to act morally and being morally motivated are not the same thing.[97] For, in order for me to experience my desire for the world to be a better place as a matter of morality, I must experience this desire not simply as *my* desire, as advancing my interests or to my taste, but rather as a response to the *fact* that the world should be a better place. Which is, incidentally, one of the reasons why the expression "Murder is wrong" (or even "Would that no one committed murder!") is bound to strike us as very different in form from "I don't like oysters".

Stevenson, as we saw, at least draws a distinction, if only in terms of intensity, between a moral response and other kinds of liking: the 'rich feeling of security' at moral action, and the indignation and shock at the immoral. However, Stevenson, like Barnes and Ayer, is similar to Russell in this: all four present the highly counter-intuitive emotivist thesis as if it were simply a matter of unacknowledged common sense (as if, that is, only a misguided professor of ethics in search of 'The Good' would dream of dissenting). When a person says "This is good", according to Russell, what they 'really' mean is 'I wish everybody to desire this', or rather 'Would that everybody desired this'. However, this will not do. What the person really means is what they say – "This is good" – and no paraphrase that introduces an interest will faithfully reflect this meaning. For, while I agree that the report of a moral response does not describe the world, but only express the way the speaker feels about it (so that Russell's paraphrase may, indeed, be all that such an expression could meaningfully signify), nevertheless, it is only the expression of a moral response insofar as the speaker *feels* that they are really describing the world. We would not feel them as moral responses if we did not feel them to be responses to facts.

There is, however, a certain amount of obvious coat-trailing in the treatment of ethics in Britain during the 1930s.[98] Given the relationship between moral responses and the moral judgements already described, there must be an element of exaggeration in any claim that the emotional nature of moral responses renders ethical debate meaningless, even given that this same relationship renders the language of that debate (and the conviction that *may* accompany it) highly problematic. There was, as we have already noted, nothing particularly controversial about referring to 'moral emotions' outside of philosophy in the previous century. However, it seems to have been the new emphasis on language itself within philosophy in the twentieth century that brought on the crisis; for, moral language appears to either report, or at least depend upon the existence of, intuitions of objective value, and yet objective value is an impossibility. To some extent the immediate reaction within ethics to the highlighting of this disparity was very much beside the point. 'Emotivism' and 'expressivism' were answered with a variety of demonstrations of the ways in which ethical propositions do not behave like expressions of emotion – a strategy that rather overlooks what might be the point of highlighting the disparity in the first place.[99] At the same time, however, it must be acknowledged that the emotive theory of moral language is also an assertion of the epistemological innocence of that language: if it is not assertive, then its appearance of realism is unimportant. Thus, emotivism and expressivism could be interpreted not as assaults upon the implicit realism of moral language so much as defences of the rationality of employing such language. It seems to have only been after Mackie, in the second half of the century, uncoupled the discussion of moral language from the outright assertion of an emotional origin, and emphasized instead, as had Wittgenstein, the epistemological offences of that language, that the debate really began to involve, if often only indirectly, the more fundamental question of the status of the response itself. Insofar as 'moral judgements' implicitly claim to point to 'something objectively prescriptive', Mackie declared, they must be 'false'.[100]

The idea that moral language is systematically erroneous is still, of course, a thesis about language and, as such, open to various responses that can simply ignore the implications for the moral response itself.[101] (We have already seen how moral *judgements* can be truth-apt for a given context.) However, what happened in practice at the end of the twentieth century and the beginning of the twenty-first, and largely it seems in response to Mackie's thesis, was that avowedly subjectivist philosophers, in seeking to reassert a sense to moral language and moral debate, began to introduce into their accounts of moral experience whatever distortions were necessary to make that experience square with the defensibility of moral language – a process facilitated by the confounding of moral responses and moral judgements already described. Moreover, this concern with the rationality of moral language was often accompanied by what appeared to be a revival of the nineteenth century's fear of the effects of *acknowledging* the subjectivity of moral feeling, albeit now recast as a concern over the subjectivity of moral feeling being "misunderstood".

There are, indeed, two basic ways in which certain trends in recent metaethics have sought to come to terms with the way that, given the untenability of realism, moral experience seems to embody a systematic misperception. The first is to circumvent this undesirable conclusion by suggesting that common sense already acknowledges the subjectivity of moral experience, so that there is actually no such thing as moral realism, except as a linguistic convention, for subjectivism to be contrasted with. (There is, of course, one prima facie difficulty with this position: precisely what function a subjectivist account of morals is supposed to serve if it is already the common sense. We do not after all require subjectivist "explanations" of such things as food preferences or nostalgia.) The second way, which allows considerably greater variation, is to present subjectivism itself as somehow equivalent to realism in every significant respect.

Given the current influence of these two strategies, it will not be possible to carry on with an investigation into the problem of the moral response until we have demonstrated that these strategies do not, in fact, solve that problem. The next task, then, is, in effect, to defend subjectivism against several prominent contemporary versions of subjectivism.

2

Defending subjectivism against subjectivists

The arguments examined in this chapter are those developed by ostensibly non-realist philosophers who wish to be able to make an assertion like "Causing gratuitous suffering is wrong", without having to make the philosophically indefensible claim that it is a fact that causing gratuitous suffering is wrong (though some of the positions we will examine later sail fairly close to just such a claim). The first such argument we shall deal with, developed it seems largely in response to Mackie's error theory, is a more developed version of an idea we encountered in Russell at the end of the last chapter: the idea that subjectivism is merely unacknowledged common sense.

Fictionalism

Fictionalism, largely, though not completely, eschewing questions of mental states, deals with the question of the apparently realism-committed nature of moral language very much in terms of language. It argues that moral statements need not be taken as assertions of belief in mind-independent properties, and that it is only a 'systematic ambiguity in our representational idiom' that leads us to unwittingly mistake fictional truth for genuine truth.[1] In short, fictionalism is the thesis that a statement like "Causing gratuitous suffering is wrong" is not actually intended to assert that it is a fact that causing gratuitous suffering is wrong. In at least one form, then, fictionalism holds that, although we appear to talk as if rightness and wrongness exist independently of our feelings, that is not, in reality, what we mean: we are only speaking *as if* they were. Thus, when someone says '*x* is wrong' they are to be understood as expressing an attitude towards *x* (as Ayer, Stevenson, or Russell might have said), and our agreement or disagreement with the statement is to be understood as an assertion that we either do or do not share that attitude.

Kalderon, who has championed this thesis, argues that while moral sentences may express moral propositions, 'just as the realist maintains', nevertheless, in uttering them speakers are not asserting the moral proposition expressed but rather using the words both to convey how they 'feel' about something and to implicitly demand that others 'come to respond affectively in the relevant manner'.[2] This is not, however, simply a matter of the standard noncognitivist claim that the content of a moral sentence is its conveying the noncognitive attitude involved in its acceptance. Rather, Kalderon believes that the moral content can be representational without agreement with it being a matter of belief in the moral proposition expressed, and thus without its utterance being an assertion of that proposition.[3] It is a mistake, he claims, to interpret moral utterance as assertion or the acceptance of a moral assertion as a belief.[4] Thus the apparently realist 'fiction of a moral subject matter' is not an error; rather, it is simply 'the means by which the noncognitive attitudes involved in moral acceptance are conveyed by moral utterance'.[5] In this way, Kalderon argues, fictionalism can vindicate noncognitivism without having to make the extreme and counterintuitive claim that moral sentences are all systematically false.[6]

This is not, at least according to Kalderon, a matter of revising our account of the 'feeling' that is conveyed by an utterance like 'x is wrong'. Feeling the wrongness of x, he holds, is equivalent to accepting that there is a reason to avoid doing x, that this reason takes precedence over non-moral reasons that might be salient in other circumstances, and that this reason is not contingent upon my acceptance of it (hence the implicit demand for others' acceptance of x's wrongness).[7] The 'relevant affect', then, is 'nothing over and above the tendency for certain features of the circumstance to become salient in perception, thought, and imagination, and for these to present a certain complex normative appearance'.[8] This is uncontroversial enough. Indeed, Kalderon himself describes his specification of the attitudes involved in moral acceptance as 'circular': the affect involved in the acceptance of a sentence ostensibly asserting that something is wrong is the feeling that something is wrong.[9] It may be, he concludes, that moral discourse is 'fictional' precisely because there is no way to specify in non-moral terms what is being conveyed by a moral utterance: it may be that moral language is 'indispensable in specifying the attitudes involved in moral acceptance'.[10]

However, while the realist would hold that in reporting this feeling – 'x is wrong' – I am expressing a belief about a property of the world, the fictionalist holds that this is not how we should understand such language. (Indeed, Kalderon suggests that it is only the convention of using such language that gives rise to the 'epistemological posture' or 'stance' of moral realism.[11]) A sentence like 'x is wrong' should be understood, according to Kalderon, as a 'quasi-assertion': an utterance that is not an assertion of the proposition expressed, and thus not a matter of stating a belief.[12] Quasi-assertions, he holds, exist not to describe beliefs about the world but as representations that are somehow good or interesting or useful independently of their truth-value.[13] Such assertions belong to a variety of discourses, from stories to, for example, the discussion of the details of star signs by one who does not actually believe in astrology, with the distinct way in which an utterance may be a quasi-assertion varying with context.[14] What is important for Kalderon is that a quasi-assertion can be divided into the proposition expressed (its 'fictional content') and the proposition asserted (its 'real content'). In the domain of morality, then, according to Kalderon, the fictional content of utterances would be the attribution of mind-independent moral properties to things, while the real content would be the expression of emotional attitudes, or, in the case of agreement, the expression of a sharing of that emotional attitude.[15]

> Moral propositions, propositions that attribute moral properties to things, play a role in moral acceptance and utterance, not by being the objects of belief and

assertion, but by being apt moral tropes that frame the perspective of a virtuous moral sensibility.[16]

The world of real (mind-independent) moral properties is, then, a fictional one. Within this moral fiction, there are, however, facts about the existence and distribution of moral properties, just as there are facts about Sherlock Holmes within the fictional world of Sherlock Holmes. It is only within the moral fiction that the acceptance of a moral sentence counts as a belief about the attributed moral property: it is 'fictionally true' that we *believe* '*x* is wrong'.[17] 'In accepting a moral sentence', according to Kalderon, 'a competent speaker does not so much believe the moral proposition expressed as he makes as if to believe that proposition.'[18] Making as if to believe is here equivalent to being disposed to respond affectively to *x* in the way described earlier. What moral debate aims at, concludes Kalderon, is not moral truth but rather 'moral transformation'.[19]

It is important to note that Kalderon is here claiming to describe moral discourse as it actually is, rather than prescribing for moral discourse.[20] As already mentioned, he suggests that moral realism, as a philosophical position, arises not from the experience of believing the world to have moral properties but rather as the result of an overliteral interpretation of the way we customarily speak. Nevertheless, he concedes that it may seem incredible that we should be using moral language in this fictional way without being aware that we are doing so.[21] It happens, he claims, not only because it is an instance of the general truth that our attitudes and actions are not always fully transparent to us but also because there is no way to distinguish between realist and fictionalist accounts merely by reflecting on the content of moral vocabulary.[22] (Particularly so, of course, where actual talk of "moral beliefs" is part of the moral fiction.) This is why Kalderon asserts that the very nature of moral language tends to conceal its fictionality. Moral sentences are representational in nature, and it is natural, therefore, to think that we believe the propositions expressed and are asserting them when making moral utterances: to mistake noncognitive moral fiction for the cognition of moral facts, making as if to believe with belief.[23]

> The conditions that make a moral claim pretense-worthy for a competent speaker, if they obtain, also make the ascription of moral belief to that speaker pretense-worthy. That people believe the moral claims that they accept would be part of the extended moral fiction.[24]

Moral realism, then, by this account is merely a mistake made by philosophers when they reflect upon the way in which we customarily talk about how we feel.[25]

One objection to Kalderon's fictionalist thesis that we may dismiss at the outset is the argument from moral language itself. Joyce, for example, in arguing for the *intentionally* assertoric character of moral language, puts forward a list of linguistic conventions governing moral discourse that appear to establish its realistic claims:

1. They (moral utterances) are expressed in the indicative mood
2. They can be transformed into interrogative sentences

3. They appear embedded in propositional attitude contexts
4. They are considered true or false, correct or mistaken
5. They are considered to have an impersonal, objective character
6. The putative moral predicates can be transformed into abstract singular terms (e.g., 'goodness'), suggesting they are intended to pick out properties
7. They are subject to debate which bears all the hallmarks of factual disagreement [. . .]
8. They appear in logically complex contexts (e.g., as the antecedents of conditionals)
9. They appear as premises in arguments considered valid[26]

However, there is no insuperable difficulty in translating any of these into noncognitive terms of the kind Kalderon would favour: as reports on having a feeling, asking after another's affective state, generalizing from specific instances and so on. If numbers 4 and 5 appear at first problematic, it is only because of an ambiguity: they are either not strictly speaking matters of linguistic convention (but rather glosses on the implication of the other conventions) or, if we understand 'considered' to mean 'treated as', they are already potentially fictionalist. While all ostensibly assertoric, then, these characteristics could also be considered 'pretense-worthy' aspects of an intentionally fictional discourse. Indeed, as I have argued in dealing with the distinction between moral responses and moral judgements, with the latter – that is, with the domain of moral discourse – even if our intention is not fictionalist, insofar as we may not be referring to the reality of any particular moral responses of our own, it often might as well be. In a limited sense, then, fictionalism actually does accurately describe large areas of moral discourse.

If, however, we turn to moral responses themselves, upon which the ultimate intelligibility of moral judgements rests, more serious problems emerge. When pushed to justify a moral utterance that is the report of a moral response, the average person does not resort to talk about their feelings about x but rather to a simple assertion of the "plain" inherent wrongness of x. Thus, while there is nothing exceptional in asserting both "Frodo takes the Ring to Mordor" and "In Tolkien's story, Frodo takes the Ring to Mordor" with an analogous pair of fictionalist sentences – "x is wrong" and "I feel a certain way about x and I feel you should feel the same" – the second of the pair will intuitively seem to many to be at least a dilution, if not an outright retraction, of the first.

However, the most telling difficulty for fictionalism – as the theory that "x is wrong" is truth-apt within a shared fiction of morality in the same way that "Frodo takes the Ring to Mordor" is truth-apt within *Lord of the Rings* – lies not in the nature of moral language but in the nature of fictional language. For, there are three characteristics of fiction that make the idea of the fictionality of our reports on moral responses problematic. First, all fictions evoke a world other than this one. The degree of divergence from reality may vary – from the description of a world that simply does not exist (*The Lord of the Rings*) to the description of what never happened in a world that has existed or does exist (*The Adventures of Sherlock Holmes*) – but this divergence is definitive of fiction. Second, fiction is translatable, in the sense that what is described can be represented in another way – a story may be illustrated, a book turned into a film, a film into book and so on.[27] Moreover, we can translate in this way precisely because fiction is ineluctably made from fact. We can understand the idea of a fattish humanoid creature with short legs, a jovial face, slightly pointed ears, curly brown hair and furry feet just as easily as we can understand the idea of an ex-army doctor looking for accommodation in London, precisely because we can know what would have to be the case for these things to really exist.[28] Even the impossible, such as time travel, can be represented in this way. Third, we value fiction for being about reality in a certain way. We weep for Hecuba or identify with Satan because they represent a *kind* of loss or a *kind* of feeling of defiance that is real: they have more or less direct analogues in our mundane experience. Fiction affects us by describing that which brings the truth of what we know or the essence of what we desire/fear vividly to mind. Which is why, incidentally, it is not uncommon to see "true" and "false" appearing as evaluative terms in connection with fiction.

If we now turn to moral fictionalism with these characteristics of fiction per se in mind, several problems emerge. With regard to the first point, what is the 'world other than this one' that moral fiction is supposed to be evoking? We might answer that it is a world in which things are really wrong independently of our feeling that they are so – just as the language of morality appears to assert. However, the feeling that is being reported is itself just this feeling that things are really wrong independently of our feelings about them. As Kalderon himself says, the feeling that is being expressed by moral language is precisely the feeling that there is a reason to avoid doing *x*, that this reason takes precedence over non-moral reasons that might be salient in other circumstances, and that this reason is not contingent upon my acceptance of it: the feeling that 'certain features of the circumstance . . . present a certain complex normative appearance'. This is equivalent to finding a thing wrong *in itself*, which is precisely what the utterance '*x* is wrong' describes. There is, then, no contrast to be drawn between the fiction of morality and the world as it is; there is no 'willing suspension of disbelief' involved. Equally, there is no question of the translatability of what is represented by moral language. This is, indeed, what Kalderon concedes when he acknowledges that since there is no way to specify in non-moral terms (say, by hypothetical imperatives) what is being conveyed by a moral utterance, moral language is apparently 'indispensable in specifying the attitudes involved in moral acceptance'.[29] Lastly, with regard to the purpose of fiction, while there would obviously be an emotional value to moral fictionalism, insofar as the realism of moral language could be seen as an emphatic way of conveying the strength of our feelings ("It is as if I were compelled by something beyond me"), in fact there is no analogy involved. Saying that *x* is wrong is not like weeping for Hecuba because I recognize the reality of a similar sorrow; rather saying that *x* is wrong is (or can be) reporting the feeling that *x* is wrong, which is precisely identical with feeling that *x* is wrong.[30] We are not living vicariously through ourselves. Indeed, from the point of view of everyday feeling (rather than philosophy), it would be easier to make a case for moral irrealism itself as a form of fictional discourse.

The same objections can be made to the idea that, even after recognizing the vacuity of the predicates employed in moral language, we might still continue to use it, though in a way that did not commit us to error. Joyce, for example, like Kalderon, holds that one could employ the discourse of morality as a fiction, that is without believing in or actually *asserting* its propositions, and, in this way, gain the 'instrumental benefits' of the discourse without accruing the 'costs of believing falsehood'.[31] Unlike Kalderon, however, Joyce does not believe that this is what we currently do; rather, he holds that it is something that a group might do once it had become convinced of the truth of the moral-error theory.[32]

> [To] take a fictionalist stance towards a discourse is to believe that the discourse entails or embodies a theory that is false (such that there is no error-free revisionary theory available), but to carry on employing the discourse, at least in many contexts, as if this were not the case, because it is useful to do so. The discourse in question may be terribly important to us – so much so that the pragmatic cost of eliminating it . . . is greater than the cost of saying things which we know to fall short of truth.[33]

Even if moral "beliefs" are not true, they are, according to Joyce, obviously advantageous in ensuring the beneficial ends of moral behaviour. Being under the impression that cooperating is 'just the right thing to do', that one has an 'inescapable obligation' to cooperate, is more likely to achieve cooperation and prevent defection than a mere belief that cooperation is instrumentally useful for some further end: 'the distinctive value of categorical imperatives is that they silence calculation'.[34] Indeed, even where cooperation is rationally advantageous in the long term, the relative tangibility of short-term advantages might often lead us to neglect that long-term advantage were it not for the 'bulwark' provided by the belief that cooperation is categorically required.[35] According to Joyce, these benefits, or at least most of them, could survive the 'shift' to fictionalism.[36]

Say, he argues, that around fifty sit-ups nearly every day are sufficient for health. I am much more likely to actually do them and avoid the slippery slope to inactivity, if I 'think' that precisely fifty sit-ups daily is requisite for health.[37] Hence, it may be that my best interests are served by my 'rehearsing thoughts that are false, and that I know are false, in order to fend off my own weaknesses'.[38] While doing my sit-ups I may 'think' that I must do fifty, but at another time I will acknowledge that forty would be sufficient. The example is well chosen, since everyone has probably had some experience of the truth of this. (My own mantra, many years ago, was 'Anybody can practice 364 days a year'.) However, what Joyce describes is not actually what is happening in such instances. Rather, it is a matter of it being easier to do fifty sit-ups every day than to decide each day whether or not one is going to do them and how many one is prepared to do. (Indeed, I might even know that practising something daily is less efficient than leaving breaks between practices, yet still choose to do so simply because it is easier.) This is not, then, a matter of 'rehearsing thoughts that are false', but rather of knowingly *behaving as if* something false were true.

Indeed, it is not at all clear what Joyce can mean by 'thinking' that a thing is so, even while knowing that it is not so. Thinking that a thing is so is, as we have seen, not actually what is taking place in entering into the world of a fiction. There is a range of ways in which fiction may affect us but only part of that range still maintains the fiction/reality divide. Crying over the film *Somewhere in Time* does not collapse the distinction, since love, time and loss are real, and thus I can respond emotionally to their evocation even while knowing that Richard and Elise are not real. Leaving the bedroom light on after watching *Alien* is more problematic; I may still know the film was fiction, but fear has temporarily produced the unreasonable idea that perhaps things like this could be real. In contrast, however, sending baby clothes to a pregnant character in a radio soap opera or picking a fight with an actor for the actions of a character he has played are indubitably symptoms of mental confusion: the collapse of the fiction/reality distinction. It may be, as Joyce says, that the fictional idea that '*x* is wrong' will be more motivating if it is 'supplemented by the thought that the action in question is just wrong' (wrong in itself) and guilt-worthy (and if this thought is routinely expressed in utterances like 'Stealing is a morally terrible thing'), but this seems to render moral fictionalism less like crying over a film and more like sending baby clothes to someone who does not really need them: in short, not really a matter of treating something as fiction at all.[39]

Since, according to Joyce, one aspect of being 'immersed' in a theory is 'thinking that being immersed in the theory is appropriate', that is 'not paying attention to the fact that one is "immersed in a theory" at all', it is not strange that the thoughts that constitute moral fictionalism should seem to the subject to be 'very much the same as beliefs'.[40] What constitutes the difference, he holds, is that the subject should remain 'disposed to deny' moral realism in the 'most rigorous context of interrogation': a person's '"moral thoughts" may be well-rooted habits of thinking that are overturned only when the person enters a very critical context of discussion, such as a conversation on metaethics'.[41] This, he asserts, is equivalent to not believing the fiction of morality, even where the person is typically unaware that they would be disposed to deny moral realism.[42] However, this must raise the question of which of the two states of mind – the person's habitual moral realism or that same person's rational recognition of the untenability of moral realism – is to be regarded as their "real" attitude of mind: the belief to which they give their real, as opposed to notional, assent. Joyce unequivocally holds that the difference between a 'thought' and a 'belief' is not a phenomenological one but, rather, 'a matter of a disposition to dissent'.[43] (Here, once again, we find that tendency to identify one's self with one's rationality.) Yet a person, for example, who habitually patronized in word and deed the sex to which they did not belong yet insisted in debate that they believed the sexes equal would not be accused of insincerity or self-deception in their habitual words and deeds but rather in their own assessment of their beliefs.

Joyce describes how a Sherlock Holmes fan may derive great satisfaction from pretending the stories are true, visiting the sites of Holmes's adventures and talking as if those adventures had actually happened. Such a fan is not self-deceived, however, so long as they can 'readopt the critical perspective' from which they know what they are engaging in fiction: so long as they can return to the world in which Sherlock Holmes does not exist.[44] Although Joyce presents this as evidence for the possibility of moral fictionalism, when we actually compare the relation between indulging the fiction and returning to the everyday world with our habitual habit of moral realism and our potential 'disposition to dissent' in a philosophical context, it is arguably the 'disposition to dissent' that has more in common with the fiction. For, while it is, of course, true that moral realism is untenable, just as the real existence of Sherlock Holmes, given what we know of the real world, is untenable, nevertheless the role of moral realism in the world, even by Joyce's own account, is more a matter of everyday reality than is its rational denial in the philosophy classroom, which is indeed very much like the entertainment of a fiction, in that, rational as the position may be, we give it, from the point of view of our habitual moral *feelings*, a merely notional and temporary assent. It may be, of course, that we do not have to decide which is the person's "real" attitude of mind – but even the possibility of such agnosticism undermines the fictionalist thesis.

Neither Kalderon nor Joyce succeeds, then, in demonstrating that viewing our moral language as fictional is or could be a matter of not ascribing moral properties to the world. In Kalderon the *fiction* '*x* is wrong' is actually representing what, for the subject, is equivalent to the *fact* that *x* is wrong. Likewise, Joyce, who believes that the 'thought' that things are wrong or right in themselves is part of our evolutionary inheritance, holds that such ascriptions are inevitable. However, a 'thought' that *x* is wrong is precisely the same, from the subject's point of view, as a belief that *x* is wrong, so that his fictionalism resides entirely in the decision to identify the self with its philosophically defensible reflections on its own mental states rather than with the contents of those mental states.

At the same time, as already mentioned, fictionalism could perhaps adequately describe many aspects of the domain of moral *judgements*, insofar as such judgements are not reports of moral responses but rather deductions based on what is taken as morally given in the context in which they are made. Moreover, the extent to which our moral language is a matter of such judgements is frequently unclear even to ourselves – after all, we can be surprised, in the event, by our own moral responses or their absence. Nevertheless, in addressing the problem presented by moral-error theory solely in terms of the status of moral language, fictionalism leaves untouched the problem towards which moral-error theory points: the states of mind that moral language either expresses, where it reports a response, or defers to for meaningfulness, in the case of moral judgements.[45]

The same may be said of a more radical response to moral-error theory that I will touch on before passing on to those approaches that systematically attempt to salvage realism. This is the rejection of the use of moral language altogether. Thus, Garner, explicitly subscribing to Mackie's 'error theory', proposes a position that he calls 'amoralism' or 'moral abolitionism'.[46] Given, he argues, that there is 'no fact of the matter about what is morally right or wrong', no 'objective morality' that exists 'independent of anything we think, say, desire, or decree', then morality is no more than a harmful myth, so 'flawed' that we should abandon it: should 'stop talking and thinking in moral terms'.[47] However, the recommendation is not quite so radical as it appears. We need not worry, he claims, that abandoning 'morality' will 'send us into a life of crime or destroy our compassionate impulses'.[48] For, 'moral beliefs', which explicitly appeal to the objectivity of moral values, can and should be replaced by what he calls 'ethics': a 'collection of the non-moralized (but moralizable) components of ... our "motivational set"'.[49] This 'ethics', according to Garner, is an aggregate of our 'inhibitions, routines, policies, and . . . ever-shifting personal values' that will allow us to make better decisions than we do when we allow 'ignorance, fear, and morality' to intrude.[50] 'Morality', he claims, is unnecessary, since 'we evolved to have helpful impulses and to value and nourish relationships'; when we feel an impulse to help a stranger it is because 'we are capable of being moved by something other than "moral considerations" and self-interest'.[51] (It is a lack of compassion – 'a built-in aversion to the suffering of others' – not a lack of 'morality' that allows us to be cruel.[52]) We naturally have, or have acquired, 'pity, sympathy, empathy, fellow feeling, care, concern, solicitude, sensitivity, warmth, love, tenderness, mercy, leniency, tolerance, and kindness', and it is these rather than 'a sense of moral obligation' that we should act upon.[53] Indeed, as the allusion to making 'better decisions' (with its assumption of a standard) implies, he is arguing that moral abolitionism is more 'objective': 'Our moral compass may be as subjective, relative, and fictional as morality itself, but we each have a fully functioning collection of dispositions, habits, policies, and principles that make up our ethics.'[54] 'When amoralists *are* faced with genuine hard choices', he concludes apropos a variety of standard moral dilemmas, 'they can make decisions [about what is the best thing to do] *at least* as efficiently and intelligently as moralists'.[55]

Thus, Garner clearly does consider there to be facts of the matter about what is the right thing to do; he is just averse to the language of morality, no doubt as a reaction against his milieu's penchant for moralism. (To clarify: morality is, however indirectly, a valuing of the welfare of others, an 'aversion' to their suffering; moralism is a valuing of one's own self-image as a "good person". Moralism, since it is essentially a matter of concern for the regard of others – present or notional – is prone to dependence on the letter of abstract conventional principles: the public face of morality, which, like the public face of anything, tends to caricature.) Garner has come to identify morality so closely with moralism that he seems unaware that, under the name of 'ethics', he is describing precisely those feelings the experiencing of which gives rise to the notion of 'moral experience'. The very fact that he believes the 'non-moral' feelings he describes can do, and do more 'efficiently', what others think of as the task of morality, clearly demonstrates that his programme is cosmetic. We can imagine that, in practice, his post-moral-abolition world would be indistinguishable from the current one, aside from the (admittedly welcome) absence of moralistic expressions like "moral beliefs", and the existence of a variety of circumlocutions for 'right', 'wrong', 'should' and so on. Garner's alternative to the felt and asserted objectivity of moral experience is to jettison moral language but retain the felt and asserted objectivity, albeit on the basis not of an external authority but of an internal, 'built-in', one.[56]

However, to return to fictionalism, we may conclude that the thesis that we either already do or possibly could experience our own moral responses as subjective, so that the realism of our moral language either should or could be taken as fictional falls down at the demonstrable fact that a moral term is only being used correctly in so far as it is used to denote an internal state that others would recognize as of a certain distinct kind. (In the case of a moral judgement, of course, this is a matter of its denoting a hypothetical instantiation of such a state.) Thus, if I say something like "That's not fair; I wanted to win" I can very properly be taken to task for misusing the word "fair", since I am so obviously using it to mean "What I want".[57] Moreover, it does not matter whether or not, as a matter of logic, anyone's commitment to fairness can be demonstrated to be founded in self-interest. To use the word correctly, I must use it to report an internal state that I do not *experience* as a matter of purely self-interest. Subjectivism commits us to the belief that things are wrong because we disapprove of them. I do not wish to dispute this view of the matter. However, for a response to qualify as a moral response it must be experienced as a feeling that quite the opposite is the case: we must feel that we are disapproving of something *because it is wrong*. There is a very good reason why moral realism, untenable as it is, is yet the default "theory" of morals: moral realism reflects, albeit somewhat inadequately, the feel of moral experience. It is for this reason that the forms of fictionalism described above cannot provide a way around the lack of epistemological justification for the propositions moral language contains.

So far, I have been defending the integrity, or identity, of the moral response against those subjectivist accounts that tend to misrepresent the way that response is actually experienced. When someone asserts the wrongness or rightness of a thing, they may very well be doing no more than expressing or reporting their emotions, but those emotions must take the form of, and be experienced by the subject as, a response to how the world *is* in order to be experienced as moral. It should be clear, then, that this defence is in no way an argument against subjectivism itself. I am not suggesting that a moral response really is the registering of a moral fact, only that moral responses *feel like* the registering of moral facts: that is how we identify a response as moral.

The misrepresentation of moral experience by professed subjectivists generally seems to be generated in response to the very natural fear that subjectivism may weaken the hold of morality upon us. Thus, for example, it is in addressing this concern that Russell puts forward the thesis that since moral behaviour 'generally resolves itself into a desire to be approved, or, alternatively, to act so as to bring about certain general consequences which we desire', a belief in moral facts is actually unnecessary to the existence of morality.[58] This, as we have seen, is not so: whatever constraints or motives might actuate one who did not experience moral responses, we could hardly in justice call them "moral". For, unless the wrongness or rightness is felt as a fact, it is not a moral response. Indeed, the only authenticated instances of people who are apparently genuinely capable of *feeling* all moral values as relative, conventional or expedient are to be found in the case notes of sociopaths.

Another motive for the misrepresentation of moral experience by subjectivist philosophers may perhaps lie in an overcommitment to the idea of human beings as essentially "rational animals". The subjectivist account of moral responses posits that we cannot avoid automatic, non-rational responses that, necessarily, involve an illusion, yet which we experience as imperative. Rather than acknowledge, then, that a vital area of human concern is grounded in the perception of what is not there, such theorists prefer to deny that we actually do experience moral responses as perception, or at least to distance themselves from this fact by identifying solely with those moments in which they philosophically reflect on the illusory nature of that experience. This, as we have seen, will not do.

We shall now turn to some examples of the other way in which many non-realist thinkers have tried to circumvent the conclusion that moral experience implies a universal and incorrigible habit of projection: the perception of our feelings about a thing as intrinsic properties of that thing. In contrast to fictionalism, the way we shall consider here does not involve misrepresenting the response itself; indeed, it relies heavily on the felt objectivity of that response. For, rather than suggesting that we may console ourselves with the thought that, despite the way we talk, we do not *really* experience moral responses as objective, it addresses the other part of the perceived problem by suggesting that even though such responses are not objective in the sense posited by realism, we are yet somehow justified – epistemologically rather than merely pragmatically – in regarding them as if they were. I would call this strategy *trivial realism*. The rest of this chapter will examine the variety of forms such "realism" may take.

Moral perception

What many recent philosophical attempts to lend some form of objectivity to moral experience have in common is that starting from the thesis that moral experience is fundamentally a matter of emotion, they then attempt to somehow collapse reacting to a phenomenon with perceiving a phenomenon. Perhaps the most straightforward example of this way of undermining one's own non-realism is to be found in an approach exemplified by Prinz's 'constructive sentimentalism'. Prinz unquestionably regards himself as a subjectivist: the very title of his work – *The Emotional Construction of Morals* – nails his colours firmly to the mast. An action is only morally wrong or right, he asserts, if 'there is an observer who has a sentiment of disapprobation (approbation) toward it'.[59] Thus, we should 'give up on moral objectivism': 'If being real entails being objective, then moral realism is false'.[60]

However, he then adds that, although 'moral properties' must be said, in one sense, to be constituted by 'motivating states in us' (things are wrong because we find them so), nevertheless, such properties are also, in another sense, 'features of the world'.[61] They are features of the world insofar as what we respond to are certain situations existing outside the mind that 'elicit' these responses in us. Thus, according to Prinz, it is legitimate to talk of the 'moral properties' of the world, since certain things do possess properties, albeit 'emotion-dependent properties' (in the sense that, for example, likeability, scariness or funniness are emotion-dependent properties) 'causing us to engage our moral sentiments'.[62] Therefore, he concludes, we may say that 'emotional judgements refer to real facts'.[63]

This characterization of 'moral properties' leads Prinz to a position he calls 'constructive sentimentalism'. Morality, he says, is a social construction. Moral facts are like facts about monetary value – they only obtain by virtue of our 'current dispositions and practices'.[64] Thinking of them in this way, he asserts, helps us to resolve the conflict between the idea that they are projections (dependent upon our sentiments) and the idea that they are facts (something we merely respond to):

> Things that we construct or build come from us, but, once there, they are real entities that we can perceive. [. . .] I think moral facts are a special kind of construction: they are made by our sentiments, and, once made, they can be perceived. You

can perceive that it's wrong to kick a dog. When someone kicks a dog, it causes an emotional response, and that response is a manifestation of a sentiment that constitutes the conviction that animal cruelty is wrong. The sentiment makes it wrong, and it also makes the wrongness palpable to us when we encounter it. Sentimental constructions reconcile projection and perception.[65]

This position, he believes, makes it meaningful to subscribe to the idea of morality being emotion-dependent, while still allowing us to talk of 'moral facts'; for such facts affect our behaviour, and do so 'in virtue of being moral facts'.[66]

The wrongness of stealing plays a causal role in preventing us from stealing and in punishing those who steal. The wrongness induces emotions in us, and those emotions impact our behavior. If stealing were not wrong, we would not avoid it. I conclude that moral properties are perfectly real in this sense. They are part of the causal fabric of the world. [. . .] We should be antirealists. But realism can be understood in other ways. Moral statements can be true; there are moral facts; moral properties are causally efficacious; and, therefore, we can quantify over them. For these reasons, it makes perfectly good sense to call the kind of subjectivism that I favor a form of moral realism.[67]

The first problem with this standpoint lies in the way Prinz moves from the observation that the world possesses certain properties (murder, rape, contradicting an elder, eating meat on a Friday, same-sex marriage) that 'elicit' moral responses in us, to the proposition that the world contains 'moral properties'. By his own theory it is our emotions that transform these properties into moral ones. Indeed, he himself here characterizes such properties as 'emotion-dependent'. Nevertheless, having apparently eschewed the simple "x is wrong" of realism, he then collapses "I respond to the fact that I feel x is wrong" into "I respond to the fact that x is wrong" to arrive back at "x is wrong".

However, while it is palpably a fact that the world contains properties that elicit moral responses in me and you and him and her, these properties are not moral properties unless I or you or he or she actually respond to them in a certain way: there being moral properties for you depends entirely on whether or not you have that response. (And even then, they are only moral properties *for* you, and not necessarily for me or him or her.) So, while emotional judgements do certainly refer to real facts, nevertheless, those are not 'moral facts' unless we feel them as such. And a 'fact' about the world that is only a fact if we feel a certain way about it is not a fact. When Prinz asserts that 'moral properties exist, but they depend on us', then, he can really be saying no more than "moral properties exist for us", which, since it is a statement about us rather than the world independent of us, is in no sense moral realism.[68]

The real problem with this confusion between "properties that cause a moral response (in someone)" and "moral properties" comes out in the way in which the moral subject in such an account is, as it were, *overpopulated*. This subject becomes at once the subjectivist (me_1) who experiences the moral response to certain properties of the world and, at the same time, the realist (me_2) who responds to the fact that he or she has responded morally. Even if we decided that such a split was justifiable, the realist *me* in this scenario is still in no position to talk of "moral properties", since he/she is depending entirely on the response of one – the subjectivist – who is responding not to moral properties but, rather, responding in a moral way to properties that only become moral to him/her by virtue of his/her own response.

Moreover, having implicitly created this division, Prinz then collapses it again in his discussion of moral experience. For, he goes on to speak as if the moral response belonged to me_2 (the realist), thus cutting out the subjectivist me_1 and making right and wrong matters of fact. So, he can say, for example, that it is possible to 'perceive that it's wrong to kick a dog', in the sense that feeling it is wrong 'makes the wrongness palpable to us when we encounter it'.[69] But who exactly is the 'us' here? If it is me_1 (the subjectivist), then we certainly cannot speak of *perceiving* a moral fact, since we are responsible for the feeling that the thing is wrong or right. On the other hand, if it is me_2 (the realist), then we would have to say that me_2 was also capable of moral responses – specifically a sense of moral obligation to the moral response of me_1. But, in this case, me_2 now requires a further observer (me_3) to play the role of realist, responding to the responses of me_2 as to "moral properties" of the world and so on ad infinitum.

As we have seen, Prinz himself says that his 'constructive sentimentalism' is intended to reconcile perception and projection.[70] What we project, he says, comes from us, but once the qualities have been projected, they are then 'real entities that we can perceive', in the sense that we feel they are real and this feeling affects our behaviour.[71] This, however, gives moral qualities no more claim to be 'real entities that we can perceive' than, for example, such *perceived* qualities as God's handiwork, ghosts or the intrinsic inferiority of certain races.

The problem here, and it is common to many invocations of the concept of projection, is that projection is not supposed to be reconciled with perception. Rather projection is a form of perception: unacknowledged desire or fear *as* perception. It is, by definition, a perceiving of what is not there to perceive. If the qualities really are there to perceive, then it is not a matter of projection. The fact that the projection is based upon 'real entities' (murder, rape, contradicting an elder, eating meat on a Friday, sexual preference or skin colour) does not make the value that is projected any more of a 'real entity'. Moreover, the notion that we can *consciously* project, as is suggested by the analogy with the value of money, not only falls foul of all the objections to a consciously subjective morality dealt with in connection with fictionalism but also empties the concept of projection of meaning. For, one does not consciously choose to project x onto y, rather one experiences y as x – and that *is* the projection.

We cannot turn the fact that we feel something is wrong into the fact that the thing is wrong in this way. Since, then, the existence of real moral properties is not compatible with Prinz's own emotion-dependence standpoint, the question must arise as to why he proposes such properties. That is why, having denied the existence of the cake, he should then try to eat it too. Given that he does not arrive at any moral realism that would satisfy a moral realist, and given that, with the observation that moral responses feel like responses to moral properties, he merely arrives back at the non-realist starting point of his enquiry, we should perhaps look at what position this 'realism' is intended to exclude, that is, what he feels emotion-dependence would entail if it were not 'a form of moral realism'.

Looked at in this way, we can see that his concern is very similar to that of the authors considered at the end of the last chapter: he is anxious to demonstrate that his form of emotivism does not in some way undermine morality.

> It would not undercut morality to say that moral rules issue from human preferences. Indeed, if morality comes from us, then morality is fundamentally important. We can be neutral about things that do not depend on our responses, but we can't be neutral about morality. Morality is, by its very nature, something we care about.[72]

But this is rather like saying that what we object to about pain is that it hurts. That is, even put this way, the analysis is still overcrowded. For it is not that we have a morality and we cannot be neutral about it; rather it is having a morality that is itself our lack of neutrality. Morality is not something we (morally) care about; rather it is our caring about certain things that *is* morality. (Caring about morality per se is not morality; it is moralism: a quite different thing, as I have already had occasion to remark.)

This last is, indeed, just what non-realism implies. Prinz's reassurance, then, contains a covert appeal to a philosophically indefensible moral realism – one that becomes more overt as he develops his theme. He talks, for instance, of the way in which morality 'places demands on us'.[73] This is certainly how we sometimes experience morality – as a check on other impulses – but who exactly is the 'us' here upon whom the demand is placed? For, if it really is a matter of moral response, then we are as much responsible for the check as for the original impulse. Morality, according to an emotion-dependent view such as his own, is not a separate entity from us. If we are committed to an emotional basis for moral responses, then we cannot speak of having "demands placed on us" (unless we hold that they are purely physiological in origin), but only of conflicting impulses. If, for example, I have a chance to watch film *A* and film *B*, but not time to watch both, I must choose between them. The hesitation I may feel over watching *A* comes from a desire to watch *B*, but I cannot say that film *B* is placing a demand on me. My desire to watch *B* is no more imposed on me from outside than is my desire to watch *A*.

There are two ways in which such a scenario may at first seem disanalogous with the case of the moral response. First, there does not appear to be any desire involved in the moral "demand". However, whether or not this is actually the case is an open question at this point, so it would be prejudging the issue to allow this as an objection. Second, while my motives to watch film *A* are very probably roughly similar to my motives to watch film *B*, in the case of morality, while we may have no clear notion of what motives might lie behind our desire that something *should* or *should not be*, we certainly experience that desire as qualitatively different from other desires. (Even to the extent of experiencing it as, in a sense, unmotivated.) If the moral response is a matter of emotion, then we must at some stage allow that desire is involved. Indeed, the fact that morality feels different is not, in any case, an argument against the analogy with conflicting desires. There are, after all, cases where we do feel it is appropriate to say that demands are placed on us even though we are still ultimately responsible for those demands. We may, for example, talk of the "demands imposed by" an exercise regime, a job or a difficult course of study, even though these too are ultimately a matter of our own election: they arise from the desire to be fit, or solvent, or better-informed or, more generally, to better conform to an image of ourselves we find attractive. Nevertheless, from the subject's point of view, such scenarios are not analogous to feeling a moral response, since that response is, as we have seen, by no means a matter of choice. Situations where we could more reasonably speak of demands being *placed* on us would be cases like being lost in a wilderness or suffering from a disease: situations in which nothing more than an instinct of self-preservation is necessary for those outside (non-psychological) forces to be experienced as demands. But to see our moral responses as equivalent to such forces is to return to moral realism.

This is, indeed, what happens when Prinz (ignoring what the concept of projection entails) identifies with the self that has demands placed on it rather than with the self placing the demand. His own non-realist position should make the conflict one between two desires, but instead, it becomes a conflict between desire and something else. The attraction of this split lies in the way it makes morals appear real, since the "I" in the equation is not responsible for them. There is, moreover, a further reward for the reluctant non-realist: it allows them to simultaneously disclaim responsibility for this morality and yet take credit for it.

A moral response, then, may be a strong impetus, and one that is in conflict with other impetuses that we have, but that does not establish that it comes from outside, that it is something not 'us' that places demands on 'us'. (That we should experience it as such is almost inevitable, since the force of a general disposition is only likely to emerge with the possibility of resistance.) The case of a moral response that is in conflict with some other interest most closely resembles, then, being torn between film *A* and film *B*, or between the desire to remain solvent and the desire to fritter away one's time writing philosophy. If this does not seem obviously the case, it may be either because, with the film example, the motivation to watch *A* and *B* seems to be of the same kind – we look forward to being entertained by both – or, with the job versus interest case, we are conscious of a conflict of desires, whereas in the case of morality we commonly conceive of the conflict being between what is (clearly) self-interest and something else (which we cannot account for): "I" want to do something but "I" do not because *it is* wrong. This is the natural way to view what is going on – but only because we are all moral realists in our feelings.

Moral responses, as we have seen, cannot feel like matters of self-interest. Yet, given that moral responses at least appear to be a matter of the emotions, there is, in fact, no reason to rule out the presence of self-interest at some point in their genesis. To contrast self-interest with morals – which gives us the formula "morals place demands on us" – is, in effect, either to give up the idea that morals are a matter of emotion or to suggest that there are matters of emotion that are not also matters of interest. This, however, is a question we shall return to later. For the moment it is sufficient to note that the rejection of realism entails acknowledging that the "demands" that morality places on us are demands we place on ourselves. Indeed, it may make more sense to say that the demands we place on ourselves are experienced as morality –

with the important proviso, however, that we are not capable of acknowledging that these demands come from ourselves, and so we do not experience moral responses as matters of our own interest. The fact that we feel that we *ought* whether we *want to* or not suggests that the desire does not come from a self that we can actually identify with. This is, indeed, just what projection entails: that we should be incapable of feeling our responses as self-generated.

This 'form of moral realism', which posits moral qualities as real on the grounds that I really feel there are moral qualities, is not, then, any form of moral realism at all. However, there are other ways of trying to arrive at some form of 'moral objectivity' starting from a notion of moral responses as basically emotional. In some instances, this may simply be a matter of allowing that a moral response is a matter of emotion but emphasizing the perceptual aspects of emotion, thus inviting a drift towards viewing that response as *essentially* a perception, or at least, functionally indistinguishable from perception.

'Rational emotions'

Nussbaum's description of emotion offers a good example of precisely this strategy with regard to emotions in general. She gives the following four reasons in support of the claim that emotions should be regarded as 'forms of evaluative judgment' and can, indeed, 'be defined in terms of judgment alone':[74]

1) Emotions are '*about* something'.[75] An emotion has an object: I am angry *at* certain person's attitude; I feel guilty *over* something I have done.
2) The object of an emotion is an '*intentional* object'.[76] That is, emotions are a result of 'my active way of seeing and interpreting': I perceive, for example, that I or another has behaved inconsiderately.
3) Emotions 'embody not simply ways of seeing an object, but beliefs – often very complex – about the object'.[77]
4) The intentional perceptions and beliefs characteristic of the emotions 'are all concerned with *value*, they see their object as invested with value'.[78] (Her own example is the way in which it is your love for someone – their importance to you – that leads you to feel fear at the prospect of their death.)

It is not immediately clear why Nussbaum should hold the third point to be separate from the second. In making the third point she gives the example of anger, arguing that in order to have anger I must have 'an even more complex set of beliefs: that there has been some damage to me or to something or someone close to me; that the damage is not trivial but significant; that it was done by someone; that it was done willingly; that it would be right for the perpetrator of the damage to be punished'.[79] This is palpably untrue – even before computers were invented, humans were swearing at (or even punishing) "recalcitrant" inanimate objects. However, while this would seem to strengthen rather than detracting from the main point – that complex ideas are involved – it does demonstrate why the mere complexity of the beliefs involved does not make this a separate point from the second: that it is my way of seeing the object that makes it the object of an emotion. This, however, is something we shall return to later.

It is, then, these four (or three) cognitive aspects of emotions – their aboutness, their intentionality, their basis in beliefs and their connection with evaluation – that Nussbaum believes justify classifying them as judgements, as a matter of cognition. Nevertheless, it might still be argued that the presence of these characteristics merely shows that beliefs and perceptions play a role – as conditions or constituent parts of emotions – rather than being identical with the emotions as Nussbaum claims. However, she rejects this notion of the emotion as somehow separate from the belief or perception on the grounds that there is, indeed, no gap between recognizing certain kinds of proposition (for example, 'that someone tremendously beloved is forever lost to me') and feeling certain kinds of emotion (for example, grief). The 'salient' proposition in the case of emotions, she adds, must always be one that has 'evaluative content'; that is, it must be a fact or something perceived as a fact about that which affects 'the person's most important goals and ends', whatever these goals or ends might be.[80] In this sense, she concludes, insofar as emotions are evaluations of events in the light of such goals or ends, in terms of 'my conception of what it is for me to live well', they are 'a function of reason' and 'can be defined in terms of judgment alone'.

Nussbaum's argument can be summarized thus: emotions can be classified as judgements because they are inseparable from evaluations, albeit sometimes only implicit, of events that we take to be emotionally significant. (The inclusion of 'emotionally significant' in this summary, despite the circularity it seems to introduce, follows from Nussbaum's own definition of the object of emotion as any event that represents to the subject the furthering or frustration of that subject's goals or ends, as that subject conceives of those goals or ends.) The first thing to note about this argument, then, is a certain lack of substance. No one would deny that emotions are judgements in this sense: in the sense that we must care about something to feel an emotion about it. The question must, therefore, arise as to why Nussbaum and others have put forward such an "argument" – that is, against what counter thesis is it directed.

Nussbaum explicitly sets her thesis against a view of emotions that emphasizes certain features of the way they are sometimes experienced: their urgency, their overwhelming force (on occasion), the way they can seem to override the claims of any kind of reasoning and so on. This view, she implies, holds emotions to be essentially irrational forces that take control of our passive selves. However, such characteristics are not incompatible with the notion that emotions are themselves forms of judgement: judgements that can be overwhelmingly motivating and which can override other forms of reasoning. Moreover, this characterization of emotion as something that sweeps away "reason" (not, of course, itself motivating, but only a tool for pursuing ends that are themselves, when not physiological, a matter of emotional motivation) is not actually a thesis about the grounds of emotion; it is rather a description of how emotions are sometimes experienced.

Nussbaum's position, then, only becomes an argument through the erection of a straw-man thesis: that emotions are 'just unthinking forces [deriving from the animal part of our nature] that have no connection with our thoughts, evaluations, or plans'.[81] This is not, of course, a thesis about the source of emotions at all but, rather, a denial that we can inquire into the sources of emotion, coupled with the obviously counter-intuitive claim that emotions have nothing to do with the way we perceive the world or what we want from the world beyond the physiological drives we have in common with other animals. It is, therefore, a simple matter for Nussbaum to argue for a more convincing alternative, and unsurprising that there should be, as we have seen, nothing particularly substantive in that argument.

Given, then, that Nussbaum only succeeds in showing that emotions are judgements in a sense of "judgement" that is quite uncontroversial in connection with emotions, we must ask precisely what she was hoping to achieve in doing so. She herself says that in seeking to establish that emotions are judgements, she is hoping 'to restore to the philosophical and political discussion of emotion a dimension that has too frequently been overlooked in debates about whether emotions are "rational" or "irrational"'. Nussbaum's own characterization of emotion does not, of course, effect this debate, since it leaves open the question of the rationality/irrationality of both the emotions I experience (which are, demonstrably, not always in the best interest of my goals and ends – at least insofar as I can perceive these) and of the goals and ends themselves that are signalled by these emotions – where the categories 'rational' and 'irrational' seem, in any case, inappropriate: what is emotionally important to me is emotionally important to me. Moreover, replacing 'emotions I experience' with 'evaluations I make' in the last sentence does not in any way change its import.

However, demonstrating the pointlessness of discussing emotions in terms of rationality is not the main drift of Nussbaum's argument. The straw-man argument against which she explicitly pits her own account is no more than a bald assertion that the emotions are not a cognitive matter. Moreover, her goal is to justify the assertion that 'emotions can be defined in terms of judgment alone', even though, as we have seen, this "judgement" turns out to mean no more than we usually mean by "emotion". This suggests that Nussbaum is seeking some rhetorical advantage from the word "judgement": encouraging us to look at emotions in a certain way. Her intention seems to be not only to get us to see emotions as judgements but also to make us feel that in doing so we are actually discovering something new about the nature of emotion. For, we usually associate the word "judgement" with a much more deliberate action than the experiencing of an emotion, which, as she herself says, is experienced principally as something that happens to us. The word "judgement", by contrast, evokes the reaching of a decision, the drawing of conclusions or the capacity to assess something according to a principle, to discriminate and to understand. The thesis that emotions can 'be defined in terms of judgment alone' appears to be trying to import some of these associations into the concept of the emotions, to make them appear both more a matter of perception and more deliberative than might otherwise be the case. In particular, it seems to allow us to equate feeling something with knowing something.

This surreptitious slide, from the obvious fact that emotional responses to things depend on assessments of the nature of those things to the assertion that emotions are a form of assessment, is so common in philosophical contexts where the stake in the emotion is high (as with ethics and aesthetics) that I feel I may be allowed to labour the significance of the difference a little here. If I find two friends, one happy and one not, by the winning post just after a race, they will probably be able to give me identical accounts of which horse won, how they know it won, how they purchased bets, the function of a bet, what the result signifies in terms of the bets they have, the usefulness of money and so on. For one of them, however, a desire has been fulfilled, while for the other it has been frustrated. The one with the big grin may be happy as a result of their assessment of the situation, but it is not *because* they have assessed the situation – the one who lost is equally capable of that, as indeed would be an indifferent bystander who had, as it were, no horse in the race. Emotions are related to facts only by desires.

The wish to align the emotional and the cognitive in a certain way explains why, when offering reasons in support of the contention that emotions are judgements, Nussbaum offers the fact that objects of emotion are intentional objects (so that my emotion is a result of my way of seeing and interpreting), and the fact that emotions embody beliefs, as two separate arguments rather than one. (Something that, as we saw, stood in need of explanation, since both refer to exactly the same state of affairs.) All this separation achieves is to make the "second" argument (emotion is a matter of often 'very complex' beliefs) seem more a matter of the rational than the first (I feel emotion because of the way I see things). Indeed, as we have seen, she illustrates the second argument by showing how, to have a certain kind of anger, she must entertain a complex set of beliefs regarding significant damage to her interests, the deliberate intent of the one responsible, and the justice of retribution ('that it would be right for the perpetrator of the damage to be punished'). To see this as somehow exclusively a matter of perception rather than emotion is to take justice (and our interests) as an emotion-independent given. The emotion of righteous anger is only a matter of pure deliberation on the assumption that justice is something to be perceived in the world itself rather than itself an ideal that only exists by virtue of our (emotional) demand for it.[82]

Inscrutability

Perhaps, however, the moral response should be seen as somehow an exception to the interest-dependence of the majority of our emotions. This is the position taken by McDowell, who feels that it is possible to both reject realism yet still establish a 'substantial notion of truth' in connection with ethics. Although our 'ordinary evaluative thought' is experienced as a matter of responding to qualities of the world, he argues, we cannot interpret those qualities as simply 'brutely and absolutely *there*', independent of human sensibilities, without invoking 'mystifying' faculty of intuition.[83] Nevertheless, he continues, this does not leave us with a choice between an untenable realism and the projectivism (as erroneous attribution) that the rejection of realism would seem to imply.[84] If it is possible to show that 'evaluative thought' is not a matter of projection, he asserts, then there is no question of error.

Projectivism, according to McDowell, certainly fits a case like the attribution of disgust, where we feel that disgustingness is a property certain things have independently of their relations to us, and our disgust simply a perception of this property: where we mistake our response for an intrinsic property of the world.[85] He questions, however, whether this model fits the domain of ethics. For, the notion of projection is employed to explain certain seeming features of reality as reflections of our subjective responses to a world that really contains no such features.[86] In order to be able to conceive of this, we must be able to mentally separate the response from 'the concept of the apparent feature that is supposed to result from projecting the response'.[87] In the case of disgust this is perfectly possible; disgust and nausea are self-contained 'psychological items', which we can conceive of without appealing to any projected properties of disgustingness or nauseatingness. In contrast, 'evaluative concepts' do not have the kind of 'explanatory priority' to moral responses that disgust has to finding something disgusting. This is sufficient, he argues, to show that moral responses are not a matter of projection.

McDowell offers a parallel with the comical. What exactly is it, he asks, that we are to conceive as projected on to the world so as to give rise to our idea that things are funny? There is no 'self-contained prior fact of our subjective lives that could enter into a projective account of the relevant way of thinking; in the only relevant response, the conceptual apparatus that figures in the relevant way of thinking is already in play'.[88] If, then, we cannot identify the 'subjective state whose projection is supposed to result in the seeming feature of reality' without appealing to that feature itself, then we cannot meaningfully speak of projection. It is not that we laugh because the joke is funny in itself (it instantiates a sensibility-independent quality of funniness), nor because we are projecting something onto it: neither the object nor the feeling has 'priority'.[89] This demonstrates, according to McDowell, that one can avoid intuitionistic realism without being a projectivist.

The advantage of avoiding projectivism, he argues, is that doing so allows us to retain a 'substantial notion of truth' in connection with ethics. If neither response nor properties enjoys a 'priority' over the other, it may be 'respectable to use the apparently world-describing conceptual resources with which we articulate our responses [existing "realist" moral discourse], in earning truth in one of the relevant areas'.[90] We can elaborate on what it is for things to be, for example, 'really' wrong from *within* our propensity to find them wrong.[91] We may, then, leave McDowell's argument for moral objectivity here, for, if this is all it was intended to achieve (and if this is the sense he is willing to accept for the expression "really wrong"), then that argument adds nothing to what we have already conceded in dealing with moral judgements: that, within a context in which certain moral propositions are *taken as given*, moral statements can become truth-apt in relation to those givens.

What is worth taking up, however, is McDowell's notion that the moral response itself is not problematic since it is not a matter of projection. This depends upon the distinction he draws between attributing a property to an object that may or may not really belong to that object (as, he claims, happens with disgust) and attributing a property to an object where that property is, for us, inseparable from the object (as, he claims, happens with the comical). A moral response, he argues, is more like finding something funny than finding something disgusting, since we cannot point to any subjective state that gives rise to wrongness (as a seeming feature of reality) other than the subjective state of finding something wrong.

McDowell's distinction between finding something disgusting and finding something funny is not, however, decisive. It is, after all, disgustingness (the property of being disgusting) rather than nausea or disgust that is projected onto qualities of the object. That is, we experience the object as objectively disgusting, in the sense that we attribute the cause of that disgust to properties of the object. Likewise, if we find something makes us laugh, we attribute the cause of that laughter to the properties of the object. (The point is clearer if we imagine someone else's disgust or amusement at objects we do not ourselves find disgusting or funny.) The state of being disgusted and the state of being amused could only be differentiated in the way McDowell suggests if it were possible to establish that certain things really are in themselves disgusting, so that some attributions of disgustingness were actually mistaken.[92] However, a thing is only disgusting if it disgusts you, in precisely the same way as a thing is only funny if it makes you laugh. Neither the one nor the other is a matter of an object instantiating a sensibility-independent quality.

What finding a thing wrong has in common with finding a thing funny is what it also has in common with finding a thing disgusting – or frightening, beautiful, moving, erotic, boring, annoying and so on. If there is a difference between being disgusted and being amused, it lies not in any relative separability of disgust and the disgusting in comparison to amusement and the funny but, rather, in the way in which disgust appears to be more *explicable* than amusement. There are several plausible theories of the grounds of the disgust response, but no intuitively convincing account of what makes something funny. (Being able to enumerate the objective properties something must possess for it to be likely to evoke a certain affective response is not the same as accounting for that affective response.) This kind of difference can be found in various forms across the range of affects to which we are prone. Some, such as fear, seem so directly linked (through danger) to obvious interests (self-preservation) that they do not seem to stand in need of explanation, though even here the affect may have a more inscrutable version, as, for example, with phobias. Others, such as sexual attraction, may manifest in mysterious ways even while the existence of the kind of response per se seems unproblematic in terms of function. Still others, such as funniness, beauty or wrongness, may appear so unaccountable that we end up positing specific "instincts" as their grounds: in effect, giving up on trying to account for them.[93] The distinction to be drawn, then, is not between those affects where the affect seems to have some kind of separate existence from any experience of it, where we can speak of "projection", and those where the affect only seems to come into existence through our experience of it, so that the term "projection" is inappropriate (as McDowell says is the case with the funny and the wrong). Rather the real distinction McDowell relies on is between those affects we feel we can explain and those we feel we cannot. In short, if 'projection' is an appropriate term for what is happening in any of these cases, then it is appropriate for all of them. The current difficulty of accounting for the nature of the projection in the case of morality (and the comical) hardly seems an appropriate reason for regarding the affect itself as unproblematic.

Consensus

If, then, we cannot arrive at objectivity by blurring the line between emotions (as responses to perceptions) and perceptions, or by positing an inscrutability that prevents us appealing to subjectivity, we might, nevertheless, try to arrive at some form of objectivity by identifying objectivity with some form of "fit" between emotion and world. Thus Wiggins, advancing what he calls a 'cognitivist formulation of subjectivism', argues that we may say x is wrong or right if x is such as to make a certain sentiment of disapprobation/approbation *appropriate*.[94] If such an appropriateness can be established, he asserts, then, even starting from a notion of moral responses as basically emotional, it is possible to show that assertions about ethical properties can have the same status as factual assertions.[95]

What, then, makes an emotion 'appropriate' to what happens in the world? Wiggins begins by disclaiming any form of realism: the properties of the world that are in question are to be explained solely by reference to 'the reactions of human subjects'.[96] Something is good or bad if and only if it is such as to arouse sentiments of approbation or disapprobation.[97] While conceding that this definition is circular, he does not see this circularity as an obstacle to establishing moral objectivity.[98] Indeed, even though the circularity of this thesis renders moral experience necessarily unanalysable, this should not, according to Wiggins, be a cause to reject it. After all, he claims, right and wrong are not the only properties of the world that have this characteristic.

He offers two analogies to the case of moral responses: colour and amusement. We can claim an object is red, he asserts, 'if and only if x is such as to give, under certain conditions specifiable as normal, a certain visual impression' – more precisely 'an impression as of seeing something red'.[99] What this shows, he claims, is that 'red' stands for something both subjective and 'unanalysable', and yet, at the same time, unproblematic. Likewise, he continues, the predicate 'funny' may also be considered 'irreducibly subjective' in the sense that there is no 'object-independent, "purely phenomenological" or "purely introspective" account of amusement': the funny is simply that which makes people laugh.[100] In the same way, he argues, a sentiment of approbation or disapprobation 'cannot be identified except by its association with the thought or feeling that x is good [or bad] . . . and with the various considerations in which that thought can be grounded, given some particular item and context, *in situ*'.[101] When it comes to ascribing value, then, '*finding x* to be φ is prior to (or at least coeval with) *thinking x* to be φ'.[102] Thus rightness and wrongness are constituted by property/response pairs that are as 'primitive, *sui generis*, incurably anthropocentric, and . . . unmysterious' as redness or funniness, or, indeed, any other property.[103]

This, we might say, is the fundamental problem. However, Wiggins sees this circularity as precisely what guarantees the objectivity or correctness of certain responses.

> [For] each value predicate φ (or for a very large range of such), there is an attitude or response of subjects *belonging to a range of propensities that we actually have* such that an object that has the property φ stands for if and only if the object is

fitted by its characteristics to bring down that extant attitude or response upon it and bring it down *precisely because* it has those characteristics.[104]

This is not, then, a particularly demanding test for correctness. Responses are 'correct' when they are 'occasioned by what has the corresponding property φ and are occasioned by it because it *is* φ'.[105] This is not a matter of the agreement in the belief that x is wrong being the criterion for x's 'really' being wrong; rather x is only really wrong if it is such as to evoke and make appropriate a certain response among those who are sensitive to wrongness. In short, I am 'correct' in ascribing wrongness to something if it is the sort of thing I usually ascribe wrongness to.

This last formula is not, however, the whole story. While in one way it appears to offer no criteria – a thing is wrong if I feel it is – in another it actually does set a more substantial criteria for correctly finding something wrong. For, it must be something I *usually* ascribe wrongness to. Wiggins is not, however, here appealing to historical (as opposed to rational) consistency as a condition for 'correct' responses. Rather the key lies in his appeal to the '*range of propensities that we actually have*'. For, while he does concede that his conditions for wrongness are relative, in the sense that it is quite possible for someone to discern the same properties I do without responding in the same way as I, nevertheless, he is really only interested in the nature of morality within an existing consensus. It is the 'we' that is crucial to his claim to objectivity. It is possible, he asserts, to treat ethical assertions as objectively true or false, as a representation of 'how things are out there independently of him or her who makes the assertion', precisely because we share them.[106] Our responses represent 'certain distinctive unforsakeable concerns', and in the course of our common dealings with these concerns, 'we arrive at our sense of what notions emerge from the crucible of shared experience as indispensable to us'.[107]

Wiggins's 'objectivity', then, is objectivity within a consensus. It is 'our *actual* collectively scrutinized responses' that establish what is really right and wrong.[108] Indeed, it is only this notion of morality as collectively scrutinized that allows him to introduce the idea of objectivity. For, just as real redness is the tendency of an object to create a certain impression under certain conditions, so, too, there are conditions analogous to normal eyesight that apply to moral 'perceptions'.[109] Since 'we' have responses in common, it is possible to be more or less perceptive about when the properties that appropriately call forth that response are really present. He offers for support of this the way in which 'real-life ethical reasoning or persuasion at its best and most convincing' can lead to moral statements that we find we must endorse – not because they express necessary truths nor because they embody sound deductions, but simply because there is 'nothing else to think' but that they are correct.[110] (We may take this to refer to the eliciting of a moral response.[111]) In this way, Wiggins concludes, an assertion can be both ethical and factual.[112]

We have now clearly passed from the realm of moral responses into that of moral judgements. As we saw in Chapter 1, there is nothing particularly controversial in the claim that moral judgements can be, in relation to an existing consensus, truth-apt. Given this, Wiggin's initial promise to provide moral 'objectivity' and his claim that 'questions of value' are 'questions of real existence or matters of fact' are misleading.[113]

He readily concedes that his definition of moral responses is circular: we respond morally to what elicits a moral response from us, and what elicits a moral response from us is whatever we respond to morally. (Indeed, the unanalysable givenness of our response is, according to Wiggins, one of the ways that allow us to recognize that we have achieved a 'result' in any debate or inquiry, and the ability to lead us to such responses can qualify someone as a 'good judge'.) What Wiggins is advancing is the idea that moral debate is possible because of the intersubjectivity of moral responses within a particular community. To refer to this intersubjectivity as 'objectivity' is inflationary. Moreover, the phenomenon does not at all bear on what is really at stake in the question of realism or anti-realism: the epistemological status of moral responses.

That Wiggins has missed the point really at issue once we reject realism comes out most clearly in his response to Russell's perplexed pronouncement: 'I cannot see how to refute arguments for the subjectivity of moral values, but I find myself incapable of believing that all that is wrong with wanton cruelty is that I don't like it.'[114] Wiggins feels that his own thesis solves Russell's difficulty insofar as it shows that what is wrong with cruelty is not that Bertrand Russell, as an individual, does not like it but, rather, that 'it is not such as to call forth liking given our *actual* collectively scrutinized responses'.[115] However, Russell's problem patently cannot be solved by the reflection that others, after due consideration of the motives and outcomes of cruelty, do not like it either. Russell is not perplexed by the difficulty of warranting what he might want to say to others about cruelty – the likelihood that others will feel the same sufficiently ensures that warrant – rather what he is perplexed by is the way in which nothing aside from his own feelings seems to underwrite his perception of cruelty as wrong *in itself*. Thus, Wiggins's further observation (based on his circular definition of moral responses) that Russell has 'no good reason to call [his response] in question' is simply begging the question.[116]

Rational norms

Gibbard is another who rejects realism, identifying normative statements with expressions of states of mind and dismissing the idea of normative *facts* as 'gratuitous', yet still believes that it is possible to determine 'what sorts of things really are ... right or wrong'.[117] Like Wiggins, he believes that the existence of moral objectivity can be established by showing under what conditions an emotional state of mind is 'warranted'. However, Gibbard rejects the kind of analogies (with colour or funniness) that we have seen used by McDowell and Wiggins to establish the unanalysable character of moral responses. While with colour, Gibbard argues, I can account for my experience simply in terms of normal vision being responsive to the way things are ('I accord my senses a *prima facie* authority'), in the case of morality 'correctness is not sheer normality'.[118] Rather my moral responses are 'governed by norms', and this is why I may see others' responses, or even, in retrospect, my own, as 'mistaken'. While my 'judgements' of what is outrageous are 'guided by feelings' – 'my judgments will fit the feelings, and I will treat the feelings as registering the content of the judgment' – it is, nevertheless, *not* purely a matter of feeling, since I can also judge when it makes sense to feel angry and when it does not; that is, I can judge whether or not the action 'merited' my feeling. In this way, Gibbard claims, 'I accord authority to myself as I am when I both have those feelings and make normative judgments accordingly'.[119] Since, then, I can judge when it *makes sense* to feel anger or guilt, then it must be that my judgements are normative in a sense that cannot be captured by the idea of 'sheer normality' that exhausts the conditions for having a genuine experience of, for example, redness.[120] This is not, however, according to Gibbard, to appeal to a separate criteria from my feelings themselves, since 'my judgments of how it makes sense to feel are guided by the feelings I really have'.

For Gibbard, then, not all moral *responses*, as I outlined them in Chapter 1, qualify as genuinely moral:

> Narrowly moral judgments are not feelings but judgments of what moral feelings it is rational to have. Feelings, we think, can be apt or not, and moral judgments are judgments of when guilt and resentment are apt.[121]

We judge our feelings to be 'apt', 'well grounded' or 'warranted', he continues, simply when they appear to us to make sense: to be 'rational'.[122] To call a thing 'rational', he argues, is to endorse it – in the sense of accepting the norms (possible rules or prescriptions, expressible by imperatives) that permit it.[123] What is important, according to Gibbard, is not what a norm is, but what it means to 'accept' a norm.[124] If we want to discover what is really rational, 'we shall have to settle what norms to accept ourselves – for that is what it is to form an opinion as to the rationality of something'.[125] Moral norms, he continues, are norms for the rationality of guilt and resentment. So, for example, 'an observer thinks an act *blameworthy*, or *morally reprehensible*, if and only if he thinks it rational for the agent to feel guilty over the act, and for others to resent the agent for it'. Thus, if my brakes fail and I kill a pedestrian the day after I have had the brakes of my car checked, it would not be rational for me to feel guilt or for others to blame me for what happened, since I am not, strictly speaking, responsible. In short, to 'think' an act morally reprehensible is to accept norms that 'prescribe', for particular situations, guilt on the part of the agent and resentment on the part of others.[126]

> An action is morally admirable, we can say, if on the part both of the agent and of others it makes sense to feel moral approbation toward the agent for having done it. An action is shameful if it makes sense for the agent to feel ashamed for having done it, and for others to disdain him for having done it.[127]

Since, then, all norms are 'primarily norms of rationality', Gibbard asserts that 'to be moral is simply to be, in the deepest sense, rational'.[128]

Gibbard attributes a particular role to language in the acceptance of such norms. Language, he asserts, can be used to formulate explicit precepts and share evaluations of absent situations, so that we will know 'what to do and what to feel' in like situations.[129] It is this *normative governance* that enables him to distinguish between merely experiencing an emotion (resentment, guilt, etc.) and being able to judge the appropriateness of that emotion against a norm one has accepted. It is through discussion and reflection that we come to accept norms.[130] Thus, accepting a norm for Gibbard, is not simply a matter of experiencing a particular emotion, rather it is, at least in part, a matter of being disposed to avow that norm 'in unconstrained normative discussion, as a result of the workings of demands for consistency in the positions one takes in normative discussion'.[131]

> From this imaginative rehearsal, then, a kind of imaginative persona may emerge, an 'I' who develops a consistent position to take in normative discussion. It is then that we can speak most clearly of what the person accepts; he then has a worked out normative position to take in unconstrained contexts.[132]

It is this imaginative persona that judges which responses – of itself and of others – are apt.

What underwrites this aptness, according to Gibbard, is 'epistemological consistency'; it is this that determines whether or not a norm is warranted.[133] For example, there may be a normative claim that revenge for its own sake is not worth having; if I accept a system of higher order norms that obliges me to accept only what I would accept 'in a cool hour', and I think that in a cool hour I would accept that revenge for its own sake is not worth having, then it is 'rational to accept' that revenge for its own sake is not worth having. According to Gibbard, then, a system of higher order norms amounts to a story of when it is rational to accept norms and when it is not. This, he claims, is equivalent to treating the higher order norm as objective, even if we cannot find what makes it objective. Part of treating it as if objective, however, is that the subject must not take themselves as, individually, the source of that objectivity: everyone's judgement 'must weigh equally'.[134] I cannot, according to Gibbard, simply tell myself that whatever I find credible is objective. Moreover, I cannot ascribe any special status to the present or reject the idea that some possible future influence might improve my judgement.[135]

Gibbard's account, like Wiggins, is evidently very much oriented towards the possibility of moral debate. Indeed, at one point in his protracted analysis of the conditions of such debate, he remarks, almost as an aside, that 'it is in discussion that we lead our normative lives'.[136] Given, however, that norms will vary from community to community, he must acknowledge that there are demands of 'rationality' we can make within our own community that we could not make beyond it. It may be, he concedes, that we cannot claim objectivity for our judgements, in the sense that they could be accepted by all rational beings, but it is still possible to 'claim all the objectivity that matters for purposes at hand'. This 'modest objectivity', he concludes, is all that is necessary for us to be able, within our own community, to 'discuss together how it makes most sense to live, what it makes most sense to believe, and how it makes most sense to feel about aspects of life'.[137]

Gibbard's 'objectivity' turns out, then, to be equivalent to Wiggins's, insofar as it refers merely to the possibility of meaningful moral debate where there is some form of moral consensus. (He does, indeed, concede that his account may 'end up missing something in our ordinary claims to objectivity'.[138]) Also like Wiggins and McDowell, he leaves the basic problem of the objectivity implicit in the response itself untouched.[139] Where he goes beyond them is in asserting that there are responses that we might justifiably call *moral* judgements that somehow take precedence over moral responses. It is this form of judgement – one that expresses the acceptance of a norm – that he holds to be neither a judgement of fact (the realist thesis) nor the entertaining of an emotion (the emotivist or expressivist thesis). However, it is difficult to see just precisely how reinterpreting morality as what is embodied in judgements that express norms would actually work in practice.

The subject, according to Gibbard, is justified in thinking his claim objective 'if he can treat it as objective and do so sincerely'.[140] However, if this 'claim' is supposed to reflect a feeling, rather than a judgement of fact, then it can only be sincere to the extent that the subject finds themselves incapable of imagining feeling otherwise. (I do not have to flay any babies to find out if I think it is wrong.) However, for Gibbard, the objectivity or rationality of a moral judgement depends on accepting that one's own judgements are open to future rectification, particularly by the community in which one finds oneself. Indeed, what he feels separates his own approach from emotivism or expressivism is precisely that I do not treat my own moral responses as objective. For, I cannot do so and at the same time allow for the possibility of future rectification. It appears, then, that he subscribes to a form of fictionalism: "Let us say that *x* is wrong, though we might be mistaken".[141] Given, this, there is no way in which we can identify such a 'claim' with a moral response per se.

In what relationship, then, do these fictionalist claims stand to moral responses? As we have seen, one of the ways in which he introduces the idea is by pointing out the way in which we may come to revise our ascriptions of blame or our feelings of guilt. This is easy enough to imagine, and, indeed, we have already considered cases where we later come to see our ostensibly moral response as adulterated by self-interest or, we might say, where we cease to sympathize with our former selves. It is, indeed, a common experience to *feel* the injustice of my recent anger, or, conversely, to *feel* that another's guilt or ascription of blame is disproportionate. This, however, is in no way fictionalist: it is a matter either of a present *feeling* failing to correspond to a previous one or of failing to sympathize with another's feelings (even though we may sympathize with their reasons for reacting with blame or guilt to the instance in question). However, if this were merely a matter of retrospect or of difference in perspective, we could hardly say that we were contrasting feeling with something else that was not feeling. I could of course lay it down as a principle that it is what *I* feel *now* that is the objective viewpoint; except, of course, that not only is this principle operative in my original feeling and in the feeling of the other person, but also it precludes the notion of entertaining our responses as provisional (open to rectification) that Gibbard makes a condition of the objectivity that belongs to judgements as contrasted with mere responses.

It must be, then, that what Gibbard intends is that genuinely moral claims can somehow override the implicit claims of moral responses insofar as these responses are *merely* a matter of feeling. One reason he wishes to establish this is because he believes that if judgements cannot be separated from responses, there will be no room for debate on what response is appropriate and, therefore, no room for even a 'modest objectivity'. However, we have already seen that this is not so. Where there is an intersubjective continuity in moral responses or an implicit agreement to speak as if there were, truth-apt moral *judgements* are unproblematic. It is not, then, necessary to relinquish the authority of moral responses (their claim to being genuinely moral) in order for the investigation of normative questions to be possible. (Indeed, moral judgements would be meaningless, and moral debate a mere word game, without a background of moral responses taken as authoritative.) It must be, then, that what Gibbard wants is a way of either rectifying or bypassing moral responses.

This is a common ambition. Indeed, if we work out the implications of Gibbard's notion of the moral as constituted by the acceptance of norms, we find that we arrive at the current state of normative ethics. Imagine, for example, what it would mean to try to establish criteria for blameworthiness. One would consider what various instances of actual blaming had in common, aside from the emotion of blame itself, and then try to establish an abstract principle of what was blameworthy. In this way, one could establish a rule for judging when blame was or was not apt. This is, of course, precisely what ethics (and lexicography) does. Indeed, Gibbard's analysis could be interpreted as a prequel to precisely the situation we currently have: one in which we have a common notion of certain moral principles and spend a good deal of time trying to decide what is right or wrong, permissible or impermissible, in terms of those principles, thereby implying that there should be a correct and incorrect of the matter, a solution to our 'moral dilemmas'. The great majority of such dilemmas, as we shall see in the next chapter, are clearly a matter of trying to reconcile our intuitive moral response to a particular case with the apparently contradictory norms that our habitual responses lead us to believe we 'accept'.

In short, then, the problems that arise from Gibbard's account are precisely the problems we already have. There is, for example, the difficulty of allowing adherence to a principle (acceptance of a norm) to override the way we feel about any particular case in hand. There is also the way in which even the most apparently systematic or rational of ethical systems must be grounded either in a feeling that is itself ungrounded or in an interest that is not itself a matter of morality. The problem of morality is not that we cannot talk about it but, rather, that, in the absence of a fixed point, an objective justification, nothing can be said with the kind of conclusiveness that the response itself implicitly demands.

Quasi-realism

We have so far considered unsuccessful attempts to consider either feeling itself (Prinz, McDowell, Wiggins) or norms (Gibbard) as such a fixed point, even if only in a pragmatic sense. Perhaps, however, such a fixed point is actually unnecessary. Blackburn, in advancing his 'quasi-realism', has argued that realism (as the belief that ethical properties exist independently of anyone's feelings in the matter) and non-realism can be reconciled without appealing beyond our feelings. Quasi-realism, according to Blackburn, is not a position in the sense that realism and anti-realism are positions but, rather, a way of considering the reality of the distinction between those two fundamental isms themselves.[142] The quasi-realist, according to Blackburn, is one who, 'starting from a recognizably anti-realist position, finds himself progressively able to mimic the intellectual practices supposedly definitive of realism'.[143]

The question is, of course, why, given that in everyday life we do inevitably talk (and feel) as moral realists, Blackburn should feel this project to be worth undertaking. He is not himself a moral realist. Rather he holds that projectivism – the thesis that we perceive the values we place on things as actual properties of the world that we are simply responding to – 'contains various explanatory advantages over other rival and alleged rival theories': it is 'consistent with, and indeed explains, the important surface phenomena of ethics'.[144] However, he is anxious to counter the charge that projectivism is 'inadequate to one or another feature of the way we think ethically'. After all, as he observes, 'our language, thought, and practice are premised on the idea that there is a normative order, a way things ought to be'.[145] Projectivism, then, appears to 'take away' too much: 'It seems to take away any notion of real normative truth.'[146] It is difficult to imagine, according to Blackburn, how any form of expressivism, which appears to regard moral reality as a myth and allegiance to it as self-deception, can give 'an adequate account of ethical language, thought, and practice'.[147] For in this practice we are frequently concerned with 'getting things right', we often think others are 'wrong', we do not 'automatically suppose that our first thoughts are our best thoughts', we recognize that 'moral truth is often "mind-independent"' and 'our thinking something is right or wrong does not make it so'. In short, it certainly feels as if our responses have to 'answer to the moral truth' rather than 'create' it.[148]

Blackburn's characterization of the 'realist surface of everyday moralizing' does not, then, distinguish between moral responses and moral judgements.[149] However, this does not, at this stage at least, effect the main point: that we certainly feel and talk as if moral values were independent of our own attitudes, as if they were not contingent on anyone's desire, preference, policy or choice.

As we have seen, it is possible to see this way of talking and thinking as simply erroneous. The error lies in the conviction that accompanies finding a thing wrong: the conviction that in saying it is wrong we are not just expressing a desire that the thing should not happen but are doing so while feeling that our desire in this matter is *right*. Blackburn concedes that, insofar as this is a claim to objectivity, it is certainly an error. However, he also claims that, from a quasi-realistic perspective, such an apparent appeal to objectivity is not so much an error as 'a proper, necessary expression of an attitude toward our own attitudes'.[150] Such judgements, he continues, are 'not something that should be wrenched out of our moral psychology', since such a conviction is 'something we need to cultivate to the right degree and in the right places to avoid the (moral) defect of indifference to things that merit passion'. We do not need to view the conviction that a thing is absolutely wrong as the embodiment of a 'second-order metaphysic of morals'; it can be 'seen instead as a kind of thought that expresses a first-order need'. So, for example, while a realist might say "Even if we had approved of it or enjoyed it or desired to do it, bear-baiting would still have been wrong", and thus be appealing to a mind-independent moral fact, the quasi-realist may make the same claim but thereby be expressing 'a perfectly sensible first-order commitment to the effect that it is not our enjoyment or approvals to which you should look in discovering whether bear-baiting is wrong (it is at least mainly the effect on the bear)'.[151]

Blackburn's point here is similar to Wiggins's argument from our experience of colour or humour: that, since we cannot actually get outside, or behind, our moral responses, the question of whether or not they are appeals to mind-independent realities is meaningless (though this is, prima facie, an odd position to take in a metaethical discussion). So, for example, while a statement like "Denying women the vote is wrong, whatever you or I or anyone else thinks" may sound like moral realism, according to Blackburn, it need not be.[152] I might be quite capable of imagining a state of mind that did not consider denying women the vote as wrong, but inevitably what I imagine will also excite my moral condemnation. Thus, according to Blackburn, I have no choice but to assert that denying women the vote is wrong, 'whatever you or I or anyone else thinks about it':

> In giving that answer one is, of course, standing *within* one's own moral view. One is assessing the scenario in the light of things one thinks and feels about such matters. But that is no objection, since there is no other mode of assessment possible. One cannot pass a verdict without using those parts of one's mind that enable one to pass a verdict.[153]

This demonstrates, according to Blackburn, that contrary to what emotivism or expressivism seem to assert, 'moral thought is not infected root and branch with philosophical myth'.[154] For it is possible, he claims, to take a starting point that sees the meaning of moral utterances as 'essentially exhausted by their role in expressing the speaker's attitude', while still 'perfectly imitating the allegedly realist thought'.[155]

> Protected by quasi-realism, my projectivist says the things that sound so realist to begin with – that there are real obligations and values, and that many of them are independent of us, for example. It is *not* the position that he says these for public consumption but denies them in his heart, so to speak. He affirms *all that could ever properly be meant* by saying that there are real obligations. When the context of discussion is that of first-order commitment, he is as solid as the most virtuous moralist. It is just that the explanation of why there are obligations and the rest is not quite that of untutored common sense [that is, moral realism].[156]

Quasi-realism is not, however, simply a matter of being able to 'imitate', or 'mimic' the language of moral realism. The projectivism to which Blackburn subscribes is more properly an account of how moral feeling comes about rather than a theory of moral language. It is, according to Blackburn, the view that we have sentiments and other reactions caused by natural features, and we gild or stain the world (as Hume had it) by describing that world as if it contained features answering to these sentiments.[157] It would seem, then, that a conscious acknowledgement of such a state of affairs as the ground of moral experience should in some way alter one's attitude towards such values. Indeed, Blackburn acknowledges that many people feel a tension between 'the subjective source that projectivism gives to morality and the objective "feel" that a properly working morality has'. Projectivism, as a threat to the 'objective feel' of morality, may be experienced as a threat to morality itself, in so far as it appears to explain away moral response as a 'phenomenological distortion'. How, he wonders, can we feel *constrained* by *obligation* and simultaneously acknowledge that this constraint is a projection of our own sentiments?

Again, Blackburn feels that a quasi-realistic approach avoids this problem. We do not need to think of our sense of morality in a realistic manner: as either the voice of God or the perception of objective moral facts, 'standing outside the natural world of sentiments and desires'.[158] From the point of view of explanation there is, he says, no problem. The individual

> has been brought up in a certain way, and a consequence of this upbringing is that he looks on certain courses of action with horror. He will keep his self-respect, be able to live with himself, only if he conducts his life in a particular way, and this prompts a range of feeling that is sufficiently strong to oppose immediate desire and that gains expression when he describes the conduct as 'wrong'.[159]

Indeed, as an explanation, projectivism has, according to Blackburn, an advantage over realism, insofar as it can both easily account for differences in sense of value and, more importantly, does not have to come up with, as realism does, an account of how values and obligations can be *cognized* in the way natural features are cognized, or why, once cognized, they should be respected.[160] As we shall later see, projectivism, as an explanation of our felt moral realism, is not quite as free of problems as this account might suggest. Moreover, the relative weakness of the explanatory power of moral realism does not make projectivism any less problematic. However, more important for our present purpose is whether Blackburn's quasi-realism can overcome what he calls the problem of 'justification'.

How, he asks, is it possible for us, as rational beings, to still entertain a sense of moral obligation once we become aware of its (projectivist) origin and nature? His answer is that rationality 'does not force one sensibility or another on us *just* because we have some belief about the origin of that sensibility'.[161] We do not, for example, cease to find something funny just because we know that being funny is a quality we project on the world. Moreover, even if the person next to us does not find it funny, we are not 'irrational' in laughing. The same applies to other projections: it is quite natural to go on valuing things – as funny, beautiful, worthwhile – even while knowing that the valuing is an expression of our own subjective sentiments.[162] Blackburn concludes, then, that we can carry on holding opinions such as that bear-baiting is wrong or that mindless violence is abominable, knowing that this is a matter of our subjective responses, since such an explanation 'in no way impugns our right to hold them, nor the passion with which we should do so'.[163] It is, he asserts, 'perfectly rational' to accept the projectivist account of morality' and yet to carry on feeling the full force of moral obligation.[164]

This seems a just observation. We do not, after all, actually experience our sense of moral outrage or obligation as desire. Blackburn offers the analogy of the contrast between the way in which a biological or evolutionary story would account for attraction between the sexes, and 'the culturally specific and surprising ways in which that attraction can emerge – the varieties of lust and love (whose imperatives often do not feel much like desire either, and may equally well be expressed by thinking that there things one simply *must* do)'.[165] However, while Blackburn's analogy certainly demonstrates that projectivism need not renounce the 'rich textures of ethical life' for any simplistic explanation of how any particular feature of that life arises, it does not demonstrate that the experience of feeling that moral values are independent of us is anything more than an illusion. That is, it does not show that projection is anything more or less than projection.

Blackburn directly addresses this question of the potentially discordant perspectives of the theorist and the participant.[166] From the point of view of the participant it is the objects of our passions that are the *immediate* object not our passions themselves: we respond to the death, the loved one or the sunset not to our own state of sadness or pleasure. Blackburn is anxious to show that projectivism does not need to 'struggle with this fact, or disown it'. There is no reason, he asserts, why we should begin to experience obligations as 'hypothetical' just because we theoretically acknowledge that 'they are properly represented as dependent upon the existence of desires'.[167] It is simply not the case that we experience what moves us and then have to tell ourselves that, since this is moving, we must feel moved: 'The news comes in and the emotion comes out; nothing in human life could be or feel more categorical.'

> Is it that we projectivists, at the crucial moment when we are about to save the child . . . will think, 'Oh, it's only me and my desires or other conative pressures – forget it'? It ought to be sufficient refutation of this doubt to mention other cases. Does the lover escape his passion by thinking, 'Oh, it's only my passion, forget it'? When the world affords occasion for grief, does it brighten when we realize that it is we who grieve?' [...] [It is a mistake to suppose that] when we deliberate in the light of various features of a situation we are *at the same time* or 'really' deliberating – or that our reasoning can be 'modeled' by representing us as deliberating – about our own conative functioning. Representing practical reasoning as if it consisted of contemplating a syllogism, one of whose premises describes what we want, encourages this mistake. But just as the eye is not part of the visual scene it presents, the sensibility responsible for the emotional impact of things is not part of the scene it takes for material.[168]

Our sensibility, he argues, is not hidden from us: we know when we are in love or grieving. However, the grounds of this sensibility are 'no part of the input, when we react to the perceived features of things'.[169] Moreover, as we have seen, 'even when we reflect on our sensibility, we will be using it if we issue a verdict: when we find our own sense of humor funny, we are not escaping use of it as we do so'.[170] This, he believes, shows that there is in fact harmony between the theoretical and deliberative points of view.

From the outside – if I watch you laughing at an unfunny joke or lusting after an unattractive person – I will certainly see your reaction as expressive of something personal to you. Likewise, if I think my love for *x* makes a claim on how others ought to feel about him/her, or if I think that my parents were 'wrong' to like different fashions, I am simply in error.[171] But, while these examples might suggest that projectivism would be morally relativistic, Blackburn does not believe that this is so. With morality, he claims, 'we insist on some responses from others, and it is sometimes part of good moralizing to do so'.[172] It is possible for a projectivist to make a statement like 'One ought to look after one's children, whether one wants to or not', precisely because ethical 'truths' do not depend on 'the existence of states of affairs in the real world'.[173] To 'see' the truth that one should look after one's children or that wanton cruelty is wrong, according to Blackburn, one must judge through the lens of one's own sensibility, but there is no other way to make such a judgement. Such a verdict does not depend on the existence of anything in the world, but only on the existence of those 'capable of making' the judgement. Thus, he concludes that 'there is nothing relativistic left to say'.[174] There is, as we saw earlier, no way to relate 'the truth of the verdict to the existence of us, of our sentiments, or of rival sentiments'.[175]

> But the strongest ethical judgements do not issue from stances that are properly variable. They may sometimes be absent, from natural causes, as if a hard life destroys a capacity for pity. But this is a cause for regret; it would be better if it were not so. In the variations of emotion, and still more of fashion, there is no cause for regret. In saying these things I am, of course, voicing some elements of my own ethical stances, but . . . it is only by doing this that ethical truth is found.[176]

This very much sounds as if Blackburn is saying that since we cannot step outside our ethical projections then, despite the truth of projectivism, we may continue to talk, act and think *as if* moral realism were correct, that is, as if those values really did exist independently of us. However, he continues to insist that his project of quasi-realism is not a matter of 'as if', not a form of fictionalism.[177]

Quasi-realism would only be a form of fictionalism, he asserts, if there really were no such thing as moral value.[178] In order to be able to say that such was the case we would have to be able to conceive of the difference between a world in which there would *really* be values and duties, and a world, such as ours would supposedly be, in which there are not.[179] If I say, for example, that it is bad to neglect children, then this is a fiction only if it is good to neglect children, or if it is a matter of indifference whether I do or not.[180] Each of these positions, according to Blackburn, is a moral position. Since there is no scope, he asserts, for holding that all three of these moral suppositions are in error, we can only hold that any one of them is a fiction if one of the other two is the truth.

However, there is palpably something wrong with Blackburn's assertion that someone who feels it does not matter how we treat children is taking a 'moral position'. Indifference is not a moral position except in a context where a moral attitude to the case already exists. Consider a less emotive example than Blackburn's:

Putting your left shoe on first is morally wrong.
Not putting your left shoe on first is morally wrong.
It doesn't matter which shoe you put on first.

The last sentence does not, as far as I know, represent a moral position in this world. Indeed, if I told you that I did not think it matters which shoe I put on first, the least likely way to interpret my statement would be as the expression of a moral position. It might appear, of course, that what prevents it from being a moral position is that – in contrast to the children example – neither of the first two propositions actually exists as a moral position in this world. However, consider the following:

Eating meat on Friday is morally wrong.
Eating meat on Friday is morally indifferent.

Here, I am sure that Blackburn would subscribe to the last proposition, but I do not see how he could call it the expression of a 'moral position'. He might hold that *caring about* whether you eat meat on Friday is morally wrong, but this would be a feeling about other people's states of mind, not about eating meat on Friday. (The same holds, of course, for cases that some people feel are more clearly a matter not, as with dietary restrictions, of obedience to a rule but of the "intrinsic value" of the action itself; as, for example, with masturbation, incest or cruelty.) Indeed, he could only advance such a position on the grounds that the second proposition – 'Eating meat on Friday is morally indifferent' – does *not* express a moral position. For, if it were a 'moral position', then it would follow that we would have say we have a moral position on every state of affairs – the weather, history, the contents of science – about which we have no moral feelings. Here, in contrast to the shoes example, then, is a situation in which it is a fact that someone holds to the first proposition ('Eating meat on Friday is morally wrong'), but this still does not make the second proposition expressive of a moral position for anyone who either does not know that the first proposition expresses an existing attitude, or, like Blackburn, does not think that it should.

If we now return to Blackburn's example, we can more clearly see that the position 'It is a matter of indifference how one treats children' is not a 'moral position' at all, except in a world in which people feel that it does matter how you treat children. The important point to note about this otherwise startlingly obvious conclusion is that Blackburn's argument turns on the fact that we do live in a world in which people *feel* that it matters how you treat children. This, however, was never in dispute. What he has not established is that we live in a world in which it matters how you treat children *no matter what you or I or anyone feels about it.* Therefore, if we assert, as he believes we are justified in asserting, on quasi-realistic grounds, that denying women the vote or neglecting children is wrong 'whatever you or I or anyone else thinks', he is necessarily asserting a fiction. Moreover, he has not succeeded in showing that there is no place from outside morality from which to view any particular moral response, since, as we have seen, it is perfectly possible to be indifferent to a state of affairs (e.g. the treatment of children or putting your left shoe on first) without, from your own point of view at least, taking up a moral position. Indeed, that is what being indifferent signifies.

We must ask, then, why Blackburn should have found it worthwhile to try to establish the existence of something – moral feeling – the existence of which was never in dispute (a question that also arises in connection with the elaborate proofs of the possibility of moral debate that we have already considered). Obviously, one target is the kind of attitude expressed by statements like "All evaluations are subjective; therefore, there are no values". However, this view, or pose, so obviously contradicts itself that it would hardly seem worth arguing against.[181] We should more charitably interpret such a statement as a problem with self-expression. (The speaker might, of course, mean that values do not exist independently of our valuing, but, in that case, none of the "answers" provided by our philosophers are pertinent.)

Blackburn, however, thinks the analysis is worth undertaking in order to show how much of everyday moral experience and discourse (with its implicit realism) survives the projectivist discourse – to show how projectivism can 'accommodate the rich phenomena of the moral life'.[182] The problem here is that in order to avoid the charge of fictionalism, he actually ends up with a form of moral realism – moral values are real because I really feel them – that appears strictly irrelevant given what is actually at stake in the realism/anti-realism dispute: whether moral values are mind-independent or not. How, then, does Blackburn distinguish between his own standpoint and moral realism?

He does so by contrasting the 'quasi-realism' that he is offering with what turns out to be a high redefinition of realism itself: something he calls 'Reealism'. The 'Reealist', according to Blackburn, is one who cannot 'put up with' the idea that values have a subjective source.[183] They cannot put up with the idea, he continues, because they 'have a defect elsewhere in their sensibilities – one that has taught them that things do not matter unless they matter to God, or throughout infinity, or to a world conceived apart from any particular set of concerns or desires, or whatever'.[184] Such 'reealism', he avers, only exists because 'a defective sensibility leads [some people] to respect the wrong things'.[185]

There are two points to make about Blackburn's distinction here between defensible 'quasi-realism' and indefensible 'reealism'. First, and perhaps of lesser importance, is the fact that his 'reealist' is fairly obviously a straw man, conceived out of a two-dimensional notion of the moral experience of others.[186] Very few people over the age of twelve will attempt to justify any moral feeling by a direct appeal to authority – and this is as true of religious people as anyone else.[187] According to Blackburn, we do not need the 'Reealist rubbish' of the 'religious myth' to keep on feeling that some things are right and wrong.[188] No doubt this is true, but *feeling* that things are right or wrong is not at issue here. The question is rather whether his own 'quasi-realistic' standpoint is actually distinguishable from such 'Reealist rubbish'. The concept of God is, of course, epistemologically indefensible (hence faith), and this would seem to undermine any attempt to make such an entity a guarantee of the mind-independence of our values. However, the problem is how to draw a contrast with this weakness of a theistic basis for morality that would make quasi-realism any more objective. For, all the "properties" that we might point to as ends in themselves in the realm of morals – justice, human rights, human dignity – are no less dependent upon wishful thinking.

Blackburn himself, for example, has subscribed to the proposition that 'human beings have the right and responsibility to give meaning and shape to their own lives'.[189] But how is he to justify the 'have' in this statement? As we saw, he does not want to say that it can be translated into "If we want (for either moral or pragmatic reasons) to achieve a certain result (human happiness, say) then we should behave *as if* human beings have this right and responsibility". Quasi-realism, he insists, is not fictionalism. All he can say, then, is that human beings have this right because they just have – and he cannot imagine feeling otherwise. As a proposition it has no better epistemological foundation than the statement "God is". The fact that Blackburn, or you, or I, might sincerely believe that the concept of human rights better serves the ends of ethics than does religion does nothing to affect this epistemological parity. For, crucially, even if it could be scientifically established that belief in human rights would lead more directly to universal human happiness than would belief in, for example, fairies at the bottom of your garden, it does not make human rights any more *real*, any more mind-independent, than fairies at the bottom of your garden.

Whenever anyone feels that something *is* wrong, they are implicitly subscribing to, or enacting, what Blackburn calls 'Reealist rubbish'. As noted earlier, and as we shall see in more detail later, all moral feelings can only be ultimately 'justified' by something like an appeal to authority – "Unfairness is just wrong" – albeit that the source of this authority is not specified. Unless one can sincerely declare that one is calling injustice "wrong" because one foresees an undesirable effect on one's interests from its existence – which is precisely *not* how we experience a moral response – then this justification ("It just is wrong") is no less of an appeal to a mind-independent entity than is the appeal to the will of God.

'Empathy'

In each of the theses we have so far considered under the heading of *trivial realism*, the writer has been seeking some way to make moral responses functionally equivalent to responses to real *moral* properties of the world, without actually endorsing the kind of moral realism we looked at in Chapter 1. They have done so either by seeking to establish that our responses might as well be responses to real properties of the world since there is no way to regard them as anything else (Prinz, McDowell, Wiggins, Blackburn) or by asserting that any particular moral response can be made to fall under the jurisdiction of what is not itself a moral response (Gibbard). With regard to the first of these strategies, it must be acknowledged that the question these approaches seek to answer would not even arise were it not that we *do* feel, as soon as we reflect on the way in which we experience moral responses, that such responses implicitly claim a warrant that cannot be substantiated. (While it is true that, as Blackburn says, the eye is not part of the visual scene; nevertheless, we are all aware that we have eyes and that our visual fields depend upon them.) Moral responses are quite different both from perceptions of such qualities as shape or colour, and even from other more demonstrably mind-dependent qualities as funniness. With regard to the second strategy, the problem is to find a warrant that is not itself dependent on moral responses – in the way that Gibbard's norms are – so as to provide a way of assessing the 'appropriateness' of moral responses that, without being circular, still leaves the moral response under the jurisdiction of feeling itself.[190]

This last is precisely what Slote attempts to do in advancing empathy as the key to morality. Starting from the idea that 'moral claims', since they are essentially linked to human sentiments, can be 'inherently motivating', he, nevertheless, believes they can also have 'genuine objective validity'.[191] If sentiment can be separated from personal interest, he holds, then sentimentalism can, like realism, 'treat moral injunctions as *categorical imperatives* in the basic sense of having validity independently of the desires, attitudes, intentions of those to whom they are addressed'.[192] If moral statements were 'merely expressive of emotions' (or imperatives), he argues, then they could not be truth-apt 'in the sense that common sense appears to assume'.[193]

Slote starts from the familiar observation that the experience of red 'serves to fix the reference of the objective term "red"'; so that, even if we cannot define 'red' we can at least say that it is an *a priori* truth that '(objective) red(ness) is whatever causes or has tended to cause, and is perceived by means of, our visual experience of red(ness)'.[194] What he wishes to emphasize, however, is the way in which one cannot understand the word "red" 'unless one has been in a position to (help) fix its reference for oneself via one's own experience of red'. Thus, it follows, he argues, that though it is only *empirically* true that red is the colour of what reflects certain wavelengths of light that we perceive as the experience of red, it is, nevertheless *a priori* that 'whatever turns out to be causally responsible for our experience of redness will turn out to be objectively red'.[195] Moral terminology, Slote believes, can be shown to be objectively fixed in a similar way.

The 'warm' feeling of approval and 'cold' feeling of disapproval, on the basis of which we ascribe rightness and wrongness, are analogous, according to Slote, to the experience of red(ness) inasmuch as they have a certain subjective phenomenology.[196] Just as the reference of "red" is fixed *a priori* by our subjective experience of redness, and it is an *a priori* truth that redness is whatever tends/has tended to cause our subjective experience of redness, so the same can be said of "right" or "wrong". The reference of "right", he claims, is fixed *a priori* by the subjective feeling of warmth we feel with regard to certain actions, and it is an *a priori* truth that rightness is whatever tends/has tended to cause such a warm feeling. It is, then, empirically true that acting benevolently is right because it is empirically true that other people's acting or failing to act benevolently is what tends to cause us to have the warm or cold feelings we have, and on the basis of which we ascribe rightness and wrongness.

However, since Slote holds it to be 'implausible to suppose that it is only an a posteriori truth that caring/benevolent action is morally right (and cruel, malicious action wrong)', in the way in which it is only an a posteriori truth that red is the colour of what reflects certain wavelengths of light, he suggests that there is a certain disanalogy with the example of colour.[197] It is not enough that the reference of "right" and "wrong" should be fixed in relation to the purely subjective feeling of warmth (approval) and coldness (disapproval): 'It can't, it shouldn't, be a mere, sheer feeling of warmth (or of chill in regard to negative moral evaluations); it needs to be something thicker or more robust, something less purely subjective and phenomenological'.[198]

Slote finds this more robust quality in empathy. It is *a priori* true, he argues, that anyone who 'has the concept of rightness and/or moral goodness' must be capable of empathy with others and capable, via empathic mechanisms, of approving (being warmed by) or disapproving (being chilled by) what others do.[199] We can, therefore, describe "rightness" and "wrongness" as whatever feelings of warmth directed at agents and delivered by mechanisms of empathy are caused by.[200] In other words, it is *a priori* that rightness is whatever causes us to be, for example, warmed by the warmth displayed by agents, and 'since it is trivial and obvious that it is agential warmth itself that causes this warming, it follows that agential warmth, as displayed in actions, is just what the goodness (or rightness) of actions consists in'. Unlike redness, then, the reference of moral terms can be fixed in a way that is both *a priori* and 'causal'.

According to Slote, it is a fact that we approve of 'fully kind actions' and disapprove of actions such as cruelty, in the sense that approval is an empathically based warm feeling directed at agents who exhibit empathy (and disapproval a chill caused by agents that do not).[201] Moreover, the reference of moral terms can be fixed without making any normative moral claims: 'what causes approval in us is morally right or good'. Thus, we can conclude that 'fully kind actions are right or good', and actions evincing a lack of empathy are wrong. These are normative moral claim, yet ones that, according to Slote, are derived from the preceding factual and semantical assumptions. The usual objection to such a deduction – to the idea of deriving an "ought" from an "is" – does not apply to the present instance, he argues, since the capacity for empathy is necessary to 'make or fully understand the claim that one can't make a genuine moral claim or genuinely approve or disapprove of something without having empathy for others'.[202] (Just as one cannot understand what red is without experience of red.) Without empathy, then, one cannot understand what approval is: 'one can't meaningfully claim that people approve of fully kind actions unless one can approve things oneself and thus possesses empathy for others.'[203] Thus, one could not understand the factual premise of the argument 'unless one has empathy and is motivated, therefore, to do the kind of thing that the conclusion of the argument says is right'.[204] The argument, then, 'doesn't lead to a conclusion that involves a certain kind of motivation on the part of someone who accepts it, from premises that *don't* involve such motivation on the part of someone who accepts *them*'. This follows from the fact that empathy, according to Slote, is at once 'a factual phenomenon, part of the world that "is's" describe', and yet one that 'underlies and powers certain sorts of motivation'.

According to Slote, it is *a priori* that kindness and love are warm, and indifference, malice and cruelty are not, and that this fact guarantees their objective rightness and wrongness respectively.[205] What, however, of those actions that seem at once moral and cold? He gives examples of actions that might be morally motivated from a utilitarian perspective (aimed at the maximization of impartially reckoned good), but which strike him as 'cold-hearted' in their impartiality.[206] A concern for 'general human happiness', where it trumps the demands of immediately perceived suffering, he argues, is certainly not malice or indifference, yet it is certainly 'chilling'. From this feeling, and his expectation that it will be generally shared, he concludes that it is 'an a priori (and necessary) truth that a basically warm-hearted agent will not prefer the general good to that of particular individuals or groups of individuals', where those individuals or groups are, for example, related by blood or vividly present. It simply is the case, according to Slote, that 'our judgments . . . follow the contours of ordinary empathy'.[207]

It is, then, our own 'empathic tendencies as agents' that seem to inform our intuitive sense of what is more or less cold or warm hearted: the same empathy that leads us to act a certain way ourselves also governs our empathic reactions of chill and warmth as spectators or contemplators of what other agents do.[208] From this he concludes that 'it is a priori (and necessary) that agential warmth consists in empathy-driven or empathy-based concern for others – and also a priori (and necessary) that agential coldness or cold heartedness consists in various specific ways of lacking such empathic concern'.[209]

Slote feels he has thus established four necessary truths: (1) The meaning of "morally good" is *a priori* fixed in relation to the experience of being warmed by the warmth of (evinced by) an agent or agents, and "morally bad" by the experience of being chilled by a lack of such warmth. (2) It is *a priori* that actions are morally good if and only if they express or reflect agential warmth. (3) It is also *a priori* for us that always preferring impartial good is not a form of warmth and is even (to a substantial extent) chilling or cold-hearted. (4) We can conclude that it is *a priori* that actions are morally good or right if and only if they express or reflect empathic concern for others on the part of the agent.[210]

What fixes the reference of moral terms is not, then, some thin, subjective notion of experience (in the manner of perceiving red) but, rather, 'certain experiences as directed toward others and as reflecting what others feel'.[211] Thus it is 'a certain phenomenon of empathy understood as a causal mechanism' that fixes moral reference in an *a priori* way. This seems to Slote more plausible that simply treating feelings of warmth and chill as *a priori* to having the concept of rightness (or goodness).

> [The] view I have been defending here holds that *there is more that is a priori to having the concept of rightness than having certain feelings*. What (among other things) is more largely or capaciously a priori to our understanding of moral judgments and to our fully having the concept of moral rightness or goodness is *our capacity for empathically feeling or reflecting what others (and, in particular, agents) feel*.[212]

Despite, then, empathy clearly being an example of a 'certain feeling', Slote nevertheless feels his account differs from those response-based approaches we have already considered in that it provides a 'much thicker reference-fixer': one that 'allows us to say that claims like "empathically caring actions are right" are both a priori and metaphysically necessary'.[213] Thus, while experiences of red fix the referent of "red", the *a priori* truth that objective redness is what is responsible for those experiences is nonetheless contingent (in that 'some other phenomenon could generally cause red sensations'), by contrast it is both *a priori* and necessary that rightness is 'whatever it is about actions that causes any empathically derived warm feelings we have in reaction to what moral agents (may) do', that 'such feelings, if they occur, are caused by empathically warm caring actions' and that 'any and all right actions will reflect warm (empathic) concern for others (or not reflect the opposite)'.[214] In short, since it is impossible that we should be 'empathically warmed by something other than (what we take to be) agential warmth or empathically caring right actions', we cannot say that 'it might have turned out that actions expressing empathic warm concern for others were morally wrong'. Thus, he feels we may confidently know that we are objectively right to, for example, prefer the good of particular individuals or groups of individuals, where those individuals or groups are, for example, related by blood or vividly present, over the general good. It may be, he concedes, that 'personal feelings can interfere with the empathic mechanisms of approval', so that the warmth we feel comes not from empathy or perception of its lack but rather from affection or antipathy, but, he asserts, this does not mean that there is not 'a fact of the matter as to whether a given feeling of warmth has the right causal origin to count as approval'.

The meaning of "right", then, is fixed, according to Slote, in relation to empathy' and is 'understood as referring to a property that causes or tends to cause approval, that is, warm feelings toward agents resulting . . . from the operation of empathy'.[215] Conversely, actions are wrong 'if, and only if, they reflect or exhibit or express a deficiency of caring motivation', and 'one can claim that actions are morally wrong and contrary to moral obligation if, and only if, they reflect or exhibit or express an absence (or lack) of fully developed empathic concern for (or caring about) others on the part of the agent'.[216] For Slote, this makes moral rightness, wrongness and goodness 'real properties of agents and their acts, attitudes, and motives'.[217] Moral claims are not descriptions of our tendencies towards attitudes of approval or towards our empathic reactions of warmth or chill; 'rather, these attitudes and empathic reactions (are used to) fix the (objective) reference of moral terms and utterances.' That is, moral claims are not 'about our observer reactions to acts and agents' (i.e. not response-dependent) but 'about the acts or agents we react to', and thus we can say that moral judgements (here, responses) are objective. The warmth or chill we feel simply pick out properties that are objectively there in acts or agents.[218] Thus we can deduce an "ought" from an "is": deduce moral claims from factual ones ('about human tendencies of approval and disapproval').[219]

One of the strengths of his theory, he believes, is that if the reference of "right" and "wrong" is fixed merely via causal (realistic) notions, then different groups of speakers may use it to 'pick out different properties', thus leading to relativism.[220] His own theory, in contrast, fixes the reference to a definite property: 'what causes our warm empathic reactions to what others (or we ourselves) do'. That is, causality is placed within rather than outside the reference-fixer.[221] He dismisses the notion of degrees of empathy; there is, he asserts, a standard 'human' level of empathy.[222] Even 'rationalists', he observes, 'have to be capable of feeling empathy if and when they make moral judgments (or show concern for their children or friends) – even if they are misled by their own rationalism into believing that this is not the case'. Moreover, individual variations are not peculiarly a problem for his thesis: every account of moral terms, he observes, must face the problem of the way in which people can be 'misled about what it is appropriate to criticize or praise in moral terms'.[223]

Slote's argument, then, yields a position that is functionally equivalent to intuitionism: in any given dilemma you may, providing you remain wary of potential contamination from self-interest, trust your emotional response to be morally "correct". Thus, he feels that he has vindicated 'our ordinary view of morality and value', which requires that we should be able to make 'true value claims'.[224]

The problem, however, is that Slote does not actually move beyond the circularity that we have already encountered in the arguments previously considered in this chapter. His 'empathy', rather than being a given non-normative emotional response, the presence of which can be used to fix the "accuracy" of a moral response, is itself already a moral response. Indeed, this much is clear from his own definition of the term at the outset of his argument, where he distinguishes empathy from sympathy. Empathy, he writes, is the capacity to, for example, 'feel someone's pain', in the sense of having the feelings of another involuntarily aroused in oneself; sympathy, by contrast, is 'feeling for someone who is in pain', that is feeling sorry for another's pain and wishing them well.[225] On this account of the two terms (there are others), the warm and cold feelings he describes should surely belong to sympathy rather than empathy, since empathy, by this definition, gives rise simply to pain. Moreover, sympathy, as it is here defined, is self-evidently a response that could only arise if one felt that what is *ought* not to be: that is, from a moral response.

Indeed, although Slote declares that his use of 'empathy' depends heavily on its use by the psychologist Batson, Batson himself is quite clear that he is using the term as a shorthand for what he calls 'empathic concern': a constellation of emotions that includes feelings of sympathy, compassion, tenderness and concern – all of which already imply that what is experienced is an interest in another's welfare *for its own sake* that belongs essentially, albeit sometimes only implicitly, to the moral response.[226]

There is a phenomenon, commonly called 'empathy' in the psychological literature, that does not have this inherent reliance on moral experience, but it would not serve Slote's purpose. This is empathy defined as the capacity to understand another person's feelings and emotions, in the sense of being able to imagine how they may view the world from their frame of reference as distinct from one's own. This, arguably, may also entail the vicarious experiencing of that person's feelings, perceptions or thoughts. ('Arguably' because it is difficult both to say what precisely 'vicarious' might mean, given that we obviously cannot *literally* experience another's experience, and also, conversely, to imagine what 'understanding' another means if it does not mean seeing something as another sees it, albeit with the addition of seeing that other.) As I have already pointed out, however, even if we define 'empathy' to necessarily include emotional contagion, this does not immediately yield the existence of the warm feeling that Slote describes. The distress that one wishes to remove in the case of emotional contagion is one's own distress at sharing the other's distress. This might or might not result in a moral-seeming action towards that other, though, even where it did, the motive would be transparently egotistic to the agent.[227]

Empathy, then, as the ability to understand that other people are distinct entities from oneself, with their own frames of reference, and to infer their mental states, and intentions from external cues (to "put yourself in their position"), would indeed be a usefully neutral psychological phenomenon against which to fix morality. However, it is also far too neutral. While such empathy may be a precondition of moral experience, it is also a precondition of such mental states as envy, vengefulness and gloating. Indeed, well-developed empathy is plainly indispensable to all the more refined ways of tormenting another human being. Empathy will only tell me that a certain epithet is likely to upset you, and, while this knowledge might lead me to refrain from using it, it might also be precisely why I choose it. There has to be something more than 'understanding' to constitute sympathy; it is only the fact that we can presume the existence of moral feeling that leads us to customarily use the one as a synonym for the other. "How would you like it if someone did that to you?" seems like a good argument against a course of action, but it does not establish a moral premise so much as appeal to one. As I have said, it is always open to the interlocutor to reply, "I wouldn't, but I'm not doing it to me". As an argument to refrain from hurting another, evoking their pain, succeeds of fails not on the basis of whether the person can imagine someone doing it to them and what that would feel like, but rather on whether, having imagined that, they feel that is somehow a reason to stop.[228] In short, empathy, in itself, does not entail motivation: it only throws any weight against self-interest where there is also already moral feeling.

Given that the phenomenon of empathy, as described above, requires a name, and that 'sympathy' is already used for *concern* for another's feelings, it would have been more appropriate for Slote to have used 'sympathy' for the feeling he describes.[229] The word 'sympathy', however, too obviously suggests an attitude of mind in which moral feeling is already operative, so that its use would make Slote's theory too obviously circular, after the manner of those other sentimentalist theories – of Wiggins, McDowell, Gibbard and Blackburn – that he rejects for their failure to give any 'substance' to moral claims. That he does use 'empathy' to describe a feeling that is already a matter of moral response makes it unremarkable that he should find 'a general correspondence between distinctions or differences in our empathic (caring) reactions and the moral distinctions we want, intuitively, to make'.[230] It is equally unsurprising that he should be able to easily account for the way in which 'moral claims are inherently motivating', since his 'empathy' is already something that 'inclines us to do what we think of as right and avoid what we think of as wrong'.[231] The fact that empathy, as it is defined in terms of comprehension alone, is arguably a necessary (though not sufficient) condition for moral feeling adequately accounts for the direct proportionality between the urgency of our moral response and the vividness of the object, or the strength of already existing attachments. This does not, however, lead to Slote's further conclusion that responses that favour the vividly present over the distant or one's own group over another's are, therefore, somehow 'objectively' correct, or that ambivalence about this 'correctness' can only be attributed to a heartless 'rationalism'. It just is the case that we sometimes have conflicting senses of what we ought to do, even without the intervention of a desire to be consistent. The notion of "following one's heart" turns out to be no more helpful in this context than it is in any other.

Moreover, and most importantly for the present context, Slote has not found a (non-moral) sentiment that will explain why we respond to acts/agents as wrong that does not already depend on the feeling that acts/agents are wrong. That is, he does not escape that circular reasoning that, as we have seen, is the hallmark of all 'subjectivist' attempts to establish some kind of moral objectivity.

Conclusion

The present chapter began by considering attempts to circumvent the problematic character of the moral response – the way in which we experience it as registering a mind-independent value – through the argument that common sense already does, or at least could, acknowledge the untenability of its implicit realism: through fictionalism. It turned out, however, that fictionalism was obliged to misrepresent the moral response. We have also considered the attempt to circumvent the same problem by employing a variety of ways to establish that the realism implicit in the moral response itself (and explicit in our moral discourse) is, nevertheless, unproblematic. Each of the positions dealt with promised to provide, in effect, a 'cognitivist formulation of subjectivism' (Wiggins) to show that, even though the moral response is mind-dependent, the world does, nevertheless, contain 'moral properties' or 'moral facts', that we can have a 'substantial notion of truth' in connection with ethics, that our responses can demonstrate 'genuine objective validity', can be 'correct' or 'rational', and that there really are 'categorical imperatives' the validity of which is independent of our desires, attitudes or intentions. In some instances, this was simply a matter of conflating reacting to a phenomenon with perceiving a phenomenon (Prinz, Nussbaum, Slote); in others the objectivity referred to turned out to be no more than the truth-aptness that moral statements may possess where there is a moral consensus (McDowell, Wiggins). In some cases, the claim was based on appeal to an independent standard (Gibbard, Slote) even though, in the event, no genuinely independent standard was forthcoming; in others it was based upon the argument that, since we are not in a position to question the objectivity of our responses, we may justifiably regard them as objective (McDowell, Blackburn) even though this argument simply returns us to fictionalism.

What we have not seen is any justification for regarding subjectivism as 'a form of realism' or 'quasi-realistic'. That, as Blackburn says, the eye is not part of the visual scene it presents shows only precisely what projection entails – that we experience our moral responses as the perception of qualities in the world. (Albeit that, as we have seen, we do so in a way that is qualitatively different from other perceptions.) That we can experience these responses (and talk about them) as demands placed upon 'us' from outside ourselves or as the qualities of objects/situations rather than as desires shows only the profundity of the illusion/subreption involved.

The fallacies in the arguments we have examined seem to arise from an unwillingness to accept the implications of the subjectivism the philosophers themselves subscribe to. That they feel, despite what some of them say, that subjectivism is somehow a threat to morality is shown by the way they often insensibly drift from metaethics into moralizing; for example, with Prinz's appeal to the way in which morality 'places demands on us', or Blackburn's belief that the claim to objectivity is something we *should* cultivate 'to avoid the (moral) defect of indifference to things that merit passion', and his insistence that realism is, in fact, 'part of good moralizing'. There appears to be a general wish to avoid the acknowledgement of projection that irrealism seems to entail. This is quite understandable: projection seems to demand some remedy. In the absence of any remedy that does not seem to somehow threaten the desired authority of moral feeling, the philosophers here considered instead either argue that no illusion is involved or they offer robust defences of the possibility of moral argument – as if the real problem lay with moral judgements rather than moral responses.

'I cannot see how to refute arguments for the subjectivity of moral values', wrote Russell, 'but I find myself incapable of believing that all that is wrong with wanton cruelty is that I don't like it.'[232] Naturally. That is what projection means: that one should be incapable of believing that one is responsible for what one perceives. We cannot, in everyday life, factor in our own projections; they would not be projections if we could.

However, there is a deliberate bathos in Russell's 'I don't like it'. It does appear absurdly reductive to characterize moral responses as preferences or even as similar in kind to other emotional responses. Blackburn, as we saw, points out that we do not expect or feel we can demand that others love the one we love, though this expectation/demand seems to be inherent to moral responses. This is not to say, however, as Blackburn does, that this somehow makes morality "more real" than affection. It demonstrates only that, with morality, there is a particularly radical division between what we experience (intrinsic value) and what is really happening (the projection of a self-interest existing at a level so profound that we are apparently incapable of owning it). There is no substance to the objection that, in contrast to affection, we do not experience morality as self-interest: it would hardly qualify as projection if we did experience it in this way. Nevertheless, it does seem that there is a difference between the way in which we experience moral value *as* a quality of the world and the way in which we experience other projected emotions (e.g. beauty or love) *as* qualities of the world: there is something inadequate in Russell's 'I don't like it' that must be accounted for.

The problem that emerged at the end of Chapter 1 – why there should be such a thing as a moral response – still stands. Indeed, the purpose of this chapter was merely to demonstrate that subjectivist or non-cognitivist attempts to solve, or circumvent, that problem have hitherto been no more successful than realism itself. Of course, the consistent failure of such attempts does not, in itself, prove that such a formulation is impossible. However, given the convoluted arguments (and occasional rhetorical appeals) that seem requisite to provide such a formulation, it seems prima facie unlikely that such a thing is possible.

For all the ingenuity of the positions surveyed, then, we have not actually advanced a single step towards accounting for the phenomenon that was our starting point. All that the various objective subjectivisms (or subjective objectivisms) surveyed here achieve is to underscore the problematic nature of that phenomenon. To the implicit realism of the way the response is experienced and the implicit realism of moral discourse, we may now add the evidence of philosophy's own urgent desire to establish the objectivity of the response, its reluctance to completely relinquish the claim to the point of view of the universe. In practice, the attempt to *justify* the existence of morality is, as we have seen, equivalent to attempting to show that the moral response is not 'merely' a matter of emotion. We may now leave aside such attempts at justification and turn instead to the nature of the emotion.

Part II

Empirical considerations

3

What do we want?

The moral response, as we saw in Chapter 1, is an emotional response – at once involuntary and motivating – in the presence of what the subject perceives, *on the basis of that response itself*, as right or wrong. It is an ascription of should-be-doneness or should-not-be-doneness to actions: the feeling that certain states of affairs, insofar as they depend on human will, should or should not be. We have now seen that this response is neither a matter of the perception of moral properties of the world nor a matter of the deliberate election of expedient norms: that right and wrong are neither discovered nor invented. We have also seen, in the last chapter, a variety of ways in which philosophers, even when they acknowledge the emotional nature of moral responses, have gone out of their way to assert, by various means, that we can be justified in treating them as if they were something else, be it perceptions or judgements. What, however, would it mean to actually consider moral feeling as an emotion?

The first thing to note is that all emotions imply a desire or an aversion; they signal that some value or goal of the person has been engaged: that the person has perceived one of their ends to be either advanced or frustrated. Emotions express a tendency to act, or at least imply a stimulus towards a definite form of behaviour, in line with the subject's interpretation of their relationship with the environment. They signal what we do or do not want of the world. This is obviously so with such prototypic emotions as anger or love, but equally so of those emotional states that are complex (grief), ambiguous (awe, determination, satisfaction) or even apparently contentless (excitement, arousal, distress, agitation). The complicating factor in the moral case is, of course, that it is also peculiarly part of that response that we should feel we are 'taking the viewpoint of the universe': that the desire or aversion are not dependent on our personal ends, are not our own. (Hence, as we have seen, philosophy's desire to either circumvent emotion or "raise" it to the status of a rational judgement.) This is something that must be accounted for, though it is worth noting here that moral feeling is not our only experience of emotions where the interest they signify is not explicit in the form they take.[1]

In one sense, it is obvious that moral responses take the form of desires/aversions. To find a thing wrong necessarily entails the desire that it would not happen. However, if we simply divide the desired state of affairs implicit in moral responses into all of the objects that elicit moral responses (instances of cruelty, injustice, unnatural acts, etc.), we are simply moving in a circle: we have an aversion to cruelty because we do not want people to be cruel.[2] The problem could be somewhat reduced if we could find something that all such instances had in common. (As a concern for one's own safety, or the safety of what one values, unites every instance of what is found frightening.) There must, after all, be a reason why we feel it is appropriate to characterize our reactions to these disparate matters as all of the same kind: "moral". Is there, then, a more general state of affairs that can be shown to be the object of whatever desire/aversion is implicit in the moral response per se?

To discover some more general object of the desire/aversion implicit in all, or at the least the majority, of moral responses would not, of course, be equivalent to explaining such responses, given that they are not experienced as desires/aversions (moral responses are responses to x, which is such that it elicits moral responses), but it would at least give us a more manageable starting point than the atomism of considering each response in isolation. The question of what precisely a moral response was a response to would still remain. Nevertheless, if we can discover a single goal implicit in the very existence of such responses, this should help to illuminate what it is that gives rise to them.

However, to discover such an implicit unifying end is a far from simple matter. Indeed, it is possible to view the greater part of philosophical ethics in modern times as an endeavour to discover such a common point – though for reasons very different from our present ones. What modern philosophical ethics endeavours to establish is an abstract *shouldness*, deducible from moral experience itself, that will serve as a standard against which to measure the legitimacy of particular instances of that experience: to "justify" certain responses. Thus, while contemporary ethics may scoff at 'the Good', it is still very much in pursuit of what *is* good. It wishes to know if x is worse than y, if z is "permissible" in these or those circumstances, should "we" do this or that, what "we" must or cannot "accept", what "we" are or are not "obliged" to do and so on. However, in the absence of any kind of realism, such questions are only meaningful if they are understood to be about the logical implications of moral feelings I already have (which is why contemporary ethics very much confines itself to the realm of moral *judgements*).[3] Indeed, given the prima facie absurdity of seeking to establish what we should do *independently of what we feel we should do*, the suspicion must arise that the real goal of this search for system in morality is not so much to discover a standard for guiding behaviour, as to reflexively establish, by the possession of such a standard, some form of de facto moral objectivity. We saw in the previous chapter how devoutly such an objectivity is desired.

Such questions are not, however, so remote from the question of the grounds of moral feeling itself as they might at first appear. For, if a moral principle, or definition of 'the Good' can be seen as the most adequate encapsulation of the principle implied in either moral feeling itself, or in the majority of our moral responses, then it should also point us towards the grounds of that feeling. That is, it would give us the desired object, the achievement or frustration of which is signalled by the emotional reaction that is the moral response. (Albeit that the view will be somewhat obscured by the fact that, as a deduction, this desire will already have had to compromise with reason to be reducible to a principle.) "What is the right thing to do?" is, then, functionally equivalent to "What would have to happen for the desire implicit in my moral feeling to be satisfied?"

In Chapter 1 we looked exclusively at the phenomenology of the response, that is, at how we recognize a particular response as moral in nature. We there eschewed any discussion of what kinds of object (action, agent or situation) such a response is a response to, on the grounds that there does not seem to be, in practice, any limit to this category. There do, however, appear to be certain necessary features, from the point of view of the subject, for what qualifies as the object of a moral response. Very broadly we may say that, as a bare minimum, the subject responds morally to what is perceived as matter of the welfare (however conceived) of another or others (however delimited) where, from the subject's point of view, it is a matter of the sake of the welfare of that other or others *in itself*. (This does not, of course, preclude the possibility of a moral response to what is merely a nuisance to oneself, so long as that response feels to one as if it is a disinterested response to the general *immoral* indifference to others demonstrated by the cause of the nuisance.) By 'welfare' I mean the greatest possible freedom from avoidable harm, including the harm of avoidable obstacles to flourishing.

We will look further into the concept of welfare shortly, but, for the moment, we may allow that moral responses are likely to be principally elicited by a perception of the diminution, whether absolute or relative, of another's welfare. Indeed, it would seem to be impossible to characterize the moral response per se without including its orientation towards such a diminution, that is, towards harm. Even where morality manifests itself in the active pursuit of harm (the urge to punish, for example), there is always a reference to a harm that *should* not have been done. What actually constitutes harm itself is a much less straightforward matter. There is a tendency to contrast "real harms" as the objects of moral responses with other objects that may elicit moral responses – infractions of codes concerned with the preservation of the sacred, social hierarchy, purity, honour and so on – but everything about the way such infractions are perceived by those who respond morally to them suggests that they do constitute harms in the relevant context. It may seem to me that *x* (homosexuality, treating people of inferior races as equal, etc.) is only a harm to someone as a result of their moral response to it, but from their point of view what they are experiencing is a *moral* response to harm *x*. If, then, we take "harm" to mean what the subject perceives as harm, rather than what I personally might feel to be real harm (excluding, that is, the real harm of being in the state of mind of feeling moral harm has been done), then we may say that a concept of harm is inseparable from the moral response.

The second minimally necessary condition for a response to be experienced as moral seems to be, as we saw in Chapter 1, that it should imply some form of *disinterested* (non-self-interested) concern for the interests of others, or at least a disinterested concern that agents should not behave in a way that implies they hold their own interests above the interests of others to an excessive degree. (What is perceived as an 'excessive degree' of self-interest at the expense of the interests of others is, of course, itself a function of whether or not that behaviour has elicited a moral response.) Though the response is emotional, it is, nevertheless, 'disinterested' insofar as the wrongness or rightness are felt by the subject to be, up to a point, qualities of the action in itself. It is not impossible to imagine a person who only responded morally to what they perceived as harm (accomplished or potential) to themselves, but if those responses did not at least take the form of stipulations of more general should-not-be-doneness, it would be impossible to identify them as moral responses. I say 'general' rather than "universal", since, while *from the subject's point of view* their application appears universal, insofar as they include all beings to which they feel the concepts of responsibility and rights can more or less equally be applied, this "universality" will, in practice, vary from subject to subject, depending on where and when they live. (One may lie to a Shudra, but not to another Brahmin; one should not treat native slaves as one treats foreign slaves; a dead civilian is a victim of terror in France, but collateral damage in Pakistan.) This does not, however, affect the point that the response itself implies what is, *from the subject's point of view*, an impartial (non-self-interested) interest in the interests of others.

Utilitarianism

Given these two minimal criteria for a response to qualify as moral, it becomes a relatively simple matter to arrive at a range of actions that, for any particular conception of the welfare of others, will count, *ceteris paribus*, as either right or wrong. (The whole of contemporary normative ethics, however, is contained precisely in this *ceteris paribus*.) It becomes possible to deduce a general principle, if not actually a goal, from the common characteristics of a very broad range of moral responses. For example, some form of utilitarian principle ('that Action is best, which procures the greatest Happiness for the greatest Numbers; and that, worst, which, in like manner, occasions Misery') will capture for us a principle that the majority of moral responses appear to imply: at least insofar as it expresses the idea of a balance of interests and a concern with the minimizing of harm.[4] Likewise Kant's principle that we should act only on maxims that could be universally legislated within a consistent system of maxims generates judgements that, for the most part, are intuitively moral. Indeed, while Kant and Mill are often presented as exemplary of two key alternative approaches to ethics (deontological and consequentialist respectively), many of the problems that Kant's approach is perceived to possess could be solved by inserting the utilitarian maxim into the place he leaves open for less abstract axioms. The concept of justice, too, insofar as it concerns the balancing of interests implied by the moral response, is comprehended by these same two conditions: welfare and impartiality.

Indeed, given these minimal conditions, it is unsurprising that the greater part of moral discourse, from the everyday to the philosophical, should revolve around questions of degrees of harm, the distribution of harm and the extent of our obligation to avoid harm to others. For, debate is only possible where the concepts of harm and of morally relevant others are, in the context, themselves taken as given. (The question of the priority of one's own interests is perhaps the most vexed of all, but, in the context of debate, even this must be treated as if representative.) Where, then, debate about rightness and wrongness is possible, it is unsurprising that the principle most likely to be appealed to is one which directly addresses the distribution (rather than the nature) of harms and benefits: utilitarianism. A moral argument or exposition that required appeal to some explicit moral absolute – the wrongness of gratuitous cruelty on the one hand or the ungodliness of cruelty on the other – would seem either redundant (if we shared it) or irrelevant (if we did not). Conversely a moral argument or exposition that appealed directly to my interests would not seem to be a moral argument at all, unless of course I could get you to see my interests as somehow morally binding on you, which would bring us back to the distribution of harm. (We must characterize this claim as 'morally binding' because if it were simply a matter of appealing to your self-interest as grounds for your respecting my self-interest, it would, of course, lift us out of the domain of recognizably *moral* discourse entirely.)

Thus, utilitarianism emerges, even among those who believe themselves to be anti-utilitarian, as the general, and generally reliable, guide to the acceptable solution of moral dilemmas.[5] It does not specify what constitutes either the happiness or the misery that are its yardstick, nor who is to count among the greatest number; it is, in effect, a merely mathematical formula into which what at least appear to be the givens of the moral context can be inserted. It asserts only that more happiness (freedom from harm) is better than less happiness, and that more misery (harm) is worse than less misery. Thus, apparently "moral" disagreements most often emerge not over whether the principle should be applied but rather over what is relevant to the application of the principle. That is, over what constitutes real happiness, who qualifies to count among the greatest number, and, even where there is consensus on these first two points, what are the likely remote results of the alternatives presently available. (These can also be seen not so much as disagreements over what is "right" as disagreements about what the world is like.)

The consequent ubiquity of utilitarian forms of argument and explanation, applied to instances of harm, within ethics (and law) easily leads to the illusion that our everyday morality is largely a matter of measuring actions against a principle: of making *judgements*. (And, incidentally, to the illusion that rationality is a large part of moral experience: an illusion to which philosophy is, naturally, particularly susceptible.) What preserves the *moral* nature of this utilitarian moral discourse, which is, after all, at least on the surface, all about the consequences or uses of particular courses of action, is the fact that utilitarianism itself does not have a utilitarian foundation. It is only my *feeling* that the interests of others are somehow binding on me, the *sense of justice* (variously conceived) implied by the moral response, that gives rise to the notion of utilitarianism as a general principle.

The basic premise of utilitarianism, then, is not arbitrary. It can apparently be deduced from what is implied by the majority of our moral feelings insofar as these feelings can be made, by the principle itself, consistent with each other. Thus, the rule that it yields is, from one point of view, a rule about what we *should* do in order to be consistent with the majority of our own feelings. (Without, of course, addressing why we *should* desire such a consistency.) From another point of view, it is a rule for discovering what is 'right' independently of how we feel, which is, as I have suggested, perhaps the raison d'etre of systematic ethics. In any case, this apparent neutrality of utilitarianism is the reason why it is so often invoked, if only implicitly, in moral discourse: moral *judgements* are only necessary where some kind of arbitration is necessary. Where we have a conflict between moral feeling and some other interest, such a principle is, of course, useless. If I am torn between the necessity to steal and a strong moral repugnance to stealing, the introduction of the idea of the wrongness of stealing is of little use to me, since it is already present in the fact that I am torn. In such a case the only useful principle of arbitration would be either a (non-moral) appeal to the consequences for myself of stealing (getting caught) or an appeal the underlying principle that makes stealing wrong, which would bring us to a consideration of the interests of others and thus back to utilitarianism. This would only work, however, if you could rely on such an appeal having some force with me: on revivifying the impulse that lies behind my repugnance to stealing (providing that repugnance is moral). Utilitarianism is simply a deduction from our moral feeling; it offers no motive as to why we *should* apply the principle. It is useful, then, only in those instances where we want to achieve what we already feel to be right but are not sure, because of the facts of the matter, which course of action will achieve that goal (as, for example, when deciding on a method of taxation).

Indeed, in deciding such matters of fact – what will lead to the best result – the application of the utilitarian principle is so far taken for granted in everyday life as to pass unnoticed. This is also why utilitarianism has received so much attention within philosophical ethics: from a normative point of view, where utilitarianism becomes problematic is precisely where ethics becomes problematic. (From a metaethical point of view, of course, utilitarianism is only as problematic as any other formulation of rightness and wrongness.) Thus, the very fact that utilitarianism has proved so contentious is a tribute to the way in which it does so successfully encapsulate the common sense of what constitutes the rightness and wrongness of actions.

If, then, we are looking for the object or state of affairs the desire for which gives rise to the moral response, perhaps this is it: the greatest happiness of the greatest number. However, before turning to the question of whether or not this is actually the case, there are two common objections to utilitarianism as a formulation of (our sense of) right and wrong that must be rebutted. The first, which is related to the question of harm, holds that utilitarianism is mistaken in holding happiness to be the only thing that people desire, and, therefore, mistaken in formulating harm in terms of the diminution of the balance of happiness. The second objection, one that is difficult to formulate without making its weakness too apparent, is that utilitarianism cannot adequately capture rightness and wrongness since, when taken strictly at its letter, it imposes far too great an obligation on the individual. Once we have dealt with these two objections, we shall return to the question of whether or not the utilitarian formulation does capture the at least ostensible object of the desire/aversion that the moral response signals.

Harm, even in its apparently most primitive form as pain, is always relative to the viewpoint of the subject (consider masochism, exercise or writing a book). Thus, it is customary to think of the avoidance of harm in terms of avoiding the frustration of another's ends – whatever those ends may be. It is this that leads to the utilitarian emphasis on the promotion of happiness. This is "happiness" understood as whatever we take to be another's view of the optimal balance of the greatest possible pleasure with the least possible pain. It follows from this that, as Mill said, happiness is the one end that every person necessarily has.[6] Though I take this view of the place of happiness in human life to be uncontroversial (almost to the point of vacuity), it is, nevertheless, a view that many object to as reductionist. It will, therefore, be necessary to digress for a moment to defend it.

There are many states of affairs – from satisfying hunger to listening to music – that we desire for their own sake, rather than as means to something else. There are even states of affairs – possessing money or power – that are the result of activities that may have begun as means to other ends, but which become ends in themselves. (There may, indeed, be no limit to what this second category could encompass.[7]) Happiness, as described earlier, would be the balance of all these things that we desire for their own sakes. For, although language may encourage us to think of happiness as a single distinct state (it is quite possible to say that we "desire happiness" and that something is "more important to us than happiness"), in fact, it is not possible to have the state we envisage except in terms of an optimal balance between the satisfaction of, or the anticipation of the satisfaction of, specific desires. Given that people's sources of pleasure – the things they desire for their own sake – differ, what set of goals constitute the projected or achieved happiness of each person will also differ, though everyone, in seeking what they conceive of as the optimal balance between pleasure and pain, can be said to be seeking happiness (as that optimal balance), and seeking it for its own sake.

Thus, depending on how we look at any particular object of desire or goal, it can be considered as an end in itself, as a means to the end of being happy, and as a part of that happiness. (The statements "I like listening to music," "Listening to music makes me happy" and "I am happy listening to music" do not contradict each other.) Indeed, what makes anything a component of happiness is precisely that it is pursued as an end in itself. What makes happiness a distinct concept is not that it is a different kind of experience, but that it is the optimal balance of such experiences: I will not be happy listening to music if I am sitting on a drawing pin or if my children hate the music I am listening to.

There are several possible reasons why this remarkably obvious point about happiness should, nevertheless, appear reductive to many: why it should appear that we do desire something other than happiness. First, as already mentioned, language itself encourages us to think of happiness as a particular state, independent of the satisfaction or anticipation of the satisfaction of any particular desires, or even an aggregate of such satisfactions/anticipations. It is only when we try to imagine such an abstract state that we realize that it must be composed of the achievement, or the anticipation of the achievement, of particular desires, or rather the mental states that accompany such anticipation or achievement – hearing music, knowing one is rich, feeling one has done right and so on. Second, when we desire something in itself – music, health, relationships, justice – it appears redundant to say that we desire it in order to be happy: it is only to the extent that the frustration of such desires leads to unhappiness that we would become conscious that they are necessary ingredients to our happiness per se. Thus, our desire for health is revealed by sickness, for relationships by unanticipated loneliness and for justice by indignation or guilt: in all cases by a diminution of happiness. Third, since we have a concept of our own happiness, or what we feel are the necessary ingredients to any human happiness, it may appear to us that certain desires of others are not actually oriented towards happiness. For example, one with a great desire to be a polar explorer may be quite willing to forfeit all those physical comforts that it would make us unhappy to forfeit, in order to undergo experiences that we ourselves would intuitively designate as unpleasant. If we were to do the same, we could certainly be said to have chosen to do something for the sake of something other than happiness, and, unless we had done so for another end, for which the polar exploration was simply a means, that behaviour would be inexplicable.[8] However, for one who has a great desire to be a polar explorer, an inability to do so would materially contribute to their unhappiness.

This last point concerns the different conceptions of what constitutes the optimal balance of pleasure and pain, which, in turn, depends upon what counts for the individual as pleasures or pains. By contrast, the fourth reason for our appearing to sometimes choose something other than happiness turns on the presence of different interests within the same person: the way in which happiness, as an optimal balance among various pleasures that we desire as ends in themselves, must involve compromise. A good example here is moral feeling itself. The hallmark of moral feeling is that it appears to represent almost the antithesis of self-interest: it is oriented towards the welfare of others apparently for the sake of those others and may actually involve the sacrifice of other interests. For this reason, it seems quite natural to overlook the fact that (for reasons we are yet to discover) we actually *desire* the right and feel an *aversion* to the wrong (however we may conceive those two things), and to talk instead of a motivation that has nothing to do with our own happiness. This way of talking may be useful when we wish to distinguish between an action arising from moral feeling and one arising from another, more obviously self-interested or primitive desire, but it obscures the fact that, as an emotional response, it is a component of happiness. (Indeed, the same apparent lack of understandable self-interest is what makes us look on misers, or those who sacrifice what we would call happiness in order to pursue fame or power as ends in themselves, as somehow deluded: we would say that they do not understand their own best interests. The difference in the case of moral feeling is that we are viewing such behaviour from *inside* rather than *outside*, so that our account of it is rather different.) Because moral feeling may lead us to sacrifice other interests, and because it has no *obvious* link to self-interest, there is a nearly universal tendency to see it as radically disinterested: as not a matter of pleasure or displeasure. Thus, we naturally talk about virtue in terms of "self-sacrifice" (just as we might talk of self-sacrifice in connection with our hypothetical polar explorer), since satisfying our desire for virtue clearly often involves the sacrifice of other interests, the frustration of which we may resent even as we sacrifice them. However, to posit this as absolute self-abnegation, that is, to demand a "genuine self-sacrifice" over and above the sacrificing of some interests to others, is to ask for the impossible: an action that arose despite the overall motivation of the actor rather than because of it (essentially, an accident).[9] It would be overstating the case to say that doing what one feels is the right thing is actually positively pleasant (though seeing the right thing done may be), but certainly the frustration of our desire for the right thing to be done becomes unpleasant; it manifests as outrage, indignation, shame or guilt. Indeed, what actions we feel these emotions in connection with, and how strongly we feel them in connection with what actions, is precisely what our morality *is*.

The idea that we desire anything other than happiness is, then, mistaken. The problem, as we have seen, lies in the tendency to think of happiness as one end among others rather than as what it is: the optimal balance of the claims of those things that we desire in themselves. As such, it necessarily follows that happiness is the one thing we ineluctably desire, in the sense that we are prepared to compromise any of our other desires for ends (love, food, sex, music, justice) that are, nevertheless, ends in themselves, in order to achieve this optimal balance between them. This becomes easier to accept once we realize that happiness can be *nothing but* the individual's optimal balance of pleasures: that happiness is constituted by this balance. As noted earlier, this means that any particular object of desire or goal that we consider an end in itself is also a means to the end of being happy and a potential component of happiness. (Indeed, it is only what is pursued as an end in itself, whether consciously or otherwise, that can be a component of happiness.) The only desire of which this cannot be said is the desire for happiness itself, that is, the desire for the combination of our different desires to produce the greatest possible pleasure with the least possible pain, since this is no more than a desire that the combination of desires we have for other things should not make us unhappy. The claims of all other desires are necessarily subordinate to this claim.

This digression has hopefully demonstrated that there is, prima facie, nothing absurdly reductive in claiming that happiness is the one overriding end that any individual can be presumed to have. Even if this gives no definite substance to the notion of happiness (since it turns out to be constituted by whatever the individual feels is the optimal balance between whatever they count as ends in themselves), it does at least allow us to more clearly conceive of what will count, for that person, as "harm": the diminution or frustration of their overall happiness or their expectation of it.

In practice, of course, our moral feelings are responses not so much to what actually are other people's conceptions of their own happiness so much as to our own conception of other people's welfare – that is, our feeling of what *should* (in both senses of the word) constitute human happiness (hence, the expression 'Cruel to be kind'). To take a simple example, we can infer from our own feelings that, since *ceteris paribus* no one likes pain, to be made to experience pain is to be harmed, that is, to have one's happiness diminished. However, for a masochist, pain may enhance, or even be requisite for, sexual gratification, and thus be a means to an end that, for the masochist, outweighs the end of freedom from pain – just as the pain of an injection or of fatigue is outweighed, for some, by the ends of health or fitness. Thus, we can perceive the masochist's pain as no more a matter of harm, in the relevant sense, than, say, the assignment of homework. However, it may also be that I feel that to invite pain solely for the end of sexual gratification is to raise sexual gratification to a level of importance that necessarily diminishes human dignity, so that, irrespective of the role the masochistic act may play in the pursuit of happiness for those involved, that act is, nevertheless, harm in the relevant sense: the frustration of the ends that I feel are most appropriate to human beings, including the masochist.

It is a failure to take into account this natural "limitation" to the meaning of 'happiness' in the utilitarian formulation that has led many commentators to blame utilitarianism for entailing morally counterintuitive verdicts that, in fact, it does not. Williams, for example, offers the hypothetical example of a small and relatively harmless minority against which the majority is so severely prejudiced that its presence is a source of distress to them.[10] A utilitarian calculation – the greatest happiness for the greatest number – would, according to Williams, issue in the removal of the minority, despite the distress it would cause to that minority: a result that he feels many (though presumably not the majority in the example) would feel to be counterintuitive. However, if one were convinced, as one well might be, that indulging an irrational and vindictive dislike would ultimately *not* lead to the happiness of the greatest number (including future generations of the majority itself), then the removal of the minority will not appear to be the utilitarian option, any more than the continual indulgence of a child's disinclination to go to the dentist would count as the utilitarian option. That is, in diminishing the happiness of a particular agent at a particular moment, I am still aiming at the ultimate greatest happiness for the greatest number. Such a standpoint will, of course, appear paternalistic from outside, but it is also inevitable (for a utilitarian), given that human happiness here can never be anything other than what *I* can conceive of as human happiness.

All this is not to say that utilitarianism never produces counterintuitive results, but only that some of these may arise from applying the formula without considering what meaning it is possible for "happiness" to bear. It may be, as we saw earlier, that it is taken to refer to an end *of the same kind* as other ends in themselves, in which case its priority can seem arbitrary. On the other hand, as we have just seen, "happiness" can be taken in too ideal a sense: simply as the agent's own conception of what constitutes their happiness, irrespective of whatever I, in the act of applying the principle, may ineluctably feel is necessary or contrary to human happiness per se.[11]

The second objection to utilitarianism that we must consider bears more obviously on the main question of whether or not the greatest happiness for the greatest number really is what we are desiring when we experience a moral response. This is the objection, also made by Williams, that utilitarianism does not allow for 'the relation between a man's projects and his actions', and is, consequently, 'alienating'.[12] If this actually turns out to be the case, then it would seem to throw doubt on the idea that it is the utilitarian object (the greatest happiness for the greatest number) that is being desired when we experience a moral response. How, after all, could we be alienated from our own desires?[13]

According to Williams, what brings utilitarianism into a potentially alienating conflict with what he calls a person's 'integrity' is the broad concept of 'negative responsibility' that it entails.[14] According to utilitarianism, in order to be doing right there is a certain state of affairs (the greatest happiness for the greatest number) that I must aim at through my actions, using the best of my knowledge to predict that outcome and whatever 'causal levers' are to hand.[15] Consider, for example, one of the test cases he uses to examine utilitarianism in general. Jim, Williams asks us to imagine, finds himself accidentally in a small South American town where a group of innocent Indians are about to be executed. The captain in charge proposes that if Jim shoots one of them, he will let the rest go free. Jim's dilemma is whether or not to shoot the single Indian.[16] The utilitarian answer, Williams believes, is that Jim is morally obliged to do so, but Jim may still feel that he cannot kill an innocent human being in cold blood, even under these circumstances. That is, he may, in such circumstances, be incapable of acting in that way that will ensure the greatest happiness of the greatest number.

Although we shall return to the question of Jim's motives, the important point here for our present concerns is that, according to utilitarianism, in choosing not to shoot the Indian, Jim becomes responsible for the multiple deaths he could have prevented. The point can be made less dramatically: insofar as, in deciding to write this rather than asking myself what, as I am currently situated, I could do that would lead to the greatest happiness for the greatest number, I can be said to be responsible for whatever diminution in happiness my choice may cause. As Williams says, utilitarianism presents me with a 'boundless obligation . . . to improve the world'.[17]

However, it does not follow from this that utilitarianism can be said to fail to capture our sense of right and wrong, since this sense of obligation is only an assault on our 'integrity' if that 'integrity' necessarily requires the belief that we are as morally good as it is possible to be. It is quite possible to morally admire someone else's actions, realize that one was not capable of giving one's moral feelings that degree of priority over one's other interests, and yet still not feel an alienating loss of consistency between one's projects and actions. Surely, we all know that we could be better than we are.

However, Williams's response – and it is a typical one – is to seek for a way around the 'boundless obligation' that utilitarianism entails, without having to admit the obvious: that there are things that are more important to us than right and wrong (a point philosophers appear to have peculiar difficulty acknowledging). His first move is to point out that if we did not have any other 'project' than utilitarianism (such as desires for things for ourselves and those we care about, or for the correction of particular injustices, or the melioration of particular flaws in human conduct and character), no goals, that is, other than the greatest happiness for the greatest number, then there would be nothing to constitute the happiness that utilitarianism has as its object.[18] This may be true, but it is not germane, since what utilitarianism entails is only that *I* should always act with the intention of ensuring what I take to be the greatest happiness of the greatest number, irrespective of what constitutes that happiness. Williams acknowledges this when he asserts that, in any particular situation, the course of action entailed by utilitarianism will depend on 'what persons with what projects and what potential satisfactions there are within calculable reach of the causal levers near which [one] finds [oneself]'.[19] However, his discussion of the projects and commitments that go to make up what people feel 'life is about' leads him into a discussion of the strength of such claims within oneself in relation to the utilitarian imperative.

It is a fact, he asserts, that 'among the things that make people happy is not only making other people happy, but being taken up or involved in any of a vast range of projects, or . . . commitments': commitments to people, causes, institutions, careers and so on.[20] It is part of our integrity, according to Williams, that we identify with our actions as flowing from 'projects and attitudes' that, for us, constitute what 'life is about'. It is important to note that he is not talking here (though he does elsewhere) about a conflict between utilitarianism and a moral feeling but, rather, between the moral feeling implicit in utilitarianism and our feelings about the projects and commitments that make us happy, or, we could say, that make life appear worth living.[21]

We must find a 'correct' balance, he continues, between the claims of utilitarianism and the claims of our other non-moral projects and commitments. He does not, however, offer any way of finding what this correct balance would be, beyond declaring that certain options are 'absurd'. This is, in effect, to leave the decision to the individual's feeling of what is absurd. The problem here is the suggestion that this is somehow a specifically *moral* absurdity, which it is not. Given that we are here dealing with all of the individual's projects, including that signalled by their moral sense (insofar as that is captured by utilitarianism itself), there could not possibly be any principle derived from another end that could arbitrate between them, aside, of course, from the desire for the optimal balance of our ends: our own happiness.[22]

Thus, Williams can only conclude with an appeal to feeling. It is 'absurd to demand' that we should always 'just step aside from' our own projects in favour of the course of action that utilitarian calculation requires.[23] To do so would be to alienate ourselves from our own actions and the source of those actions in our own 'convictions':

> It is to make [myself] into a channel between the input of everyone's projects, including [my] own, and an output of optimific decision; but this is to neglect the extent to which [*my*] actions and [*my*] decisions have to be seen as the actions and decisions which flow from the projects and attitudes with which [I am] most closely identified. It is thus, in the most literal sense, an attack on [my] integrity.[24]

I have quoted this passage in full in order to demonstrate the extent to which Williams is finally obliged to appeal to individual feeling. For, if we read the passage with a situation like Jim's in mind, then, no matter how we ourselves might have acted, it is possible to take it as a robust defence of his refusal to shoot the Indian, possibly on moral grounds that are not captured by utilitarianism. However, insofar as the 'projects and attitudes' with which one most closely identifies are not specified, and insofar as Williams does not restrict the claims of such projects and attitudes purely to those that issue in moral feelings, a different Jim could equally well appeal to the same principle in defence of his hobby of hunting Indians for sport. (Read the passage again.) This might strike us as 'monstrous' (as the original Jim found the utilitarian option of shooting the Indian in cold blood 'monstrous'), and if we had to formulate its monstrosity, we might well do so in utilitarian terms (the wrong balance between his interests and those of others). However, there is nothing *in the letter* of what Williams says that precludes the, from our point of view, cruel Jim from appealing to it. In the absence of a specific overriding principle (such as utilitarianism), the only way in which to say what is the morally acceptable balance between our projects is to make this appeal to what we *feel* it is: to what strikes us as absurd, or monstrous, or too coldly calculating, or too 'high-minded', or impossibly virtuous.

Williams, then, is quite right to concede that merely pointing out the potentially alienating effect of utilitarianism does not, in itself, establish another *moral* yardstick that might be used to provide an uncontroversial 'solution' to a dilemma such as Jim's; one, that is, that would avoid any feeling of alienation.[25] At the same time, he fails to show that the strong sense of negative responsibility, the 'boundless obligation', entailed by utilitarianism is necessarily alienating in a way that shows utilitarianism does not capture the end implied by moral feeling. It would only be such if we *felt* that the overriding goal of our lives – the purpose of life – was to do right. (There is also the question of whether or not we actually always *feel* that the right action is that which will produce the greatest happiness for the greatest number, but that is a point we are coming to.) It is only if this were the case and we found ourselves unable (rather than simply unwilling) to act on that feeling, that utilitarianism would be *necessarily* alienating. If it is simply a matter of being unwilling to act on the feeling, then what we have is not alienation but simply a consciousness of not being as good as we could be. If this is actually what Williams means by alienation, then it will apply to any sense of right and wrong that makes demands that run counter to other inclinations (and it is difficult to imagine a morality that would not) rather than exclusively to utilitarianism.

In justice to Williams, however, it must be conceded that he only *suggests* that the absurdity of utilitarianism is a moral absurdity – at least in relation to our non-moral interests. In contrast, Railton, picking up Williams's point about alienation, seeks to raise this rejection of utilitarianism on the grounds of its incompatibility with self-interest, to the level of a *moral* principle. Like Williams, he observes that, over the courses of our lives, we develop 'certain "ground projects" that give shape and meaning to our lives', and, given that that we experience them as ends in themselves, they may easily come into conflict with the verdicts of utilitarian calculation.[26] Since, he argues, such 'ground projects' as 'loving relationships, friendships, group loyalties and spontaneous actions are among the most important contributors to whatever it is that makes life worthwhile', it follows that 'any moral theory deserving serious consideration must itself give them serious consideration'. Where 'human well-being' and a particular morality come into irreconcilable conflict, we must begin to doubt the 'claims' of that morality.[27]

> If to be more perfectly moral is to ascend ever higher toward *sub specie aeternitatis* abstraction, perhaps we made a mistake in boarding the moral escalator in the first place. Some of the very 'weaknesses' that prevent us from achieving this moral ideal – strong attachments to persons or projects – seem to be part of a considerably more compelling human ideal.[28]

The person, he asserts, 'may suffer if he is alienated from his ground projects by being forced to look at them as potentially overridable by moral considerations'.[29] Such 'ground projects' are products of our background and situation, and, while it may be that we should question their right to legislate over our actions, we cannot simply override all of them for the sake of the greatest happiness for the greatest number without thereby becoming detached from our lives.[30] Whether or not utilitarianism is correct about what is 'right' or 'wrong', 'it could not be the standpoint of actual life without radically detaching the individual from a range of personal concerns and commitments'.[31] He does not wish, he says, to abandon utilitarianism ('the most plausible sort of morality'), but he does wish to expand its conception of the goal of morality, and thus what will count as 'rightness in terms of contribution to the good'.[32] The mistake of utilitarianism, he claims, is (A) its 'failure to see that things other than subjective states can have intrinsic value', and (B) its reduction of all intrinsic values to the single one of happiness.[33]

However, Railton here seriously misrepresents utilitarianism. 'Happiness', within utilitarianism, as we have seen, refers to whatever a person feels is the optimal balance in the pursuit or enjoyment of things that they value in themselves, and it is, inevitably, a subjective state. Such an abstraction is necessary because any other way of trying to capture what people want would have to specify definite ends, and there is no reason why these should not vary from person to person. It is only the optimal balance from that person's own point of view – that person's happiness – that we can definitely say *must be* an end for them. (We must, unfortunately, keep adding the qualification that, in dealing with the greatest happiness of the greatest number, this is 'happiness' insofar as I can conceive of it. The qualification must be added not because this 'happiness' could possibly be anything else but because discussions of utilitarianism so often proceed as if it could.) Thus Railton's argument that people desire things – for example, knowledge or friendship – for the sake of those things in themselves rather than simply instrumentally, as a means to happiness, is beside the point.[34] Likewise when he argues that the fact that most people would reject an 'experience machine' ('a hypothetical device that can be programmed to provide one with whatever subjective states [one] may desire') in favour of life shows that 'it seems to matter to us what we actually *do* and *are*' more than simply our subjective states, he overlooks the fact that a thing *mattering* to someone is itself a subjective state.[35] Thus, not only is his contrast between things that are intrinsically valuable to us and the goal of 'happiness' false but so, too, is the contrast he draws between 'mere' subjective states and what we feel is important to us.

Given that Railton does, however, see utilitarianism as limited in these ways, he proposes to factor in to 'the good', ends other than whatever he has in mind by 'happiness'. Some of the alienating effect of utilitarianism can be overcome, he argues, by 'a pluralistic approach in which several goods [such as happiness, knowledge, purposeful activity, autonomy, solidarity, respect, and beauty] are viewed as intrinsically, non-morally valuable'.[36] Without specifying how these intrinsic goods are to be weighed against one another, he nevertheless suggests that they 'may be attributed weights'. Once this has been done 'the criterion of rightness for an act would be that it must contribute to the weighted sum of these values in the long run'.[37] The problem here is that, if this is to be of any help in avoiding the alienation of being unable to decide what is right, or least wrong, the 'weighting' of the different goods is everything.

To demonstrate this, let us return to Jim armed with this pluralistic approach to 'the good', and bearing in mind also that simply acknowledging the claims of a plurality of goods does not, in itself, give any way of balancing their claims. To better illustrate the problem, however, let us imagine that if Jim does not shoot the single Indian, that Indian will go actually go free. This now offers Jim the choice between saving one and saving nineteen, rather than the original, arguably easier, choice of saving twenty or saving none.

The original utilitarian option (if that is the utilitarian option) of killing the one does not change, since Jim can probably safely assume their own death is not a component of the happiness of the majority of the Indians, and that their deaths are not a component of the happiness of the majority of their relatives. However, what if this is to be weighed against one of Railton's other intrinsic goods, such as 'solidarity'? Everything now depends on what constitutes Jim's sense of solidarity, and how strongly he feels the claim of that solidarity. It could be that the 'right' action, by

Railton's definition of 'rightness', now becomes not shooting the single Indian *because* he turns out to be a fellow US citizen or a fellow botanist, or, conversely, shooting him because it turns out that one of the other nineteen is one of these things. Similarly, with Railton's intrinsic good of 'beauty'. Depending on Jim's sense of beauty, and what weight he gives to that intrinsic good, not shooting the single Indian may become the 'right' action if that Indian is better-looking than any of the others, and shooting him becomes the 'right' action if he is, in comparison to the average among the other nineteen, particularly ugly. Similarly, with knowledge: Jim may decide that the value of his knowing what it is like to kill in cold blood, or conversely, to be responsible for nineteen deaths, outweighs whatever mundane revelations these peons are likely to experience during the rest of their lives. Likewise, depending on Jim's sense of what constitutes his autonomy, he might weigh every other of his goods, decide on the 'right' action according to them, and then, in order to assert this autonomy, do the opposite (shades of Lafcadio Wluiki). His 'wrong' will be his 'right'. Moreover, in none of these scenarios can we accuse Jim of neglecting the claims of morality as Railton conceives them, since he may indeed have weighed up all of the competing intrinsic goods in coming to his decision. That is, there is nothing in Railton's notion of the weighing up of intrinsic goods that precludes his calling any of these actions 'right'.

Railton might, nevertheless, object that some, if not all, of the above-mentioned justifications for claiming the action involved was 'right' were absurd: that they simply fly in the face of common sense. Such an appeal, however, throws us back on feeling as the yardstick of rightness, and this is precisely the difficulty that the reform of utilitarianism was supposed to meliorate: it was supposed to *justify* the rejection of the greatest happiness for the greatest number. The introduction of a pluralistic notion of 'right' does not actually help in any way to preclude the possibility of the kind of alienation Williams described, unless it also comes with a formula that gives some way of arbitrating between the claims of the intrinsic goods it proposes. One is tempted to say one means the greatest balance of these possibly competing ends 'compatible with doing right'. But this ends with the hardly enlightening solution that doing the right thing is the right thing to do.

Railton, even more than Williams, is anxious to avoid the 'boundless obligation . . . to improve the world' that acknowledging the utilitarian definition of 'right' and 'wrong' entails. However, Railton is committed to utilitarianism in a way that Williams is not, and it is this commitment that leads him to claim that utilitarianism does not actually entail such an obligation. He defends this claim by proposing that a distinction should be drawn between two kinds of consequentialism. The first of these, *subjective consequentialism*, he asserts corresponds to 'utilitarianism' (as I have used that term here): 'the view that whenever one faces a choice of actions, one should attempt to determine which act of those available would most promote the good, and should then try to act accordingly'.[38] (That 'the good' here no longer refers to the greatest happiness for the greatest number does not materially affect the argument.) He contrasts this with what he calls *objective consequentialism*: 'the view that the criterion of the rightness of an act or course of action is whether it in fact would most promote the good of those acts available to the agent'.[39] *Subjective consequentialism*, then, is the view that one should follow a particular mode of deliberation, while *objective consequentialism* is simply the view that an action is 'right' if it does promote 'the good'. The latter, according to Railton, does not prescribe a certain form of decision making, but rather 'deals with [sic] the question of deliberation only in terms of the tendencies of certain forms of decision making to promote appropriate outcomes'.[40]

Based on this distinction, he suggests that a *sophisticated consequentialist* need not hold doing the right thing to be a 'boundless obligation'. The *sophisticated consequentialist*, according to Railton, is someone who has 'a standing commitment to leading an objectively consequentialist life' (i.e. subscribes to *objective consequentialism*) but who does not 'set special stock in any particular form of decision making and therefore does not necessarily seek to lead a subjectively consequentialist life'.[41] A 'standing commitment to leading an objectively consequentialist life', according to Railton, means that one is committed to the idea that 'the criterion of the rightness of an act or course of action is whether it in fact would most promote the good of those acts available to the agent'.[42]

However, it is hard to see what function this distinction is supposed to serve. Having a 'standing commitment', as Railton describes it, gives no indication of what a person would feel obliged to do in any particular circumstance. A person might have a standing commitment to the idea that it is better to be physically fit than not to be physically fit, and a standing commitment to the idea that exercise is the only way to become physically fit – and still be a couch potato. It is only if we add a commitment to *subjective consequentialism*, that is, that I should act on the standing commitments I have, that we actually get any consequences from such 'standing commitments' – even if it is only an acknowledgement of my own laziness. The most that *sophisticated consequentialism* appears to necessarily entail is a feeling of disapproval towards actions that are clearly contrary to 'the good'. Moreover, this hardly counts as a consequence, since it is rather the feeling of disapproval that signals to us that the action is clearly contrary to whatever it is we feel 'the good' is.

Railton is quite consistent, then, when he describes a 'sophisticated consequentialist' as one who may 'believe he should act for the best but does not . . . feel it appropriate to bring a consequentialist calculus to bear on his every act'.[43] In other words, the sophisticated consequentialist is one who has a clear sense of what is right but does not always feel obliged to do it. We cannot, says Railton, be always preoccupied with doing right 'without this interfering with normal or appropriate patterns of thought and action'. That is, he claims not only that we do not *want* to be always preoccupied with doing right, which would be an obvious empirical observation, but also that morality does not require us to be. Insofar, then, as Railton advances sophisticated consequentialism as the 'right' attitude, this is a bizarre *solution* to the original problem of alienation, since, beyond saying that it is not necessary to always do right, it gives no way of judging when it would be wrong not to do so. Inevitably, what is 'normal or appropriate' for a person is whatever that person feels is such, so that the question of where and when a concern for 'the right' constitutes illegitimate 'interference' can only be measured by the same yardstick. In effect, then, sophisticated consequentialism throws us back on our own feelings, and, as we saw earlier, if this really were a solution, the very question of the alienating effect of utilitarianism would never arise. Moreover, it does nothing to show that utilitarianism does not capture the goal implicit in moral responses. It only confirms what was never in doubt: that whatever desire/aversion the moral response represents, it is not our only desire/aversion.

Given that Railton does fail to solve the problem of alienation with which we started, we will end by looking at why he believes he has, since this is particularly connected to the tendency for ethics to fall into the trap of presuming that moral feeling, to be such, must have some absolute priority over feeling per se. First, Railton believes he has secured utilitarianism as a reliable moral guide. Thus, directly addressing Williams's suspicion that there may be something wrong with utilitarian reasoning itself, if it leads to verdicts that ignore so much of what is important in our lives, he claims that, on the contrary, utilitarianism need not lead to such self-abnegating verdicts.[44] As we have seen, however, he achieves this only by substituting a plurality of discrete intrinsic goods for 'the good' (the greatest happiness for the greatest number) that is the goal of utilitarianism. Moreover, as we saw with the case of Jim looked at in the light of such a pluralistic 'good', this does not solve the problem of what is right: it simply warrants the application of 'right' to whatever the individual feels is right. (This may be perfectly adequate as a description of 'right', but it could hardly be said to constitute a moral position.)

Second, Railton believes he has shown a way in which the individual may *in good conscience* avoid the 'boundless obligation' utilitarianism imposes. The sophisticated consequentialist, he writes, need not consider that he is 'deceiving himself or acting in bad faith when he avoids consequentialist reasoning'.[45] He offers a variety of scenarios to justify this, such as when, if routinely faced by emergencies, the best consequences are brought about by developing a habit of not stopping to think, or where following a rule of life that you feel maximizes the good, without examining every decision you make, is most likely to bring about that good.[46] However, in none of these cases is it actually a matter of his *sophisticated consequentialism* taking precedence over what he calls *subjective consequentialism*; that would only happen, according to his own definitions of these terms, in a situation in which conditions changed such that the habit or rule of life became morally problematic but the individual did not ask themselves if they were doing the right thing. Railton's *sophisticated consequentialist* is actually just a person who has decided that his life, as he lives it now, is as compatible with the greatest happiness of the greatest number as he is prepared to make it. If he also wishes to believe he is simultaneously doing everything that morality might require, then Railton's argument offers him the appearance of a justification for doing so.[47] In short, it is a charter for self-righteousness.

That we are not always as 'good', by utilitarian standards, as we could be proves nothing about the extent to which the utilitarian definition of 'good' corresponds to the goal that is signalled by the existence of moral responses. Utilitarianism does entail a boundless obligation, but that is only because it does capture what is implicit in the moral response: its apparent selfless interest in the interests of others. However, it is simply the case that we do not feel this all the time and, even when we do, that (selfless) interest may be overridden by other interests that we have. (The whole topic of "weakness of will" arises only from the deeply irrational belief that one is identical to, or somehow "truly", one's idea of oneself.) Moreover, in practice, we experience moral responses mainly in the form of aversion: as a desire that things should be otherwise than they are or threaten to be. This, as we shall see, renders them entirely dependent on the vividness with which that harm strikes us, that is, on chance. This is also precisely what we would expect from an emotion; think, for example, of the rhythms of grief, regret or joy, which emotions may depend both on a standing desire/aversion and an enduring state of affairs but which, nevertheless, wax and wane according to the extent to which we attend to them.

Non-utilitarian moral feeling

The boundless obligation entailed by utilitarianism is not, then, an argument against its 'good' being what is desired in moral responses. What, however, is an obstacle to this conclusion is the way in which such a goal may appear morally inferior to another. That is, the existence of moral responses that appear to imply a desire for an end that is incompatible with the greatest happiness of the greatest number.

Where the utilitarian principle becomes problematic (as a description of the goal of moral responses) is where it comes into conflict with *moral* responses themselves. For, if the goal implicit in moral feeling really were the greatest happiness of the greatest number, such a conflict should not be possible. This is not, of course, a matter of utilitarianism coming into conflict with self-interest, as we have seen it do with Williams and Railton. (There is no question of moral feeling being our only emotion: the only thing we desire.) Neither is it simply a matter of means and ends: one might feel badly about a child's fear of vaccination, but one would not feel morally conflicted about it. Rather, the problem notoriously arises that the application of the utilitarian principle to a particular situation may result in a verdict on the morally best course of action that simply *feels* morally wrong.

It is worth noting, however, that this is not nearly so common as the literature would lead one to believe. Utilitarianism is the best approximation to what is implicit in the majority of moral responses. Moreover, many well-known examples of intuitively immoral utilitarian verdicts often turn out to depend on a mistake. Foot, for instance, offers the following two scenarios to illustrate what she takes to be an anomaly in moral feeling. The first is the now well-known example of the runaway tram that can only be steered onto one of two narrow tracks, on one of which there are five men working and on the other only a single man. As Foot observes, most people would not hesitate to say that the driver should steer away from the five and towards the one.[48] This general, though not universal, consensus is what makes it a useful demonstration of the extent to which some principle of the greatest good, or the least harm, is an adequate reflection of common moral feeling (or, in the present context, the extent to which the moral response signals a desire for this end). The second scenario is the following:

> We are about to give a patient who needs it to save his life a massive dose of a certain drug in short supply. There arrive, however, five other patients each of whom could be saved by one-fifth of that dose. We say with regret that we cannot spare our whole supply of the drug for a single patient. . . . We feel bound to let one man die rather than many if that is our only choice. Why then do we not feel

justified in killing people in the interests of cancer research or to obtain, let us say, spare parts for grafting on to those who need them? We can suppose, similarly, that several dangerously ill people can be saved only if we kill a certain individual and make a serum from his dead body.[49]

It is, however, only the way the cases are juxtaposed that creates the appearance of an inconsistency. The case of the runaway tram presents us with a simple choice – to produce more or less misery in the world – and almost no complicating features. It could, indeed, be reduced simply to the question "Would you prefer more or less happiness in the world?" The only way to make such a question controversial would be either by making the immediate balance of happiness represent an inverse future balance of harm – say five Klansmen versus one social worker – or by making the happiness more personal – say five strangers versus your own child (thus introducing a non-moral interest). In the first of these alternative scenarios, at least, were the one chosen over the five, it could still be on the basis of a preference for the greater amount of happiness. If we now approach the case of killing someone to create a serum with the same question – "Would you prefer more or less happiness in the world?" – the decision not to sacrifice the life of a chance bystander can be seen as actually consistent with the apparently contrary decision in the previous case. A world in which no one could enter a hospital without the threat of being reduced to a serum is not obviously a world containing a greater potential for happiness than the one we live in. That is, it is quite possible to derive the principle that people should not be treated as means from a utilitarian principle. (What is perhaps most striking here is that almost no one thinks to justify their reluctance to use someone to create a serum by appeal to such a principle.[50] Rather the majority of the literature seeks to explain this "inconsistency" in terms of contrary principles – utilitarian and deontological – or of a conflict between reason and feeling, or to somehow reconcile the apparent inconsistency in a rule regarding what is 'permissible', which is actually no more than a description of the conditions to which most actual responses conform: the average response in abstract form.)

Nevertheless, there are scenarios where utilitarianism does genuinely give rise to verdicts that many observers find morally wrong. Take another of Foot's scenarios:

> Suppose that a judge or magistrate is faced with rioters demanding that a culprit be found for a certain crime and threatening otherwise to take their own bloody revenge on a particular section of the community. The real culprit being unknown, the judge sees himself as able to prevent the bloodshed only by framing some innocent person and having him executed.[51]

She asks us to further imagine that the rioters have five hostages, so that, as with the case of the distribution of the drug in short supply, it is a matter of choosing between the life of one and the lives of five. In contrast to that case, which she takes to be uncontroversial, Foot asserts (and contemporary local research appears to confirm) that 'most of us would be appalled' at the sacrifice of the innocent man in this instance.[52] 'Appalled', that is, to the extent of seeing the death of the five as the lesser of the two evils.

This was, indeed, the source of Jim's dilemma over shooting the Indian, which we encountered earlier in discussing the notion of 'negative responsibility'. The problem for Williams was that utilitarianism entails one goal – the greatest happiness of the greatest number – that I *should* aim at if I wish to do the right thing.[53] Williams's problem with this is that it appears to oblige us to consider an action as morally "right" even under circumstances where we cannot *feel* that there is a "right" course of action: it makes, for example, the massacre of seven million the right thing to do if, by doing so, we avoid the massacre of seven million and one.[54] And, for Williams, it is simply impossible to consider the murder of seven million (or one, in Jim's case) as "right".

Williams's difficulty may strike us, at first, as artificial. The massacre of seven million, or even the murder of one, is not the kind of action that, *ceteris paribus*, we would think of as conducive to the greatest happiness of the greatest number. Is it not, then, simply that utilitarianism recommends them as the "less wrong" of the available alternatives? The problem with such a defence, at least from the point of view of the moral response as an emotional response with a single goal – the greatest happiness of the greatest number – is that, if this is what the moral response is, it should apparently not be possible for us to feel a *moral* objection to the pursuit of that goal.

Oddly, however, Williams appears unwilling to simply assert the wrongness of utilitarian rightness.[55] It may be 'a feature of a man's moral outlook', according to Williams, that he regards certain actions as *'unthinkable*, in the sense that he would not entertain the idea of doing them'.[56] Clearly this 'unthinkable' cannot mean that, for example, Jim cannot comprehend or imagine the act of shooting the Indian (as one could not imagine a square circle), since this is something he must do even in order to reject it as a course of action. However, despite his assertion that the action is rendered unthinkable by Jim's 'moral outlook', Williams also, confusingly, characterizes such a situation as one in which the person is faced with a choice that is not 'morally conceivable': a situation that presents him with a choice that is 'not a special problem in his moral world, but something that [lies] beyond its limits'. Again, however, as with his use of the word 'unthinkable', it is not possible to take this in a literal sense. If the choice facing Jim literally lay outside the limits of his moral world, it should be no more emotionally significant than any other decision to which he feels morality does not apply, such as which of two T-shirts to wear or what to have for lunch.

We have already seen that Williams cannot mean that the 'unthinkable' action is such by virtue of coming into conflict with Jim's non-moral interests. If Jim's objection to shooting the single Indian is that it will take time out of his holiday, or he does not like the sight of blood, there is no reason to present this as a special problem for utilitarianism. It is simply a fact, and one that Jim must have previously been aware of, that he does not always act so as to increase the greatest happiness of the greatest number. He is, for example, presumably not taking this particular holiday in order to ensure the greatest happiness of the greatest number: there must have been something else he could have done with his free time that would have better effected such an end. That is, he knows already that, according to the lights of utilitarianism, he is not the best person he could be. There is, therefore, no reason why neglecting his "duty" in this particular case should represent a crisis in his self-image as a morally motivated person.

In short, then, despite what Williams says about certain actions being 'unthinkable' or lying beyond the limits of the person's 'moral world', what he is actually describing is rather a situation in which the person feels that the utilitarian course of action is the *morally* wrong thing to do. Williams skirts this conclusion by talking about alternatives in a dilemma that a person 'regards as dishonourable or morally absurd' (rather than 'wrong'), and by evoking 'situations so monstrous that the idea that the processes of moral rationality could yield an answer in them is insane . . . situations which so transcend in enormity the human business of moral deliberation that from a moral point of view it cannot matter any more what happens'.[57] However, in light of the fact that, as we have seen, Williams cannot here mean by 'absurd', 'monstrous' and 'insane' either that Jim cannot grasp the concept of shooting an Indian or that Jim's reluctance arises from a conflict between shooting the Indian and another, non-moral, motivation (indifference, self-interest, or taste), we must take such terms as rhetorical inflations of the concept of morally wrong. Indeed, this is precisely why we would present Jim's situation as a *moral* dilemma: he does not want to be indirectly responsible for the deaths of the group, and he does not want to be directly responsible for the death of one. Jim really feels that he should not shoot the Indian because it is an act that he feels to be wrong in itself – so wrong that he will not consider it, irrespective of the consequences. This feeling of Jim's does, then, imply a moral end that is not captured by utilitarianism, albeit that such a moral end cannot be formulated except in very specific terms (do not take a life under these circumstances).

(It might at first appear that we could measure how far his reluctance to shoot the Indian was a matter of morality from the extent to which he would blame a travelling companion who snatched the rifle from his hands and shot the Indian for him. Even in such a case, however, his reaction would not serve as decisive evidence of the nature of his own reluctance. Universality appears implicit in the very nature of moral response, but this is only a matter of the subject's own perception of that response. It is conceivable that Jim could feel only that it is wrong for *him* to shoot the Indian.)

Williams's point is an anti-utilitarian one. We have, he says, certain feelings that we experience as part of our 'moral relation to the world'. To regard such feelings 'from a purely utilitarian point of view, that is to say, as happenings outside one's moral self, is to lose a sense of one's moral identity; to lose, in the most literal way, one's integrity'.[58] This does not mean, Williams adds, that we should reject utilitarianism as a guide to what is 'right' in many circumstances, but it does oblige us to acknowledge that 'we are partially at least not utilitarians'.[59]

What Williams has shown here is not so much that utilitarianism in itself is alienating – there is no reason for anyone to feel obliged to choose the utilitarian option just because it is utilitarian – as that certain situations are alienating, in the sense that they present us with a choice where we feel that we cannot do the right thing without also doing wrong. For, there would be no reason for Jim to experience his situation as 'monstrous' or 'absurd' if, aside from finding the idea of shooting the Indian morally unacceptable ('unthinkable'), he did not also have a strong aversion to the result of his failing to do so.[60] It is this second aversion that is captured by the idea of utilitarianism. It is, therefore, misleading to present utilitarianism as a contrast to Jim's sense of moral integrity: the situation would not present itself to him as a dilemma if it were merely a matter of choosing between his feelings and whatever feeling is the basis of his commitment to an abstract principle. There is no *dilemma* in having to choose between two alternatives only one of which is problematic from the point of view of the criterion – here feeling – by which you feel compelled to choose.[61] In short, if we are, as Williams says, 'partially at least not utilitarians' in our moral feelings, it is also the case that we partially are.

Williams ends the essay we have been considering by characterizing utilitarianism as hopelessly 'simple-minded' and looking forward to the day 'we hear no more of it'.[62] Others, however, have tried to add qualifications to the basic principle to bring its results more into line with their moral feelings. Brandt, for example, begins by asserting, even more directly than Williams, that utilitarianism has morally 'objectionable' implications.[63] If the right act is the one that brings about the greatest happiness for the greatest number, then if, for example, my father is terminally ill, with 'no prospect of good in his life', and his maintenance reduces the happiness of others, then, providing I can kill him 'without provoking public scandal or setting a bad example', it is my moral duty to do so.[64] However, many such morally counterintuitive conclusions, Brandt argues, only follow from a certain form of utilitarianism: 'act-utilitarianism'. Act-utilitarianism, according to Brandt, holds that 'the rightness of an act is fixed by the utility of *its* consequences, as compared with those of other acts the agent might perform instead'.[65] He goes on to propose that an alternative form of utilitarianism – 'rule-utilitarianism' – could avoid many such implications. He defines rule-utilitarianism as the view that 'the rightness of an act is not fixed by *its* relative utility, but by conformity with general rules', the correctness of these rules being in turn fixed 'by the utility of their general acceptance'.[66] Thus, even leaving aside the question of accommodating filial affection, it is obvious that a world in which others feel positively obliged to murder you for the sake of the general happiness will not be a generally happier world than one in which they do not. Thus, "Don't murder" is a rule, the general acceptance of which has a high utility: the existence of such a rule is more likely to lead to the greatest happiness for the greatest number than leaving the question of the rightness or wrongness of murder open.

However, Brandt's distinction is problematic. For, an act-utilitarian who did not take into account the effect of their act in, for example, setting a precedent would not actually be acting in a utilitarian way at all, since, in ignoring the remoter consequences of their act, they could not be said to be acting with the intention of securing the greatest happiness for the greatest number. (Indeed, Brandt recognizes this when he sets among the conditions of the patricide that it can be done 'without provoking public scandal or setting a bad example'.) Conversely, if rule-utilitarianism can actually be distinguished from an act-utilitarianism that is still authentically utilitarian, then it cannot itself be utilitarian. This is because every decision to follow a rule is itself an act. Thus, if I am a utilitarian, I must ask myself whether, on this occasion, following the rule will lead to the greatest happiness for the greatest number. If I do not, then it can only be that I am taking it on faith that following the rule will have this effect; that is, I am *not* asking myself what I should do to ensure the greatest happiness for the greatest number. Of course, I cannot be said to abnegating my responsibility, if we add the conditions that I must be convinced both that the rule really does maximize happiness and that following it in this particular instance will not have a contrary effect. However, if we add these conditions, then I am no longer following the rule because it is a rule but rather because it conforms with what I have decided to do on an 'act-utilitarian' basis. Thus, the distinction between act-utilitarianism and rule-utilitarianism makes no difference to the question of, for example, whether or not I should kill my father in the circumstances Brandt describes.[67]

Brandt, nevertheless, believes that it is possible to formulate a version of rule-utilitarianism that is both still utilitarian and yet excludes the kind of 'unbearable demands' (you should murder your father in these circumstances) that act-utilitarianism makes – the same 'demands' that lead to what Williams called 'alienation'.[68] The principle he proposes is the following: 'An act is right if and only if it conforms with that learnable set of rules the recognition of which as morally binding – roughly at the time of the act – by everyone in the society of the agent, except for the retention by individuals of already formed and decided moral convictions, would maximize intrinsic value.'[69] (By 'intrinsic value', Brandt means the greatest happiness for the greatest number.) Thus, if I live in a society that prohibits murder, and this prohibition maximizes 'intrinsic value', the right action will be to refrain from killing my father. As we have seen, this still leaves me with the problem of deciding whether or not the rule does maximize 'intrinsic value', though it does specify that, if I decide it does, I should not then ask the further question of whether or not the current situation is one in which following the rule will actually maximize that value. That is, I should never ask whether following the rule in this particular instance will actually accomplish that for which the rule exists. This is why, as I said earlier, we cannot describe Brandt's principle as utilitarian, since utilitarianism entails that I should always act with the intention of maximizing the value. If, however, one could rest content with not asking the second question concerning the particular instance, then this would be a way of avoiding moral dilemmas, albeit one that requires a certain amount of bad faith.

However, this is not all there is to Brandt's formula. Conformity with generally accepted contemporary social rules insofar as they tend to maximize happiness for the greatest number is not his only criterion of rightness. He also makes an exception for 'the retention by individuals of already formed and decided moral convictions'.[70] One can see why he should add such an exemption if his aim is to avoid a concept of rightness that yields 'unbearable demands'. It might be unlikely within a single contemporary society that anyone would have moral convictions that ran counter to those that were generally accepted but it is a possibility – say, for example, with the settled moral convictions of a religious minority. Such convictions might, according to his formula, give rise to actions that were 'wrong' from the point of society at large, but still 'right' in terms of the formula. Obviously, then, his formula cannot be a reformulation of utilitarianism, since there is only one way of doing right according to utilitarianism: to act with the intention of securing the greatest happiness for the greatest number.

Brandt's principle, then, potentially allows two conflicting actions to be 'right'. Moreover, including both a semi-utilitarian principle (utilitarianism minus one level of decision making) and an opt-out clause (for settled moral convictions) from that principle within the same rule means that the rule itself does not offer any indication as to how we might weigh their claims. For example, if one of my settled moral convictions was utilitarianism, this would then oblige me to kill my father (according to Brandt, at least), even though another part of the same rule forbids it.

Brandt himself concedes that his reformed 'utilitarianism' still leaves cases too complicated to legislate for.[71] He, therefore, proposes a 'remainder-rule': that in cases that prove insoluble by application of the reformed utilitarian formula, one should 'take whatever course of action would leave morally well-trained people least dissatisfied'.[72] This, of course, begs the question. The concept of a morally well-trained person would only make sense if Brandt adhered strictly to utilitarianism, since utilitarianism has a single goal. Therefore, a person might be more or less adept at seeing what actions would best achieve that goal and able to elucidate the reasons for their judgements. However, in the absence of a single goal, with potentially competing 'right' actions, a morally well-trained person could only be one who demonstrably consistently makes the 'right' choices. This leaves us with the problem that there would be no way to tell who is 'well-trained' and who is not, since it is the very question of what counts as 'the right choice' that is at issue.[73] We might, of course, fall back on our feeling of who is a good judge. The problem here, however, is that if one had complete confidence in following one's feelings, the question of measuring one's action by a moral principle such as utilitarianism would never have arisen. That is, the problem left over by Brandt is precisely the problem utilitarianism is supposed to solve.

Brandt's difficulty in formulating an alternative principle to utilitarianism – one that could replace utilitarianism, or at least reconcile it with common moral feeling – is one that is repeated across the literature. The urge to reduce the "anomalies" to a principle ('killing is worse than letting die', 'respect for rights overrides utilitarian calculation' and so on) is, of course, strong within normative ethics, but the emotion is recalcitrant. Consider, for example, the fate of the scenario – the runaway tram – that Foot proffers as evidence of our intuitive assent to utilitarianism, before she goes on to problematize that assent with her examples of *moral* reluctance to sacrifice the one for the many. There are genuine "anomalies" (from a utilitarian perspective) to be elicited from the variations to this scenario later introduced by Thomson. Thomson notes, for example, that one possibly significant variation between the tram case and Foot's more controversial cases is that the single man on the track does not have to be there in order for the five to be saved, whereas the presence of the healthy donor is indispensable in the serum case.[74] To level out this disparity she proposes a variation on the basic tram situation in which the track containing the single man loops back to join the track on which the five are standing. In this 'Loop' variant what stops the tram from hitting the five is the fact that the single man is big enough to effectively brake it before it reaches them.[75] She notes that some people feel it is now less 'permissible' to divert the tram, though she herself asserts that 'we cannot really suppose that the presence or absence of that extra bit of track makes a major moral difference as to what an agent may do in these cases, and it really does seem right to think (despite the discomfort) that the agent may proceed', despite the fact that this has now brought the case much closer to that of Foot's genuine dilemmas: the one is being 'used' to save the five.[76] Therefore, she concludes, it cannot be the notion of 'treating a person as a means only' that makes the difference between the cases. To make her point more forcibly she invents another tram case, which she refers to as 'Fat Man'. Here, the only way to stop the tram from hitting the five is to push a fat man, standing next to you on a footbridge overlooking the line, into the path of the oncoming tram.[77] Everyone she asked about this scenario agreed that it would be 'impermissible' to do so.

Thomson's conclusion is that our intuition in this case is a matter of the 'rights' of the fat man. Moreover, she believes that this ascendancy (or right) of rights over utility represents a 'general moral truth' (in this context, a desire of this particular 'our').[78] Despite her confidence here, she proposes a further scenario, which turns out to render her conclusion problematic. Imagine the bystander at the switch has, in all good faith, previously given an assurance to the man on the single track that the track may safely be walked upon. In such a case, according to Thomson, it would be 'impermissible' for that bystander to divert the tram onto the line containing the single man, since that man 'has a right against' the bystander generated by the assurance.[79] Thomson confesses to being greatly surprised by the fact that not everyone agrees with her on this, commenting that she must conclude 'they think the right less stringent than I do'.[80] Of course, once it becomes a question of the relative stringency of different rights, and thus the necessity of another standard by which to arbitrate, we must give up hope of having here discovered a principle *universally* implied by the moral response. From the perspective of the normative ethicist, the prospect of a "solution" to the dilemma disappears.

This last is brought out by the way in which Thomson now asserts that the rule derivable from most responses to the tram problem demonstrates the rightness of most responses to situations commensurable with Foot's magistrate problem:

> If A threatens to kill five unless B kills one, then although killing five is worse than killing one, these are not the alternatives open to B. The alternatives open to B are: Kill one, thereby forestalling the deaths of five (and making A's moral record better than it otherwise would be), or let it be the case that A kills five. And the supposition that it would be worse for B to choose to kill the one is entirely compatible with the supposition that killing five is worse than killing one.[81]

Even among those who chose not to kill the one, it is doubtful that this rationale would be found convincing.

Explanation aside, however, more systematic research into the way in which people of a similar background to Thomson do respond to her scenarios has largely born out her intuitions regarding many people's feelings about the more basic cases.[82] Moreover, other research into the same kind of dilemmas only seems to compound the moral "inconsistencies". There do, however, emerge certain operative principles implicit in the majority of responses: harmful actions are judged morally worse than harmful omissions (the action principle), harm intended as the means to an end is judged morally worse than harm foreseen as the side effect of an end (the intention principle), and harm involving physical contact is judged morally worse than harm without contact (the contact principle).[83] Indeed further research has suggested that this last principle is even odder (in terms of understanding moral responses as determined by sensitivity to the distribution of harm) than it first appears. A study by Greene et al.

discovered that, while the majority of test subjects did not find it morally acceptable to push someone into the path of the tram (the Fat Man scenario), people generally found it more 'morally acceptable' to push the person off the footbridge using a pole and considerably more 'morally acceptable' to pull a lever that would result in the person falling from the bridge (suggesting that the elements of physical contact, and, even more, the employment of personal force, were taken as morally significant).[84]

Such thought experiments do not draw a distinction between moral judgements and moral response – the subjects may be making either – but, given that the cases are hypothetical, we might reasonably expect a greater proportion of the former than would normally be found in daily life. Given that utilitarianism does so successfully capture what can be codified in what the moral response itself seems to imply, the presence of the aversions described earlier, *experienced as moral responses*, even at the cost of greater harm, is striking.

Vividness

There is an even more fundamental determining factor in moral aversion, which the research, with its dependence on hypothetical scenarios, is ill-suited to eliciting, though it does, nevertheless, reflect it to some extent. This is the dependence of the moral response on the vividness of the harm involved. It is the importance of this factor that makes the version of the tram scenario in which the tram is diverted onto another line, killing the single workman as a result, much more acceptable (for this group) than the Loop variant, in which we must envisage the same workman smeared along the tracks as an impromptu buffer, which is, in turn, more acceptable than the effectively identical Loop Weight variant, where the presence of a weight behind the single workman makes it even more difficult for us to *fail* to imagine the violent death that our action will entail. For the same reason, both of these are still found more acceptable than having to envisage pushing the man onto the track: a scenario that makes the idea of our own responsibility for the result still more vividly present to us.

It was the opinion of Diderot that so dependent are our moral feelings upon 'the sensations we receive, and the degree by which we are affected by external things', that, were it not for fear of punishment, 'many people would find it less disagreeable to kill a man at a distance at which he would appear no bigger than a swallow, than to cut an ox's throat with their own hands'.[85] Indeed, we positively *expect* the vividness with which we encounter an acknowledged wrong (either in reality or imagination) to effect the strength of our reaction. When, in *The Third Man*, the hero is trying to awaken a sense of guilt in the racketeer, Harry Lime, he does so with the most natural of questions: 'Have you ever seen any of your victims?' Lime, indicating the people far below them as they ride the Wiener Riesenrad, appeals in turn to the same effect of distance:

> Look down there. Would you really feel any pity if one of those dots stopped moving forever? If I offered you twenty thousand pounds for every dot that stopped, would

you really, old man, tell me to keep my money, or would you calculate how many dots you could afford to spare?[86]

The subsequent action of the film bears out the general truth of this observation. It is only after the hero has himself seen Lime's victims (children brain-damaged with meningitis) first-hand that he finally agrees to help the police arrest his old friend. There is nothing psychologically unlikely in all this. If the character of Lime in this scene is particularly memorable, it is only because his response is so suavely articulate, in contrast to the defensiveness or special pleading we would normally expect from someone similarly situated. That, and the fact that *despite ourselves* we suspect he is right.

Yet, moral feeling itself rebels against the suspicion. Thus, Chateaubriand, writing of the ineluctable authority of conscience (as a proof of the immortality of the soul), asserts that even if he could 'by a mere wish kill a fellow-creature in China, and inherit his fortune in Europe, with the supernatural conviction that the fact would never be known', and even if that person were to die instantaneously and painlessly, or was so overwhelmed with disease or trouble as to himself desire death, or, indeed, was actually on the very brink of death, and despite the fact that no one else would thereby lose the man's fortune, still his conscience protests 'against the mere idea of such a supposition'.[87] But why put it like this? Why say that one would still find killing unacceptable *even if* no one were to find out, *even if* it happened far away, and *even if* the "victim" wished to die, were it not for the fact that, in practice, such factors usually do make a difference?

Morality, however, is a matter of what we should do, not what we actually do. As Singer says, 'we can't decide moral issues by taking opinion polls'.[88] The problem, of course, as we have already seen, is that we cannot decide them any other way either. Our touchstone is inevitably feeling, but what the feeling implies (the viewpoint of the universe) in one context turns out to be contradicted by what we actually feel in another. Moreover, this applies equally to how we feel about the contradiction. Even with a position like Railton's 'sophisticated consequentialism', or those arguments, which we shall meet in the next chapter, to the effect that since it is 'natural' to prefer kin over strangers it is therefore 'right' to prefer kin over strangers, the matter always comes down to what one *should* or *should not* do or *should* or *should not* feel guilty about. A purely descriptive ethics is a contradiction in terms.

Nevertheless, a striking feature of the role of vividness in determining moral responses, unremarkable as it is from the point of view of the moral response as an emotion, is the way in which it is universally rejected as morally relevant. Smith, for example, having conceded that it would be perfectly unsurprising for the average humane European to be more upset over the loss of their own little finger than over news that an earthquake had killed hundreds of millions in China, nevertheless asserts that, despite this disparity, 'the world, in its greatest depravity and corruption, never produced such a villain as could be capable of entertaining' the idea of sacrificing millions of distant lives to prevent such a 'paltry' misfortune to themselves.[89] Yet Smith was living in a time when distaste for the slave trade might not extend so far as foregoing the cheap sugar it provided, and in which, largely for the sake of property, the application of capital punishment had been extended to 160 crimes.[90] It is not only those who would be indifferent to the immediate reality of a sweatshop or a slaughterhouse, for example, who are content to benefit from both. Hence, the *resentment* they may evince towards anyone who renders the reality of such things vivid to them.

The most interesting modern case in this regard is the reaction to Singer's well-known essay 'Famine, Affluence, and Morality', in which he argues that those living in developed countries act wrongly in not giving more to charity. Singer's argument is straightforward. We all accept, he says, both that 'suffering and death from lack of food, shelter, and medical care are bad', and that 'if it is in our power to prevent something bad from happening, without thereby sacrificing anything of comparable moral importance, we ought, morally, to do it'.[91] Given, then, he continues, that it is within the power of those living within prosperous, developed countries to alleviate the suffering and prevent the deaths of those in poorer areas of the world by giving more to charity than they currently do, and to do so without any significant sacrifice, they ought to give more to charity. It is, he concludes, as wrong not to do so as it would be to ignore a drowning child for a reason as trivial as the wish not to ruin one's shoes.

Singer specifically says that he is not addressing those who would not accept his first two fundamental premises – that the suffering and death of others is bad, and that if we can prevent it at little trouble to ourselves, we should – and, indeed, it is not these premises that proved the sticking point with his audience. (One might easily rebut his argument simply by denying or qualifying one of them; for example, by arguing that the badness of what happens depends on who it is happening to, or, à la Railton, that my integrity as a person trumps any moral obligation apparently implied by "my principles".) Rather Singer's argument has been most widely rejected, unsurprisingly, on the grounds that it is too demanding: that what Singer calls an 'obligation' is actually supererogatory.[92] It is unsurprising because this is actually how many people feel, and, whatever the soundness of the argument, if they do not feel guilty, then they do not feel guilty: their "position" is no more open to refutation than a tear or a giggle are open to refutation.

Unfortunately, but again predictably, dissatisfaction with Singer's conclusion has, nevertheless, led to the unedifying spectacle of any number of philosophers trying to discover a flaw in his argument – as if that were the problem. For, the conviction that what Singer holds to be morally obligatory is actually supererogatory implies some strikingly counterintuitive operative principles: for example, that 'It is at least sometimes permissible to let others suffer great harms in order to secure incomparably small benefits for yourself', or that 'It is at least sometimes permissible to let others die in order to secure additional luxuries for yourself'.[93]

According to Singer, his argument is one for what we *ought* to do in order to achieve consistency between our expressed principles and our actions: to, as he says, bring 'theory and practice' into harmony.[94] This same harmony could, however, be achieved by simply acknowledging that, although we may still admire the principle Singer takes as implicit in the response to the case of the child drowning in the pond – 'if it is in our power to prevent something bad from happening, without thereby sacrificing anything of comparable moral importance, we ought, morally, to do it' – in fact, though we hitherto professed it, it was never actually our own. The problem here, of course, is not that such a solution is cynical but, rather, that it would feel cynical: a misrepresentation of what we feel are our "true feelings" in the matter. According to Singer, if we 'accept any principle of impartiality, universalizability, equality, or whatever, we cannot discriminate against someone merely because he is far away from us (or we are far away from him)'.[95] That, however, is simply not true: we can. Rather what it seems we cannot do is acknowledge to ourselves that this is what we are doing; we cannot feel that it is only vividness that makes the difference. Moreover, this is not because we have 'accepted a principle' but, rather, because the very experience of a moral response, as we saw in Chapter 1, seems to imply impartiality and universalizability. Hence the reaction to Singer's argument: it cannot be, his critics feel, that it is *only* distance that accounts for my relative indifference. No one wants to admit, even apparently to themselves, that what makes all the moral difference between a child dying in front of them and one dying 2,000 miles away is simply that the second is not in front of them.[96] And this, even though the effect is so commonplace as to be perfectly predictable.

The influence of vividness on moral response is not, of course, confined to the strength of our sense of obligation. It also affects the intensity of our response to "wrongs". Thus, mass murder can even serve as the basis for comedy, providing it happened long enough ago. Conversely the portrayal of fictional suffering, provided it be vivid enough, can move us more than our knowledge of real instances of suffering that have become too familiar to be noteworthy.[97] Likewise causing suffering to the conspicuously vulnerable (children, the old) can seem more culpable than causing suffering to others, even though these others may be no less vulnerable to the particular kind of suffering involved.

Incommensurable responses

This disjunction between what we feel, in the abstract, can or cannot be morally relevant and what actually emerges, in practice, as morally relevant is also a feature of the results of the tram experiments reported earlier. Cushman et al. discovered that subjects' ability to justify their decisions depended greatly on the principle implicitly employed. ('Justify' here meaning being able to express, or at least recognize, the implicit general principle in one's pattern of responses/judgements: not, that is, actually being able to give a reason *why*, for example, a harmful act is worse than a harmful omission, but at least recognizing that one has made this decision because one feels a harmful act is morally worse than a harmful omission.[98]) The subjects of Cushman et al.'s experiments were largely successful in identifying that they had followed the action principle (an act is more culpable than an omission).[99] By contrast less than a third of those who applied the intention principle (harm intended is worse than harm merely foreseen) appeared to be conscious of having done so. Many confessed uncertainty about how to justify their responses, denied that there were any morally relevant differences between the cases, justified them on the basis of unwarranted assumptions about the scenarios or provided justifications that implied a principle that would not account for their actual choices. That is, even while they consistently generated a pattern of moral responses implying a certain principle, they were incapable of articulating that principle.[100] Unsurprisingly, while subjects were twice as good at articulating the relevant principle they were employing in contact-principle cases (harm is worse if it involves physical contact), they were relatively unwilling, once apprised of the actual principle implicit in their own verdict, to endorse that principle as actually "moral". About the same number could identify the principle employed as with the action principle, but the proportion who felt, on reflection, that contact actually constituted a moral difference was far smaller, suggesting that while the contact principle was implicit in their moral responses, in an explicit (conscious) form it was not recognized as morally relevant.[101]

The apparent inconsistencies, from a utilitarian point of view (wrongness determined by total balance of harm), revealed by responses to these hypothetical dilemmas are not, then, the only "problems" to emerge. The original thought experiment was concerned with the incommensurability of different implicit moral principles within the individual: with what are, given the intuitive "correctness" of utilitarian verdicts in most cases, apparent inconsistencies in the individual's moral responses. They do, indeed, demonstrate such an incommensurability between different implicit desires/aversions within the individual that are, nevertheless, all experienced as moral feeling. However, what the experiments also demonstrate is the existence of desires/aversions – the implicit reason why a thing is felt to be morally worse – that, when made explicit to the subject, appear to that subject as morally counterintuitive.

I have already had cause to mention philosophy's tendency to look for the effects of reason where it is unreasonable to expect them. We have seen it at work in ethics own readiness to conflate moral responses with moral judgements. However, if philosophy appears the worst offender in this regard – doubly so, given that its raison d'etre is arguably to discover the unreasonable in thought – it is only because philosophy treats its themes in an explicit, extended and systematic way. The common sense of any particular milieu may be just as caught up in this illusion of the explicability of feeling in terms of the reasonable application of consciously held principles. (Remember Nussbaum's "defence" of emotion.) It is, then, unsurprising that subjects, when challenged to justify their moral responses, should appeal first to what appears (for the reasons already outlined) the given of our shared context: utilitarianism. Subsequently they may also appeal to another principle they feel enjoys universal acceptance – such as the greater wrongness of commission than omission – before finally falling back on "It just is". This comes out more clearly, of course, where it is not simply a matter of the distribution of harm, as with the tram case, but rather where it is a matter of the presence of harm per se.[102]

The very fact that vividness, like several of the other determining factors (e.g. physical contact) that emerge from the tram problem, should imply, in their explicit form, operative moral principles that appear morally counterintuitive even to those whose responses they determine might appear, in itself, a kind of "solution" to the problem of which competing response *should* take priority. (That was, after all, the purpose of the original thought experiments: to use intuition to discover what was 'permissible', irrespective of the apparent rational consistency from a utilitarian perspective.) However, no problem is solved. Finding the principle morally counterintuitive is itself a moral response: it does not take us outside the domain of moral responses. Moreover, to now appeal to rational consistency (in the form of utilitarianism) would only return us to the beginning of the problem, with precisely the same aporia in prospect. The only way to escape from this vicious circle on a moral plane would be to decide that some moral responses represent intuitions that are "correct" and some intuitions that are "false" (in the sense of not really being moral intuitions at all): by moral realism. This would not, of course, remove all moral dilemmas, but it would at least produce the sense that they had discoverable solutions: solutions in terms of the situations themselves rather than simply how we happened to feel about them at the time. Moreover, it would be in harmony with the way we experience our own moral responses: with our instinctive moral realism.

After all, Foot presents her scenarios (the runaway tram, the magistrate, the doctor) as dilemmas – as problems with a solution. Such dilemmas, she says, are a question of being 'confused about the general question of what we may and may not do where the interests of human beings conflict'.[103] She is looking for a principle by which an action can be justified to 'most reasonable men'.[104] Indeed, we should not overlook the legal context of much of this discussion. Some notion of the contemporary consensus on right and wrong, some idea of what can count as 'given' in a particular context, is indispensable for the purpose of codifying what is to count as *justice* in that context. As we saw when dealing with difference between moral responses and moral judgements, so long as a consensus can be established there is no need to invoke moral realism, nor a single formula (after the manner of Brandt) that will capture the principle behind every instance of a correct judgement. A rough hierarchy of implicit principles is sufficient for such a purpose.[105]

We must not forget, however, that such principles (unlike the utilitarian one apparently implied by the very form of the moral response) are revealing only of the moral sense of that group whose moral responses imply them. For example, the aversion implicit in the difference between the results for the tram scenario in which someone must be pushed onto the track to effect the saving of the five and the results for the scenario in which the person will inevitably be pushed onto the track in order to effect another action (pulling a lever) that will save the five appears in Greene's study as a minor if interesting variation between scenarios where the majority nevertheless reject taking action in both cases. However, this principle may appear much more justifiable, and be more strongly operative, in some sections of the population than in others. Where I live, for example, I universally find that, while most people would steer onto the one track if they were actually the driver, *no one* would switch the tram onto the less-populated track if they were a bystander – on the quite consciously held grounds that in doing so they would be making themselves responsible for someone's death. (And, so long as they have done nothing, they are not responsible for the five deaths.) In light of the fact that many of the subjects in the experiments described earlier found the diverting of the tram in the bystander scenario not only 'permissible' but even 'obligatory', this represents a wide divergence in moral feeling. The important point, however, is that the implicit principle that produces this "immoral" (from a utilitarian perspective) result is nevertheless operative as a *moral* principle in the American experiments; hence the contrast in results between pushing the man to effect the rescue and having to push the man to achieve another action that effects the rescue, and also, perhaps, the less than unanimous result even for simply throwing the switch to divert the tram. What we have here, as with our original problem with utilitarianism, is an irreducible difference in the operative strength, and perception of the justifiability, of two incommensurable moral feelings, two contradictory desires/aversions – and no way to adjudicate between them.

I do not mean to suggest, however, that what these seekers after the solutions to moral dilemmas are principally interested in is the discovery of a consensus that may be employed for a practical (legal) end. What most are seeking is what normative ethics is always seeking: a fact of the matter. When Thomson revisited Foot's scenarios a few years after their publication, it was to ask whether or not it was 'true' that, as those scenarios implied, killing is worse than letting die.[106] While much of Thomson's talk of discovering what is 'permissible' could, of course, be interpreted simply as a convenient way of discussing how we might account for our responses, rather than as the expression of a theoretical moral realism, such an interpretation is precluded by her comment that 'One's intuitions are, I think, fairly sharp on these matters': as if the response could be measured against the *real moral fact* of the matter.[107] This, as we saw in the last chapter, is what ethics seems irresistibly drawn to. But while there may be, as we have seen, a fact of the matter about what principle best captures what, as a fact of the matter, most moral responses imply, and a fact of the matter about the consensus in any particular time or place on what is the right thing to do, none of these is equivalent to a moral *fact of the matter*.

Indeed, the idea that there is a correct solution to such dilemmas is a tribute to our inevitable adherence, on a visceral plane, to moral realism: our first instinct is to look for *the* right thing to do. Thus, an intuitionist like Huemer can appeal to the most common response to Foot's scenarios as evidence of the truth of intuitionism.[108] For Huemer, what the apparent disparity in our responses to Foot's cases shows is that moral intuition does not depend on what we *believe* about morality (in this case, our apparent *a priori* commitment to the greatest happiness for the greatest number): that only intuition itself can sort out the true from the false.[109] However, as we have seen, such an argument must presume what it claims to establish: the only proof that the intuition is correct is that it agrees with the intuition. Nevertheless, such cases do serve to show the extent to which we are, indeed, all moral intuitionists in our feelings, in the sense that we feel things are wrong and right in themselves independently of whether we can justify them by appeal to any general truth about right or wrong other than that embodied in the instance itself: we *cannot* relinquish our moral response for anything other than another moral response. (I mean, of course, the response itself, not any action such a response might appear to entail.) Indeed, it is precisely the felt authority of the emotional response per se that these cases are designed to elicit.[110]

At the same time, the appeal to rationality or consistency in itself (in relation to the supposedly moral given of utilitarianism) fares no better. Singer, for example, fixes on just this "unreliability" of moral intuitions, which manifest only as emotion, in advancing his own claim that there is a solution to such dilemmas. He is particularly struck by Greene and Haidt's observation that, when subjects were debating with themselves over whether to push the man onto the track, the parts of the brain associated with emotional activity were more active than they were when the subjects were asked to make judgements about the less controversial cases.[111] Conversely, he notes, the minority of subjects who came to the conclusion that it would be right to push the man, thus minimizing the overall harm, demonstrated more 'activity' in those parts of the brain associated with cognition and took longer to reach their decisions than those who said they would not push the man. His conclusion is that, while some are unable to 'overcome' their emotions, 'those who are prepared to save as many lives as possible, even if this involves physically pushing another person to his death, appear to be using their reason to override their emotional resistance to the personal violation that pushing another person involves'.[112] According to Singer, while we may share with other social mammals an evolutionary-determined tendency to avoid personal violence, the ability to overcome this heritage in order to minimize harm is peculiarly human. It is, according to Singer, a 'moral judgement' that arises from our capacity to reason.[113] While a large part of our morality may reflect the automatic emotional responses of the social mammal, he continues, some of it reflects the fact that we can 'reflect on our emotional responses, and choose to reject them'.[114] Morality, he asserts, is not, and should not be, simply a matter of emotional or instinctive responses, 'unchecked by our capacity for critical reasoning'.[115] It may be, he concludes, that we can only reject our emotional responses on the basis of other emotional responses, but the involvement of reason and abstraction should lead us to 'a morality that is more impartial than our evolutionary history as social mammals would – in the absence of that reasoning process – allow'.[116] As with intuitionism, however, this requires that there be a fact of the matter: real moral properties or objectively better actions that can, like any other facet of the world, be more surely discovered by more diligent research. For, otherwise, there is no force to the foregoing "should" – except, as we saw in Chapter 1, the non-moral "should" of expediency.

Singer is not alone in this view of the "solution" to the dilemmas, though I imagine few would suggest, as he seems to, that the rational course is superior because it is open to us but not to other social mammals: that we *should* because we *can*. Sinnot-Armstrong, examining the same experiments, is particularly struck by the way in which subjects react with "That's so horrible that I can't even think about it".[117] Plainly, he comments, emotion is preventing subjects from considering the factors involved. If this is so, he concludes, then it may be that 'many pervasive and fundamental moral beliefs result from emotions that cloud judgment'.[118] But, again, what form of "judgement", and in what sense are moral responses, such as those of Williams's Jim, the expression of "beliefs"?

There is, of course, a case to be made for seeing the instinctive response in any given situation as maladaptive: as frustrating its own ends. It might be that, on reflection, we come to feel that pushing the fat man was a better thing to do. (Just as a distressed parent who may have been physically forced to relinquish the body of an injured child so that child can receive medical treatment is unlikely to resent that forcing in retrospect.) 'Better', that is, in the sense that once we have viewed the results of our choice – say perhaps the fat man, now revealed as a paparazzo, eagerly taking snaps of the five mangled corpses – we feel that it would have been better to choose otherwise. It is worth noting, however, that in the absence of such an *emotional* confirmation of the "rightness" of our choice, we would be left with only the mathematics, and perhaps a sense of accomplishment in overcoming what we have chosen to regard as our own squeamishness, to satisfy us.

More importantly, however, the 'more impartial' or 'clearer' moral judgement, that is, the judgement that appears to owe least to moral response only derives its authority, only counts as a moral judgement at all, insofar as it conforms to a principle that is itself grounded in a moral response. Why care about the greatest good? Why not treat people as means? After all, faced with a choice between letting one die or five, or killing one for five, or whatever other ingenious combination one could come up with, why bother doing anything? Why bother going to the trouble of pushing a fat man, or even a switch, when there is nothing in it for you? The very concept of a *moral* judgement, as we have seen, only exists by virtue of the existence of moral responses. It might still be argued that, in some of these scenarios, the emotional response that would be in line with the (utilitarian) principle derived from responses in general is being blocked by another non-moral emotion. However, this would be to overlook the fact that several of the non-utilitarian operative principles that emerge (that the degree of harm depends on how vivid it is to us, that actions outweigh omissions, that harm intended as a means is worse that harm merely foreseen as a side effect, that harm caused through physical contact outweighs harm caused remotely) are clearly enduring aspects of moral responses rather than momentary aberrations.

In short, "It's not fair that five should die for one" is a more *morally* convincing reason for redirecting the tram than any reason that might be advanced for its being a reason. Likewise, "You should not use a human being as a means" is a more *morally* convincing reason for not pushing the fat man than any reason that might be advanced for its being a reason.[119] They are equally irreducible. If it turns out that these moral responses are in conflict in certain situations, the fault lies not with their incommensurability but with the situation. There is no reason why there should be a "solution" to some moral dilemmas. The feeling that there should is merely a reflection of that moral realism that is intrinsic to having moral responses at all. (That is, if morality is part of the fabric of the world, it does not make sense for there not to be a morally better course.) The conflict is not produced by some *fault* in the moral sense; it is produced by a problem in the world. The world is not adapted to our emotional comfort.[120] Once we have accepted that moral realism is at once a necessary condition of moral responses *and* an illusion, there should really be nothing particularly surprising about the discovery that the same person can experience moral responses that express what appear to be incommensurable desires.

It might still be that we expect a certain logic in, or at least to, our emotions. If the world is not adapted to them, then at least we might expect them to be somehow adapted to the world. After all, anger can be rationalized as a self-defence mechanism, and love (by some) as a way of preserving our genes or recreating our primordial attachments. We have, however, already dealt with the inadequacy of evolutionary explanations of moral experience. Here we may merely make the further point, contra Singer, that whatever it is that fundamentally separates us from other social mammals, it is certainly not the employment of our more developed powers of reason. It is hard to think of any more self-destructive emotion than human anger, or anything more guaranteed to lead to devastating loss than human love. Or anything more self-deceiving than stoicism.

It is a lurking commitment to moral realism (such as we have already witnessed at work in Chapter 2) that causes this whole debate about the explication of moral "anomalies" to drift towards the false dichotomy of reason versus emotion. Utilitarianism is no more than a deduction, a rationalization, from what is implied by moral responses, which are themselves a matter of emotion. We cannot justify utilitarianism itself *in moral terms* without appealing to a non-utilitarian criterion. The kind of confusion experienced by those trying to account for their own radical *moral* departures from utilitarianism (Williams, Railton, the subjects in the tram experiments, dissenters from Singer's argument for charity) is not, then, peculiar to certain intractable instances of feeling; rather, it is intrinsic to moral experience itself: we will always be at a loss if called upon to account for the moral justification of the principle underlying our moral justification.

Conclusion

The most puzzling aspect of dilemmas such as Jim and the Indians or the various tram cases is not, then, that they elicit responses that appear to be inconsistent with a principle that, in other cases, appears intuitively sound but, rather, that this should appear to anyone as inconsistent: that such inconsistencies should be taken as exemplary of moral "anomalies". The way in which we experience moral responses clearly implies they are connected to an aversion to the existence of *harm*, as we conceive it, in the world. (More particularly, harm as the result of human agency, though we shall have more to say later on the extent to which this is a necessary condition.) This aversion, coupled with the disinterest (impartiality) implied by the response's apparent lack of reference to any self-interest, is what is captured by the utilitarian formula. In every example we have looked at the 'anomaly' arises from an instance in which the course of action that appears to conform to this formula necessitates the subject becoming an actual agent of harm in a particularly vivid manner. Indeed, the moral unacceptability of the utilitarian option, as we have seen, becomes increasingly likely in proportion to the vividness with which the subject is required to become the agent of the harm. The perceived immorality of the utilitarian option, then, arises from the same aversion that gives rise to the utilitarian concept of right and wrong. Moreover, it is not simply a matter of not wishing to be the agent of harm ourselves; we would look askance at anyone who could unhesitatingly choose the utilitarian option in some cases precisely because it would seem to us to display an insensitivity to the very foundational elements of moral experience, an absence of the relevant aversion.

The fact that many of the instances described earlier, in which the non-utilitarian option is commonly perceived as more moral, are instances of extreme jeopardy should not mislead us here. It is not simply a matter of not having time to think. Consider the opprobrium that traditionally surrounded the public executioner even in societies where capital punishment was a norm, or that has historically been attached to butchers in meat-eating Buddhist societies. In some cases, a group may come to accommodate itself to tolerating a harm, particularly where that harm is symbolic, on utilitarian grounds – as, for example, with the mutilation of corpses in autopsies – but, in others, so vivid is the harm that it is difficult to see how such an accommodation could be possible. Say, for example, that it turned out that the surest way to reduce crime was to execute the families of the perpetrators. The only people one can imagine, at the present time, able to choose the utilitarian option in this scenario are precisely the kind of people one would expect to enthusiastically put themselves forward to be the executioners.[121]

The notion that our feelings either *show* us what is really right (as with Williams or Huemer) or, conversely, that they *obscure* from us what is really right (as with Singer) both depend on the idea that something can be really right. The first viewpoint implies intuitionism, which we have already dealt with, while the second depends on identifying the really right with the principle encapsulated in utilitarianism. This second point of view must make a distinction between feeling you are responding morally and actually responding morally, which latter is to be identified with the undesirability of harm in the world from an impartial viewpoint (i.e. the viewpoints posited by either a supernatural or a naturalistic explanation, such as were examined in Chapter 1). The problem here is that this concept of right, despite numerous attempts to identify it with rationality, rests ultimately on the way in which such a concept appears to be operative in the majority (though not all) of our routine moral responses and, more importantly, the way in which it appears implicit in the way in which we experience moral responses as impartial aversions to harm (through human agency). However, for all this, it is not, as we have seen, and despite the character of this experience, actually implicit in every moral response – even of a single subject. Given that right and wrong exist only in my feeling that certain things are right and wrong, we cannot discount any response for failing to conform to a principle deduced from feeling.

Here is where the analogy with the parent who will not relinquish their child for preservation out of an instinct to preserve their child falls down. In such a case we must imagine someone so overwhelmed by emotion that they cannot reason about the best way to pursue their own (emotional) interests. Yet in such a case there is one clear interest at stake: the parent's desire to preserve their child. By contrast, in the case of moral responses, there is not one clear interest at stake: no amount of reasoning or cajoling will make Jim feel he would be doing the right thing in shooting the Indian. Shooting the Indian is, for him, the wrong thing to do. Likewise, we may see, and even feel, that vividness should not make a difference – but it does. A parallel situation would be the parent refusing to relinquish the child even while fully cognizant that this would lead to its death. In such a case we would have to conclude that preservation of the child's life was not the motive underlying their refusal to relinquish it.

We may conclude, then, that the moral response, despite what it appears to imply, does not signify our desire for the greatest happiness, or least harm, for the greatest number – even allowing for sufficient flexibility in the definitions of 'harm' and 'greatest number' to accommodate the different ways in which people may perceive these two factors. However, we may also conclude that, aside from a fundamental aversion to harm, the vivid sense of which is, as our dilemmas have shown, sufficiently aversive for many to feel a greater amount of harm in the world morally preferable to having to entertain the thought of it, no other desire/aversion emerges as more successfully capturing what moral responses imply. There is too great a variation, and too little consistency even in a single subject's responses, for us to replace the utilitarian formula with a more inclusive one. There can be no end to the pursuit of what *is* right: the futility is an essential condition of the pursuit itself.

The aspiration to system within ethics, then, while it may have a pragmatic value for lawmakers, and though it can be an interesting mental exercise, will never amount to anything more than the description of a local consensus or the occasion for exercising one's powers of analysis. For, what the innumerable inconsistencies in our actual responses suggest is that the goal, or function, of moral responses – the desire their existence signifies – rather than being revealed by the character of the moral response as we experience it, is actually somehow obscured by that character: that whatever goal the moral response per se appears to imply, this is not its actual goal. Thus, no system that is built upon what is consistent in moral experience will ever reveal what underlies that experience: the desire that gives rise to the moral response. This last can only be discovered by looking at the totality of moral experience and treating the apparent inconsistencies not as the anomalies they appear to be from the point of view of any normative ethics based on the way the response feels but rather as the phenomenon to be explained: to allow that the "distortions" of the system may actually be the system. For, our problem is not simply that the utilitarian (or, indeed, any) abstract moral formula does not manage to successfully capture the desire/aversion that gives rise to the emotion involved, but that we must account for why we should feel some formula could capture (in a concept of 'the Good') that desire/aversion.

To this end, the following two chapters will focus on moral responses that exhibit not merely the relatively straightforward "anomalies" that we have examined earlier in connection with moral dilemmas but, rather, responses that exhibit the absence of elements that appear ineluctably constitutive of moral responses (from the point of view of what the feeling implies), yet still retain the character of moral responses. For, as we shall see, it is not that moral responses appear to escape any principle that might be deduced from the form they take; rather even the seemingly most fundamental implicit operative principles of the moral response – sensitivity to consequences and the perception of responsibility – turn out to be themselves constantly overridden in practice by responses that are experienced as moral. For, it is not simply a matter of any consistent principle running up against conflicts between judgement and response, or even of the conflicting moral responses of different people; rather it is a matter of the moral responses of the same individual failing to square with each other in terms of any consistent ethical principle of the sort that the moral response per se might seem to imply.

The next chapter, then, will deal with moral responses that appear to disregard the consequences of an action – not, that is, in the way that Williams's Jim disregards them as a matter of painful moral necessity, but rather the deliberate intent to disregard them, accompanied by a feeling of positive moral self-admiration in doing so. The second will deal with responses that ignore what would, prima facie, appear to be the essential condition of human agency within the domain of blame or praise, and with moral responses that disregard both consequences and agency.

4

Disregarding consequences

The last chapter approached the question of the grounds of the moral response by considering the goal apparently implied by the occasions of those responses. Such an approach is arguably unavoidable, given that the emotion itself – the feeling that something is wrong or right – is actually experienced as what it simply cannot be: "disinterested". It emerged, however, that even the most plausible implicit disinterested goal (the greatest happiness of the greatest number) is not the actual goal. Moral feeling may appear to imply utilitarianism, but utilitarianism does not exhaust what is implied in practice by moral responses. The greatest happiness for the greatest number is *not* the object implied by our experience of moral responses, despite being the most consistent "Good" that can be deduced from the way the response is experienced as a desire that, *independently of my own goals or interests*, harm (however conceived) should not happen. This, indeed, is why the question "What is right?" is so very familiar, for, given that what can be consistently deduced from our moral feeling does not actually match our experience of moral feeling, this question itself can never receive anything other than a temporary, local and contingent answer. At the same time the moral response is experienced as precisely not temporary, local or contingent. Thus, ethics finds itself perpetually in pursuit of its own tail. To make sense of moral experience, then, it may be that we must stop demanding that moral experience make sense in terms of the way in which we experience it. Perhaps, that is, the desired object, the "Good", that we are looking for is not one that we will recognize as morally "good", albeit that our desire for it somehow gives rise to the concept of moral goodness.

However, we must now turn to those moral responses that do not claim to be consistent from the point of view of what is implicit in moral feeling itself. After all, utilitarianism is simply a deduction from what *appears to be* implied in moral feeling. The fact that it has sufficient predictive power for us to be able to automatically assume it as the consensus, as given, in the great majority of moral debates, should not blind us to the fact that, as we have also seen, it does not capture the whole of moral experience. A few of the possible alternative aversions/desires that might be *constitutive* of a moral response emerged in the last chapter. Some of these may be readily acknowledged as such and perhaps easy to explain in terms of at least some accounts of the grounds of the moral response itself – as the aversion to being an agent of harm, even where this indirectly causes greater harm, can be accounted for in terms of the everyday phenomenon of emotion frustrating the goal that gives rise to it (trembling at the idea of falling causes us to fall).[1] Others, and particularly those demonstrably determining factors, such as the effect of distance, in the perception of what is or is not moral, which are yet explicitly rejected as such by those for whom they are determining factors, are more difficult to account for. Here again, however, it may simply be a matter of reluctance to own one's own immorality. There are, nevertheless, broad swathes of moral experience in which the implicitly desired goal appears to be the particular behaviour or attitude *in itself*, irrespective of any consequences. These present us with a variety of 'goods' that both escape utilitarianism and yet apparently fail to imply either any alternative single object of desire/aversion to account for their being experienced as moral or any obvious "extra-moral" motivation.

This, indeed, is the usefulness of such responses from the point of view of discovering what desire/aversion gives rise to moral feeling. For we have already seen how the moral sense fails to correspond to what we can either systematize or, in many instances, even own as moral. Moreover, given that, as we saw in Chapter 1, morality does not "make sense" even in the way we experience and profess it, what we need is the evidence of what does not make sense even according to the sense we feel and say it makes. Thus, it is those implicit desires that are both routine and demonstrably present on the occasions of moral feeling, yet, when reflected upon, morally counterintuitive, that will be the most useful here. (Though, in practice, routine aspects of moral feeling are rarely experienced as counterintuitive, since we customarily attribute them to "human nature": the secular equivalent of an appeal to *mysterium fidei*.) It is here, in what are routine anomalies from the point of view of what we feel (however, wrongly) is uncontroversially, "explicably" moral, that we will find the true desire/aversion – in just the same way as one might suddenly gain insight into the true motives of an apparently impartial judge were that judge to be visibly disappointed by incontrovertible proof of a defendant's innocence, or into the real feelings of one who, professing a keen desire to go jogging, was yet visibly relieved on learning that it was not possible to do so. We must, as it were, surprise the motivation, as a boy I once knew would toss a coin on difficult decisions and then decide on the basis of how he felt about the result.

The customary distinction drawn within ethics between consequentialism and non-consequentialism is largely capricious. (What, after all, are supposed to be the consequences of the greatest happiness for the greatest number?) However, insofar as the utilitarian goal *appears to be* implicit in moral feeling itself it appears to be common sense; or at least it would were it not, as we have seen, for certain hard cases or "anomalies". Thus, to ask after the reason for having a disinterested concern for others' welfare is perceived as equivalent to stepping outside of morality entirely. As I remarked before, the question "Why should I be good?" allows for only amoral answers. We can say, then, that, in practice, some moral responses more obviously ignore consequences than do others. These are instances where the perception of the implicit operative principle involved in an action elicits one kind of moral response even where the actual action, considered in itself, would normally elicit the opposite moral response in the same observer, and, indeed, may actually be doing so on precisely this occasion. Moreover, in certain instances – much as with the cases in the last chapter – the implicit operative principle in the moral response may be one that the observer finds difficult to recognize as their own: they find it hard to *morally* justify (i.e.

justify in terms of what their own moral feeling apparently implies) their approbation or disapprobation of the motive displayed.

Vice

Consider, for example, the way many people respond to hypocrisy. It would be a simple matter to show the very great moral value (from a utilitarian point of view) of the practice of pretending to be better than one is. Indeed, so defined, hypocrisy is obviously essential to good parenting; it would be hypocrisy to deny it. Yet, pretending to be better than you are is generally considered not only a particularly distasteful vice but also one that seems exacerbated rather than meliorated to the extent that you endeavour to improve others by your, albeit fictitious, example. Indeed, hypocrisy is generally held in far greater moral *distaste* than many other traditional vices, such as greed and lust, which not only seem more forgivable but which may even be considered endearing. There is no endearing form of hypocrisy. This may be because hypocrisy seems motivated by pride and the desire to deceive – both motives that we feel should be more under the agent's control than are those apparently more natural appetites that give rise to either greed or lust.[2] (This perceived potential of the agent will turn out to be significant to what follows.) Whatever the reason, however, hypocrisy tends to elicit a degree of moral disapprobation that is, at least from the point of view of utilitarianism, quite disproportionate to the amount of actual harm that it either does or could do. Indeed, this disapprobation may go as far as holding avowed wickedness to be somehow the morally superior, or at least more attractive, position.[3]

This tendency to respond morally to the mental state of the agent rather than the consequences of their actions reaches its apotheosis in that tendency to morally judge mental states in themselves, irrespective of whether or not they are connected to motivation. Although we might most readily associate such a tendency with certain more archaic and usually religiously based approaches to morality ("sins of thought"), it is also one that appears as an implicit operative principle in many common moral responses. Moreover, this implicit principle is not without its explicit defenders.

Gaut, for example, observing that 'much of our ethical assessment is directed at what people feel, even though these feelings do not motivate their actions', asserts that such assessments are justified: a person 'can be ethically criticized for what she takes pleasure or displeasure in'.[4] It is the case, he continues, that 'experiencing immoral feelings with pleasure' is itself 'an immoral action'.[5] (The use of the expression 'immoral feelings' here does seem to rather prejudge the issue, but let us take it to mean any pleasure in the thought of an immoral action.) The essential thing here is that it is the enjoyment itself that is condemned. A man whose sexual life consists entirely of rape fantasies, according to Gaut, 'stands ethically condemned for what and how he imagines, independently of how he acts or may act'.[6]

Gaut is here guilty of what might be called 'the fallacy of the appeal to the unimaginable'. This is precisely the same fallacy that Mill commits when he thinks that the consensus response to his question 'Which would you rather be: Socrates unsatisfied or a pig satisfied?' proves that we would all actually prefer to be Socrates unsatisfied. In fact, however, this consensus arises only because the great majority of people, like Mill, actually fail to imagine what they are being asked to imagine. That is, what most people imagine is not *being* a satisfied pig but rather *their current self* as a satisfied pig. If you are Socrates, then you are Socrates and not yourself as Socrates; if you are the pig, then you are the pig and not yourself as the pig. Therefore, the only real choice you are being asked to make by the question is "Would you rather be satisfied or unsatisfied?", which answers itself.[7]

Gaut, too, relies on the unimaginable. It does, indeed, seem impossible not to feel moral revulsion at the thought of a person whose sexual fantasy life consisted entirely of rape fantasies, irrespective of what he does or may do. But is this not precisely because we cannot actually imagine such a case: a case in which there could be no possible practical effects arising from such a compulsion, in which such a taste did not also imply a propensity? It is all but impossible to imagine such a person without imagining them as also representing a real danger of harm (if not actually of rape, then at least of the exhibition of offensive attitudes). Likewise, it is very difficult to imagine anyone who could be both habitually amused by the idea of sadistic cruelty and yet truly harmless. We condemn or are disgusted only because we cannot help but feel that such tastes reveal more general character flaws. Thus, it is the implicit threat of harm that is the real inspiration of the moral response, even though it is not ostensibly its object. Its ostensible object is the *harmless* fantasist himself. In short, if we intuitively assent to Gaut's condemnation of the rape fantasist, it is probably only because we do not, in fact, imagine such a figure 'independently of how he acts or may act'. It is perhaps this inability to truly imagine the case that leads us to overlook the actual letter of Gaut's thesis. For, it is quite conceivable that even those who might intuitively respond with moral revulsion to Gaut's rape fantasist would also find the principle that this revulsion serves to establish – that we are justified in morally condemning individuals irrespective of their actions or intentions – morally counterintuitive.

There might, of course, be all sorts of egotistical reasons for feeling that one may condemn others on the basis of what they are rather than what they do, but it should be noted that this condemnation may also be self-directed. It is quite possible for a person to respond with disapproval to their own feelings when they discover themselves enjoying what, on reflection, is morally repugnant to them. We may feel guilty when we find ourselves cheering on the bloody and excessive retribution of a fictional hero, or more impressed by the sublimity of a disaster than mindful of the suffering it implies, or sexually aroused by the image of a minor or by our own fantasies of being raped.

Devereaux, for example, on finding herself responding positively to Leni Riefenstahl's *Triumph of the Will*, is led to reflect that 'certain kinds of enjoyment, *regardless of their effects*, may themselves be problematic'.[8] The concern, she believes, is not about what one may become – what motivation the pleasure might be revealing – but rather about 'who one is *now*': 'If virtue consists (in part) in taking pleasure in the right things and not in the wrong things, then what is my character now such that I can take pleasure in these things?'[9] Again, as with Gaut's ascription of 'immorality' to the mere possession of certain feelings, 'virtue' here floats quite free from either action or intention.

There is nothing mysterious about the way in which this concern for "right feeling" arises. One discovers that one has impulses or potentials that could lead to acts that one finds morally repugnant. What happens next, however, depends on one's view of the world. One might just accept it. After all, having the potential to be a brute, an egomaniac or a Nazi is not the same thing as being one. Being a human being, on the other hand, is the same thing as having the potential to be any of them. However, this is not how everyone sees it. Some feel that the world may be divided into 'the good' and 'the bad', with no crossover in kind. (Moralism, as we have seen, is a matter of congratulating yourself on being a certain kind of person.) It is understandable, then, how for such a person the discovery of their own urges might lead to panic, and how this panic would give rise to a moral response to the feeling itself, and even to the positing of the problematic concept that certain feelings can be morally culpable in themselves.[10] ('Problematic' in the sense that the harm to others is, by definition, intangible.) However, from a pragmatic point of view, the assumption implicit in this concept – that the human race may be divided into those (the vicious) who have such potential and those (the virtuous) who do not – strikes me, since it is as much a matter of conviction as of impulse, as embodying a far greater potential for tangible harm than any involuntary response ever could.

This response to the feelings of others, or even ourselves, as if those feelings were actions, and the philosophical justification of that response dealt with earlier does, then, imply a morality that I doubt most would subscribe to on further reflection: that there is another way of being a morally better or worse person other than doing, or even being inclined to do, morally better or worse things. Even where the immorality of thinking certain things is simply felt – as is done by Gaut and Devereaux – it is evidently extremely difficult to make consistent. It is an attitude towards the private mental world that often calls forth the response "Where would the application of such a principle end?" But we might equally well ask – given that one must first think of the thing one is not to think – where, in good faith, the application of such a principle could begin. Surely it is a recipe for neurosis rather than morality.

In short, while it is quite common to instinctively react with moral disapprobation to the tastes of others, it seems clear that this is always a matter of, as it were, sneaking in an imagining of the consequences of this taste understood as evidence of actual motivation. It can take, then, almost an effort of will to remember that fantasizing about raping no more makes one a potential rapist than fantasizing about being raped proves that one really wishes to be raped.[11]

Since this is, necessarily, a topic that can arouse the kind of emotions that "cloud the judgement", let me make quite clear what I am not saying here: that fantasy has no connection with reality. It is, indeed, the case that sometimes fantasy does express ideology, particularly perhaps when that fantasy is a collective one.[12] Ideology, by definition, must lead to consequences – harmful or otherwise. There is, then, a kind of fantasy that may reflect and thus *potentially* serve to reinforce ways of considering the world that do lead to action. The enjoyment of that fantasy, *insofar as it is grounded in a feeling that this is the way things should and could really be*, could then be quite consistently taken as evidence of a motivation to acts that do fall within the domain of morality. However, what we have been dealing with here is a kind of emotional spillage – equivalent to, for example, "punishing" a recalcitrant computer – from responses that can be traced to such a perception of the implications of the enjoyment. For, both

Gaut and Devereaux make a point of saying that we are justified in condemning certain feelings even if what they seem to imply – a propensity to immoral actions – is not actually what they imply. However, while fantasy may express ideology, an "ideology" that is never reflected in practice is just fantasy.

Why such emotional spillage might occur is something we have already glanced at. There is the very difficulty, at least in some instances, of imagining that one could take pleasure in imaginatively contemplating something that one would not also be drawn to in reality. However, put this way, it is obvious that this division between fantasy and reality is, in fact, a common phenomenon. Indeed, where the fantasy scenario does not produce some kind of revulsion – as it does, for some, in the case of rape fantasies or slasher films – we generally take it for granted that the pleasure a person derives from the fantasy arises from its symbolic value for them rather than from their desire to have it literally reproduced in reality.[13] We do not, for example, take the popularity within fiction of life and death struggles or star-crossed love as proof that most people would actually be thrilled to have their lives really threatened or their strongest desires really thwarted.

Where, however, we do feel a strong revulsion, it appears to be very difficult not to have an intimation of the threat of harm. This may be what prevents Gaut from fully imagining the figure of the rape fantasist as he himself posits that figure. For, if he really did fully imagine such a person, according to the letter of his own description, surely the result would be the perception not of a dangerous, and therefore immoral, person but rather of a perfectly harmless one suffering from some form of psychopathology. What he is probably imagining when he imagines the rape fantasist is the kind of person he would have to be himself if his entire erotic life consisted of rape fantasies, which, given the way I presume he feels about rape, is not actually a thing that it is possible for him to imagine unless he also imagines himself possessing a strong motivation to find the idea of raping pleasurable. Naturally, the easiest motivation to imagine in such an instance is the desire to rape. This same difficulty of sufficiently distinguishing between a person who feels certain pleasures or aversions and the self we imagine being if it were we ourselves that felt these same pleasures or aversions leads to many misperceptions, both in the aesthetic and the moral domains.

This is not, however, a work of normative ethics. It is by no means my intention to lead this analysis to the conclusion that we *shouldn't* judge other people on the basis of their private fantasy life. I only wish to establish that we do respond in this way (and, with regard to my feelings about the fans of slasher films or the novels of James Ellroy, I include myself in this 'we') despite the fact that this implies an operative moral principle – that the agent can be immoral irrespective of their actions or intentions – that is very difficult to sustain in terms of any professed morality short of one that simply asserts the existence of feelings that are "immoral" in themselves.

The same tendency to unjustifiably extrapolate out from a state of mind to a potential for harm seems to be naturally exaggerated where there is some pretext in the behaviour of the agent. There are certain actions that seem almost inevitably to lead us to infer a state of mind that we perceive as a potential for harm, even where it may be difficult to demonstrate what actual harm is involved in those actions. Cannibalism is an obvious case. We may be intellectually capable of perceiving cannibalism itself as morally neutral in certain circumstances, but it is more difficult, even in those same cases, to perceive the cannibal themselves as actually harmless. Or, if that perception seems too culture-dependent, imagine the case of a man who has charge of corpses just prior to their burial or cremation who routinely smashes in the faces of those corpses with a hammer. Assuming that no one knows about this, it is rather difficult to point to any tangible harm. At the same time, I would predict that the majority of readers would still perceive such an action as wrong *in itself* and would do so precisely because they could not help inferring from the action a state of mind from which they did extrapolate a potential for harm.

The tendency can also be seen even where the actions involved are uncontroversially harmful (immoral) but are so to such a degree or in so vivid a manner that the state of mind, and thus the felt potential for harm, appears to somehow exceed the normal limits of the moral domain. In such cases we feel an intimation of a transcendental or supernatural wrongness: we perceive either the agent, as the cause of such an act, or the act itself, as the expression of an agent capable of such an act, as "evil". (This is precisely why Arendt thought it worthwhile to remark on the actual banality of evil in practice, and why many of her more slow-witted readers responded to this by accusing her of not taking evil seriously.)

Indeed, it is because the perception of evil is determined by spontaneous reference to the inferred mental state of the agent that our use of the word, despite how we might be inclined to define it, does not correspond to the *amount* of harm involved.[14] For example, the random sadistic murder of a child is more likely to immediately evoke a perception of evil, than the career of one who has murdered dozens but done so painlessly and for profit. This is not to say that, on vividly envisaging the mind of the latter agent, we could not perceive that agent as evil, but only that, in the case of the random sadistic child murder, we do not have to consciously envisage such a mind: the act itself appears to embody it. There is more to infer in the case of the cold-blooded killer acting out of an interest one can empathize with, so that the element of shock comes not from any image of the particular result but at two removes: first we must reconstruct the character, then we must feel it as a threat. By contrast, in the former case, the threat is immediately present in our horror at the sadistic act itself. This is why one could, eventually, make even a generally popular comedy film from the second kind of case but not from the first.

Evil, then, is not a matter of "extreme badness" in the sense of quantity of real harm. (I suspect many would react with more outrage to the idea of the hypothetical mortuary attendant with a hammer, than they would to the actual spectacle of the real harm of a mild insult to a living person.) Rather we call something "evil" on the basis of the image of a human agent we infer from the nature of the act, where the act is such that we infer an agent with a great potential to cause harm. An evil agent is an agent who could *will* this. The very possibility of their existence is a source of fear to us. To feel a thing is evil is principally to feel a certain kind of shock, arising from fear, in response to the symbolic qualities of objects or actions, as they appear to embody the malevolence of an agent. Thus, for example, we would most likely feel a sense of relief if what we at first thought was the aftermath of a murder turned out to be the result of a bear attack. For the same reason, we generally prefer to contain evil by concentrating responsibility for it into a single individual (as happens, for example, with Hitler).

The key element in distinguishing what kind of acts inspire, when perceived as intended, a sense of evil is the presence of disgust and fear. With regard to disgust, the act must be such that it obliges us to imagine an agent devoid of, or able to overcome, inhibitions that we take to be universal, or at least fundamentally constitutive of a bearable life (hence the tendency to call such acts or their agents "inhuman"). For this reason, the proximity of the agent to the results of their actions is important. We would expect a person to be more reluctant to confess to having tortured cats as a youth, than to confess to once flying bombing missions against civilian targets. The harms in the two cases may be, when viewed from the perspective of most definitions of harm, incomparable, but so too, and in inverse proportion, is the degree to which the whole personality of the agent is implicated. What we call 'evil', then, is that which apparently forces on us the image of a fellow being with an appetite for producing repulsive results – with the qualification that this repulsiveness is connected with either uncontroversial human harm (the sadistic murder) or what can easily symbolize human harm (cannibalism).

In this way, the very existence of the perception of an act or agent as evil is another instance of the mechanism that is at work in the idea of culpable states of mind. In this case, of course, uncontroversial harm is usually (though not always) involved. However, the very violence of our reaction in ascribing 'evil' (transcendental badness) to the act/agent, and the fact that this violence is not explicable in terms of either the amount of harm or the real threat of harm (the object of the response may be either past or fictional without altering the strength of that response), points to the same overspilling of emotion in response to a hypothetical agent and the potential for harm the very possibility of their existence presents to the imagination.

Virtue

In terms of negative moral responses that ignore consequences the above-mentioned examples are fairly easy to account for, if we allow that in many cases that response only seems to ignore consequences. (That is, the condemnation can be plausibly traced to an inability to *not* imagine consequences.) Likewise, certain positive moral responses that seem at least incommensurate with consequences can be understood in a similar way. However, there are instances of moral responses that do seem to genuinely discount consequences and thus presents a far greater degree of "inconsistency" than any of those responses so far considered. This is most strikingly the case with the moral admiration of certain predispositions *in themselves*: virtues.

Before demonstrating how the admiration of virtues may involve the morally problematic discounting of consequences, it is worth noting that it is only the phenomenon of admiration for virtues *in themselves* that is the issue here. It takes no very great ingenuity to see how certain apparently discrete virtues, such as either justice or *caritas*, might be defined in such a way as to encompass an ideal of moral action per se, nor to see how either or both, depending on how they are defined, could be said to be presupposed by a systematic ethics like utilitarianism. Our topic here, however, is not virtue itself but, rather, virtues: those character traits that are discretely objects of moral approbation. The perception of virtues as such arguably plays a far greater role in everyday moral experience than is reflected in the literature of ethics, with its urge to unify such experience into a single principle. Indeed, one reason that many people find philosophical ethics remote is that we principally seem to experience "good" or "bad" actions as expressions of an admirable or deficient aspect of the agent's character rather than as the fulfilment or contravention of a principle.[15] Hating the sinner seems inseparable from hating the sin.

With this emphasis on common experience in mind, the virtue I will examine here is one that has remained tenaciously popular despite its absence from any of the canons of virtues that have informed the Western ethical tradition: loyalty.

The first thing to note about ascriptions of loyalty is that they are ascriptions of a certain motivation rather than a course of action. We describe actions as "loyal" only on the basis of an inferred motivation. So, two generals might fight equally "loyally" – that is, with equal zeal and apparent indifference to self-interest – for the sake of Ruritania. However, if one of them switches sides in the face of Ruritania's imminent defeat, then it becomes clear that, whatever his motivation had previously been, it was not the loyalty that we ascribed to him, or at least that this loyalty has now come to an end. We cannot, of course, say that he was not originally acting out of loyalty, since his actions may have arisen from what was indeed loyalty to, for example, a superior, or to his hometown, or to a certain idea of Ruritania – the interests of any of which are indeed best served by his changing sides – but only that he did not, in fact, possess the particular loyalty we originally attributed to him. (It was loyalty to some other thing that led him to act *as if* he was loyal to Ruritania.) If, however, we were to discover that his original zeal arose purely out of a desire for career advancement and that he had changed sides from the same motive, then we would simply say that he was never "really" loyal: that his previous behaviour was not a matter of "acting loyally" but of acting *as if* he was loyal, while not, in reality, being so. In just the same way, an employee's apparent loyalty may be simply a matter of no one else ever offering them more money to do the same job, and a spouse's no more than a want of libido, opportunity or enterprise. In neither case, were we aware of the actual motivation of their actions, would we describe them as acting out of loyalty, no matter how much like loyalty or faithfulness their outward behaviour appeared. Whenever, then, we attribute loyalty, we are doing so on the basis of an inferred motivation.

What kind of motivation, then, constitutes loyalty? To display loyalty to an object (person/group/institution/ideal) is to place the interests or welfare of that object above both perceivable self-interest and above the interests of other comparable objects. An instance of loyalty emerges by a contrast with three potentially conflicting motivations: self-interest, loyalty to something else, and a concern for the common good.[16] Interestingly, it does not emerge as a contrast to any one of them in isolation: one may overcome perceivable self-interest out of love or hate, one may fail to demonstrate loyalty to anything and, of course, one may place self-interest above the common good. It is only when a person displays the habitual tendency to prioritize the interests or welfare of a particular object over a combination of all three – self-interest, the interests of comparable objects, and the common good – that we actually describe them as loyal to that object. It is not, of course, necessary for a person to actually behave in a way that would establish such a prioritization; it is enough that they signal a disposition to do so.[17] (Thus, one of the most common forms of self-conscious loyalty appears to be patriotism, even though the greater part of the evidence for its prevalence is purely verbal.[18]) To attribute loyalty to oneself is to be conscious of feeling disposed to such a prioritization, and to experience it as a virtue is to respond with a feeling of approbation towards such a prioritization in oneself or others.

This characterization of loyalty, accurate though I take it to be, does raise a problem. According to what has been said so far, it should be possible for a person to be, from an observer's point of view, loyal to an object, without that person actually being conscious of this loyalty. I do not here mean what is sometimes referred to as "unconscious loyalty", as when someone fails to recognize that they are demonstrating partiality simply because they are unaware of an emotional influence on their judgement. ("My child is careful, yours is timid, hers is cowardly.") Rather what I mean here are those cases where, even if a demonstrable partiality, from an observer's point of view, were pointed out, the agent, even while acknowledging the prioritization, would not recognize it as partiality. That is, the agent may prioritize the interests of a certain object over their own interest without either recognizing that there is such a thing as a *comparable* object, and without distinguishing between the interests or welfare of that object and the common good. In short, they take the interests and welfare of the object of their loyalty to be identical to the common good. So, for example, I once saw two women spend some time each politely insisting that the other take the one of two empty train seats that was not next to a person of a conspicuously different race to themselves and the other occupants of the carriage. Although this was done in full view of the man, if you had asked the women what they were doing in each insisting that the other should not have to take the seat next to him, they would have said that they were endeavouring to be "polite". Moreover, they could have said it with perfect sincerity, since that was precisely their intention; it was simply that the common good they were respecting in being polite genuinely did not include the feelings of the outsider. (Any more than your sense of the common good would incline you to extend the franchise to toddlers or divert a runaway tram towards one human in order to save five rabbits.) Breathtakingly rude as their actions were from some observers' viewpoints, these same actions were, from the women's own point of view, genuine expressions of just its opposite: politeness.

Likewise, with loyalty. From a non-human standpoint, responses that were commensurate with such an apparently "universal" principle as, for example, utilitarianism would necessarily appear to constitute loyalty to the human race.[19] However, from a human standpoint it would be a misnomer to refer to such an implicit predisposition as an expression of loyalty, since there is neither a comparable object over which humanity in general could potentially be preferred nor a concept of a more *common* good. (Thus, the current disagreement over whether or not it is possible to speak of "loyalty to the human species" – in contrast to loyalty to life – must turn upon how far it is possible to take a non-human standpoint.) As we have seen, loyalty only gets its identity as a separate, identifiable motivation from its contrast to the common good – however that common good is conceived. Thus, it would not make sense to speak of loyalty to one's family if one's concept of the common good only extended as far as the limits of one's own family. It would, however, be possible to speak of loyalty to one's brother within such a context, if one were self-consciously disposed to prioritize his interests over those of the rest of the family. Regardless of the extent of one's recognized common good (family, race, nationality, species, etc.), it only makes sense for the agent to themselves be conscious of loyalty in relation to an object that exists discretely within this ethical universe – the realm to which they feel morality applies – and has interests that may conflict with the common good of that universe.

Thus, when Rorty asks if it would not be a good idea to 'treat "justice" as the name for loyalty to a certain very large group, the name for our largest current loyalty, rather than the name of something distinct from loyalty', we can only answer that it would not. What would be lost in doing so are precisely those limits to the meaning of "loyalty" that currently make "loyalty" a meaningful word, for the word could no longer be used for any loyalty other than this one.[20] The distinction between being loyal and being motivated by a sense of justice or morality or concern for the common good (however "just" and "moral" are defined in any particular context, that is, however restricted the community included in the particular "common good") is a distinction that points to a real difference. That, indeed, is why we have a concept of loyalty. In what follows, then, we will be dealing with loyalty only in the normally accepted sense of that word – the prioritization of the interests or welfare of a subset of that which is taken to belong to the realm of the common good.

Given, then, that loyalty only exists as a contrast to concern for the common good, the inconsistency that must immediately strike us is the way in which loyalty is so widely held to be a morally admirable quality, a virtue. Certainly, for the one who is loyal it is, necessarily, in line with their values, but even for them there is a perceived divergence from the standard of common good, alignment with which would seem to be essential to perceiving one's actions as moral. It is not, of course, that any particular loyalty necessarily brings one into conflict with the common good – that is a matter of chance – but rather that the very consciousness of possessing loyalty is consciousness of feeling a counterweight to a common good. (Hence the element of, paradoxically, self-directed moral defiance – "My country; right or wrong" – that is the hallmark of expressions of loyalty, and which we shall return to later.) Indeed, where chance operates to make this conflict obvious, the moral status of loyalty may indeed be questioned. Thus Hume, reflecting on history, observes that 'a strict adherence to any general rules, and the rigid loyalty to particular persons and families, on which some people set so high a value, are virtues that hold less of reason, than of bigotry and superstition'.[21] Keller, too, concludes his analysis of loyalty by affirming that 'there is no guarantee that if something counts as a loyalty, then it counts as something good, or something that merits our approval or encouragement', and offers the obvious example of the loyal Nazi.[22]

Yet, loyalty is generally accounted a virtue, and its display will tend to meet with some form of admiration, no matter what the loyalty is loyalty to.[23] Indeed, so admirable does loyalty generally seem that its possession has even been accounted the chief virtue: 'the heart of all the virtues, the central duty amongst all duties'.[24]

Thus Royce insisted that 'our traditional moral standards ought to be revised', to take account of the fact that 'in loyalty, when loyalty is properly defined, is the fulfilment of the whole moral law', and that 'justice, charity, industry, wisdom, spirituality, are all definable in terms of enlightened loyalty'.[25] One would be justified in expecting at this point some form of definist manoeuvre – yielding a special kind of "loyalty" that is not loyalty – to make good this claim. What we get, on the contrary, is precisely the same loyalty we have so far been considering:

> Loyalty shall mean, according to this preliminary definition: *The willing and practical and thoroughgoing devotion of a person to a cause.* A man is loyal when, first, he has some cause to which he is loyal; when, secondly, he willingly and thoroughly devotes himself to this cause; and when, thirdly, he expresses his devotion in some sustained and practical way, by acting steadily in the service of his cause. [. . .] The loyal man serves. That is, he does not merely follow his own impulses. He looks to his cause for guidance. This cause tells him what to do, and he does it. His devotion, furthermore, is entire. He is ready to live or to die as the cause directs. [. . .] There is only one way to be an ethical individual. That is to choose your cause, and then to serve it, as the Samurai his feudal chief, as the ideal knight of romantic story his lady, – in the spirit of all the loyal. [. . .] For nobody has anything better than loyalty, or can get anything better. But one [loyalty] alone can you live. No mortal knows which is the better for your world. With all your heart, in the name of universal loyalty, choose. And then be faithful to the choice. So shall it be morally well with you.[26]

This is all perfectly consistent as a "moral law", and we might surmise that it perhaps encapsulates the "moral law" of bushido and, if not chivalry, then at least pre-Christian feudalism. (It is also, of course, the morality implicit in every concept of honour.) What it does not encapsulate, despite what Royce believes, is Royce's own sense of the moral. For he goes on to say that 'we must consider what are the fitting objects of loyalty', and by 'fitting' he means morally worthwhile.[27] In sum, then, loyalty per se is to be the touchstone of morality, and the moral worth of the object of the loyalty is to be the touchstone of the moral worth of the loyalty. As if a teacher were to say, "Your grade will depend on the results of the exam, and the exam score will be determined from your grade".[28]

It is Royce's love of the sound of the word 'loyalty', the images (knights, samurai, self-sacrificing patriots, captains going down with their ships) it evokes, that lead him into proposing loyalty as the key to morality and hence into nonsense. It is not, however, necessary to make loyalty as key as Royce makes it, in order to find oneself in philosophical difficulties. It is enough to try to justify its moral status.

Ladd, for example, though he begins his treatment of loyalty by acknowledging that there at least appear to be examples of bad loyalty (the usual Nazis), nevertheless, claims that the implications drawn from such disreputable associations are 'ill-founded', and that, in fact, 'loyalty is an essential ingredient in any civilized and humane system of morals'.[29] Moreover, as with Royce, he does not, at least initially, resort to redefining 'loyalty' in order to make his point. Loyalty, he says, is 'wholehearted devotion' to such objects as a friend, one's family or a highly organized group such as a political, priestly or military community. Further, this devotion is based not on a perception of the virtues of the object but on the existence of the relationship itself; I am loyal to X 'because he is *my* friend', not because he possesses any other characteristic: 'purely personal characteristics of *X*, such as his kindness, courage, amiability, honesty, or spirituality cannot serve as *grounds* for loyalty'. A relationship of loyalty to any object is grounded, then, in a 'specific kind of relationship or tie' that arises from the agent's belonging to a group 'distinguished by a specific common background and sharing specific interests'.[30] Unsurprisingly, then, Ladd concedes that it would not appear that loyalty has any 'inner value', since, if it did, we would have to say that the Nazi's loyalty had as much value as anyone else's and such a conclusion 'outrages our moral feelings'.[31] His quandary, then, is that he feels it is 'impossible to separate logically the moral quality of devotion from the moral quality of its object', yet at the same time, seeing the value of loyalty as dependent on the value of its object 'robs loyalty of any special moral significance'. And he does not want to rob loyalty of its special moral significance, for, if we do so, how are we to justify, for example, 'the admirable side of a mother's loyalty to her son even when, considering the total picture, it is not entirely justified morally'. (It is not clear why he wants to call this "loyalty" rather than "love", nor why he presumes our admiration is equivalent to moral approval.) His solution is, ultimately, to redefine "loyalty". Loyalty, he now says, is 'strictly speaking' only loyalty when it restricts itself to 'what is morally due the object of loyalty' and what is morally due is 'defined by the roles of the persons concerned'.[32] Thus he can conclude that 'a loyal Nazi is a contradiction in terms, although a loyal German is not'.

There is, of course, nothing in his original definition of loyalty that would allow him to draw such a distinction, and even his redefinition does not make clear how such a distinction is possible. What principle makes loyalty to nationality somehow 'morally due' and loyalty to a body that embodies a particular set of political, ideological or moral principles somehow not loyalty at all? Moreover, if, as his choice of examples (child, nation) suggests, the criterion of legitimate loyalty is to be whether or not something is a given of one's situation rather than something one has chosen, then why, for the German, must it be Germany rather than, say, Stuttgart or Europe? His is, however, a common assumption. Thus, Maistre dismissing cosmopolitanism:

> In my lifetime I have seen Frenchmen, Italians, Russians, etc.; thanks to Montesquieu, I even know that *one can be Persian*. But as for *man*, I declare that I have never in my life met him; if he exists, he is unknown to me.[33]

This is clever enough as a piece of rhetoric, but by the same argument Maistre never met a Frenchman either, since this too is an abstraction. There is no Frenchman without a specific age, socio-economic background, birthplace and so on. If, therefore, being French disqualifies one from counting as a man, surely being born in Paris disqualifies one from being French. For, if there is such a thing as a Frenchman (irrespective of where one is born in France), then surely there is such a thing as a man (irrespective of where one is born in the world). In short, if Maistre has never met a man, he has never met a Frenchman either. The point is not that nationality is not a given category, but only that it is no more a given category than any other, so that using its givenness as the basis of an "ought" that might override an "ought" deriving from any of these other categories is arbitrary. (That concept of "identity" that has so infatuated recent generations presents the same paradoxical wish: the wish to *elect* what is to *determine* one.)

However, even if Ladd could somehow establish that there are objects to which loyalty is 'morally due' and objects to which it is not, this still would not establish that loyalty to these other things is not loyalty and thus would not help to support his claim that loyalty per se has, as he says, 'inner value'.

Fletcher, too, asserts that we *should* be loyal, that there is a distinct 'ethic of loyalty' and that we must 'recognize the legitimacy of loyal bonds in the ethical life'.[34] Loyalty, he claims, 'is more than a habit of attachment; it is based on a recognition of duty'.[35] Unlike Ladd, however, he does not seek to extricate himself from the moral dilemmas that inevitably follow by redefining 'loyalty', though he does, like Ladd, assume that natural categories are somehow essential to the establishment of the moral status of loyalty per se. The idea of the existence of natural ethical categories is, indeed, essential to his argument about the moral value of loyalty. Our obligations, he claims, are determined by our particular 'identity', which is the 'historical self' we acquire by birth and upbringing.

> [The] historical self generates duties of loyalty toward the families, groups, and nations that enter into our self-definition. These duties may be understood as an expression of self-esteem and self-acceptance. To love myself, I must respect and cherish those aspects of myself that are bound up with others. Thus by the mere fact of my biography I incur obligations toward others, which I group under the general heading of loyalty. [. . .] In acting loyally, the self acts in harmony with its personal history. One recognizes who one is. Actions of standing by one's friends, family, nation, or people reveal that identity. The self sees in its action precisely what history requires it to do.[36]

Thus he claims that, while we cannot properly speak of those French soldiers who fought in the American War of Independence out of a commitment to the ideal of an American republic as fighting out of "loyalty", we can, nevertheless, legitimately claim that loyalty was the motive of those American Jews who went to fight in the 1948 Arab–Israeli War.[37] He thus extends Ladd's group of "natural" categories – family, nationality – to include ethnicity and, like Ladd, seems to exclude from "identity" any conscious choices you might make as an adult. It is not clear why this should be so, since such choices obviously both spring from what he calls one's past 'historical self' and constitute one's ongoing 'historical self'. (Does he feel that one's history is finished at a certain age?) Fletcher's claim that ethnicity is a relevant ethical category – that colour of skin *should* trump contents of character – is as much a matter of fiat as Ladd's claim for nationality.[38]

What is more puzzling, however, is his claim that we are morally obliged to be loyal. For he does not say merely that our particular upbringing leads us to feel certain obligations (which would be true), but rather that it actually morally obliges us to have those obligations. The only motive he mentions is the imperative to 'love myself'. However, while it has become a cliché that self-love is a precondition of loving others, there is no way this formula can be reversed, so that self-love becomes the goal of loving others, and still claim the status of a moral imperative (at least as measured by the apparent disinterest implicit in moral feeling) except, again, by fiat: loving yourself is, per se, a moral thing to do. Likewise, the consequence of acting loyally that he puts forward as justification – that 'One recognizes who one is' – does not seem to offer any way of morally discriminating between any kinds of behaviour. It might be, of course, that "Be what one is" is, for Fletcher, a categorical moral imperative, but it is hard to see anything like an imperative in an injunction to do what is, in any case, unavoidable.[39]

In fact, of course, Fletcher's conflation of what is with what should be, and his tautological imperative do run up against other aspects of his own moral sense. He is not actually prepared to defend the letter of his own avowed morality. (Rather as the implicit operative moral principles of some of the participants in the tram experiments turned out, when made explicit, to be morally counterintuitive to those same participants.) As already noted, Fletcher does not take Ladd's route of effectively redefining "loyalty" to mean "loyalty that does not produce bad consequences", and this leaves him with the obvious problem that there exist loyalties that do lead to consequences that he feels to be morally wrong. The case for loyalty, he says, requires 'modification': 'We could hardly insist on total commitment regardless of the evil that might follow.'[40] Moreover, there may come moments when 'the duties of [one's own] loyalty reach their limits', and 'the flattening pitch of moral impartiality overwhelms what we once thought were clear and compelling tones':[41]

> There is a moral danger in thinking that any concrete person or entity could become the ultimate source of right and wrong. . . . To counteract this danger, exit remains a critical supplement to the loyal voice. The commitment to voice could become a moral trap unless there are limits beyond which exit becomes the sensible turn.[42]

Interestingly, he cannot bring himself to say 'disloyalty' or 'betrayal', though this is precisely what the 'supplement' of 'exit' means in the present context. (Neither does he reflect on how comfortable he might feel about using an expression like 'the flattening pitch of impartial morality' were he describing, for example, a concentration camp guard's change of heart.) This need for euphemism and emotionally loaded language is a measure of his dilemma, which he describes as the difficulty of finding a way to establish 'the proper balance of loyalty and independent moral judgment'.[43] What, he believes, makes this question – 'When should justice and when should loyalty prevail?' – so hard even to formulate is that 'the ethic of loyalty is itself a species of morality'.[44]

However, the question is not so much hard as impossible to formulate. For what Fletcher is asking for is some form of moral sense capable of adjudicating between the sense that exhibits what he calls 'impartial morality' and the sense that exhibits what is, by his own definition, the "partial morality" of loyalty. It is here, in this incomprehensible phrase – "partial morality" – that we can discover the root of his problem. In the greater part of his account, he forestalls the problem by consistently drawing a contrast between the 'ethic of loyalty' and what are straw man caricatures of 'Kantianism' and 'Utilitarianism': cold, calculating attitudes, unconnected with human feeling. However, ultimately his 'species of morality' turns out to conflict, at least on the level of reflection, with other aspects of his moral feeling: his moral sense is in conflict with itself. It is inevitable that what he himself perceives as a *partial* morality should come into conflict with his own conception of morality.[45] The significant point, however, is that even after reflecting long enough on the topic to have written a book about it, he cannot help but feel that loyalty is a moral virtue.

Moreover, it is not the case that the feeling would be inexplicable except as a moral response. In some places in Fletcher's account, it is evidently simply affection that accounts for the strength of the feeling. What perhaps makes it easy to mistake affection for a 'species of morality' is the way in which it is almost universally acknowledged as something that must be taken into account with regard to morality. So that, for example, were I, in the tram situation, to choose my own child over five strangers, this would appear more *forgivable* than if I were to choose a single stranger against five strangers or my successful stockbroker over five strangers. You might feel that I had done wrong, but you would not brand me as a moral imbecile. You might wish to punish me, but the fact that it was my child would almost certainly count as a mitigating circumstance. This is not, however, because affection is a separate species of morality: if it is brought into the balance here, it is brought in precisely as a *counterweight* to the perceived demands of morality.

At one point in his exposition, Fletcher approvingly quotes the remark famously attributed to Camus: 'I believe in justice, but I will defend my mother before justice.'[46] He approves of it because he sees in it evidence of the way in which we are 'blessed with the capacity to reject the sirens of abstraction and to commit ourselves to the bonds of our immediate and concrete lives'.[47] However, in the context in which Camus said this – in answer to a question about where he stood on the Algerian question – it is wrong to speak of 'the sirens of abstraction', since, as an Algerian, he knew quite well that 'justice' in this context meant self-determination for a country that France had conquered by violence and was currently holding onto only by means of abuses of human rights that he had himself spoken out against. There is no question of abstraction here. He is saying that if it is necessary for a village suspected of aiding guerrillas fighting for independence to be bombed in order for his mother to remain safe, then he would prefer it to be bombed.[48]

Let us, at the risk of creating a rather absurd image, reduce this to a more fundamental level. Imagine Camus is at the controls of a runaway tram; he has a choice either to steer onto a line containing five people or onto a line containing his mother. Since he is, in Fletcher's words, 'blessed with the capacity to reject the sirens of abstraction', he steers the tram into the five. (I do not, of course, wish to suggest that Fletcher's thesis enables Camus to do so without any moral qualms, even if it does recommend that these qualms should be less if the five are, for example, not French or not of European ancestry.) Frankly, if you were to replace Camus's mother with my father in this scenario, I would do precisely the same thing. For, even if Camus never did say exactly the words that are attributed to him, nor ever actually acted on the principle they imply, I do say them and I have acted on that "principle": I prefer my father to justice.⁴⁹ Now imagine that Camus and I are together in the cab of the tram and the choice of who is to die on the tracks ahead is between his mother and my father. We will, of course, fight each other for the controls, though perhaps with little sense of animosity. The point is, of course, that not every conflict is a moral conflict.

Only if I were to fight him for control of the tram in order to steer it into his mother in order to save five strangers would it be possible to posit that one of us is acting morally. If such an action on my part seems somehow cold, particularly in contrast to the warm glow of admiration Camus's statement about his mother seems to elicit, it is only because he is present in this scenario and it is his feelings about his mother that we have been contemplating for the last few paragraphs. There is no reason to suppose that each of the five strangers is not also the mother of a loving child. There is, then, a certain asymmetry here. Camus's pronouncement strikes Fletcher and has struck many others, precisely as the statement of a moral standpoint: the expression of a principle. Yet once that principle is applied to practice, it becomes self-evident that there is nothing recognizably moral about it.

Might there, however, be some way to establish the moral status of loyalty (independent, that is, of the *feeling* that it is a moral feeling)? One way, of course, is by moral realism. Thus Waal, who defines "loyalty" as a bias in favour of the those nearest to us in natural kind (ourselves, our family, our community, etc.), asserts that this is a bias we *ought* to have – 'Loyalty is a moral duty' – and "proves" this, in fine circular fashion, by appealing to the fact that 'we find treason morally reprehensible'.⁵⁰ The claim is further underpinned by the thesis that evolution has "designed" us to be loyal, that is, that loyalty has a survival value for the species – making Waal's argument (unless he is recommending self-preservation as the goal of morality) another striking instance of the tendency among contemporary moral realists to make the "intentions" of evolution perform the role once played by the will of God.⁵¹

All moral feeling must, of course, come to this realist sticking point: "It's wrong because it's wrong". However, this appeal to a foundational feeling, a given of the context of any particular ethical discourse, seems strikingly absent in the case of loyalty. Other commonly acknowledged virtues (humility, kindness, temperance, honesty, rectitude, etc.) turn out, in contrast, to be relatively easy to justify in terms of their contribution to a common, and therefore uncontroversial, good. This is why, perhaps, the paeans to loyalty we have considered so far have been paeans: there is no *ethical* argument to be made in favour of loyalty.⁵² Is there, however, some way in which we could defend loyalty in terms of some form of common (or at least more common) good? Let us return to Royce's claim that there is 'only one way to be an ethical individual' and that is to choose your cause and stick to it. This formulation has at least the advantage over Ladd's or Fletcher's notion of natural loyalties in leaving you free to make an initial choice of what you feel is a "good" cause. The problem is, of course, that Royce also, and quite consistently with the notion of loyalty, makes it a further requirement that, having chosen your cause, you must then stick to it. For, it is the adjuration of further choice that constitutes loyalty. What I wish to pick up here, however, are two possible moral justifications for such a course of action that he hints at but does not develop; namely, that there is 'nothing better' than loyalty and that, among loyalties, 'No mortal knows which is the better for your world'.

Let us imagine that, given that we cannot be sure of the consequences of our action, we decide that the best thing for us to do to achieve the common good is to choose whatever seems the best existing cause at the moment and add our weight to that. On the same principle of lack of omniscience, we might continue to add our weight to that cause, despite misgivings, from the same doubts about our power to discern what really will ultimately turn out to have been for the greatest good.[53] (A more plausible kind of Pascal's wager in which what is committed is behaviour rather than belief.) Loyalty might then be morally justified by appeal to the common good: perhaps the greatest good for the greatest number of those included in my common good will come about if we all opt for and stick with what at least at one time seemed the most likely route to that common good. We can see that some of what this commitment entails may appear to run counter to the present common good, and it may increasingly appear so with the passage of time, but, given the initial difficulty, with our limited foresight, of choosing any commitment, we remain with the one we chose, with the moral satisfaction of knowing that thereby we are at least trying to, remotely, achieve a greater good even if we cannot be sure we have chosen the best way of doing so.

This may, indeed, be a fair picture of a good deal of the experience of loyalty. However, there are two problems with the motivation outlined as a justification of loyalty. The first is that if such a thing as an initial moral choice is possible, there is no reason to preclude the possibility of further choices. If one really is aiming at the common good, there is always the possibility of a moment arriving in which one perceives that the balance of probability has tipped against one's loyalty to this object being the best way to achieve that common good. At this point, the choice becomes the familiar one between loyalty and the common good.

The second problem with this defence of loyalty is that it is not, of course, a defence of loyalty. One has only been 'acting as if' loyal to a certain cause. While your behaviour, as "loyalty", appeared to prioritize your cause above the common good, in fact it was motivated by the belief that the success of that cause would enhance the common good: the cause itself, then, was a means rather than an end. This moral justification of loyalty is then only a justification of a fictionalist version of loyalty, not of the real thing.

What, however, if your cause really does serve to enhance the common good? In other words, surely, loyalty to a good cause is good loyalty. Here again, however, what we are dealing with is a fiction of loyalty. For, as with the scenario described above, if the common good really is the object aimed at, then we would expect the agent to betray that cause ('exit the loyalty', as Fletcher might say) the moment it palpably came into conflict with the common good; in other words, we would not be justified in expecting them to display loyalty for loyalty's sake at all. What is good about such apparent "loyalty" to a good cause is precisely that it is not really loyalty at all but rather a settled habit of acting for the common good. The appearance of loyalty is merely a side effect.

It might, of course, be argued that loyalty is pragmatically necessary to achieve a balance of everyone's interests. Thus, for example, in a world where partiality towards one's own children is almost universal, we do not blame a person for partiality towards their own child, since, in the context, anything less would be tantamount to positive neglect. However, such an argument presumes a bird's-eye view of the general good

– from which viewpoint loyalty takes on a purely instrumental value in terms of that good. The loyal individual, by contrast, is precisely not motivated by a desire for the common good. There is, therefore, no more reason to admire loyalty on these grounds than there would be to admire the motivation of an arsonist just because their actions *unintentionally* prevented the spread of a plague.

How, then, does loyalty come to be regarded as a virtue? What is the lure that can lead even professors of philosophy and law in their reflective moments into making so elementary a mistake as collapsing that distinction – between what *is* and what *should be* – upon which the very idea of the thing we call "morality" depends? There are two phenomena to account for here. First, how it is possible to experience one's own self-conscious loyalties as moral responses. Second, how it is possible to admire loyalty in others.

The difficulty of accounting for the moral tenor of loyalty should not be underestimated, given the way in which it can be so obviously self-serving. There are, for instance, those cases where, while the agents themselves may take pride in their own loyalty, to the spectator the motivation appears to be no more than an extension of self-interest to include what one considers one's own. Consider, for example, the abusive parents who nevertheless fiercely, and with obvious partiality, uphold the rights of their children in the public domain – and admire themselves for doing so. Similarly self-deceptive, though more readily socially sanctioned, is the pride that people can take in their loyalty to their own "natural" groups (to the extent, as we have seen earlier, of trying, vainly, to identify this loyalty with a general moral principle). Though here again the self-deception may be quite apparent to an observer. For the palpable motive is that one values x (country, race, institution, group) precisely because one belongs to it: asserting its superior value to comparable objects is simply a way of asserting one's own superior value. In short, it is a form of snobbery.

Moreover, the very prestige of morality itself (the "value" of morality) as a brute fact of the context in which every moral response occurs should not be overlooked. One obvious way in which a problem such as Fletcher's might arise is not so much from a desire to champion the claims of affection (pointless though such a championing might be) but rather from the desire that in doing so one should also be championing morality. Fletcher, for example, wants his desire to 'be what he is' (whatever that may be) to be a moral matter; he wants the triumphs of affection to be moral triumphs. He could avoid the aporia of his conclusion simply by not trying to assert that we 'should' be loyal, or that there is such a thing as an 'ethic of loyalty'. The problem, then, might not be what it at first seems. Perhaps it is not that Fletcher is too eager to sacrifice morality to loyalty, but rather that he is too attached to the *appearance* of morality to allow that he is strongly motivated by and admiring of something that is, even by his own account, an obstacle to morality. (It is not enough for Fletcher that Camus is simply stating a fact – "I will defend my mother before justice" – he must also, impossibly, be positing a principle.) However, this conviction that one's own strongest impulses must be, by virtue of their strength, justifiable in terms of the common good (i.e. self-righteousness) is still a moral feeling.

What motive might be strong enough to allow one to deceive oneself in these ways? Affection might easily do so, of course, but affection cannot be identified with loyalty.

(No one admires themselves for their *sincere* affections.) Fletcher seeks to identify the two in quoting Camus, but I know it is quite possible to be aware of having such a preference without feeling it is necessary to morally justify it, let alone raise it to the status of a virtue.

Such aggrandizement of the self through the masquerade of selflessness is unlikely to appear admirable to anyone but the agent themselves. It is only where the self-deception is truly profound that an observer is likely to agree with the agent in the agent's ascription of loyalty (as a virtue) to themselves. The sense in which it is more profoundly self-deceptive, is that, while the proprietorial, snobbish or self-righteous forms of loyalty are mainly experienced as a sense of one's superiority to others and principally oriented outwards, towards the admiration one feels is one's due, this "purer" loyalty is that loyalty that is mainly experienced as a demand made on oneself and is oriented inwards, towards securing one's own approval.[54] At this point some form of self-sacrifice, or at least the experience of feeling disposed to make some form of self-sacrifice, becomes absolutely essential to securing this approval. For here one seeks to avoid both the trouble of choosing and the possible pain of taking responsibility for what one chooses, by identifying one's will with something more "objective" than one's will. I assert to myself that some object is placing demands upon me merely by existing. In this way, all loyalty seems to feed on the very prestige of the common good that the agent still recognizes but quite self-consciously rejects. This rejection itself is, from the agent's point of view, part of the way in which the value of their object of loyalty "asserts itself".

It is, then, the very commitment to the object of loyalty that gives the object its value, which value then justifies the commitment. This is what those who champion loyalty as the appropriate moral response to certain "natural" or "appointed" objects overlook: that it is the followers who make the leader.[55] Loyalty, it is said, ennobles the self by subordinating self-interest. But it is in the interest of the self to create an object loyalty to which will ennoble that self. The object becomes a thing worth sacrificing one's life to because it is an object that people (oneself, for example) will sacrifice their lives to.

There is, then, an obvious draw to a suprapersonal good in terms of the subject's desire to somehow objectify their willing, even while taking responsibility for that willing. Indeed, this trap of self-deception is unavoidable from the moment one begins to think of oneself as somehow responsible for one's morality: when one starts to think of one's moral response as something one is choosing rather than something that is happening to one. Even Kant does not escape:

> [So] *little displeasure* is there in [respect for the law] that, once one has laid self-conceit aside and allowed practical influence to that respect, one can in turn never get enough of contemplating the majesty of this law, and the soul believes itself elevated in proportion as it sees the holy elevated above itself and its frail nature.[56]

The loyal person, in electing their good as something separate from the sense of common good that just comes to them, is aiming for just this consciousness of possessing an "elevated soul".

We have already seen, in the last chapter, that a *disinterested* desire for the common good, implicit though it appears to be in the way the moral response is experienced, does not exhaust what is implied by the full range of such responses. We must be wary, then, of disallowing the agent's experience of the virtuousness of their loyalty from the domain of morality. Loyalty is, after all, experienced as concern for a suprapersonal good. Moreover, there remains the question of how we can admire loyalties we do not actually feel – the spectacle of loyalty – which is also the question of how the obvious self-interest underpinning the manifestations of loyalty outlined earlier can be disguised from the self. For loyalty would obviously not bind anyone were it not a potential draw to everyone. That is, it is evident that, in feeling loyalty, the agent is, in a sense, admiring the spectacle of their own loyalty.

First, however, there is one possible explanation that must be dismissed. This involves our admiration of what is only "loyalty" from our point of view, but not from that of the agent themselves: not unconscious loyalty as it was defined earlier (which strikes us simply as epistemic failure) but rather what is loyalty from our point of view but commitment to the common good from the agent's point of view. It may not correspond to our own common good, but we perceive it as the agent's concern for the common good *as far as they can conceive it*. What the spectacle presents us with, then, is what is, even for us, a "good" motivation. There is, however, no way in which this could be the grounds of admiration for self-conscious loyalty, nor, indeed, for the strength of affection exhibited in Camus fighting me for the controls of the tram. There is no way *we* can make the common good identical with the survival of Camus's mother. Indeed, not even Camus can do this, which is precisely why he can draw a contrast between the welfare of his mother and justice.

Our potential admiration for this particular spectacle of "loyalty" is, then, not germane insofar as it is, by definition, not loyalty from the agent's point of view. Neither is it the kind of "loyalty" that could be recommended to any agent within the context of that conception of the common good, since, within that context, the actions entailed would not be the exhibition of loyalty: they would represent not the possession of *a* virtue but simply of virtue. This, then, is an instance in which we admire loyalty as a spectacle but only because it is not loyalty. Moreover, it is not a "loyalty" one could admire in oneself, since it does not appear to the agent as loyalty.

Perhaps the simplest explanation of our admiration of the spectacle of what is genuinely loyalty would be that we identify with the motive – the desire to possess a clear "objective" good that both simplifies choice and appears to render an increased "significance" to our actions. However, since it is not necessarily our own loyalty that we are admiring, there must be something to prevent us fully acknowledging this identification: logically at least, somebody dying for *x* hardly shows us that *y* is worth dying for. How, then, is the spectator (like the agent) distracted from acknowledging the motive of loyalty?

Here again, the champions of loyalty are themselves inadvertently helpful. For, as we have seen, the aspect of loyalty that they constantly emphasize is the extent to which it involves a transcendence of self-interest.[57] Thus Royce, in exemplifying loyalty, reaches at once for the martyr, the patriot dying for their country, and the captain ready to go down with his ship.[58] As he says, 'Loyalty without self-control is impossible'.[59] Foremost in his mind, then, when he thinks of loyalty is the (cause-unspecified) martyr rising above his desire for life, rather than that martyr's executioner, who may be equally loyally struggling, in the name of civic or national duty, to rise above a deep-seated repugnance to taking human life in cold blood. Both may be acting out of loyalty but, from the spectator's point of view, it is easier to imagine that it is the martyr who is making the greater sacrifice.[60] Where, then, it is this aspect of self-sacrifice that most strikingly appears in the scenario of loyalty, it may be that what is brought most vividly to mind is precisely one of the ways in which we measure the effect of morality per se: the overcoming of self-interest.[61]

There is another aspect to this identification of sacrifice per se with morality; one that also depends upon the vividness of the impression. It appears in the way in which Ladd and Fletcher anchor their arguments for the morality of loyalty in notions of natural categories or the 'historical self'. If we approach loyalty from this side, we are prone to see it principally as a consequence of what would generally be considered natural affections – which is, indeed, the motive of much, though not all, of the behaviour we would generally characterize as loyalty. (Even though to the agents themselves – Ladd's hypothetical mother, or Camus, for example – their motive is not loyalty but love.) Given this perception, then, disloyalty will necessarily appear principally as a sign of a deficiency in natural affection. Moreover, a deficiency in natural affection appears so clear an indication of a lack of human sympathy – that willingness to balance self-interest with the interests of others – that it seems impossible that a person who exhibits it could be capable of moral feeling at all. (That is, we imagine ourselves, with our affections, in their place and judge this hypothetical other as we would judge ourselves.) It is not, then, that loyalty to any particular thing is evidence of the kind of acknowledgement of others' claims that appears essential to a moral disposition, but rather that disloyalty, seen as lack of affection where it might be expected, seems evidence of the lack of such a disposition.[62]

The attractiveness of any particular instance of what we discern as loyalty appears to depend, then, not so much on the object of the loyalty as on the comparative vividness of either the motive or the imagined consequences. So that, for example, if I told you that I had once, during wartime, flown several dangerous bombing missions over foreign cities, this piece of information might elicit a range of reactions from admiration, through grudging respect, to an enquiry about the justice of the war. Conversely, if I told you that I had once, during wartime and under orders, entered enemy territory and there taken a brick and smashed out a baby's brains in order to intimidate the enemy into surrendering, I might reasonably expect the reaction to be quite different. And yet the fundamental difference, measured in consequences, is that in the latter case it was only one baby. Moreover, if we presume that I possess what is (by contemporary standards) a natural degree of squeamishness, the actual degree of loyalty I demonstrate in the latter case is far greater. Once again, distance, if only imaginative, turns out to be decisive.

This is also, of course, a matter of whether the loyalty strikes us from the viewpoints either of the loyal agent or the object of that agent's loyalty or from the viewpoint of one who suffers from that loyalty. In this connection, it is worth considering the fate of the words "loyalty" and "duty" in many countries since the beginning of the twentieth century. Royce, in 1907, might have felt irresistibly drawn to the word "loyalty", insofar as it principally conjured up for him images of knights and stalwart captains, perhaps Poynter's *Faithful unto Death*, but by the middle of that century this positive moral aura had been fairly well dissipated by the vividness of examples of what loyalty per se might entail. This is a matter of the "moral climate" of the place and moment. However, moral responses, as I have observed before, *happen to* us, not irrespective of, but certainly not determined by, the self we wish to identify with. Thus, for example, one may judge the fictional representation of a particular loyalty as morally objectionable, on the grounds that the loyalty that is represented is loyalty to a cause that morally repels one, but one does so precisely because one has found that representation of loyalty per se so alluring. Indeed, the vehemence of one's objection may be directly proportional to the degree of allure one experiences.[63]

Conclusion

I have suggested that, while no system built upon what is consistent in moral experience will ever arrive at the desire/aversion that underlies that experience, this desire/aversion might still be discovered through looking at moral experience in its totality: including both what appears amenable to systematization of the kind that makes moral *judgements* possible and also what renders such systematization impossible, in the sense of producing conflicts between particular moral judgements and that experience of moral responses from which the principles underlying those judgements are derived. A *moral* aversion to being personally responsible for harm, even at the cost of greater harm, is one aversion that emerged in the previous chapter. In terms of morality as the desire that, independently of my own goals or interests, harm should not happen, this aversion, as a specifically moral aversion, is an anomaly, yet its effects are also so predictable as to be routine: it constitutes a norm, the contravention of which would predictably appear cold-blooded. Moreover, as I suggested in the last chapter, it could not be called "anomalous" in every culture, since in some it is an avowed moral principle. Furthermore, it will not do dismiss such an aversion as "the human element", since the principle (the minimization of harm) it comes into conflict with is simply the abstract formulation of what is also a "human element", one that is implicit in the form of the moral response itself. Such conflicts are never a matter of feeling versus rationality, for there is no moral response that is not anomalous in relation to what we perceive as our own interests: no rational moral response. This is precisely what is meant by calling moral responses "disinterested".

In the present chapter we have encountered two more instances of moral feeling that are difficult to reconcile with what the moral response itself appears to imply. The first was the tendency to morally condemn agents for their mental states, either irrespective of their actions or, in the case of evil, disproportionately to any conceivable mental state. The second was the perception of certain states of mind as morally good *in themselves*, irrespective of the potential consequences of those states. However, before turning to the similarities between this phenomenon and that examined in the last chapter, it is worth noting the differences. Principal among these is that there we encountered an aversion/desire that gave rise to the apparent moral anomaly of finding more harm morally preferable to less, if it means avoiding a vivid sense of that harm or one's own responsibility for it, while here the anomaly (the conflict between two apparently implicit goals in the responses of the same subject) arises from the way in which we experience as moral responses feelings that set aside the balance of harm for an object that is clearly *dependent on our own goals or interests.*

In the case of the perception of "sins of thought" and of evil, the response is clearly motivated by fear. That is, the fear is not a distortion of the response but a constituent of it. It cannot be said, then, to be fear of the immoral (since the moral, as other moral responses imply it, is clearly itself overridden by the ignoring of consequences) but rather by fear of the existence of harm itself, to the extent that what is merely symbolic of such harm becomes itself the object of moral condemnation but purely *as symbolic* (i.e. even in the absence of the possibility of concrete harm). It could be argued that what is involved here is merely 'emotional spillage': that the condemnation can be plausibly traced simply to an inability to *not* imagine consequences. Thus, the feeling might be said to still evince a disinterested concern that harm should not happen. After all, fear can express itself as anger or love as jealousy; perhaps this is a case of a disinterested concern that harm should not happen expressing itself as fear expressing itself as a moral response. However, the analogy is misleading. We say that this anger arises from fear and this jealousy from love; however, the anger is not itself fear nor the jealousy love. By contrast, in the case of the moral response, what is experienced in these instances of finding a state of mind per se "immoral" is precisely a moral response. This suggests that whatever the moral response is it is already something other than the disinterested concern that harm should not happen that it appears to imply.

It is not, then, a matter of one feeling mistaking itself for another. We cannot make a mistake in our responses, unless, in attributing them to the effect of a certain object, we have misperceived that object. There are those who, both immediately and on reflection, really feel that a mental state can be wrong in itself, just as Williams's Jim, both immediately and on reflection, really feels it is wrong to shoot the Indian. Moreover, it is important to constantly bear in mind that it is not a matter of the "human element": that the utilitarian option, or, in Gaut's case, the consequentialist option would somehow itself be more "rational". No moral response, as we have seen, is explicable, except in terms of what we feel is given (and, thus, exempt from the domain of rationality). These mental states are, for the subject who finds them so, wrong in themselves, just as the greatest balance of happiness or misery appear as right or wrong in themselves in those responses that do appear to manifest these objects as their goals. What this seems to indicate is that, in certain instances, fear is actually *constitutive* of the moral response.

The same point also holds for the perception of certain mental states as virtuous in themselves, even though, as we have seen, in this case the element of self-interest is far more explicit than is the case with the objects of condemnation discussed earlier. Indeed, the desire that gives rise to our admiration of loyalty, both as we feel it in ourselves and, under certain conditions, as we perceive it in others, is so plainly exhibited by the character of loyalty itself (as 'partial morality') that it must be counted something of a wonder that it could ever possibly be perceived as sufficiently "disinterested" to count as moral feeling. Yet, it is. For, as we have seen, despite the obvious self-interest that gives rise to loyalty, it is principally experienced as a demand made on oneself (or, where admired in others, as a demand made on the self). It is experienced as *not* a matter of pleasure or interest but as a response to an external demand arising from the mere existence of what is "bigger" than oneself: an objective value. Thus, it objectifies my willing, though, since I choose loyalty, it allows me to still experience that willing as my own and, thus, take credit for it: it is not merely my choice and yet I am choosing. The same, of course, is true of the canonical ascetic virtues – temperance, chastity, patience – which, like all ascetic practices, smack of a covert will to power. Indeed, all of the virtues, not as they might be abstractly defined, but as they are *consciously* practised and admired, may be interpreted in terms of self-interest. Diligence, as rejection of autonomy, may be the most intense sloth; conscious humility is palpably a form of pride and so on. (Indeed, the non-canonical but currently popular virtue of *integrity* would have done just as well as loyalty to illustrate the theme of this chapter.) However, there are two ways we might regard the kind of standing motivations that are usually referred to as "virtues": as instrumentally valuable in relation to the morally valuable or as morally valuable in themselves. It is only in the latter, and perhaps more common, sense that virtues give rise to the kind of moral anomalies that we are currently pursuing.

At the same time, the moral anomaly contained in loyalty forms an even greater contrast with the cases examined in the last chapter than do the anomalies involved in condemning mental states or in other potentially self-deceiving virtues. For Williams's Jim it was a matter of recognizing a common good but feeling that it demanded an action that was felt to be morally worse than the neglect of that good. Loyalty, by contrast, is not perceived simply as a matter of the lesser of two evils; rather, it is regarded as a positive good. The loyal individual may be ashamed of the consequences of their loyalty but never of the loyalty itself. Loyalty is something people positively take pride in (it might, indeed, be defined as "pride in one's own partiality") even if, as we have seen, it often contains an element of defiance that bespeaks some consciousness of culpability or, at least, inconsistency. Philosophers have even championed loyalty, despite the difficulties that emerge once one tries to assert its moral status in a form of discourse (ethics) that must, necessarily, contain a more common good as a given. Indeed, there is an inherent absurdity in trying to *sell* loyalty per se through argument; hence the way in which the authors considered here must constantly fall back on rhetoric. This is not, of course, to claim that normative ethics can ever be anything other than rhetorical, but only that, where it is a matter of principles that could be made universal, it is much easier to rely on one's audience's existing moral feeling, so that the rhetoric is far less conspicuous than in the case of a partial morality.

If moral responses do point to a single desired goal, then the moral condemnation of states of mind and the moral admiration of partiality do appear to demonstrate that most characteristically human trait: the preference for what is symbolic of an end over what might actually be a real contribution to that end. This might suggest that the ostensible goal is actually a cover for the real goal that the totality of our real moral responses points to, though such a hypothesis still leaves us with the problem of accounting for that ostensible goal, particularly given that, as we saw with loyalty, the feeling that the virtue is a good in itself may come into conflict with our sense of another end that is also, and incompatibly, good in itself. It might also, of course, be that the admiration of certain virtues represents the subject's lack of faith in the possibility of whatever wider end is implicit in the rest of their moral responses and consequent willingness to settle for what can vividly represent it in imagination. However, it must be born in mind that all moral responses appear to be responses to what is symbolic. That is, unless the harm involved is a harm to me or to those upon whose welfare my own depends, then the response has already exceeded what interest might account for except in terms of that harm's symbolic value to me.

It is important to emphasize that the anomalies examined in this chapter and the last have not been a matter of any consistent principle running up against conflicts between judgement and response, or even of the conflicting moral responses of different people; rather, they have been a matter of conflicts within the moral responses of the same individual. This is why I previously suggested that the real implicit "Good" (the object of the desire/aversion registered by the moral response), if it can be elicited in the same person by what are, even for that person, incompatible "goods", may not actually be one that, where it made explicit, they would recognize as morally "good". That is, what is desired must be capable of inspiring other desires for what is instrumental but not acknowledged as such. Thus, it appears that the desire or aversion that the moral response signifies is not explicit in the form that response takes *from the subject's point of view* (most clearly, of course, in instances such as the obviously self-interested virtues of others). Hence, the systematization of the way in which the moral response is experienced does not generate a desire/aversion (greatest happiness/least harm) that will actually cover all moral responses. Moreover, we should not forget the perennial struggle of philosophy to bring the world into line with our feelings about it by showing that the moral response is somehow not a matter of desire/aversion at all.

5

Disregarding intentions and materialist ethics

Disregarding intentions

The last chapter dealt with the way in which moral responses can be responses to an inferred state of the agent's mind. We saw there both how the symbolic value of this inferred state of mind can *morally* outweigh consideration of real consequences and how this symbolic value appears to be rooted in self-interest (fear, self-aggrandizement). From the point of view of what the moral response, in its felt character, appears to imply (the disinterested desire that harm should not happen) this phenomenon may appear a form of fetishization of the will. However, this "perversion" (from the point of view of what can be systematized in ethics) is one that might appear to spring quite naturally from the emphasis that must inevitably fall upon the will once we begin to reflect on what qualifies a response as a *moral* response. For, although it is quite natural to speak of morally good or bad actions, a little reflection soon reveals that "good" and "bad", in a moral sense, apply unconditionally only to the intentions of the actor.[1] That is, no matter how good an action is in its effects, we do not attribute a moral intention to the person performing it if we know that they are acting from self-interest, nor do we hold somebody morally responsible for what is beyond their control, for what *happens to* them. This is why rationales for acting morally – in terms of social usefulness, rationality, personal happiness, our own aversion to harm to ourselves and so on – will, unless they are put forward merely as side effects, inevitably sound amoral. It is also why, if we try to imagine scenarios in which such apparently definitively "bad" actions as, for example, lying, stealing or killing might be the right thing to do, we inevitably find ourselves mentally experimenting with the possible motivation of the agent. It appears, then, that moral responses are essentially responses to the manifest or supposed motivation of the agent involved.

Thus, without claiming that the phenomena dealt with in the last chapter actually are instances of the ideal of moral willing implied by the way in which we perceive such willing (the implicit self-interest prevents that), nevertheless, it is fairly easy to see how they can appear to be such. What are perhaps more difficult to account for are those moral responses that are the subject of the first part of the present chapter: moral responses that are predominantly determined by the consequences of an action irrespective of motivation.

For, despite the fact that a reference to intention appears to be an operative principle necessarily implicit in moral responses as such, and is certainly embodied in those "moral principles" that most would be willing to consciously espouse, it is quite commonplace for our actual moral responses to fail to be commensurate with such a reference. Think, for example, of a woman who gets into a car drunk and drives home. It is reprehensible, no doubt, but it is unlikely to inspire more than a few raised eyebrows among her acquaintances, and, retrospectively, a sense in herself either that she was a little irresponsible or that she is a bit of a card. Now, think of the same scenario, but this time she hits and kills a child – an accident she could have avoided if she had been sober. For most people, what she has done in the second scenario feels worse than what she did in the first: the act of drunk driving seems to become more culpable *in itself* if the driver hits someone. (And even more culpable *in itself* still if the person hit is perceived as especially vulnerable – as if some human beings stood a better chance than others against 2 tonnes of metal travelling at 90 kilometres per hour.) Indeed, it is not unusual for us to spontaneously assign culpability to an action in proportion not to the intentions of the agent but to the seriousness of its consequences.[2] So commonplace is this "inconsistency" that it is even institutionalized: many legal systems reserve a heavier penalty for murder than for attempted murder, which may give rise to such prima facie counterintuitive situations as the culpability of x's action towards y depending entirely on the medical skill of z.

There is, moreover, a corresponding tendency to excuse intentions that would otherwise appear culpable, where there are no consequences, though this is generally more idiosyncratic in operation than the tendency to blame by consequences. The same person who might fantasize about righteously beating to a pulp the person who has picked his pocket could equally be merely amused at someone trying to pick that same pocket when it was empty. (Of course, extreme ineptitude in a criminal attempt also seems to lessen our urge to blame, though here it seems to be a matter of our sense of the ineffectuality of the will involved. Significantly, however, this mitigating effect ceases to operate – emotionally, if not legally – where the actual consequences, even if unintended, are dire.) Even the law may reflect something of this indulgence. Rescher offers the example of the innocent villain, who burgles the house of his absent grandfather, only to subsequently discover that the old man had previously died and made him his heir: so that the property he has "stolen" was already his own.[3] (The law, however, as we shall see later, may be a poor guide to general feeling in such matters.) Where the consequences are positively good, the effect will be more pronounced. Consider, for example, the probable response to promise breaking in the case of a child who, having expressly undertaken not to spend any of its lunch money on lottery tickets, nevertheless did so and won enough to keep its family in luxury for the rest of their lives, compared to the probable response to the same promise breaking where the child had lost or won just enough to make itself sick on sweets.

The same inconsistency is to be found with praise. Imagine that a man risks his life by diving into a dangerous flood to save a baby. No doubt, he would be universally praised for his selfless courage. But imagine if, upon reaching the infant, it turned out to be merely a life-sized dolly of a baby. His kinder acquaintances, even if they had been present and also believed that the dolly was a real child, would probably avoid mentioning the incident ever again. Yet, the virtue in the previous case lies entirely in the man's motivation rather than in the consequences. For, if he had died in a failed attempt to save a real child – so that the consequences of his action would be identical to his having done nothing – he would still be honoured as someone who had done a good thing. Nevertheless, in the case of the dolly, the very same motivation and courage that appears to be the source of the admiration now counts for nothing. All this is not to say that we would not think that we *should* measure the worth of the action by the man's motivation, but only that we would have to consciously remind ourselves to do so.

Of course, this assigning of blame or praise by consequences irrespective of intentions may be carried to absurd lengths. There are people (I wish I were making this up) who, if you were in a train accident and became disabled, and your disability caused them inconvenience, would blame you for not having caught a different train. There are even people who will blame you for the immoral actions of your ancestors or take pride in the moral achievements of their own: who will assign guilt and assume merit where there is not even the possibility of intention/responsibility. However, even this side of such egregious stupidity, the tendency to assign blame and praise in terms of consequences is still sufficiently general for us to discern an operative moral principle in that tendency – even though it is, on reflection, morally counterintuitive. This principle is that moral culpability is proportional to consequences irrespective of intention.

Although there is a temptation to extend the instances of this phenomenon to the history of the law, even the most apparently glaring examples of blaming the innocent may in fact be other than they appear. Where, for example, the idea of collective responsibility is codified into law, it may be a matter either of deterrence or of a genuinely held belief that if one member of a particular group has revealed themselves to be capable of the crime, this is proof of the criminal nature of the whole group to which that individual belongs. The punishment of animals, on the other hand, would seem a fairly clear case of misplaced blame, though it, too, can become problematic on further inspection.[4] For example, tempting as it would be, from the point of vivid anecdote, to bring forward Evans's *Criminal Prosecution and Capital Punishment of Animals* to show that blame by consequences can be more than merely a momentary aberration, it must be granted that most of the cases Evans considers take place against a background of either sustained antecedent anthropomorphism or belief in demonic possession and are, therefore, quite "rational" in terms of the normal parameters of blame.

Moreover, as was suggested earlier, what appears to be punishment cannot always be equated with blame. That the innocent are made to suffer does not necessarily indicate that they are not thought to be innocent. The punishment of the children of the guilty, for example, may be decreed simply because it is perceived as a particularly effective deterrent and thus necessary for the greater good.[5] (Many today, of course, still do appeal to this argument to justify the destruction of the harmless, even at the risk of the loss of innocent life.) This deterrent intention is particularly evident where, as is often the case, the causing of harm by negligence is punished as seriously as the same harm caused deliberately – as, for example, in the case of the accidental breaking of a taboo that is felt essential to the maintenance of the greater good.[6] A concern for the greater good also lies behind the "punishment" of a blameless agent who is the cause of harm that is yet acknowledged to be both accidental and unavoidable, where this "punishment" is seen as the only way to appease the feelings of those – living, dead or immortal – who suffered the harm.

It is easy, then, to misinterpret the extent to which any particular law actually embodies the principle of blame by consequences, either because we may overlook the extent to which agency is conceived to be involved (as with the animal cases) or because we may mistake the intention of the law (as with cases where considerations of deterrence or appeasement outweigh questions of culpability). The French court's decision to raze the house of Henry IV's assassin to the ground has an obvious propaganda purpose that Xerxes's thrashing of the Hellespont for destroying his bridge (if it happened) does not.[7] Nevertheless, several codes of law do, in fact, indirectly provide evidence for the ubiquity of the phenomenon of consequentialist blame, simply by virtue of containing express prohibitions on actions arising from such blaming; thus demonstrating both that the phenomenon is common enough to warrant prohibition and that it is perceived (in terms of the systematic application of that community's concept of justice) as itself culpable.[8]

Indeed, the lack of moral justification for blaming by consequences can often be found implicitly recognized even by those who are doing the blaming. As Kames says, 'human nature is not so perverse' as to punish the innocent 'without veil or disguise', and the 'disguise' that we find in blaming by consequences takes the form of a *wilful epistemic failure*.[9] That is, blaming by consequences is not a matter of seeking redress irrespective of any perception of the agent's guilt. Rather, it seems as if the perception of the harm involved *causes* the ascription of responsibility: it really is a case of blaming, and the harm sought or willed as redress is genuinely conceived of as punishment. Thus, not only does the vividness of the harm distort (from the perspective of the subject's usual criteria for responsibility) the subject's perception of how responsible the agent was, but it also leads to a distortion (again from the perspective of the subject's usual criteria) of what will count as evidence for another's state of mind. In short, the worse the outcome, the more likely the agent is to be credited with a deliberate intention to produce that outcome, or the more likely normal behaviour is to be interpreted as negligence.[10] It appears, then, that the subject strives to avoid the moral perversity of blaming the innocent by whatever epistemic shifts are required to justify the ascription of responsibility to the agent. From the point of view of a more impartial spectator, or even from the point of the same subject in a calmer mood, such dodges may appear absurd, but under the influence of the desire to blame they pass for justice.

It should be noted, however, that although I have described this epistemic failure as 'wilful', nevertheless, since it is not a matter of error, we must presume that, like any other cognitive bias, it is not something the subject consciously elects to do but, rather, something that happens to them as the result of a strong interest. Indeed, we most naturally associate blaming by consequences with situations in which the subject responds under the palpable influence of, for example, anger, fear or grief. Ironically, then, the very culpability of blaming by consequences presents a problem (one shared by cognitive biases in general) for the concept of responsibility. This, however, is a question we shall return to later.

The best-known twentieth-century treatment of the perceived inconsistency of consequentialist blaming is that by Nagel, who took up the issue under the slightly misleading title of 'moral luck': 'Where a significant aspect of what someone does depends on factors beyond his control, yet we continue to treat him in that respect as an object of moral judgment, it can be called moral luck.'[11] He observes that while it is 'intuitively plausible that people cannot be morally assessed for what is not their fault, or for what is due to factors beyond their control', in fact the 'irrational tendency' to do so is commonplace.[12] He distinguishes four ways in which 'the natural objects of moral assessment are disturbingly subject to luck': the kind of person one happens to be, the kinds of circumstances one finds oneself in, the way in which 'one is determined by antecedent circumstances', and the way in which one's actions and projects turn out.[13] The first and third of these appear to be effectively identical in terms of the extent of responsibility involved and also to raise problems about the notion of responsibility per se that go beyond the present topic of inconsistencies within the same moral sense. The second – circumstantial luck – does not seem particularly problematic; given that moral responses are emotional, we would expect there to be such a "discrepancy", since we receive a far more vivid impression from the accomplishment of an action than from the intention or potential to accomplish it. This leaves us with the fourth category: 'luck in the way one's actions and projects turn out'.

Nagel's examples are analogous to those we have already considered: the difference in the perceived culpability of negligence depending on the result, blame for blameless accidental harm, lack of admiration for unsuccessful as opposed to successful heroism and so on. 'From the point of view which makes responsibility dependent on control', Nagel observes, such 'judgments', as he calls the moral responses involved, must appear 'absurd'.[14] Yet, such 'judgements' are also incorrigible; 'we may be persuaded that these moral judgments are irrational, but they reappear involuntarily as soon as the argument is over'.[15] At the same time, Nagel feels that we cannot simply conclude that the 'condition of control' is false, since this condition is not merely a generalization from certain clear cases but, rather, seems intuitively correct however far it is extended: we instinctively feel that we can only be held responsible for what is within our control.[16] The distinction that I drew earlier between moral responses (which routinely embody a principle of 'moral luck') and moral judgements (which cannot) would certainly be helpful here but would not actually solve what Nagel describes as the real 'philosophical problem' that the existence of 'moral luck' represents. For even calling an intended action "good" or "bad" is a matter of moral response.

In what sense, though, is this inconsistency, this 'absurdity', actually a philosophical problem? After all, the fact that I will swear at a frozen computer hardly seems to represent a philosophical problem (unless I believe my feelings in general to be essentially rational in relation to my interests). Similar inconsistencies run throughout our feelings, not just our moral ones. There would only be a philosophical problem here if this were a matter of a conflict between beliefs; but, as we have seen, while a moral response may appear to express a conviction that something is the case independently of how I feel about it, it is also significantly unlike the formation of a belief. What seems, then, to make the inconsistency appear to Nagel in the guise of a philosophical problem is a certain underlying commitment to moral realism on his part, a reflex that, as we have seen, runs through even the most 'subjectivist' ethics.

Thus, Nagel introduces the example of leaving a bath running with a baby in it, precisely to make the point that 'one will realize, as one bounds up the stairs toward the bathroom, that if the baby has drowned one has done something awful, whereas if it has not one has merely been careless'.[17] This ability to give a 'moral verdict' in advance of the event shows, according to Nagel, that these kinds of consequence-dependent moral responses are 'genuine moral judgments' rather than simply the 'expressions of temporary attitude'.[18] But 'genuine moral judgment' here means no more than that we can predict this is the moral response we are likely to feel. Moreover, a moral response *is* an attitude. The very fact, then, that the feeling we have done something terrible (as terrible as causing a death) is going to dissipate on our finding the baby safe shows that this contrast between 'genuine moral judgments' and 'expression of temporary attitude' relies on moral realism (embodied in the idea that the more enduring attitude is somehow closer to "the truth"). Similarly, he asserts that there is 'a morally significant difference' between reckless driving and manslaughter and between rescuing someone from a burning building and accidentally dropping that person twelve storeys while trying to rescue them.[19]

But 'morally significant' to whom? 'Genuine' in what sense? As I have said, if a response feels like a moral response to the agent, then it fulfils every condition of a moral response. Why would we also expect more from them? Twice Nagel describes it as 'irrational' to take or dispense credit or blame for matters over which a person has no control.[20] Yet, while there may be, as we have seen in Chapter 1, such a thing as a rational moral *judgement*, there is no such thing as a rational moral response with which to draw such a contrast as he draws. Blaming by consequences may depart from an emotional norm that does appear to defer to the control principle – we generally blame people only for what they are responsible for – and do so sufficiently to appear anomalous from the perspective of that norm, but that establishes nothing about the rationality of that norm or the irrationality of departures from it. Certainly, moral *judgements* may be irrational, since moral judgements take certain principles as given and these principles are premises from which sound or fallacious arguments may be constructed, but there is no question of moral responses themselves, even those that ground such principles, being a matter of rationality.

However, rather than asking why variations in circumstances beyond the agent's control should influence how we feel about the merit or demerit of an action, Nagel appears to drop the middle term (feeling) and examine the problem in terms of why variations in circumstances beyond the agent's control should influence the merit or demerit of an action. This could be justified insofar as, since the merits and demerits of actions do depend entirely on how we feel about them, there is little point in distinguishing between the two things: feeling and the ascription of merit or demerit. In practice, however, this removal of the reference to feeling leads to a view from no one's perspective and thus to a search for justification in terms of moral realism.

This tendency to interpret the inconsistency in terms of the problem of what we *should* feel becomes even more pronounced in responses to Nagel's paper. A surprising number of these take Nagel to have been arguing that we *should* take luck into account in our moral appraisals and thus seek to "refute" him simply by pointing out the very inconsistency his paper draws attention to.[21] Other commentators take the more radical route of suggesting not that we *should not* feel it but, rather, that we *do not* – providing an object lesson in what can happen to the reality of moral experience once one comes to identify that experience solely with one's moral judgements.[22] Some commentators, however, even though interpreting Nagel as endorsing moral assessment by consequences, treat the phenomenon of such assessments more in terms of a corrigible inconsistency in feeling. That is, they see such assessments as at once moral yet less 'rational' than those that conform to the control principle.[23]

Leaving aside the question of the ultimate "rationality" of even those responses that do conform to a control principle, we may certainly agree that, in terms of any particular prevailing moral consensus, for a response to appear as a matter of 'moral luck' it must also appear as anomalous in terms of that consensus. As noted earlier, even the subject experiencing such a response implicitly seeks to defer, as far as possible, to a "rational" concept of responsibility by *perceiving* a degree of control in the agent that, in a calmer mood, they certainly would not. Hence, the often defiant nature of expressions of blame by consequences, their air of unhappy consciousness: the embattled subject is caught between what they experience as the epistemic sacrifice necessary to blame where there is insufficient responsibility for blame, and the epistemic sacrifice necessary to discover responsibility where it does not exist.[24] It seems that we blame by consequences, irrespective of motives, because *we want to blame*.

Although I have described the perceived perversity of 'moral luck' as depending on what counts as legitimate responsibility in any particular context, it is difficult to imagine any consistent pattern of blame/approval ascription that depended entirely on the consequences of actions, irrespective of intentions, that would still take the form of a "moral sense". That is, such ascriptions are, to the observer, not simply counterintuitive in terms of any particular moral sense, but in terms of the very way in which we experience moral responses. There is not only a perceivable inconsistency in our responses, but it is also one that we perceive as arising from the response's departure from norms of responsibility rather than from something counterintuitive in those norms themselves.

Often, indeed, we find that instances of blame by consequences are corrigible. For example, I may be spontaneously outraged by the "selfishness" of someone who rings me at the climax of a film but will fairly quickly acknowledge to myself the unfairness of my own response, which I now attribute purely to frustration. Moreover, it is clearly possible to respond negatively to the expression of consequentialist blame, to feel, for example, outraged at those who seek to take revenge on the innocent causes of their misfortune. Where, conversely, we sympathize with someone whose sense of misfortune overwhelms what we take as a normal (moral) assignment of blame, we are not sharing their moral response to the unwitting agent of that misfortune but, rather, *making allowances* for their feelings.

We do strive, from a sense of justice, to correct what we can recognize on reflection as our own consequentialist responses and blame them (as wilful unfairness) when they are incorrigible in others. Moreover, this is not a matter of moral judgements, with their implicit ideal of consistency, coming into conflict with spontaneous moral responses: I do genuinely now feel the unfairness of my previous moral resentment of an innocent individual. However, although my previous moral response has now evaporated and although I perceive another's incorrigible consequentialism as itself immoral (the effect of blind anger or unacknowledged envy), it would obviously be a mistake to disqualify such responses from being genuinely moral, to say that what I previously felt or what others feel could not be actually a moral response since, despite the way in which I or they experience those responses, they do not square with my current moral response, or lack of it, to the same object. As we saw in the first two chapters, if moral responses must pass the test not only of feeling like moral responses but also of a logical compatibility with other moral responses, or with a principle that serves some particular end (e.g. the maximization of each member of the community's chance to pursue their own interests), we will never be able to call any response "moral". Consistency is a dominant theme in ethics, where the goal is most often the justification of some system of generating rational choices, but an ethical system is not anybody's actual morality. To understand what morality is, we must allow that the feeling that we are experiencing a moral response is the only consistent criterion for the claim that we are experiencing a moral response. For, we must not lose sight of the fact that, as we saw in Chapter 1, morality in itself, for all its quotidian familiarity, presents us, philosophically, with one great inconsistency.

From this point of view, such local "inconsistencies" as blaming by consequences are obviously not best approached either as dilemmas to be ethically adjudicated on, or as antinomies to be resolved in terms of a concept of morality that is already given. It is unsurprising, then, given that Nagel raised his 'problem of luck' within the context of philosophical ethics, that so many of the responses to his account should be beside the point. For the existence of consequentialist blaming is not really a philosophical problem at all. It is, however, a very interesting aspect of real moral experience: moral experience as it is, rather than as what, according to philosophical ethics, it morally should be.

Seen thus, it is unsurprising that the 'moral philosophy' of the eighteenth century, with its decidedly psychological bent, does rather better at focusing on the significance of the phenomenon. (So common and conspicuous an "inconsistency" was not, of course, a discovery of the late twentieth century.) Indeed, Smith devotes a whole chapter of his *Theory of Moral Sentiments* to what he calls 'the influence of fortune upon the sentiments of mankind, with regard to the merit or demerit of actions'.[25] He begins from the observation that whatever praise or blame is due to an action must belong to the 'intention or affection of the heart from which it proceeds'.[26] The physical action that is performed cannot be itself the object of praise or blame, since identical actions – shooting a bird or shooting a man – are obviously morally different. Still less can it be the actual consequences of the action, since these depend not on the agent but on chance, and so 'cannot be the proper foundation for any sentiment, of which his character and conduct are the objects'.[27] That neither action in itself nor the consequences of action can be the foundation of praise or blame is, according to Smith, 'abundantly evident; nor has the contrary ever been asserted by any body'.[28] It is generally agreed, he continues, that the only consequences for which we are 'justly' answerable are those we somehow intend, or which at least show (as perhaps negligence does) some 'agreeable or disagreeable quality in the intention of the heart'.²⁹

> But how well soever we may seem to be persuaded of the truth of this equitable maxim, when we consider it after this manner, in abstract, yet when we come to particular cases, the actual consequences which happen to proceed from any action, have a very great effect upon our sentiments concerning its merit or demerit, and almost always either enhance or diminish our sense of both. Scarce, in any one instance, perhaps, will our sentiments be found, after examination, to be entirely regulated by this rule, which we all acknowledge ought entirely to regulate them.³⁰

This, he continues, is an 'irregularity of sentiment', which everyone feels, though few reflect on or even acknowledge.³¹

Smith accounts for the phenomenon by appealing to the fact that all sources of pain or pleasure become objects of resentment or gratitude; a dog hurt by a stone will bark at it, a child hit it, an adult swear at it.³² Reflection may modify our feelings in the matter – we soon see that what is inanimate is no proper object of revenge – but, as Smith says, where the mischief is very great we may be unable to 'correct the sentiment'. We would be unlikely, for example, to carry on using an everyday object that had accidentally been instrumental in the death of a friend.³³ Likewise, according to Smith, we feel something like gratitude towards even inanimate objects if they have been the cause of great or frequent pleasure to us.³⁴ This holds true also for our feelings towards animals, which seems slightly more reasonable insofar as, even though we cannot attribute good or bad intentions to them, at least they can, unlike inanimate objects, benefit or suffer from our gratitude or resentment.³⁵ Where the object is human, and thus a fully appropriate object of gratitude or resentment, the tendency for pleasure or pain in themselves to arouse these feelings is even more likely; even to the extent, where those pleasures or pains are great, of causing us to overlook the actual intentions – or meaningful responsibility – of the source of that pain or pleasure. In sum, chance affects our moral responses in two ways. On the one hand, it diminishes our sense of the merits or demerits of actions arising from the most laudable or blameable intentions, when those actions fail to produce the intended effect (as in the case of the man who risks his life to save a dolly, or the thief who ends up stealing from himself). On the other hand, it increases our sense of the merits or demerits of actions, beyond what would normally be due to the motives behind them, when they accidentally occasion either extraordinary pleasure or pain; for example, negligence appears more culpable if it leads to a fatal result, we feel unreasonably grateful to the bringer of good news and so on.³⁶

Here again, then, what the inconsistency appears to turn on is a sense of vividness. As Smith would say, the 'calm judgments of the mind may approve' the actions of one such as the man who risks his life to save the dolly, but the result lacks the 'splendour' necessary to 'dazzle and transport' it.³⁷ Although the object of our admiration is actually the implied virtues and talents of the agent, in practice the 'superiority of virtues and talents has not, even upon those who acknowledge that superiority, the same effect with the superiority of atchievements [sic]'. Where someone tries but fails to harm us 'the joy of our deliverance alleviates our sense of the atrocity of his conduct'.[38] Conversely, where we are actually harmed, the 'grief of our misfortune' tends to increase our feeling of the agent's culpability – so that the punishment we feel appropriate for any particular crime may be very different before and just after we have ourselves been the victim of it (though generally it will tend to eventually return to what it once was). Moreover, while an impartial spectator might try to calm us, they would also probably feel some indulgence towards our own unjust degree of resentment on the grounds that it was "only human". Our own harm is naturally vivid to us, but, as we have seen with the majority of cases so far, it is enough for a harm to be great for it to arouse a sense of indignation sufficient to overwhelm our normal sense of culpability – at least as measured by how we would respond to the same negligence without fatal consequences.

Although, as I have said, Smith's approach to the question in terms of 'irregularity of sentiment' is more germane to what is problematic here than are those twentieth-century approaches previously examined, which view the matter as an ethical problem to be solved, nevertheless, his appeal to the way in which consequentialist blaming is of a piece with our more general tendency to respond to all sources of pain or pleasure with resentment or gratitude is not actually an explanation. While his account does bring out the *normality* of consequentialist blaming – there is, indeed, nothing at all remarkable about the way in which feelings of anger, fear, grief, relief or pleasurable anticipation become directed towards objects that are merely associated with what are the real (in the sense of adequate) objects of those feelings – nevertheless, "It's human nature" is not, in itself, an explanation. Smith's account does, however, focus on a point worth pursuing: that not only is it a simple matter to find parallel instances of implicit untenable ascriptions of responsibility and the urge to punish or reward beyond the recognizably moral domain, but that moral responses appear to, as it were, *follow* such feelings.

Generally, we believe that we are angry with someone because we blame them for some action or omission and only blame them for that action or omission insofar as we hold them responsible for it. The ideal model of a moral response would thus be:

perception of harm → perception of responsibility → blame (feeling that the agent acted immorally in causing this harm) → anger directed towards the agent

('Acted immorally' here means acted with an egotistical disregard for the welfare of others or the proper order of the universe, as measured against what you feel is the acceptable mean of the balance between egotism and the welfare of others or the proper order of the universe.[39]) Although the word "blame" can serve equally to denote both the holding of someone responsible and the negative feeling one has towards that person for being responsible, we can, nevertheless, distinguish between the perception of responsibility and blame itself, given the possibility of perceiving a person as unintentionally responsible for a harm and thus blameless. At first sight, it might seem as if consequentialist blaming follows the same process but simply breaks down epistemologically at the second stage (the subject misperceives the agent's degree of responsibility) or at the third (the subject erroneously attributes culpability to this degree of responsibility). However, consequentialist blaming is not a matter of making an error: even where it is corrigible, such corrigibility does not depend on acquiring new information but rather on calming down. What appears to happen in consequentialist blaming is that the perception of the kind of responsibility necessary for blame is worked up from the desire to blame itself: it is this desire that motivates the cognitive bias involved in perceiving the appropriate kind of responsibility where it does not exist. (All cognitive biases require some kind of pressure – desire or fear – to overcome the demands of reality; this is what distinguishes them from mistakes.) In contrast to the ideal model presented above, in consequentialist blaming, the blame, impossibly it would seem, actually precedes the attribution of the appropriate form of responsibility.

If, however, blaming precedes, and gives rise to, the attribution of the appropriate kind of responsibility, then it must itself somehow arise directly from the perception of the harm. This is not, however, so strange as it sounds. Smith, as we saw, draws attention to the way in which it is commonplace for us to act towards *any* source of pain or pleasure with feelings that are indistinguishable from resentment or gratitude, no matter how inappropriate, on reflection, that object may be as the object of such a feeling. Children may react with aggression towards anything, animate or inanimate, that has hurt or frightened them. Moreover, as we have previously noted, consequentialist blaming is always associated with a certain kind of emotional context. (Hence, its conspicuous absence from the domain of moral *judgements*, which is perhaps why philosophical ethics is unable to deal with it adequately.) It is merely common sense to attribute someone's unfair blaming on their state of mind: to their being upset or afraid. With consequentialist blaming, then, the priority of responses appears to be:

perception of harm → anger directed towards event → blame (feeling that something immoral has taken place) → construction of appropriate form of responsibility blame directed towards agent → anger redirected towards agent

In most cases, the agent involved will be responsible for the harm, in the sense that they will be the cause of it (as the weather is *responsible for* a cracked pipe), though not in a way – through intention or negligence – that would normally qualify for blame. However, the connection between the agent and the harm may be even more tenuous, as, for example, in the common phenomenon of a small and economically negligible minority being blamed for the general condition of the economy, or where one who has by chance escaped a certain harm is blamed by those who have not (though precisely what that person is blamed *for* is ambiguous). Not only are we capable of resenting a stone, but it also seems that we are capable of resenting a person for the same reasons we would resent a stone.

Indeed, there is one further manifestation of consequentialist blaming, involving an even more far-fetched attribution of responsible agency, that serves to bring out yet more forcibly the degree to which the moral response may be determined by the way we feel about the harm irrespective of a warranted occasion for blame. This is the way in which, when faced with the spectacle of another's suffering, we may, when either unable or unwilling to blame the responsible agents or circumstances, or when predisposed to hostility towards the victim, blame that victim themselves for what they suffer. Just as in the previous examples of consequentialist blaming, here the subject, in the face of vivid harm, appears to cast desperately about for a way to justify attributing responsibility for that harm, though here it is a matter of finding some means of being able to hold that the victim has *deserved* what has happened or is happening to them. This is, incidentally, perhaps why harm to a child or an animal is peculiarly distressing: it is not only that their vulnerability is vivid but also that their lack of agency prevents us from falling back on the comfort of feeling that they might in some way have deserved what is happening.

This tendency to seek to blame people for their own misfortunes, irrespective of evidence, has been investigated within psychology under the title 'the just-world hypothesis'. The expression, coined by Lerner and Simmons, refers to the way in which they account for this particular cognitive bias in blaming. People, they assert, need to believe they live in an essentially "just" world, secure from random misfortune, able to plan rationally, and, thus, ultimately able to get what they deserve.[40] Thus, the spectacle of 'innocent victims of undeserved suffering poses a threat to that fundamental belief, and as a consequence, people naturally develop and employ ways of defending it': where eliminating the injustice is not judged possible (or perhaps desirable), they will blame the victim in order to maintain the illusion of the "justice" of the universe.[41] In short, the cognitive bias, which posits responsibility in the behaviour or characteristics of the one who suffers, serves the end of lessening the feeling of our own vulnerability that the spectacle of undeserved harm inspires.[42]

However, despite the neatness of this explanation, it is, nevertheless, possible to take issue with two aspects of the 'just-world belief' hypothesis. First, and perhaps pedantically, what is involved appears to be not so much a *belief* in a just world as a *desire* for one. Belief, where it is not a matter of affect, is open to rectification. (It is not the case that the suffering of the innocent baffles us, though it is certainly true that, irrespective of whether or not we blame the victim, we *resent* the existence of such suffering.) Second, and more importantly, it is not at all clear that the kind of world that is desired is actually a 'just' one. Victim blaming, as a matter of cognitive bias, involves emotionally committing oneself to an ascription of blame that is only possible insofar as one recognizes and yet overcomes the fact that such an ascription is unwarranted. In short, the assertion of the existence of the 'just world' in these circumstances requires a self-conscious 'injustice' on the part of the subject. If the aim of the response were really to assert that reality is morally determined, the very form it takes would seem to undermine what it is seeking to achieve. For, one's own response is instantiating, in the most intimate possible manner, a denial of such determinism.

Certainly, there is a desire involved and this desire manifests as what is, to most intents and purposes, a belief in a 'just world', but such a world does not seem to be the object of the desire. Indeed, given that the response appears to be a way of avoiding the sense of our own vulnerability that the spectacle of undeserved harm has inspired, it would be more accurate to describe the object of the desire as our own security. Blame, then, appears to enter in here, as in the other forms of consequentialist blaming already considered, as a way of giving the fear-inspired anger the harm provokes, an appropriate object. Thus, the process of attributing blame to the victim of the harm follows the same order as the previous kinds of consequentialist blaming considered, differing only in the extra degree of cognitive bias necessary to manage to attribute the 'appropriate form of responsibility' to the one who is harmed:

> perception of harm → anger directed towards event → blame (feeling that something immoral has taken place) → construction of appropriate form of responsibility → blame directed towards "agent" → anger redirected towards "agent"

Before leaving this topic of consequentialist blame, there is one last manifestation of it to be examined for the light it throws on the influence of social norms on the corrigibility of such blaming.

Although blaming in proportion to consequences rather than motivation is an everyday occurrence and, as we have seen, it is easy enough to bring to mind examples one has encountered, it is much more difficult to envision moral responses that demonstrate the reverse: praising by consequences irrespective of motivation. (Certainly, it is not uncommon to admire others and oneself for matters of chance as if they were achievements, but such admiration is not the same as moral approval.) It is not, however, unknown, though its roots appear far more obscure than the simple resentment and desire for redress that obviously underpins blaming irrespective of consequences. I will confine myself to a single example here, though, insofar as it occurs in the course of a self-conscious reflection on the nature of ethics and involves the first-hand report of a moral response, it is a striking one.

Sidgwick notes that terms like 'duty', 'ought' and 'moral obligation' imply 'at least the *potential* presence of motives prompting to wrong conduct' and are therefore not applicable 'to beings to whom no such conflict of motives can be attributed'.[43] We might reasonably infer from this that the greater the temptation to wrongdoing, the greater the degree of virtue demonstrated by its overcoming, which is indeed the common perception. As Sidgwick remarks, we feel that the virtue of veracity, for example, has been 'manifested in a higher degree' in a case where the agent had strong temptations to lie.[44] We only praise certain actions because we presume in most agents 'powerful seductive motives' operating against the performance of those actions: 'there is no virtue in doing what one likes'. However, a few pages later Sidgwick remarks that 'in our common moral judgments certain kinds of virtuous actions are held to be at any rate adorned and made better by the presence of certain emotions in the virtuous agent' quite apart from actual volition.[45] 'Thus the Virtue of Chastity or Purity, in its highest form, seems to include more than a mere settled resolution to abstain from unlawful lust; it includes some sentiment of repugnance to impurity.'[46] That is, despite what he has said about the dependence of virtue on volition, in this particular case the agent becomes more virtuous in proportion to the weakness of the temptation. This Sidgwick takes to signal the presence of an 'emotional element from the conception of Virtue' that is 'irrational' but, nevertheless, part of 'the common sense of mankind'.[47] Moreover, this initial 'perplexity' in common sense throws up the further paradox of implying that the more successfully we learn to control some potentially vicious inclination, 'the less virtuous we grow'.[48]

Sidgwick suggests that the difficulty may be resolved by considering that 'our common idea of Virtue includes two distinct elements, the one being the most perfect ideal of moral excellence that we are able to conceive for human beings, while the other is manifested in the effort of imperfect men to attain this ideal'.[49] Thus the naturally 'chaste' provide an image of the former, the 'true moral ideal', the contemplation of which in itself prompts a moral response, irrespective of the fact that this image (the 'chastity' of the naturally 'chaste') does not actually represent what it symbolizes: a will to avoid the harm to others that would follow from the absence of chastity.[50] This is what Sidgwick refers to as the other element in our idea of virtue, and it is this that makes virtue equivalent to the exhibition of that kind of willing that, as we have seen throughout this chapter, is the object of our more consistent notion of moral praise or blame.

Sidgwick's problem with the way we can morally admire an "agent" in the absence of any demonstrable moral volition does then demonstrate the existence of consequentialist moral praise that parallels the consequentialist blame we have principally considered so far in this chapter. Just as, in the latter, it is anger at the harm itself that is transmuted, through desire, into moral agency, so here it appears to be a desire for a certain good (or the avoidance of a certain harm) that is similarly transmuted.

Moreover, virtue, too, can appear in corrigible and incorrigible forms. One can grow out of a sense of machismo or cool that once seemed good in themselves, or one can come to see a virtue as frustrating the achievement of a more desirable good, or even its own *ostensible* goal.[51] Nevertheless, as we saw with loyalty in the last chapter, consequentialist admiration, as the moral admiration of virtues *for their own sake*, is, or at least appears to be, generally far more incorrigible than consequentialist blaming. (No matter how repulsive Roman *virtus* may appear when we think of it in terms of the actions a Roman would have used to exemplify it, when considered in the abstract it may still appear admirable.) From this point of view, the use of Sidgwick on chastity is opportune. For, at least some readers will have found his assertion that we find 'natural chastity' (lack of sexual appetite) in itself virtuous, to be counterintuitive. I have taken at face value Sidgwick's claim that chastity is for him only morally admirable, only a virtue, insofar as it serves the end of morality conceived as something more general (the production of the greatest average happiness). However, if we do not share his admiration of 'natural chastity', it is difficult to see how it could arise, whether Sidgwick is aware of it or not, from anything other than a feeling that sex itself is a harm. For, it might seem that only if sex in itself were a harm would a lack of sexual appetite be functionally equivalent to possessing a 'will to good'. (Most people, for example, can disapprove of gluttony without considering eating itself to be a moral failing.) This notion of the very existence of a physical phenomenon constituting a harm is one we shall return to later in this chapter. More germane to our present concerns is the way in which the admiration of chastity suggests a grounding in self-interest more nearly equivalent to that evinced by consequentialist blaming.

Apropos such self-interest, there is, most famously, Hume's contention that the common emphasis on female chastity arises from the fact that, given human infants require extended care, in order to reconcile men to this burden 'they must believe that the children are their own, and that their natural instinct is not directed to a wrong object, when they give a loose to love and tenderness'.[52] Indeed, Hume puts forward chastity as a 'conspicuous' instance of his contention that our sense of justice, and of virtue and vice, 'arise merely from human conventions, and from the interest, which we have in the preservation of peace and order'.[53] This is not to say that we consciously refer the valuation to self-interest. According to Hume, while those who have a direct 'interest in the fidelity of women' will inevitably feel it is a virtue, even those who have no such direct interest 'are carry'd along with the stream, and are also apt to be affected with sympathy for the general interests of society'; this includes women who are educated into regarding chastity as a virtue from an early age.[54] Thus the feeling of the desirability of chastity and the viciousness of its opposite become widespread, even where there is no obvious direct interest, since, once a 'rule' of this kind is established, as Hume remarks, 'men are apt to extend it beyond those principles, from which it first arose'.[55] Moreover, he continues, it is precisely because we have 'an implicit notion' that this response is linked to reproduction, that we place less emphasis on male chastity (though this, too, is not a matter of indifference from the point of view of the 'interest of civil society').[56]

In Hume's model, then, the moral response is transmuted regard for the peace and order of society, which is, in turn, transmuted self-interest: we admire chastity as a virtue (or at least respond negatively to its absence) because we have internalized an interest of society that is grounded in self-interest though that social interest in itself may not actually be in our own immediate interest. (It should be noted, however, that Hume's initial anthropological scenario also implies a female self-interest, albeit more remote than the male's, quite independent of the self-interest that will subsequently arise from chastity becoming perceived as virtuous.) There might appear to be a certain weakness in his premise that it is in the man's interest that the children he rears should be his own, since every function of a child, except the transmission of genetic material, can equally well be fulfilled by children fathered by another. Moreover, mutual attachment – 'love and tenderness' – follows from familiarity and care rather than from consanguinity. However, such metaphysical materialism (the extrapolation of essence from biology) is sufficiently common to justify Hume's appeal to it as given.[57] Nevertheless, a more substantial implausibility in the account is that the self-interest is too concrete (we are conscious of the interest in paternity), and therefore transparent. Thus, while it is easy to see how it could give rise to a rule, it is more difficult to see how it could generate a moral response. The fact, moreover, that we know such a response is more likely to occur in men than women, and, in contrast to other moral failings, to be more vehemently felt in proportion to personal attachment to the "agent", naturally adds to the problem of perceiving that response as disinterested. Though we saw with loyalty that the transparency of the self-interest involved may not be an obstacle in this regard, nevertheless, the case of chastity is somewhat different: here the virtue seems more oriented towards the avoidance of what is perceived as a particular harm rather than, as with loyalty, the promotion of what is perceived as a positive good. This, indeed, is what the case of this particular virtue shares in common with the kinds of consequentialist blaming considered in this chapter, and why, as Sidgwick noted, it can, in practice, so easily take the form of what is, in effect, consequentialist praising.

What, then, is the harm to be avoided, if, as I would maintain, the plain interest in perpetuating one's biological self is too explicitly avowed an interest to require, or perhaps even permit, sublimation into a moral response? Why, that is, does the subject find it necessary to transmute "I want" into "it is"? I would suggest that here, as elsewhere in human experience where we run up against the concept of disinterested evaluation, this transmutation is the result of a reluctance to relinquish a desire for what one yet must acknowledge to be impossible.

There are two preliminary points to make. First, we are concerned here only with the perception of chastity in women; it is no coincidence that "female virtue" was once a synonym for "chastity". Male chastity, though it may occasionally be an institutional rule, never seems to have been of particularly burning moral concern to the generality of males in any culture. Likewise, historically there appears to be little in the female response to male lack of chastity that corresponds to the male concern with its female equivalent. Where their own immediate interests are not threatened, women are most likely to find male sexual promiscuity either contemptible, amusing or aphrodisiac.[58] The second preliminary point to note is that, as Sidgwick's discussion inadvertently demonstrates, chastity appears to be counted a virtue only insofar as it is seen as the avoidance of a harm: it has, we might say, no positive value. Thus, while the concept of "female chastity" now seems hopelessly outdated, nevertheless, when we consider contemporary mores, it is clear that it is only the expression itself, the emphasis on the positive, signalled by its status as a virtue, that has gone out of fashion: the ideal that gave rise to it remains implicit in the enduring response to evidence of its absence. It is there, for example, in the enduring myth that women are incapable of enjoying sex with a man they do not like on short acquaintance. The element of wishful thinking in this apparently empirical observation is revealed by its paradoxical concomitant: that a woman who *is* capable of this is a proper object of opprobrium.

The impossible desire that is at work here is the male desire for the sexual act to mean more than it can possibly mean. What precisely that meaning is does not concern us here, for we are interested only in the way in which a harm to the *amour soi* (or possibly *amour propre*) can become a moral matter. It is sufficient for our present purposes simply to recognize that the autonomy of female desire per se undermines this sense of that meaningfulness.[59] This happens most intensely, of course, where there is a strong attachment to a particular individual, where sexual access comes to signify most intensely, though it is also to be found, naturally, in association with the desire for "conquest". Moreover, it extends to the whole of the sex, insofar as each woman appears a token of all. Thus, even while, at various times and places, this sense of the "value" of sexual access may be restricted to a certain social group, nevertheless, the lack of "sexual value" of women outside that group will not be a matter of indifference: insofar as they are still women, they will be objects of contempt or disapproval on precisely these grounds, since their very existence represents a threat to the meaningfulness of sexual access to other women.[60]

It would be a mistake to confuse this "meaning" of the sexual act with any easily quantifiable interest. As mentioned earlier, women are generally sexually jealous only where they are emotionally attached and see sex as evidence of a real alternative attachment and, thus, a threat to an existing or potential relationship.[61] Hence, with that impeccable instinct for misunderstanding one another (born from judging by analogy from our own feelings), a woman, faced with a lover's dismay over her infidelity, will "defend" herself with "But, John, it didn't mean anything".[62] From John's point of view, however, that is precisely the problem. Indeed, men are liable to react most hysterically to what instantiates quite the opposite of meaningfulness (in this pragmatic sense): the more casual the sex with another, the worse. The more closely attached he is, the greater the value he places on access to the woman's sexuality, and the more devalued that access is by a perception of the ease by which it may be had by others. Moreover, since this is a matter of a far more intangible 'meaning', obscurely connected to a harm to self-esteem, his jealousy is not time-dependent: it does not appear to be simply a practical matter of the present and the future.[63] A man can be equally jealous of the past; jealous, that is, even of what, to all appearances, he is currently enjoying. This dismay at one's lover's past sexual activity is so *normal* that, while women may perforce become accustomed to negotiating its strange topography, men themselves will rarely reflect on that strangeness. Where their outrage is not socially sanctioned, the best they can do is to notionally acknowledge the operation of a double standard, social or personal, and strive (in the interest of self-esteem) not to leave themselves open to the further humiliation of a public display of their vulnerability.[64] John may wish to demand "How could you do this to me?", but the question is far too revealing.

All of this is almost too commonplace to remark, yet the desire for what a woman's (or, at least, this woman's) sexuality should signify that is implicit in these feelings is clearly a desire for what simply cannot be the case. This, indeed, is what Sidgwick's puzzle over his admiration of a certain kind of chastity, which is not even strictly chastity, shows. For, if chastity becomes a virtue simply by being the negative of an ease of access that is perceived as devaluing where value is desired, then his greater admiration for an indifferent or even frigid "chastity" makes sense: for what the man wants is simply that the woman should not *want* another. This is impossible. However, given the normality of the feeling described here, and the obscurity/intangibility of the interest involved, with its lack of any apparent reference to present or future, it is easy to see how such a feeling could become a moral matter: it has the same quality of apparent disinterest (if only by virtue of making no sense). Moreover, it has clear parallels with the forms of consequentialist blaming previously considered: it involves a "harm" that is not intended as a harm – she has, most obviously where it is a case of his resentment of the past, done nothing to him – and it involves the conversion of anger at a state of affairs into blame of an "agent" (the woman).

Where it differs from those cases of consequentialist blaming so far considered, aside from in the obscurity of the interest involved, is in the way in which it has historically been held to be a moral matter: a matter of "female virtue". In the previous cases of consequentialist blaming, it was almost invariably the case that the feeling would be "rectified" once the subject calmed down, and certainly, from the outside, it was easy to see both the unreasonableness and the transparently self-interested, if involuntary, motivation of the blaming. However, we must now imagine a situation in which, since the feeling is commonplace, there is no reason to think of it as irrational. (The fact that it cannot be justified is no obstacle to this; as we saw in Chapter 3 and will see again when dealing with disgust, there are a host of uncontroversial moral responses where the "harm" is similarly obscure.) Mill, having remarked our tendency to indiscriminately resent whatever causes us hurt, claims that such resentment can become 'moralized by the social feeling' where it 'acts in the directions conformable to the general good': people come to feel that the anger they feel is moral only insofar as it is directed towards a harm 'of the kind which society has a common interest with them in the repression of'.[65] (So that what is 'moral' for Mill is not the desire to punish in itself but rather the subordination of that desire, through 'intellect and sympathy' to our 'social sympathies'.[66]) This 'common interest', in view of what will count as 'common' given the historical balance of power between men and women, is sufficient to account for the institutionalization of the feeling into the *virtue* of female chastity.[67] The "value" in terms of self-esteem becomes a moral matter because we want the universe to be on our side in this perception of the woman's sexuality. Indeed, we have already seen a similar phenomenon, of common self-interest becoming morality, in the way in which it is *shared* loyalty that is most easily perceived as virtuous.

Nevertheless, the harm to which the approval of chastity is the response is strikingly intangible: it is only sufficient for a man to imagine for a moment his lover entertaining the same feelings about his sexuality, that is, for him to see his consequentialist blaming from the outside, for him to realize the utter absurdity of those feelings. Thus, female chastity is currently not a virtue that many societies do explicitly endorse. However, another modern tendency – to externalize the self-destructive as "social pressure" – leads many to misattribute the feeling itself that gives rise to the idea of 'female virtue' solely to the influence of patriarchy or religion.[68] Hume's explanation in terms of inheritance is of a piece with such accounts, which, along with the ease with which it may be aligned with an evolutionary explanation, is probably why it continues in popularity to this day. However, such explanations are not commensurate with the vehemence of the feeling involved, nor would they solve Sidgwick's conundrum over why chastity, unlike other virtues, should appear more admirable in inverse proportion to the temptation overcome.[69]

It was suggested earlier that what consequentialist blaming reveals is a standing desire to blame. As we have seen (and as is, in any case, plain from experience), what grounds this particular area of moral experience is anger. Perhaps because anger is generally counted as a "basic" emotion, insofar as it has its own signature facial expression and physiological correlates, it is easy to overlook that anger itself presupposes an antecedent response: frustration. By 'frustration' we may understand any experience of the world as other than we wish it to be: in essence, the world as a source of harm to ourselves (including, of course, not only physical pain itself but also the pain of the deprivation of an expected pleasure, and the pain of fear, or the pain of the threat of pain). Anger, unlike the other possible response of avoidance, is an outwardly directed predisposition to action that will remove the source of the pain. It is a reassertion of the desire for the world to be as we would wish it to be, in the face of what we experience as opposition to that wish. To this extent, anger itself implies the most primitive form of blame, insofar as, just by virtue of being anger, it presupposes that, in some sense, the check *should* not have happened, and that something is responsible for the ensuing frustration. It also, of course, seems to presuppose an appropriate response to that frustration, even though anger is a notoriously impractical emotion in most contexts. This last is the case even apart from its role in consequentialist blaming in all its forms – from the child's indiscriminate revenge on inanimate objects to the more mature psychological dodges we have chiefly been considering – though consequentialist blaming renders this impracticality particularly conspicuous. Nevertheless, even where impractical, anger is unavoidable insofar as it is not merely the reassertion of the thwarted desire but also, as a predisposition to act, a reassertion of the efficacy, or potency, of the self, which is precisely what the frustration has temporarily thrown into doubt. Anger, then, is necessary to our feeling that the world might be as we wish.

Consequently, it would seem perfectly natural for anger to try to fasten on the most appropriate object it can find. Folk psychology takes it for granted that consequentialist blaming, "finding someone to blame", is an expression of the subject's need to "vent", and thus relieve, their distress at the harm suffered, threatened or even, as in the 'just-world belief' scenarios, fearfully contemplated as the possibility of harm per se. (This would appear to apply most obviously to situations in which the act of blaming was also the assertion of the appropriateness of punishment, but mere condemnation in itself also seems to fulfil this purpose of relieving the feelings.) How it is possible to relieve one's feelings about one object (the harm) with a response directed towards a different object (the blameless culprit), even when, as in consequentialist blaming, one is necessarily aware that the unwitting, or even elected, "agent" is not really responsible, is not a problem for folk psychology, since such displacement is a signature of "human nature" (a given for folk psychology). However, this glosses over another aspect of "human nature" that would seem to render this particular form of displacement problematic. That is, the way in which the idea that someone is responsible for a harm we suffer demonstrably *increases* our anger at that harm makes the harm worse. From this it would seem to follow that it would be in the subject's interests not to infer responsible agency where they do not have to. (Which is perhaps what we see with the consequentialist excusing already considered.) Yet, in consequentialist blaming, rather than avoiding this aggravation of their distress, as reality permits, the subject prefers to make such an inference even at the cost of epistemic sacrifice. What this suggests is that *moral* blame itself satisfies some desire, and that this satisfaction is sufficient to outweigh both the aggravated distress of feeling that the harm was *intended* and the cost of the epistemic sacrifice that is necessarily involved in doing so.

Given, however, that anger represents the recoil of one's *amour de soi* in the face of what threatens it, there is clearly an advantage to attributing that threat to another human will. To do so is to both assert the evitability of the harm (the agent might have done otherwise) and to direct the anger towards an object that might, in principle at least, be amenable to the influence of one's anger. (The perceived evitability of human actions, as a contrast to the inevitability of "acts of nature", may be an illusion, but it is an inescapable one.) If, however, a human agent is to be responsible, this now becomes a matter of *moral* blame: an ascription of excessive egotistical disregard for the welfare of others or the natural order *from the viewpoint of the universe*. Moral blame is clearly more than simply holding someone responsible for the harm that has caused one's anger; there is a world of difference between "I did not want this" and "This should not be". There is, however, a marked continuity both in formal structure and in feeling, between the most primitive form of anger, as a protest against the frustration of one's wishes or expectations, with its implicit claim that this frustration should not be, and the moral response's implicit claim that, from the viewpoint of the universe, certain things should not be.

What seems to distinguish anger from blame appears to be that the latter is supposedly a *disinterested* antipathy. However, this would be to overlook the extent to which anger itself, as a predisposition to action even where no action is possible, is experienced as disinterested: in the sense that it is an assertion of the self purely for the purpose of the assertion of the self. (We are so familiar with anger that it is difficult to appreciate this aspect of the emotion; it may help here to think of the behaviour of most other animals in response to the kind of serial checks that would anger a human, or, indeed, simply of the difference in meaning between the word 'check' and the word 'frustration'.) We do not normally think of anger as a disinterested feeling only because there is always clearly an interest involved. This, however, obscures the extent to which anger is, in terms of the accomplishment of any particular concrete goal, always excessive.

This continuity, or consanguinity, between anger per se and moral blame serves to explain one of the problematic aspects of the model proposed for consequentialist blaming:

perception of harm → anger directed towards event → blame (feeling that something immoral has taken place) → construction of appropriate form of responsibility → blame directed towards "agent" → anger redirected towards "agent"

The problem here is that moral blame (as the feeling that something immoral has taken place) actually precedes, and, indeed, serves to determine, the ascription of responsibility to an agent, despite the fact that it would seem a responsible agent would be a necessary precondition of the feeling that something immoral had taken place. However, this becomes less problematic if we see anger and moral blame as actually continuous in kind; with anger, by its very nature, already directed towards an as yet undetermined agency and moral blame as anger that has fastened on a human object. Thus, we might be tempted to see instances of consequentialist blame as examples of situations in which the force of the emotion is sufficient to overcome the constraints of reality in our election of a responsible agent (we morally blame where moral blame is not possible), and "normal" blame as simply the same process (harm/frustration-anger-blame) without the need for any epistemic sacrifice in order to fasten on a culpable agent.

Against this extension of the process implicit in consequentialist blaming to blame per se, it might be objected that, insofar as consequentialist blaming is so obviously emotion-driven, so obviously a breakdown in the norm, it cannot provide any kind of model for "justified" blame. After all, as we have seen, consequentialist blaming is often corrigible in a way that justified blaming is not. That is, while the force of our feeling may gradually abate over time in the case of justified blaming, it is never the case that it actually gives way to a retrospective sense of our own unfairness, as is the case, and often on short notice, with consequentialist blaming. Moreover, while we *make allowance* for those who blame by consequences under the pressure of fear, hurt or grief, at the same time we do not share their response in the way that we share (feel in ourselves) the wrongness of a deliberate injustice done to another. However, as already noted, blaming only appears consequentialist, and culpability a matter of 'moral luck', against the background of a particular prevailing moral norm (personal or social). Thus, it is unsurprising that where a particular instance of blaming appears consequentialist it should also turn out to be corrigible. (Though, as the example of chastity illustrates, this corrigibility can, on occasion, be largely notional.) However, this is very much a matter of appearance; once we look beyond our own norm it becomes an easy matter to find instances of incorrigible consequentialist blaming: examples of contexts in which what may seem to us to be unacknowledged fear, disgust or envy masquerading as morality is experienced by those within the context as the justified (disinterested) ascription of moral culpability.[70] This point would scarcely need to be made were it not for the fact that our usual response to such blaming outside of what is recognized as "just" by our own norms is to deny the moral nature of that blaming, that is, to perceive it as a matter of something other than morality.

This last brings us to the second answer to the objection that since consequentialist blaming is emotion-driven it is fundamentally different in kind from "justified" blaming. That is, the argument that 'justified' or truly *moral* blaming cannot be a matter of any feeling other than moral feeling. What, however, is moral feeling, at least in terms of blame, apart from an antipathetic feeling towards instances of what are, *for the subject*, instances of the egotistical disregard of the welfare of others or the proper order of the universe? (I emphasize the subject here, for this definition is intended to cover everything from genocide to eating meat to espousing this or that system of taxation to breaking a taboo.) It is, of course, possible to abstract a purely descriptive definition of immorality from this (e.g. 'egotistical disregard of the welfare of others'), but this is only an abstract from instances that have inspired the feeling of antipathy. Indeed, what counts as immorality for a particular subject is what has been found to inspire a certain kind of antipathy: the kind that, as we saw in Chapter 1, somehow includes the conviction that one's viewpoint is universal. However, that the object of this emotion *can* be, at least to a certain extent, defined in abstract terms means that it is also possible to perceive it separately from the feeling itself. Hence, the possibility of moral *judgements*. Given this possibility, it then requires only a tendency to identify moral experience with the formation of such judgements (in which any feeling, other than those "moral feelings" that are supposedly consequent upon such judgements, can appear only as foreign matter), to obscure the fact that moral blaming is, in essence, a species of anger.[71] It is not, then, a matter of choosing between giving anger precedence over a perception of immorality (which suggests consequentialist blaming) or giving the perception of immorality precedence over anger (which suggests moralism); rather it is a matter of recognizing that the "perception" of immorality is a form of anger.

The tendency to see feeling as an accompaniment to moral responses rather than constitutive of them is one that, as we have seen, runs deep. The dictionary of the American Psychological Association, for example, lists the triggers of 'anger' as frustration, injury *and* 'perceived injustice', thus suggesting, with a curiously debonair assumption of moral realism, that our perception of injustice, and presumably our feeling of the injustice of injustice (whatever that may be), is a more primitive psychological fact than anger itself.[72] However, what makes "unjust" or "cruel" intrinsically evaluative words is not any possible description of the situations they customarily designate that might contain no words that were themselves evaluative, but rather the antipathy that gives rise to the need for the word in the first place. What, for example, makes the spectacle of a person inflicting harm on another solely for the satisfaction it gives them to do so an instance of *cruelty* is the feeling of antipathy that the spectacle inspires. (So that, for example, the ancient Romans could not have used "cruelty" as it is here defined as a term of moral disapprobation.[73]) However, in a context where the wrongness of such behaviour counts as a moral given, where there can be no morally neutral instances of cruelty, it is naturally extremely difficult to grasp this emotion-dependence. It is only from outside the context of such dependence that we can perceive the gap between description and evaluation ("traitor", "slut", "wimp", "infidel", etc.).

What, then, constitutes the wrongness of injustice is not anything that can be described aside from reference to the feeling of a certain kind of paradoxically disinterested antipathy it inspires in someone. It is strictly absurd to say that a perception of, for example, cruelty or injustice makes us angry. There is no cruelty or injustice there to perceive unless we feel this state of affairs is cruel or unjust, and that feeling is inseparable from anger. We would take a person who could reliably point to instances of injustice yet still sincerely ask what was wrong with injustice, as deficient in *feeling*, not understanding. As we saw in Chapter 1, insofar as it *is* possible merely to discern (as opposed to feel) wrongness, after the manner of discerning a property like symmetry or correct numerical order, it is only on the basis of discerning what we believe someone else would feel antipathy towards: moral judgements are only possible because of the *existence* of moral responses.

What, then, emerges from a consideration of the forms that consequentialist blaming takes (both in its direct form and indirectly in the celebration of such virtues of restraint as chastity, temperance or patience) is the way in which the moral experience can be *constituted* by emotions we do not, and apparently cannot, own. That is, the way in which we can experience self-interest as the conviction that "This, *from the point of view of the universe*, should not be". As was already remarked, the most common response to instances that render this conspicuous – as, for example, with other's consequentialist blaming – is to claim that such instances are a matter of mistakes or of self-interest masquerading as morality. This, we might say, is not what morality *should* be; we *should* not blame this way. However, this 'should' appears to be precisely the same "should" that drives everything that people experience as morality. (We could, of course, arrive at a theoretically universal *should* as utilitarianism does, or even through self-interest itself, by means of a Rawlsian 'veil of ignorance', but this would only be theoretical: while it could generate judgements, it would not determine responses.) Thus, it is arguably morality itself that masquerades as morality, in the sense that our moral realism, inseparable from moral experience itself, leads us to disqualify from morality any experience that seems to contravene what that realism implies – even though that realism is, as we have seen, itself untenable.

Materialist ethics: Disregarding consequences and intentions

Before finishing with moral responses in practice, there is one last form of moral 'inconsistency' to look at: those responses that appear to be determined by neither the motives of the agent (irrespective of consequences) nor the consequences of an act (irrespective of motivation), but rather are determined by the physical properties of objects in themselves. We might, then, call this the realm of *materialist ethics*, and what we are chiefly concerned with here is the relationship between moral responses and disgust.[74]

We must begin, however, by delineating precisely what constitutes disgust in an uncontroversially non-moral sense. Disgust, then, is a strong involuntary aversion: the antithesis of desire or appetite. The recoil, or urge to evade, that we experience is very much like the state of alarm except that, with disgust, the threat appears to come not so much from outside as from within ourselves. That is, what we appear to wish to avoid is not some external danger but rather a certain state of our own consciousness. What disgusts us feels invasive, contaminating or polluting; hence the way in which the fear that disgust produces is a fear of contact or, worse, ingestion. Nevertheless, the disgust is not this fear itself; rather, the fear follows from the disgust. (Thus, while we might feel reluctant to touch even a photograph of a disgusting object, a photograph of a dangerous object is not necessarily frightening.) We cannot neutralize disgust, as we might neutralize a fear by removing ourselves from what we perceive as dangerous, by endeavouring to meet the danger or by reflectively reassessing the extent of the threat, for with disgust it is the very mental state we are experiencing that we wish to avoid. An object may cease to frighten us without changing its appearance, but, with disgust, it is appearance itself that is the essence. The "harm", then, is in the very perception itself. We have, therefore, no defence against the disgusting object: our disgust represents a desire for the object to simply not exist, or, more precisely, for it to be not possible for the object to exist.

The futility of any possible response to disgust is, however, essential to the experience of disgust. For, as noted earlier, an object or idea is disgusting only insofar as we are disgusted by it, and it is disgusting just precisely because we are disgusted by it. Finding a thing disgusting, then, is not something that we can be wrong about, any more than we can be wrong about finding something beautiful or moving. This is not, however, to say that we cannot learn to be disgusted – it seems that many even apparently universal disgusts, such as that of faeces, are either learnt or only develop after a certain age – but only that, once we have acquired a sensitivity to whatever it is that stimulates our disgust, the response is involuntary.

While the experience of disgust appears to be universal, there is, nevertheless, considerable variation in the objects that elicit the feeling. This variation is not so great, however, as to preclude tracing certain tendencies in what is likely to be found disgusting. Perhaps the least controversial example is the decomposing corpse. Decades after the "event", I still recall the visceral shock of the closing lines of Poe's 'The Facts in the Case of M. Valdemar', in which the narrator reports how the protagonist, dead though still animated through hypnosis, changes upon being "wakened", within the space of a minute, from a speaking body into 'a nearly liquid mass of loathsome – of detestable putridity'.[75] The decomposition appears to be the key point since equally dead bodies in the form of mummies or skeletons are rarely found disgusting. It is rather a matter of the visible *active* transition from the body that is still sufficiently lifelike to evoke the living individual to the body as something else: the oozing, putrefying liquefaction of the organic. Indeed, the rotting of even a part of the body, as with purulence or gangrene, is a generally reliable elicitor of disgust.

The process of decomposition in other animals is also commonly found disgusting, as indeed are those animals that, even in a state of integrity, suggest such a process: slugs, worms, maggots or mould. Excrement, vomit, urine, mucus, earwax and dandruff are also often found disgusting. Blood is a problematic case, since it is, as a signal of damage, likely to provoke an alarm that may be difficult to distinguish from disgust. Nevertheless, some people seem to find blood disgusting even in forms – blood samples, menstrual blood – where damage is not in question. McGinn instances the interior of the body: its 'disgusting assemblage of grisly organs, damp tissues, and noisome fluids', the 'soggy monstrosities' of the heart, lungs, intestines and brain.[76] However, these do not seem a universal elicitor of disgust in themselves – that is, aside from the idea of these objects being visible, which suggests radical damage to the body. Just as, while there is nothing disgusting about the human head, since we are used to seeing it, a severed human head is a general elicitor of disgust.

Indeed, the appearance of harm in the form of the disfigurement of a phenotype (decapitation being an extreme example) covers a broad range of possible elicitors of disgust. We are often disgusted by evidence of mutilation, dismemberment, wounding, disease or ageing, or at least whatever suggests these things by its appearance (such as boils, warts, pimples, moles, wrinkles or areas of discolouration). This same response to "abnormality", or the falling away from what we are accustomed to think of as the intact, fully functioning phenotype, can also shade, for some, into disgust at the elderly, the handicapped, the obese, the excessively thin or those of a conspicuously different race.

Curiously, the ideal of the intact, fully functioning human phenotype may go well beyond what is actually natural to that phenotype. Generally, it appears that the human body is felt to be improved in the direction of an ideal phenotype – up to the point where it does start to become uncannily unfamiliar – by the absence of excrescences: by the degree to which it does exhibit a smooth uniformity while still retaining its phenotype. This is the raison d'être of soft-focus photography, of the peculiarly statuesque quality of what the nineteenth century called the 'chaste nude' (Leighton's 'Bath of Psyche', for example), and of the *sfumato* of the Renaissance. The same tendency can be seen carried into life in, for example, the appearance of current Japanese and Korean pop idols.

The idealization of the body appears, then, to consist of its reduction, as far as possible, to mere form, to what we have in common with the inorganic, which is never disgusting except insofar as it mimics the organic. (The limit to this tendency towards the inorganic is the necessity that the body retain both life and its basic phenotype.) This apparent urge towards a minimally embodied form of embodiment (mere 'soul and form') has led some commentators to suggest that it is signs of organic physicality per se that are the most reliable elicitors of disgust, though this thesis requires qualification – an idea that we shall return to later.

The sexual organs, too, are often included in lists of reliable elicitors of disgust. Here, it seems rather to be the association of the organs with sex that is the key to the disgust. Indeed, McGinn asserts that it is generally characteristic of sex 'to want something urgently that generally elicits aversion', that 'attraction-in-repulsion' is essential to sexual pleasure.[77] Counterintuitive as this seems, one need only reflect on the "dirty joke", or the hysterical tone of pornography copywriting, or, indeed, the way in which, in some cultures, many people's sexuality appears almost inseparable from either a sense of aggression (concomitant to the overcoming of an aversion) or abasement, to see that this may commonly be the case. Indeed, disgust is often quite directly expressed at any sexual activity beyond a certain narrow region of the possible spectrum – suggesting that this acceptable region is indeed beleaguered along fragile boundaries by the outright disgusting. Miller, for example, includes the 'self-defilement' of masturbation in his list of what is disgusting.[78] Oral sex, anal sex, homosexuality, group sex, sex between people of different races, sex between people of widely different ages, consensual incest, interspecies sex and even sex in certain positions have all been at some time, or still are, common elicitors of disgust. All of this, then, suggests that, for many people, a certain disgust at sex itself is constantly ready to emerge once the social pressure to *not* find sex disgusting is removed by the manifestation of sexual impulses in what one's society designates a "deviant" form.

The example of sex, where, in contrast to the elicitors so far discussed, the question of agency starts to become relevant, leads naturally into those cases where disgust appears to overlap or accompany moral responses. McGinn, for example, includes under the heading of 'moral disgust proper' the disgust people may feel at instances of cheating, corruption, cruelty, bullying, deception, selfishness or hypocrisy.[79] Elicitors of moral disgust appear, however, to be even more idiosyncratic than the physical examples dealt with earlier. Thus, McGinn extends this list of elicitors of moral disgust to include that which for others might be simply irritating – cliché, plagiarism, bad grammar – suggesting, given that McGinn is an academic, that what is found disgusting in the moral realm may crucially depend on the virtues one is most concerned with seeing exercised.[80] The character Marlow in Conrad's *Heart of Darkness* avers that he detests lying; it makes him 'miserable and sick, like biting something rotten would do'. (Interestingly, Marlow acknowledges that the strength of his feeling is disproportionate to any moral justification he could offer.) Generally, however, those who report disgust at actions that are generally taken to be, independent of this disgust, immoral actions also feel that they may somehow justify the intensity of their response in moral terms. (This phenomenon will become crucial later, when we deal with instances of "moral disgust" that prove difficult to morally justify.) Nevertheless, despite this felt moral justification, it is difficult to discover examples in the moral domain that are as reliable elicitors of disgust as those in the physical, regardless of the broadness of consensus there may be about those same phenomena as elicitors of blame. Hypocrisy, for example, is often cited, but, as mentioned before, I struggle to see hypocrisy in itself as a particularly serious wrong, let alone a disgusting one. Conversely, spite and contempt, which I do find disgusting, are never cited.[81]

The one thing instances of "moral disgust" do seem to have in common is the way in which those who report them perceive the fault in relation to what they take to be fundamental or essential to the preservation of the common good. Yet, at the same time, disgust seems to be elicited by actions that are, in one sense, trivial (bad grammar, hypocrisy, spite) when compared to the kind of actions we would most readily reach for to illustrate immorality. What seems to generally characterize the group of faults that are most regularly chosen to illustrate what is disgusting in the moral realm is an apparent lack of sufficient motivation. It seems that we are least likely to feel disgust at those actions that, however immoral we may find them, nevertheless appear to be the result of motives that we can potentially sympathize with. Thus, murder or robbery in themselves are unlikely to be found disgusting except where we feel the action far outweighs the discoverable motive; as, for example, killing someone because you do not like the way they are dressed, stealing from a charity box or increasing your company's dividends at the expense of public health or welfare. Thus, where certain values have become for the individual central to their sense of the common good then certain specific faults (cliché, lying, contempt) will necessarily appear to that individual to be disproportionate to any imaginable motivation. It is not that the faults could easily be indicted as particularly heinous in comparison, say, to the murder, theft and exploitation examples given earlier, but rather that, given the particular individual's heightened sense of the importance of the principle involved and the apparent ease of avoiding these faults, it seems evidence of a profound meanness of spirit *not* to avoid them: "There is no excuse", we would say. Moreover, so vivid is our sense of this falling away from what we feel is a basic minimum of moral sense that we are also likely to feel (very probably wrongly) that anyone who is capable of such meanness must also be capable of any degree of immorality.

Despite, then, the idiosyncrasy of our examples of "moral disgust", it is possible to see how such non-physical elicitors of disgust nevertheless relate to the relatively uncontroversial examples of human decay and the falling away from a perceived physical phenotype discussed earlier. For, it is meanness rather than either the immoral demonstration of a self-interest that we can sympathize with (even as we condemn the agent for not overcoming it) or the immoral demonstration of what we perceive as the *active* nature of positive evil that comes closest to a disfigurement of our phenotype of human nature. We may describe the evil agent as "inhuman", but what we mean is that the agent is something *other than* human. With the meanness that elicits moral disgust, by contrast, what we experience is a symbolic dissolution of what we take to be fundamental to humanity on an affective plane. That we have different senses of what constitutes this human affective phenotype – different senses of human nature – depending on when, where and how we live, is the reason why it is more difficult to find a consensus on "moral" elicitors of disgust than it is to find the same for physical elicitors.

The criteria for the formation of this ideal phenotype (physical or cultural) are more easily formulated in negative terms: whatever does not suggest vulnerability to dissolution. (The limiting factor for how far this invulnerability can be manifest is set by the requirement that the organism should still exhibit an optimal aliveness.) However, perceived vulnerability is not, of course, in itself sufficient to elicit disgust. Indeed, both cuteness and sweetness also depend on the perception of vulnerability. Indeed, the very "perfection" of the infant appears to be an implicit ideal towards which those techniques for suppressing the impression of organic vulnerability, such as *sfumato* and soft-focus photography, could be said to aim. Rather, what elicits disgust is a sense not of any specific corporeal vulnerability but rather of the fundamental vulnerability of being corporeal at all.

It is not, however, merely a fear of death (the inevitability of which is embodied in our embodiment) that lies at the root of disgust. It is, as Kolnai says, not death itself, nor a similarity to death, nor the approach of death that elicits disgust; rather, it is 'the terminating section of life in death'.[82] What inspires the kind of inescapable fear that is disgust is the vivid presentation of the idea of active decay, that is, *dissolution as a possibility of experience*. This is why the putrescent corpse, which still has so much of life about it, is disgusting while the skeleton is not, and why even live flesh, when it begins to sag, likewise becomes disgusting. However, despite the evidence of this urge towards a minimally embodied form of embodiment (mere 'soul and form'), it would be a simplification to view disgust as purely a matter of consciousness' fear or resentment of the bodily and the fate embodiment entails.[83] The bringing to mind of the idea of dissolution as a possibility of existence that lies at the root of disgust is as much a threat *to* the corporeal as it is a threat *from* the corporeal: it offends the body as much as the soul.

Having outlined the nature of disgust in itself, we now turn to its relationship to the moral response. Those instances of "moral disgust" (at cliché, hypocrisy, lying, contempt and so, idiosyncratically, on) considered in the previous enumeration of elicitors of disgust appeared to be very much a matter of disgust *accompanying* a moral response. Likewise, the contribution of disgust to intensifying our sense of the severity of the wrongdoing has also been alluded to. (Indeed, it could be argued that the difference between "bad" and "evil", where it does not turn on the extent of harm done, tends to turn precisely on the extent to which the act or its consequences are perceived as disgusting; so that one murder followed by cannibalism outweighs several ordinary murders.) What we must now consider are those instances where disgust appears to somehow actually constitute the moral response.

The most striking feature of the debate on this topic in recent years is the way in which that debate turns on the question of whether or not we can morally justify identifying some disgust responses with moral responses. In other words, it is, for both sides of the debate, a normative argument about what counts as normative. Thus, what we have to deal with here is less a philosophical disagreement than a clash of wills.

Among those who have advanced the idea that disgust can be equated with morality, there is, for example, Kass, who, in the course of arguing against human cloning, appeals to a 'wisdom of repugnance'.[84] The revulsion 'we' feel at human cloning, he asserts, arises not from its strangeness but rather because, in the very idea of it, 'we intuit and feel, immediately and without argument, the violation of things that we rightfully hold dear' (a definition that, janus-like, points simultaneously to disgust and to moral outrage).[85] While conceding that revulsion might not be an argument, he, nevertheless, asserts that in 'crucial cases . . . repugnance is the emotional expression of deep wisdom, beyond reason's power fully to articulate it'.[86]

The debate on cloning, therefore, cannot be 'reduced' to a matter of benefits and harms, rather cloning must be regarded primarily as 'a matter of meaning', and, since cloning is a 'pollution and perversion' that is 'fittingly' regarded with widespread horror and repulsion, that should be sufficient to close the debate.[87] Thus, while he does present some utilitarian arguments (repugnance, he says, 'need not stand naked before the bar of reason'), the main thrust of his case is an appeal to the way in which cloning affronts 'our' sense of the 'deep mysteries of nature and of life', and in particular 'our' sense of the 'profundity of sex' and the 'soul-elevating power of sexuality'.[88]

Conversely, Nussbaum argues that the degree to which a society separates disgust from indignation, the degree to which it bases its laws and rules on substantive harm rather than on 'the symbolic relationship an object bears to our anxieties', is actually a measure of that society's 'moral progress'.[89] In order to be 'really civilized', we must 'make a strenuous effort to counter the power of disgust, as a barrier to the full equality and mutual respect of all citizens'.[90] There is no subconscious wisdom in disgust, she asserts; it is neither an inarticulate morality nor a continuation of morality by other means. Nussbaum thus contrasts disgust with what she holds to be the genuinely moral response of indignation. While indignation, she asserts, is oriented towards harms that can be recognized as such by everyone, disgust is oriented towards the more idiosyncratic feeling of contamination.[91] Moreover, indignation is 'typically based on ordinary causal thinking about who caused the harm that occurred, and ordinary evaluation, about how serious a harm this is'. Disgust, by contrast, is grounded in 'magical thinking'. Thus, she argues, while indignation responds to the demonstrable fact that we are vulnerable to real harms that may be caused by others, disgust, in contrast, 'revolves around a wish to be a type of being that one is not, namely nonanimal and immortal', and involves us irrationally ascribing dangerous (immoral) properties to whatever brings our fear of mortality to mind.[92]

McGinn is similarly insistent on the distinction between disgust (an 'aesthetic' response) and condemnation (a 'moral evaluation').[93] Though many people confuse the two, he argues, we should bear in mind that there is no inconsistency involved in finding an activity disgusting from one's own point of view, while at the same time finding it 'morally permissable'.[94] His own example is homosexual sex from the heterosexual's point of view.[95]

Kelly, too, though he starts from a different grounding of disgust to either Nussbaum or McGinn, also holds that the emotion 'deserves no privileged status in ethical thought and should be regarded with deep suspicion in the moral domain'.[96] Since disgust, according to Kelly, is rooted in a defence mechanism against toxins and diseases what disgust 'properly' responds to are cues indicative of poisons and parasites.[97] Moreover, disgust appears to follow a "better safe than sorry" rule: we are disgusted even by what suggests the poisonous or infectious, whether it really is or not, and even when we know it is not. In short, the emotion, rather than representing an inarticulate wisdom, is rather 'a fairly blunt instrument', one that is clearly extremely susceptible to false positives. Given this unreliability, Kelly feels that, though disgust obviously does often influence moral responses and can seem quite 'authoritative' when we are in its grip, it should not have this influence: 'repugnance is simply irrelevant to moral justification.'[98]

The weakness of Kass's position in defending a 'wisdom of repugnance' in the matter of cloning is clear: if cloning does not outrage your sense of 'the profundity of sex', or if you do not have this sense to begin with, his argument falls flat. Moreover, even if you did share such a sense, you might still feel that the benefits of cloning outweighed the harm of the offence to sensibility – in precisely the same way as autopsies or medical dissections, though by no means a matter of indifference to the average sensibility of a population, may, nevertheless, be seen as morally neutral by that population by virtue of their practical value. All Kass can do is point to the idea and ask us to agree with him that, whatever the benefits, it is too disgusting to put into practice. If we do not agree, he can do no more.

However, those who argue against Kass's position, such as Nussbaum, McGinn and Kelly, are in a similar position. For, to exclude disgust from the moral domain proper, they must assume that this domain is itself a given. Thus, Nussbaum contrasts the 'magical thinking' of disgust with the authentically moral response of indignation, pointing to its connection to universally acknowledged and quantifiable harms. However, we have seen how, even where morality *can* become a matter of rational discussion, it can only do so on the basis of agreed principles that themselves derive their authority from immediate experiences of feeling that certain things simply should not be. Moreover, what these things are can only be "argued for" by pointing at them while inviting others to feel about them as we do. It does not matter that we might agree with Nussbaum that a society in which regard for equality and mutual respect outweigh the claims of disgust would be a better society, for if there is a consensus on the unacceptably disgusting this too will count, for that consensus, as one of the given principles of any rational moral discussion. What is "moral progress" for Nussbaum is "moral decline" for others.

Both sides of the debate, then, appeal to a reality underlying their responses. Indeed, McGinn specifically makes the demonstrable relativism in perceptions of what is disgusting into one of his arguments against acknowledging disgust as constitutive of morality, asserting that 'moral judgments *cannot* have such relativity built into them'.[99] However, moral responses (excluding disgust) clearly do have such a relativity built into them, so the argument can hardly be used to justify the moral disenfranchisement of what appears to us to be "merely" disgust where the subject claims that their disgust is moral in nature. The realism implied by Kass's notion that disgust is a special insight into human nature is mirrored, then, by the realism of his opponent's arguments that moral responses cannot be relative or 'mistaken' and still be moral.

As we have seen, while moral *judgements* may strive towards an ideal of what is rational and right, the moral *responses* on which they depend, and from which they derive their identity as specifically *moral* judgements, obviously owe no allegiance to such an ideal – or indeed to anything but themselves. Ethical systems, such as utilitarianism, might seek to bring some order to them and help us to find "solutions" to moral dilemmas where no immediate moral response is forthcoming, but, necessarily, they cannot legislate on the very moral responses on which they are grounded or which might be employed to test their application.[100]

There is a further, though perhaps minor, problem with drawing a distinction between moral responses to "concrete" harms (like pain or deprivation) and moral responses to what merely offends "symbolically" (sacrilege, pork, desecration, homosexuality), that is, to that which creates only an unwelcome mental state in the subject. It misleadingly implies, since the symbolic is clearly a more nebulous category than the physical, that when we talk of harm in the symbolic realm we are talking, as it were, metaphorically. This is misleading not because harm in the symbolic realm is not really harm (which, as we shall see, it is), but rather because the 'moral response to harm' with which it is contrasted is, as we have had occasion to remark before, not exactly what that description suggests. That is, the majority of what we might call moral responses to harms are not in fact made in response to harm; they are, rather, responses to harm to others or to the natural order, that is, to the idea of harm. (A *direct* response to harm would be something like annoyance, fear, pain, illness or death – that is, those responses that actually constitute being harmed.) A moral response takes the form "I do not want this to happen", not "I do not want this to happen to me". Indeed, the latter form, with its appeal to self-interest, obviously does not in itself constitute a recognizably *moral* response at all. (Likewise, with a response that was consciously a matter of "I do not want things like this to happen because, if they do, they might happen to me".) Moral responses to "concrete" harms, then, even where they are the *moral* responses accompanying the harming of myself, are no less a matter of the symbolic, no matter what kind of harm is involved. This, after all, is how tales of long-ago infamy can still inspire a moral response. In short, so long as the response is oriented towards a threat to myself (insofar as it is a threat to myself) it fails the test of disinterest; so long as it is disinterested it is not a matter of a "response to harm". The whole range of moral responses, then, from concern for other's welfare to concern for fairness to concern for "purity norms" (as evidenced by "moral disgust") is not amenable *from the subject's point of view* to the distinction, invoked in the discussion of disgust, between concrete (literal) versus symbolic (figurative) harm.

However, it is not necessary to appeal to either the circularity of non-disgust moral responses or their own ineluctably symbolic orientation, in order to establish the moral relevance of disgust. For, the contrast drawn, for example, by Nussbaum, between real harm and disgust (even understood as the expression of a wish to be a certain type of being) is a false one for a much more straightforward reason. There is evidently a harm in being disgusted, just as there is a harm in such other unwelcome experiences as boredom or embarrassment. Moreover, where we take it that an agent is responsible for such negative mental states, there is a tendency to feel that agent to be in the wrong. This is obviously so if we feel that the production of these states in us is either a matter of indifference to that agent or, worse, the actual intention of that agent's actions. It would be convenient here if we could simply draw a line, in terms of subjects' responses, between such intentional, or culpably negligent, instances of the production of disgust and instances of the wholly "innocent" production of disgust: to say that while we may be disgusted by the wound we are not, therefore, offended by the person suffering from it. To a large extent, this is, of course, the case; where there is no sense that the disgusting object is being gratuitously displayed or displayed precisely to elicit disgust, we are inclined to attach no blame, and certainly, as we saw in dealing with blame itself, it would be difficult to justify doing so on any intuitive moral principle. Nevertheless, as we also saw in dealing with blame, it is not necessary for there to be either negligence or malicious intent for a moral response to be elicited. For, in practice, many moral responses obviously do not defer to 'intuitive moral principles'.

That the operative principle in some moral responses to disgust is, yet, largely counterintuitive can be seen from the extent to which the subject will tend to appeal for justification not to the disgustingness of the object itself but, rather, to the more intuitively acceptable criteria of the gratuitous display of what is disgusting. The young and fit express moral outrage at the old and infirm "parading" themselves about. Thus, the very dynamic of the experience of disgust, as a form of rejection, can be carried over into the moral response to it – the subject does not even wish to acknowledge that what they really object to is the way in which the object functions as a memento mori for them; they prefer to be offended by a person than by a fact.

Cases such as these, where it appears to be the excessive insecurity of the subject (in effect, that subject's squeamishness) that is the operative principle rather than a response to any intended or avoidable "real harm" on the part of the agent, might lead us to believe that it should be a fairly simple matter to distinguish disgust from moral response. We might, for example, say that while disgust is an offence to the senses, a moral response is only properly such if real intended or avoidable harm is involved, or at least an offence against the sensibility, by which I mean the generating of a thought of that which undermines the subject's sense of human dignity (the "misuse" of human cadavers, dwarf tossing, pornography, reality television). However, there are two problems here. First, as I have remarked before, we cannot disenfranchise responses that subjects experience as moral responses on the grounds that they do not square with any theory of what is properly the domain of the moral – not in a context, such as the present one, where it is the nature of this very domain that is under examination and where the subject's own sense of what kind of response they are experiencing is the only sound guide to what that response actually is. Second, given that disgust is, as we have seen, a matter of the symbolic properties of objects, there is every reason to suppose that there will be circumstances under which, though no intended harm is involved, the disgust will nevertheless be experienced as an offence to sensibility, that is, as 'harm' even by this strict definition, within a certain community. (So that the list of that which undermines 'our' sense of human dignity must be extended to also include the old and infirm, cloning, etc.) For, it is obviously the case that one person's squeamishness is another person's respect for human dignity.

The appeal to disgust as a moral matter does not, then, have to equate the disgusting and the immoral directly. There is already a potential link in the fact that disgust is itself an unpleasant mental state, so that the deliberate or culpably negligent causing of it can fall within the moral domain even when that domain is defined in terms of harms. So far, I have alluded only to controversial cases, that is, cases where some would dispute either the disgustingness of the object or, more importantly, the right of others' disgust to *count* as moral. However, there are other cases – for example, desecration or sacrilege – where, even if we ourselves have no investment in the symbols involved, we nevertheless perceive a real harm to those who do have an emotional investment in those symbols. Moreover, it is difficult to imagine a human community in which nothing was held sacred. I do not mean the word 'sacred' to refer to anything religious; I use it only because it is the most appropriate word to describe what any particular community holds to be symbolic of an irreducible value. What is sacred to you is that the mockery or denigration of which causes you to feel profound offence – and that feeling of profound offence is precisely the measure of what you hold sacred. Generally, the objects of such a feeling are connected to the subject's sense of an intrinsic value to human life, to their sense of human dignity, with 'dignity' here meaning, in inescapably circular fashion, that quality of a thing that makes it worthy of respect. For example, the human body, as the most obvious natural symbol of the human being, has commonly been held to be sacred in this way. Thus, even when no longer alive, it is often felt that the body must be shown respect, as symbolic of the value of the human per se. (In the sense that it is commonly felt to be the natural object of the sentiments living people evoke in us.) So, for example, the same community that might accept the use of human corpses for medical research might yet baulk at using them as substitutes for crash test dummies; it might agree to abortion yet object to the use of aborted foetuses as dog food.

In the case of profound offence, it is the very idea of the existence of the thing that is found unacceptable. I do not feel it is wrong because I am disgusted; rather the disgust and the offence are apparently simultaneous. I may not be able to point to any harm (beyond employing a slippery-slope argument concerning the general effects of "dehumanization" that itself must presume the present instance to be dehumanizing), but neither am I in any doubt that this should not be, and this for reasons other than anything I can recognize as my own self-interest. I feel as if I am taking offence on behalf of everyone. Moreover, as we have seen, if someone reports themselves to be 'morally disgusted' by something, it is not open to us to say that what they are feeling is precisely equivalent to the kind of disgust they might report at a mere offence to the senses – "pure" disgust, as we might say. Only they are qualified to pronounce on what kind of feeling it is they have – no matter what explanations (as, for example, fear) can be offered to show why they might feel as they do. Furthermore, because the objects of this feeling depend on the symbolic qualities of matter, that is, on what, given who we are, things *mean* to us, we can expect no universal consensus on what these objects will be.

'No one in his right mind', asserts Feinberg, 'could claim that lewd indecencies or even privately performed sexual deviations that are shocking merely to think about are some sort of menace to individual or collective interests, a threat from which we all urgently need protection at any cost to the offenders.'[101] However, even if we agree with Feinberg and are happy to accept as a criterion for 'being in one's right mind' the conviction that these things, disgusting or not, are not a matter or real harm – as, indeed, we must if we do – then the problem still remains of what one might morally owe to those who are not in their right minds. Thus, for example, while arguments against homosexual marriage on the grounds of concrete harms (i.e. harms *anyone* could recognize as such) are easily dismissed, the argument that the existence of homosexual marriage harms insofar as it *devalues* heterosexual marriage is unanswerable.[102] For, the soundness of the latter argument depends entirely on the existence of people who *feel* that this is so. To say that someone *should not* be offended or that their offence *should not* count in any moral debate is not, then, to make an argument about the scope of morality, but rather to make an argument from one side of what is already a normative debate. This is why I claimed at starting that what is involved here is fundamentally a clash of wills: a matter of "We feel this, and, if you don't, you should" versus "We don't feel this, and, if you do, you shouldn't". No doubt a more abstract moral principle, of the kind that can yield moral judgements, could be agreed upon by the two parties, but the application of that principle, its "proper" domain, can only be determined by feeling itself.

Part III

Conclusion

6

The origin of morals

Moral responses happen to us. They are emotional responses, that is, motivating ascriptions of value, that cannot be reduced to another emotion – even where other emotions (anger, resentment, contempt, disgust, admiration, gratitude) may appear, at least to an observer, essentially constitutive of them. They are experienced as *necessarily* connected to the situations to which they are responses. Thus, we feel, and speak, as if rightness and wrongness were qualities of actions, and our responses had universal application, in the sense of being applicable to everyone perceiving the same action. We feel them as responses to a *reality*, or at least to a value that is quite independent of our interests (valuing). This is not to say that a moral response must be demonstrably disinterested, but only that it is definitive of the response that it is *experienced as if* it were not a matter of personal interest. The response is not, however, detached: as a feeling of *this should not be*, it is experienced as a disposition to act (to do or to undo), or at least a wish to see action taken. Paradoxically, then, a moral response feels very much like a desire, though a desire that is, given its felt disinterest, not mine. Hence the appropriateness of talking about the experience in terms of taking 'the point of view of the universe'.

The emotional nature of moral experience is obscured not only by the subjective experience of moral responses themselves, which feel like responses to moral *properties* of the world, but also by the place of morality within social life. Even the most supposedly etic of viewpoints – that of metaethics – tends to collapse back into the emic. Indeed, as we saw in Chapter 2, this remains true even where the emotional nature of morality is acknowledged. As we also saw, this tendency is exacerbated by the use of a single term, "moral judgement", to describe both moral responses and consciously drawn conclusions about the implications of assumed moral givens.

Thus, despite its paradoxical form – as a disinterested emotion, an anorexic desire – the cause of the moral response is largely unproblematic to common sense. Intuitionism may be viewed as the explicit form of the common-sense view of the grounding of moral feeling, insofar as it takes moral responses to (potentially) be exactly what they appear to the subject to be: intuitions of the *intrinsic* wrongness or rightness of actions or states of mind. This is, indeed, what is implied by our everyday discourse: that we *perceive* the morally right and wrong, and that these properties provide motives for action irrespective of our individual interests (i.e. motives that are, somehow, not desires). The arbitrariness of this position was examined in Chapter 1, where we saw that belief in moral properties is epistemologically gratuitous. In this it is like faith, and, like faith, it implies beliefs that possess a *greater* degree of conviction than those derived from mere perception.

The philosophical untenability of moral realism, and of those appeals – to God or evolution – that attempt to ground the moral in a suprapersonal reality (the divine or the biologically expedient), has given rise, as we saw in Chapter 2, to various attempts to either deny that the character of our moral responses actually implies moral realism or ascribe some form of de facto objectivity to the object (the wrongness) of those ostensible 'responses': in effect, to either deny that moral feeling implies moral realism or to arrive at moral realism by alternative means. The former approach gives us fictionalism, which claims that we either are or at least could become conscious of *finding* things wrong because we disapprove of them. This requires, however, a fundamental misrepresentation of moral experience. The latter approach – trivial realism – takes a variety of painstaking forms, though all can be ultimately reduced to the sophistical erasure of either the difference between reacting to a phenomenon and perceiving a phenomenon or the difference between a moral response and a moral judgement. That the recent and current philosophical scene should manifest, and accord respect to, so many such isms in the service of 'moral facts' is a testimony to the strength of our desire that moral values, even on reflection, should have some form of independent reality. This resistance of moral experience to philosophy together with the desire to *justify* such experience philosophically (in the form of ethics) are phenomena that themselves stand in need of explanation when we explain the existence of moral experience.

The moral response is neither a matter of a necessary response to the perception of moral properties in the world nor the product of the deliberate election of expedient norms. It is an emotional response. However, there is, as we have seen throughout the present work, a great deal of resistance to the idea of moral responses as emotional. Part of this arises, naturally, from the way in which we experience those responses *as* qualities of the world (the wrongness of the action), though I have suggested that the very excess of our "conviction" in this realm actually undermines the identification of moral response with perception/belief. Equally, there is the way in which the emotions most readily brought to mind by the word "emotion" are those that register the achievement or frustration of a goal, or the belief that one of these two things is likely to happen: joy, relief, disappointment, sorrow, longing, anxiety, regret, anger, fear and so on. Such emotions will usually be easily referable to the interests of the individual who experiences them, even if that individual is not always consciously making such a reference while in the grip of the emotion. In contrast, the moral response – disapproval, outrage, indignation, contempt, guilt, shame, remorse – while it certainly gives rise to desire (even where, as with fictional wrongs or with remorse, no action is possible), is experienced as arising quite independently of our own goals and interests (except insofar as those interests are themselves moral). Thus, while it is quite natural to say, "It makes me happy" or "I felt sad about it", the realm of moral discourse is a matter of "It *is* wrong/right/good/bad/just/unfair".

At the end of Chapter 2, then, having established that the moral response is an emotional response, the task we had ahead was to discover what goal was implied by that emotion. The method for undertaking this task was to turn to actual moral experience, and, in particular, those areas of moral experience that appear to throw up what are, from the point of view both of our reflex moral realism and the philosophical ethics that echoes it, anomalies. Thus, though we have traversed many "problems" that are already familiar from normative ethics, we have done so not, as in that discipline, in order to solve them but, rather, to see what their "problematic" nature implies about the moral response. For, one striking characteristic of the moral response is its apparent "disinterest", which is to say that we have no direct subjective access to the interest it expresses: we cannot analyse it through an examination of our own moral experience.

Despite this felt "disinterest", it was suggested in Chapter 3 that if the moral response really were a matter of emotion, then there must be some goal implicit in the form that the response takes. We began, in that chapter, by considering a goal (the greatest happiness of the greatest number) that seems implicit in very wide range of moral responses, even though that goal itself could hardly be said to imply what we would usually think of as an *interest* of the subject. Nevertheless, insofar as that goal appeared to be implicit in a wide range of moral experience (to be 'the Good'), it would at least have given us a general state of affairs that would be the object of whatever desire/aversion was implicit in the moral response per se, which would, in turn, help to illuminate what the interest involved might be.

I explained at length in Chapter 3 why I believe utilitarianism is the best *generalization* about what counts as "good" and "bad". However, as we saw there, while it does appear in perhaps the great majority of cases that the moral response is an emotional response to the threatened frustration (or, to a much lesser extent, promised fulfilment) of a desire for the greatest happiness for the greatest number, in fact, such a goal does not exhaust what is implied in practice by moral responses. For, it is possible to experience the more utilitarian of two options as *morally* inferior. Moral responses can imply desires for ends that are not only separate from but also, on occasion, incompatible with the greatest happiness of the greatest number. As we also saw, these other ends appear to be highly specific: for example, the avoidance of performing certain actions (e.g. killing) per se. Thus, there appears to be too great a variation, and too little consistency even in a single subject's responses, for us to replace the utilitarian formula with a more inclusive one. (It scarcely needs remarking that, if we were to try to deduce a general principle – an implicit goal – from what these ends, taken together, most *consistently* imply, we would end up back with utilitarianism.)

Moreover, as we tacitly acknowledge everywhere except, it seems, in ethical discourse itself, the relative vividness to the senses or imagination of the harm involved is also a determining factor in the eliciting of a moral response. Not only will the vividness with which we encounter (either in reality or imagination) what we would profess to be wrong influence the strength of our reaction, but it may even determine whether we react at all. Thus, what the moral feeling implies (the timeless, impartial viewpoint of the universe) in our experience of it in one context turns out to be contradicted by what we feel in another. We cannot *feel* that vividness is morally relevant, which is why, while its role in our responses is tacitly acknowledged in daily life, it presents an insoluble problem to deducing 'the Good' – as the implicit desired goal responsible for moral feeling – from the totality of our responses, which is the only way 'the Good' can be deduced.

What first emerges from consideration of what desire might be implicit in the moral response is that it is not a desire that can be identified either from the situations that elicit it or from the way in which it is experienced. With regard to the object of the response, it is not possible to identify 'the Good' even with the most plausible deduction (utilitarianism) from the common characteristics of what is routinely found wrong. With regard to the way the moral response is experienced, we discover that a moral response may contain an implicit desire/aversion – the operative 'principle' of the response – that, when made explicit to the subject, appears morally counterintuitive to that subject. Examples of such routinely operative yet counterintuitive principles would be that the degree of harm depends on how vivid it is to us, that actions outweigh omissions even where outcomes are identical, that harm intended as a means is worse than harm merely foreseen as a side effect, that harm caused through physical contact outweighs harm caused remotely and so on. None of these, we feel, from what our own experience of responding morally seems to imply, should make a difference, yet they demonstrably do. In practice, the moral response, then, rather than implying a single (albeit 'disinterested') desire, such as the greatest happiness for the greatest number, appears to express, at least from the point of view of the goal we feel we can discern ('the Good'), several incommensurable desires within the same individual. However, this incommensurability is only such from the perspective of the subject themselves – from the point of view of the way in which they experience their own moral responses – or from the perspective of a systematic ethics that takes the existence of 'the Good' as given, as indeed any ethics must if it is to be systematic. (Something must be taken as given, and that something must be itself recognizably moral.) We must not forget that moral realism turned out to be both an illusion and a necessary condition of experiencing moral responses. Thus, we should not expect morality to be understandable from a moral perspective.

What the innumerable inconsistencies in our actual responses suggest is that the goal, or function, of moral responses – the desire their existence signifies – rather than being revealed by the character of the moral response as we experience it, is actually somehow obscured by that character: that whatever goal the moral response per se appears to imply, this is not its actual goal. Thus, no system that is built upon what is consistent in moral experience will ever reveal what underlies that experience. This last can only be discovered by looking at the totality of moral experience and treating the apparent inconsistencies not as the anomalies they appear to be from the point of view of any ethical system based on the way the response *feels*, on moral intuition, but rather as constitutive of the phenomenon to be explained. For, our problem is not simply that the utilitarian (or, indeed, any) abstract moral formula does not manage to successfully capture the desire/aversion that gives rise to the emotion involved, but that we must account for why we should feel some formula could capture (in a concept of 'the Good') that desire/aversion. For, if it is not possible to identify what is desired in the moral experience with what we might recognize as 'the Good', we must still account for how our desire for it gives rise to the feeling that there is a Good.

The last two chapters, then, have dealt specifically with "problematic" responses: responses that exhibit the absence of elements that appear, in terms of how the moral response is experienced, ineluctably constitutive of moral experience. The first example of an "anomaly" that we considered was the way in which we may morally condemn what merely brings harm to mind, even where no harm is possible. Such is the case with the moral disapprobation of thoughts and feelings: the idea that a thought or feeling can be in itself immoral, irrespective of whether it is linked to the potential existence of any real harm in the world. That is, where the very existence of the state of mind is treated as the harm, as culpable. Moreover, the violence of the reaction is not commensurate with either the amount of harm (as we saw with evil) or even the likelihood of harm (the object of the response may be either past or fictional without altering the strength of that response); rather the strength of the reaction appears to be directly proportional to the amount of fear the occasion inspires. It is fear that causes the moral sense to overspill the limits that the moral sense itself appears to implicitly posit in the way in which the subject experiences that sense. Hence, its appearance, on reflection, as an anomaly.

A similar discounting of consequences in favour of the symbolic value of an implied state of mind was also discovered to take place in the domain of moral approval. This we saw with loyalty, which, despite being experienced as morally admirable, only exists as a contrast to the general good that the moral sense implies: it is, impossibly from the point of view of the way in which morality is usually experienced, a 'partial morality'. Moreover, while the agent themselves may experience the loyalty as morally admirable, it is, where there is no motive to identify with that agent, patently self-serving. This is not, of course, to say that it is consciously such: it could scarcely be experienced as morally admirable if it were experienced as interested. Rather the perception of loyalty as a virtue seems to lie in an unacknowledged desire to objectify the will, to perceive the self as driven, or even *determined*, by suprapersonal values, the following of which one may nevertheless congratulate oneself on *freely choosing*. Just as fear apparently "overrides" what the moral response implies in the case of responding morally to states of mind in themselves, so here, self-interest overrides the same. In both instances the symbolic value of the inferred state of mind *morally* outweighs consideration of real consequences. Most importantly, however, is that both responses exist only as *moral* responses. That is, fear and self-interest are constitutive of the moral response, though not as the subject experiences it.

The same conclusion can be drawn from a consideration of those moral responses that, in contrast to those discussed above, fix on the consequences of an action and assign culpability (or, more rarely, admiration) in proportion to the seriousness of the consequences irrespective of the intentions of the agent. As we saw, this tendency runs so counter to what is otherwise implicit in moral responses that it requires what appears to be an almost wilful epistemic failure: the ascription of responsibility – deliberate human agency – where the subject knows it cannot be ascribed. For, even the subject experiencing such a response implicitly seeks to defer, as far as possible, to a "rational" concept of responsibility by *perceiving* a degree of control in the agent that, in a calmer mood, they certainly would not. What such cases reveal is a standing *desire* to blame in response to harm. Moreover, as comes out perhaps most clearly in the 'just-world hypothesis', this harm also includes the harm of the threat of harm.

Consequentialist blaming is not a matter of being mistaken – of misperceiving the agent's degree of responsibility or the degree of culpability – rather the kind of responsibility felt to be necessary for blame is worked up from the desire to blame itself; the cognitive bias is an effect, not a cause. The blame precedes, as it were, the attribution of the appropriate form of responsibility. The schema for the moral response thus takes the following form:

> perception of harm → anger directed towards event → blame (feeling that something immoral has taken place) → construction of appropriate form of responsibility → blame directed towards agent → anger redirected towards agent

Indeed, it is not even necessary that the agent should actually be responsible for the action. This we saw with the 'just-world hypothesis': the tendency, when faced with the spectacle of another's suffering, where we are either unable or unwilling to blame the responsible agents or circumstances or when predisposed to hostility towards the victim, to blame that victim themselves for what they suffer. Here the desire to blame is even more pronounced, and the harm itself – irrespective of real responsibility – is more clearly the object of the response. We *resent* the very existence of suffering – the mere idea of it is experienced as a frustration – and the action of blaming appears to be a means of lessening the feeling of our own vulnerability to it. As with consequentialist blaming in general, blame is here a way of giving the fear-inspired anger the harm provokes, an appropriate object. We will deal later with why such an object might be desired. For the moment, we may note that the standing desire to blame that consequentialist blaming reveals can be seen as expressing a tendency to enlist the universe to one's point of view: to convert "I do not want this" to "This should not be", to transform personal resentment into *disinterested* antipathy.

Anger presupposes frustration: any experience of the world as other than we wish it to be. That is, it presupposes an experience of the world as a source not only physical pain itself but also the pain of the deprivation of an expected pleasure, and the pain of fear, or the pain of the threat of pain. Anger is an outwardly directed predisposition to action that will remove the source of the pain, a reassertion of the desire for the world to be as we would wish it to be. Even where impractical, anger is unavoidable insofar as it is not merely the reassertion of the thwarted desire but also, as a predisposition to act, a reassertion of the efficacy, or potency, of the self, which is precisely what the frustration has temporarily thrown into doubt. Moreover, insofar as anger appears to be an assertion of the self purely for the purpose of experiencing the possibility of such an assertion, it is, in one sense, itself disinterested. For, while it is obviously the frustration of an interest that inspires anger, the extent to which the emotion as such exceeds any practical response to removing that frustration shows that it is, in fact, at least partly an end in itself. That is, anger serves to ameliorate the frustration insofar as the frustration has a symbolic element: anger is a reassertion of the general potency of the self in the face of the sense of impotence or vulnerability that the particular frustration, as a token of that vulnerability, invokes. Anger, then, is necessary to our feeling that the world might be as we wish. It is our *acting as if* the world might be as we wish – even where that action is clearly futile. It is a protest we apparently cannot help making. As such, the very existence of anger reveals an element in our relationship to the world relevant to the moral response.

Blame is distinguished from anger in being perceived, where it is not obviously consequentialist, as *disinterested*: it is anger 'from the point of view of the universe'. Anger itself, however, as a predisposition to action even where no action is possible, is experienced as "disinterested" insofar as, while it expresses a strong interest, it does so even in the absence of any practical recourse: it is an assertion of the self purely for the purpose of feeling the sense that the self can be asserted. Anger and blame, then, are continuous in kind. Anger, by its very nature, is already directed towards an agency, even before that agency may be determined. Moral blame is anger that has fastened on a human object. Consequentialist blame arises where the force of the emotion is sufficient to overcome the constraints of reality, that is, the force of the anger overcomes the constraints of morality, as perceived by subjects themselves (and, thus, as a social phenomenon), in our election of a responsible agent (we morally blame where moral blame, according to what we might deduce from our experience of it, is not possible). "Normal" blame, then, can be seen as the same process – harm/frustration → anger → the enlisting of the universe (blame) – but in cases where the ascription of responsibility does not involve, *according to our own perception of morality*, any cognitive bias. That is, there is no need for any epistemic sacrifice in order to fasten on a culpable agent.

Indeed, blaming can only appear consequentialist against the background of a particular moral norm. As such, where the subject inhabits such a norm, this blaming is often, though not always, corrigible; it is simply a matter of the subject calming down or perhaps realizing they are alone in their response. (This latter makes it more difficult to entertain the response as moral.) Hence the way in which consequentialist blaming only turns out to be corrigible where it is perceived as consequentialist, that is, against the background of a particular prevailing moral norm (personal or social). However, across moral norms, there are clear examples of incorrigible consequentialist blaming: examples of contexts in which what may seem to someone outside the context to be unacknowledged fear, disgust or envy masquerading as morality is experienced by those within the context as the justified (disinterested) ascription of moral culpability. (All of those emotions/sensations are responses to the threat, symbolic or real, of harm, which is why they can so readily present as moral feeling.) Not only is it a simple matter to find instances of incorrigible consequentialist blaming (Sidgwick's 'chastity' was one), but even our own norms, when we reflect upon them, can appear mysterious to us in terms of precisely what, by our own professed standards of harm, is the harm involved – but appear so without losing anything of their normative force. The literature of ethics is full of those supposedly hard cases, even within our own moral consensus, in which we "know" an action (sacrifice of the innocent for the greater good, incest, cannibalism, etc.) is "wrong" without being able to provide a plausible account in consequentialist terms. However, this simply reproduces on another level the fundamental circularity of ethics: cruelty, injustice and so on are also only wrong because they are wrong. The words "cruel" and "unjust" only exist to describe/evoke the antipathy certain actions arouse. The 'reality' and 'rationality' mentioned earlier only apply to what is 'real' and what is 'rational' about feeling *within any particular moral consensus*.

This last phenomenon has appeared particularly clearly with the relationship between the moral response and disgust. We have already seen how the kind of harm that elicits a moral response can be understood to be symbolic (insofar as it is not direct harm to myself), but this has mostly been a matter of actual tangible harm to another, or, in the case of responses to inferred states of mind, the implicit threat of such tangible harm. In dealing with disgust, in contrast, the harm involved exists at yet another symbolic remove. The harm is the very sense of vulnerability that renders an object disgusting: to be disgusted is the harm itself.

This comes out in the way in which we cannot establish the wrongness of what morally disgusts us other than by pointing to the object itself and inviting others to find it wrong. (The case is the same, of course, with everything that is simply "wrong in itself", as indeed something *must* be if anything is to be "wrong" at all. Where the disgusting differs is that it cannot be incorporated into a system that will yield abstract principles, though more general concepts, such as "natural", "dignity" and "taste" are sometimes appealed to.) Hence the ease with which the argument from the 'wisdom of repugnance' can be dismissed by those who do not share that feeling about whatever object is being promoted as the proper object of repugnance. Those who argue against such 'wisdom' can easily point to the absence of any harm in the matter, with 'harm' here defined as what is rationally analogous to any of the harms acknowledged as such by the consensus to which they appeal (a consensus that naturally excludes the particular harm that their opponents perceive). However, there is no universal consensus, nor even, as we saw in Chapter 3, any actual individual moral sense that is comprised entirely of harms that are "rationally" analogous to each other. Everyone has something that is simply "wrong in itself", not merely in the way that what can be abstracted from moral experience (injustice, for example) is wrong in itself, but separately and, as it were, autonomously wrong in itself. Everyone has something that can profoundly offend them and which they feel *should* offend everyone. The self-interested ground of this feeling hardly needs to be remarked, for the harm involved (except in those instances where we are principally concerned with the harm of offence to others) is purely a matter of a state of our own consciousness.

Thus, in the course of the last three chapters, and particularly in the last two, we have seen a variety of ways in which the moral response is related to other emotions: fear in the case of responses to inferred mental states in themselves, self-aggrandizement in connection with the virtue of loyalty, anger in the case of consequentialist blaming and, lastly, disgust. Indeed, it could be argued that all these phenomena are united by the same dynamic: perception of vulnerability → fear (including disgust) → anger → moral response. While, however, I have argued that in each case this is a matter of the non-moral emotion constituting rather than adulterating the moral response, nevertheless, it would be a mistake to reduce the moral response to these other emotions. From an observer's point of view, the moral response can at times certainly appear to occupy the same functional position as, for example, anger (in the case of consequential blaming) or disgust (in the case of "harmless" offence) might for someone else, but this is not equivalent to the moral response being indistinguishable from these other emotions. That is, it is not a matter of the moral response being "really" another feeling in disguise; there is something more in the moral response, an extra element that obscures whatever self-interest might be present.

Moral feeling (as blame) *is* a feeling of antipathy towards instances of what are, *for the subject*, the egotistical disregard of the welfare of others or the proper order of the universe. What counts as immorality for a particular subject is what has been found to inspire a certain kind of antipathy: the kind that somehow includes the conviction that one's viewpoint is (or should be) universal. That this feeling of antipathy is, literally, essential to moral experience is something that may be obscured by the possibility of *moral judgements* and the way in which moral experience is often identified with the formation of such judgements. (This is not only a matter of ethical discourse; within a moral consensus it does appear possible to appeal to "reason" in these matters.) This tends to obscure the obvious: that blame – the perception of immorality – is, in essence, a species of anger. It is strictly absurd, then, to say that a perception of, for example, cruelty or injustice makes us angry. There is no cruelty or injustice there to perceive unless we feel this state of affairs is cruel or unjust, and that feeling is inseparable from anger. (We may, of course, make a moral *judgement* about the cruelty or injustice of a particular case without feeling anything whatsoever, but, as we have seen, such judgements are only meaningful in so far as they refer to the possibility of a moral *feeling*; a moral judgement declares that, for the sake of consistency, we *ought* to have a moral feeling about the case in hand.)

Unless we are to opt for a transcendental explanation, we must admit that to call the moral response "disinterested" is only to say that we have no direct subjective access to the interest it expresses. Moral realism, philosophically untenable though it is, is implicit in the way we experience moral responses. This suggests that whatever goal the moral response per se might appear to imply (the greatest happiness for the greatest number, for example) is not its actual goal. The actual goal, then, must be "surprised" by seeing precisely what does not make sense in that experience *from a moral point of view*. I have argued that, by coming to see such "inconsistencies" and "anomalies" as reflections of the actual grounds of the moral response, we might come to see that response not as we experience it but rather as it is.

What emerges from our examination of such anomalies (from the points of view both of moral experience and of systematic ethics) is that the moral response is an emotional response to the very existence of harm (pain, frustration, fear). The very idea of harm per se appears to act as a frustration: an experience of the world as other than we wish it to be. In this sense, the moral response appears very similar in function to anger: as an outwardly directed predisposition to action (even where no action is possible) directed towards removing the source of the frustration, and thus a reassertion of both the desire for the world to be as we would wish it to be and the efficacy, or potency, of the self, temporarily thrown into doubt by the original frustration. Like anger it is a reassertion of the general potency of the self in the face of the sense of impotence or vulnerability that the particular frustration, as a token of that vulnerability, invokes.

Each of the "anomalies" that we have dealt with – the role of vividness, consequentialist blaming, the extent to which the moral response can be provoked by what is merely symbolic of harm and so on – represents a point at which this response to vulnerability implicitly evokes a morality that exceeds (if only from the viewpoint of one's conscious ethics or from the viewpoint of another) that impartiality, the identification with the viewpoint of the universe, that appears constitutive of morality per se.

The basic problem to be solved is why there should be such a thing as morality: why it should appear to us that certain things are right or wrong *in themselves*, even while there is no way that things can be right or wrong in themselves. The very role of "rationality" in mature moral responses – the way in which, for example, a very broad range of them can be reduced to a principle ('the golden rule', utilitarianism, etc.) that itself seems self-evident – is, as we have seen, misleading when it comes to accounting for the existence of morality. In considering such phenomena as 'moral luck', loyalty and disgust we have already encountered the ways in which fear and desire outrun any conception of "reasonable" morality without ceasing to be part of *moral* experience. Rather as a zoologist must be ever watchful for inappropriate anthropomorphism, so in dealing with human values, we should be ever watchful for inappropriate ascriptions of rationality. Our holding of something to be of instrumental value is a matter of reason, since the degree to which an instrument is adapted to a specific end is a question of fact. But what I take to be valuable in itself has nothing to do with reason.[1]

There is another potential hazard in accounting for moral experience, aside from the tendency to ascribe to rationality whatever can be (in part) rationalized – that is, the tendency, arising from the nature of moral experience itself, to explain that experience in moral terms. Such is the conviction attendant on the moral response that it is difficult not to take certain moral responses as perceptions of self-evident truth. This is why intuitionists can believe that their position actually constitutes an argument and why, as we saw in Chapter 2, subjectivists seem to have such a difficult time remaining consistently subjectivist. As a result of this characteristic of the experience, many writers on the subject approach the question of the grounds of moral experience in terms of accounting for our 'ability' to think in moral terms – as if what were to be explained was the possession of some particular skill, rather than, as is actually the case, a propensity to certain kinds of involuntary response. Likewise, many seem to feel it is meaningful to account for moral experience simply by appealing to the existence of altruistic desires. In effect, they posit that we become moral because we are moral: as if our possession of a moral sense was the solution rather than the problem. Circular arguments are ubiquitous within metaethics.

This inability to *not* take the moral as given, and thus the tendency to confuse problem with solution, has a related consequence: a reluctance to recognize as a potential solution any account that does not itself have a moral cast. As if, having had the workings of the internal combustion engine and transmission explained to them, a person was then to announce that, clear as the explanation was, they still did not see how a car could cause all that to happen just by moving.

The moral experience is peculiarly hermetic. This is, indeed, what we would expect from what appears to be an almost universal projection. (We may readily see what appear to us to be "extra-moral" factors at work in the responses of others, but the moral nature of our own responses is simply given.) We cannot "get behind" our own moral responses: cannot see our own eyes. It is in this sense that we are all moral realists. Nevertheless, we may still attempt to *infer* a grounding for morality from the data that we have: from the nature of the response itself and from the kinds of features of the world that elicit these responses. There is, moreover, a third source of data: the history of reflection on moral experience – metaethics itself – which shows us what, on reflection, we *want* the experience to signify. These are sufficient to give us an input and an output for the mechanism that is the object of our investigation. This mechanism is also, obviously, the human mind. We might reasonably expect, then, that we could take into account what is already known of this mind, and, to a certain extent, this is true. What we know of what the mind is capable of cannot be irrelevant to the nature of the process that leads from stimulus to moral response. However, although we have seen how moral experience may overlap with other areas of experience (affection or disgust, for example), that experience is, nevertheless, sui generis. From this it follows that accounting for moral experience may be a matter of extending our conception of what the mind is capable of. What we absolutely do not need, of course, is a concept of human nature. If we already had a concept of human nature that could accommodate moral experience, there would be nothing theoretically problematic about that experience. Such a concept is our goal, not our starting point, and the form it takes will depend upon the account of moral experience itself.

The desired world

The moral response, as we saw in Chapter 1, is an involuntary feeling that something *should not be*. It is experienced as necessary, or immediate, in the sense that we feel we are responding to properties of the world, independently of any personal interest. (It is not simply a matter of *this should not happen to me*: it is exemplary.) At the same time, it also has the character of a disposition to act or see action taken – irrespective of whether or not action is even possible in the particular instance – in the manner of a desire.

This, then, is the first and most fundamental point: that even while moral responses do not, from the subject's point of view, take the form of desire, they, nevertheless, imply a desire. The desire they imply is a desire for the existence of a world without a particular object. (This object is most commonly an action, though, as we have seen, it is not necessarily such.) Moreover, moral responses imply a desire for a world without this object even in connection with objects – past wrongs – that no longer exist in the world. More strictly, then, we might say that moral responses imply a desire that certain *kinds* of objects should not be. That is, each object, each harm, is a token of the possibility of harm in itself. The *desired world* implicit, then, in the response, that is, the goal of the desire implied by the emotion, is simply a world without the possibility of these harms.

It would, of course, make no sense to say that the implicit *desired world* is desired because it is *morally* preferable.[2] For, we would then have to explain what makes this world morally preferable, which would take us back to our beginning: to the response itself. We cannot explain moral responses with moral responses. There must, then, be another interest at work here. To see what this interest might be, we must look at the kinds of objects that elicit moral responses. These are, essentially, what the subject perceives as instances of harm – deprivation, pain, death, disruption of the "natural order" (as a harbinger of deprivation, pain or death), along with those mental states that symbolically evoke such harms – insofar as they are the results of the actions of human agents. (Though, as we have seen, under the pressure of the moment we are prepared to extend the concept of responsibility even to the inanimate.) There is, of course, every reason why we should desire a world free from such things for ourselves: this follows from their very nature. However, a moral response is not a *direct* response to such threats to myself; the appropriate response to the direct threat of any of these things is rather fear and avoidance.

Aversion to deprivation, pain and so on, as they might affect the self, does not stand in need of any further grounding. Yet, what actually elicits the moral response is not the direct threat to ourselves of such harms but, rather, the very idea of their existence as brought to mind by any token of them. This we have seen not only in those moral responses to the obviously symbolic (as with disgust) but also in responses that discount consequences or intentions in a way that does not square with what the moral response takes itself to be. (That is, those instances where the desire to blame outruns the very conditions that make "blame" meaningful.) This sensitivity to the symbolic is also unproblematic, since every instance of such a harm, even where it does not seem to touch remotely on my self-interest, is, nevertheless, a reminder of the possibility of such harm to myself (hence, the importance of vividness). What it does, however, clearly point to is the grounding of the moral sense in an enduring *fear* of harm to the self. Every moral response may thus be seen as an occurrent state of this *standing* fear, brought into existence by an appropriate stimulus: a token of the kind of harm through human agency that we fear. In short, it is not that I do not wish to live in a world in which cruelty, for example, exists because I feel cruelty is morally wrong; rather, I feel cruelty is morally wrong because I do not wish to live in a world in which cruelty exists.

However, from a practical point of view, such fear in itself would merely produce behaviour that superficially resembled morality, insofar as it would take the form of an aversion to the idea of harm to others.[3] Moreover, so long as we were aware that this self-interest was the grounds of our aversion to the idea of harm to others, we would not experience that aversion as a moral response. Squeamishness and sympathy, while obviously closely related, are not identical. In other words, this standing fear alone would not explain why we are all moral realists in our feelings: why such a thing as moral feeling exists.[4]

Despite implying a desire (*this should not be*), a moral response is not principally experienced as a sense that something is not – as we might expect if that response were principally a perception of the distance between the *desired world* and the world as it is – but rather as a sense that something is: "This is wrong". To the subject the response appears to represent not so much a wish as the perception of a mind-independent reality (apprehended by the 'moral sense'). We experience the desire that arises from the difference between the world as we would have it (i.e. safe) and the world as it is as a property of the world, as a perception of what has value (undesirability) *in itself*.

This perception of our feelings about an object as intrinsic properties of that object, this projection, is a function of the strength and the futility of the desire. Just insofar as I do not acknowledge to myself that the object (the harm) represents a de facto denial of the possibility of my desired (harm-free) world, just to that extent I assert the possible reality of that desired world. The desired world, my response affirms, is not merely a matter of my desire, since what runs counter to it (even if only symbolically) is something that, from the point of the universe itself, should not exist. (Thus, I cannot even acknowledge to myself that I possess this image of a desired world.) Moreover, since I respond in this way as much to *tokens* of the harms I fear (in the form of harms to others even distant, past or fictional and in the form of the undermining of human dignity itself) as to potential real harms to myself, the very "disinterested" or impartial appearance of the response serves to support the projection. As, of course, does the fact that I am immersed in a community that similarly projects.

It follows that, to sustain the projection, with its assumption of the viewpoint of the universe, I must experience moral responses to my own behaviour also. (For some, as we have seen, this may even extend to experiencing moral responses to their own unwelcome desires.) If morality were merely a matter of unmediated fear, without this objectifying projection, there would, of course, be no reason why this would be the case. The viewpoint of the universe must apply to the harm itself, no matter who the agent. Thus, I am reluctant to be the agent of the harms I fear because, by doing so, I myself weaken the reality of the desired world – the world in which such things do not exist.[5] Moral realism implies that the laws implicit in my responses are somehow equivalent to laws of nature. Insofar as I feel myself capable of breaking such laws, to that extent I weaken my own sense of their status as natural laws, which are laws that, by definition, cannot be broken.[6] Fundamentally, I do not wish to live in a world in which such things can happen. Thus, self-interest gives rise to impartiality, a hypothetic imperative to a categorical one. Indeed, it may give rise to what appears to be much more than impartiality; people are prepared to die for "what is right". That is, they would rather not have the world than have it without the reality of the value that doing otherwise would entail.

Many writers discuss the tendency to respond morally to our own behaviour in terms of "sacrifice" or "obligation". Again, as with the notions of "moral beliefs" or morality "telling us what to do" that we saw in Chapter 1, this way of speaking strikes me as peculiarly detached from moral experience itself. I have never really wanted to do anything that I felt was morally wrong. This does not, of course, mean that I have never wanted to do anything that I knew others felt was morally wrong; that is a different matter. What I mean when I say that I have never wanted to do anything that I felt was morally wrong could equally well be expressed by saying that I have never felt that anything I really wanted to do was morally wrong. It is the distress I feel at the idea of another's distress that stops me from pursuing an advantage that would cause that distress. (Remorse occurs where I only have this idea too late.) I can understand why some should wish to, as it were, allegorize this feeling of distress into an external entity – Morality – but I do not see that this is either necessary or particularly natural. Indeed, while such allegorization would seem to follow from our instinctive moral realism, at the same time it also seems to undermine that moral realism in bypassing the strongest guarantee of that "reality": my own immediate feelings.

There is a sacrifice involved in moral experience, but it is an epistemic one – the repression of my own role as a desiring subject in that experience – rather than a sacrifice of desire itself. The non-moral desires remain in play, but they must compete with the very fundamental desire – for a world without the possibility of harm – that grounds moral experience per se. Given, however, that the only function of rationality is to help us achieve what we desire, it is unsurprising that we should be prepared to make this sacrifice. (Moreover, it is by no means unique to morality; witness the endemic biases that constitute human perception or the tendency to innumerable fallacies that must belong to any complete account of human reasoning.[7]) However, the very fact that rationality requires autonomy from desire in order to function at its best, and we have a general interest in its functioning at its best, means that such a sacrifice can never be completely successful. Thus, moral experience takes a form (the intuition of objective value, a motivating perception, etc.) that, as soon as we begin to reflect on it, ceases to make sense from any point of view except the moral itself (hence the tendency in philosophical ethics to constantly slip back into an inappropriately emic point of view).

We might, however, wonder why this epistemic sacrifice should be restricted only to a certain range of sources of harm: why it is only human agents or implied human agents that are the objects of moral responses. For, it is not immediately obvious why, if the moral response is grounded in the desire to avoid certain fundamental harms – deprivation, pain, death, the disruption of the "natural order" – we should not respond morally to instances of these harms that do not involve human agency. Why do we respond morally to murder but not to disease? To some extent, of course, we have found that blame *does* tend to spill over even the limits that morality itself implies, generating responses that can appear to observers, and even subjects themselves in retrospect, counterintuitive – from kicking the object on which you stubbed your toe to measuring responsibility by consequences. Indeed, the feeling that the universe itself should respect our moral sense is not uncommon. However, in all these cases an attribution of agency seems to be implicit in the blame. After all, we do go to the trouble of *punishing* the inanimate object.

There is, nevertheless, a limit to how far rationality can compromise with desire before the attrition to rationality becomes too obviously disadvantageous to desire itself. Responding morally to harms that do not arise from human agency would seem to go beyond this limit (though we are more likely to blame a cat than a poisonous plant). Harms arising from human agency are, in contrast to other harms, evitable; we automatically ascribe our own freedom of will to others. Thus, the protest against the existence of harms arising from human agency that is the moral response does not have the obvious futility that it would have as a protest against natural harms. Asserting prohibitions, in the form of laws of nature, against the very empirical conditions of nature would involve a contradiction so blatant that its origins in my desire would be difficult to conceal from myself with any amount of epistemic compromise. This does not, however, stop us from making that protest insofar as we feel able – irrationally attributing agency (and, thus, evitability) on the basis of consequences, from cases as simple as unintended and unforeseeable harms that yet have some connection to human agency right up to full-blown resentment of the universe itself. Moreover, it is a common supposition that we will be recompensed for the natural harms we suffer in this world by a future existence in another world without them – just as if the universe did indeed have a sense of justice. Such emotional overspill should not surprise us, given that moral experience is itself grounded in such an overspill. (Kant was right that the existence of the moral sense is the strongest argument for the existence of God.) Additionally, as we have seen, since moral responses assert an efficacy to our desires on the basis of the supposition of agency there is a strong motive to create even the illusion of agency if it will enable us to respond to harm as if it were a moral matter.

To some extent, of course, the harms that come to us through human agency, which is also part of our environment, might also be thought of as "natural". Indeed, it has been observed that blame per se is a theoretically problematic concept.[8] Generally, we feel that it is absurd to blame inanimate objects and intuitively feel in most situations that it is unfair to blame people for being instrumental in unintended and unforeseeable harms. Moreover, we tend to blame in proportion to the extent to which a person is compelled by motives with which we can sympathize. All things being equal, most would regard a boy who stole a loaf as the only way of preventing his little sister from dying of starvation as less blameworthy than one who stole it just for the thrill or out of malice towards the baker.[9] In general, the more we know about the motivation behind a crime, providing it does not turn out to be simple malice, the less we tend to blame. (This is why *ceteris paribus* we are most forgiving, most morally permissive, towards ourselves.[10]) The more, then, the action seems determined by circumstances beyond the agent's control, the less we blame. Conversely, as we have seen, it is common to feel that it is blameworthy to possess certain inclinations even if one does not act on them, and virtuous to lack certain inclinations, even where the virtue would only seem to lie in the *overcoming* of that inclination. (The reason lies, of course, in the relation in which the imagined potential for harm or the real harmlessness stand to the *desired world*.) Yet, this principle of agency, which seems constitutive of moral responses, at the same time serves to undermine them. For, all our actions are determined by what is beyond our control, in the sense that they depend upon antecedent circumstances, including those that form our character, that are necessarily beyond our control.[11] My intentions are determined by what is beyond my power of intention. My action may be voluntary, in the sense that I was not coerced; yet, if I am not responsible for what I am, how can I be responsible for what I do?

Yet, we do blame. We do not respond to the harms produced by others merely with a wish that the harm had not happened or that the person was different. Rather, we blame the agent as an agent: as someone who could have done otherwise. The moral response, then, is, in effect, an assertion of the reality of human agency. The kind of an entity that a human being must be in order to be the proper object of moral responses is precisely the kind of entity that I feel myself to be: a free agent. At every point at which I am conscious of being "determined", I am, by definition, not determined. At every point at which I am determined, there is simply 'I': the "free agent". I am not, therefore, capable of seeing my actions as merely a series of events: they are *my* actions.

We might think here of Sartre's claim that only existentialism gives dignity to human beings, since the 'first principle' of existentialism is that 'Man is nothing else but that which he makes of himself', and it is only this freedom that lifts us above the level of, for example, moss.[12] It follows from this, he claims, that, of all philosophical schools, existentialism 'alone is compatible with the dignity of man, it is the only one which does not make man into an object'.[13] Dignity, however, is a comparative concept, and it is difficult to know just precisely what we might be said to have to celebrate in realizing that we possess more dignity than moss, which is, after all, equally incapable of lacking dignity. Nevertheless, Sartre's existentialism can be said to be very much a common-sense philosophy, insofar as it expresses how we do, indeed, experience our own lack of determination, our freedom. At the same time, however, it is only half of common sense. The other half is the ineluctable feeling (manifested in moral, aesthetic and affectionate experience) that there are things that are valuable in themselves: our spontaneous election of what will determine us. Thus, though Sartre's objection to those who demonstrate 'bad faith', in appealing to their own lack of freedom in order to escape responsibility, is salutary where this evasion is a conscious choice, there is, nevertheless, a sense in which an element of spontaneous bad faith is a necessary condition of being human.

It follows from my own sense of agency that I must extend this same sense of selfhood to others like me or resign myself to solipsism. Some solipsism does, of course, result from the way in which we conceive of the selfhood of others, as we have seen in connection with our tendency to respond morally to the actions of agents in terms that would only make sense if it were we ourselves who were the agents of those actions. Nevertheless, in order to be a person, I must regard others as persons, and this, given the existence of the desired world, necessarily entails that I ascribe moral responsibility to them.[14]

As mentioned before, the very fact that this community of free agents also asserts the reality of moral properties to the world is another way in which the reality of the desired world is affirmed – even where some in that community are "mistaken" in their attributions of rightness and wrongness. As we saw with Hume in Chapter 1, the profession of any kind of recognizably moral experience tends to be taken as a warrant of the validity of our own moral experience. We are used to the phenomenon of "seeing things differently"; it does not undermine our faith in things being there. What is more significant is that we can all agree that there is such a thing as moral experience. Indeed, the very fact that, even as we all agree on its existence, we can, nevertheless, not articulate how it can be possible only seems to underline its "objectivity" – in the manner, as we have seen, of colour perception or the truths of mathematics.

The way in which moral experience depends upon the supposition of a community of free agents, and the relation of that community to our desired world, emerges clearly from the desire to punish that appears intrinsic to the moral response itself. Removal of the agent's power of agency, either through their destruction or by depriving them of the power to harm, would seem to be the rational response to their being an agent of harm. However, we must remember that every harm is also a token of the possibility of harm. (This is why the most vivid – most gratuitous or frightening – harms can inspire a desire for *revenge* even in those ostensibly not directly affected by them.) It is not enough, then, that the particular agent should cease to be a real threat, for it is not as a particular real threat that we respond morally to them. What resentment aims at is that the agency of the harmful agent should be brought into line with our own: that, having undermined our desired world, they should now, as it were, contribute to its repair: atone. Thus, while asserting the efficacy of our own desire by causing them harm in turn may go some way towards achieving this, what we ideally want is for them to restore the reality of our desired world by acknowledging its validity. We want them to regret, to see the harm as we see it. (All of this is, naturally, even further exaggerated when the harm is done to ourselves.[15]) Resentment, then, insofar as it is part of moral experience, that is, insofar as we feel justified (from the point of view of the universe) in entertaining it, enables us to carry on defending ourselves against a harm even after that harm has been done.

Despite, then, the passivity implied by moral realism – the ostensible resignation of autonomy involved in positing objective value – one of the interests that moral experience appears to serve is the enhancement of our sense of our own agency. If we were to experience the outer world solely in terms of acknowledged desires – merely responding to the threats or promises of that world – the sense of being something separate from our environment, upon which the feeling of agency rests, would be difficult to sustain. (We naturally baulk at the idea that our choices are determined by antecedent conditions – despite the fact that an event must be either determined or magic.) We might fulfil our desires, but it would not be as *our* desires. A means of suppressing my consciousness of being merely a desiring subject is thus necessary to preserve my sense of being an agent. This sense of being an agent is necessary, in its turn, to underpin my sense of the efficacy of my desires. By identifying with a point of view (*what should be*) that appears not to take my individuality as a desiring agent into account, I can thus recuperate a sense of my own agency. ("Ought" implies "can".) Moral experience, as unacknowledged desire, enables us to feel a sense of our own agency insofar as, in taking rightness and wrongness as *given*, we assert our individuality as identifiable with a universe that is not merely the flow of our desire and satisfaction, which flow threatens to dissolve our sense of agency, and thus our sense of self, into the environment. Hence, as we have seen, we both do and do not experience rightness and wrongness as themselves properties of that environment. We experience them as properties of the environment in the sense that we feel we are merely responding to their mind-independent reality, and we experience them as compelling, yet *we do not experience them as determining*. What, then, from one point of view might appear as a compulsion or restraint, from another point of view actually serves to enhance our sense of autonomy.

The preceding description of how the desired world gives rise to moral experience has been exclusively concerned with negative moral responses, feelings that something *should not be*. This still leaves the problem of positive moral responses – feelings of approval and admiration – and we must address these before we finish. To some extent such responses may be accounted for in terms of harm avoided. (Certainly, the word "approval" suggests a response to an action made against a background of potential wrongdoing.) When the word "right" appears in the realm of moral *judgements* it seems to do so exclusively in this sense: the right, or "permissible", is the lesser of whichever two evils are being balanced against each other. Thus, "good" is more often a judgement than the report of a response and is determined by a negative response to an alternative. Nevertheless, there can be an intensity to our admiration of goodness that seems to exceed the perception of what is, by contrast, *mere* justice. There is, however, almost no symmetry between negative and positive moral responses.[16] The desire to punish that accompanies the negative moral response is not balanced by a desire to reward in the case of the supererogatory; rather, the latter inspires admiration or affection.[17]

Another sign of this lack of symmetry, even within the experience of moral admiration itself, is that it does not take the form of a feeling that *this should be*, as we might expect it to if it were simply the reverse of a negative moral response. Negative moral responses imply a conviction, a belief in the reality of something (wrongness), that positive moral responses do not. We are more conscious of willing the right precisely because it arises only as a contrast to the wrongness that we posit as a property of the world as it is. In some ways, conspicuous goodness is taken as a token of the possibility of the desired world. However, since we cannot acknowledge to ourselves that it is such without simultaneously acknowledging the irreality of that desired world (its dependence on our own desire), we experience this token as a feeling of yearning that does not appear to have an object. Conspicuous goodness *moves* us, even to tears. This is because, even as we are overwhelmed by the promise of the desired world, we at the same time "know" it to be impossible. Thus, while positive moral responses would appear to merit the appellation 'moral' by virtue of being elicited by the actions of human agents in connection with (the prevention or relief of) harm, they are rather, in essence, aesthetic responses.[18]

We might say that while negative moral responses derive directly from the desired world implied in our fear of harm, positive moral responses imply a desired world that is desired for, as it were, moral reasons. That is, they have as their object not escape from harm but, rather, a desired world derived from what one desires from the world after non-moral impulse, self-interest, has been transformed into moral feeling.

One last incidental lack of symmetry between negative and positive moral responses is also worth noting. While the urge to the altruistic performance of good acts may be viewed, according to the grounding I have outlined, as a form of magical propitiation of the universe, an involuntary ritual performed in order to make the desired world come into being, it may nevertheless be contrasted with the same magical thinking as evinced in blame, in that, to some extent, in the case of altruism the magic actually works.

I have spoken already of moral experience being grounded in our fear of harm: in our desire for a world without harm specifically for ourselves. Given that moral experience, by contrast, takes the form, at its weakest, of impartiality, and, at its strongest, of altruistic feeling, I can foresee the foregoing account, with its assertion of the key role of fear and thus self-interest, appearing to some as reductionist (in the pejorative sense): as in some way denying the "reality" of moral feeling. It would, however, be nonsensical to take the inference of self-interest from the phenomenon of moral feeling as, in some way, proof that there is no such thing as moral feeling. Without moral feeling, as we experience it, it would not be possible to infer the grounding here proposed: one can hardly use the existence of a thing as proof that it does not exist. I cannot say there is no such thing as moral outrage or altruism because their origins lie in what is not moral outrage or altruism – for this is only a meaningful thing to say if moral outrage or altruism really exist. Debates about whether moral feelings are sui generis or have a non-moral foundation are otiose, since these are not mutually exclusive theses. Moral feelings are self-evidently sui generis (hence the expression "moral feelings"), *and* they are grounded in feelings that are not themselves moral. This is not a matter of reducing something to something else but, rather, of explaining, in a non-circular manner, why something is the way it is.

We might, nevertheless, say that this grounding in self-interest at least shows that moral experience is not what we think it is. Again, this would be a mistake. Moral outrage really is moral outrage and not another thing; impartiality really is impartiality and not another thing; altruism really is altruism and not another thing. Although I have used the expression "self-interest" to describe the goal of the drive that ultimately motivates moral experience, we must avoid anthropomorphizing this drive into another little person inside ourselves who is acting out of self-interest in the way a person, as we understand the concept "person", could be said, in any particular situation, to be acting out of self-interest. (Likewise, of course, a drive is not something that can possess or, therefore, lack a moral sense.) Indeed, the very use of "self-interest", insofar as we do inevitably think of it as a conscious motive in a context in which acting otherwise is possible, is perhaps inappropriate. It is as odd as describing the instinctive act of ducking as "motivated by self-interest", yet there is an almost insuperable difficulty in finding a replacement.

The problem is, of course, that all our vocabulary of motives comes from conscious experience. (This is true even when we speak of someone being "unconsciously motivated" or someone being "unaware" of their own real motives.) By contrast, the self-interest that is involved in the genesis of moral experience does not belong to the self *as I can experience it*. Indeed, it is constitutive of that self. (It is the tendency, found in both ethics and aesthetics, to identify this 'I am' with everything that happens to one – the 'arrogance of consciousness' – that gives rise to the kind of painstaking irrationality we encountered in Chapter 2.[19]) It is, therefore, a misnomer to refer to it as "my self-interest", since the 'my' here necessarily stands for something to which the self-interest does not belong. The self-interest is operative at a level of my being that cannot possibly be part of my sense of self: a level that I cannot, as the agent I feel myself to be, identify with. Moral feeling is not a matter of egotism because it is not a matter of the ego: it happens to us.

This is, indeed, the point with which we began: that moral feeling is involuntary, emotional. While, then, the foundation of moral experience lies in the instinct for self-preservation, the function of that experience in relation to this instinct requires that we really do feel desires, such as those inspired by sympathy, that are the very antithesis of selfishness. Self-interest gives rise to altruism, but the altruism is real. There is, then, no sense in which the grounding I have offered is equivalent to an assertion that there is no morality, or that we are all basically immoral, or that morality is "nothing but" something else.

At the same time, it is naturally difficult to think of a phenomenon like projection other than as an instance of epistemic failure, as self-deception and, therefore, as something necessarily standing in need of correction. But who is the *we* who would be in a position to make such a correction? Several philosophers, finding themselves committed to subjectivism, have gone on to argue that we should, nevertheless, not "abandon morality" (whatever that might mean), on the grounds that in doing so we would lose much of what we value. This does not, of course, make sense. If they mean we have good self-interested reasons for preserving morality, then what they are talking about preserving is not morality. It is only from a moral point of view that there would be any "loss" in no longer distinguishing between accident/inevitability and intention/agency, that is, in the loss of a moral point of view. But, if morality were "lost", how could we miss it?[20] It is another tribute to the instinctive nature of our moral realism that some have felt able to argue, in good faith, that we would lose much of value by ceasing to value what we find valuable. There is no "we", no recognizable "us", who stands to benefit from rectifying the epistemic failure inherent in moral experience. It is not a matter of whether we should or should not try to get outside our tendency to experience the world in moral terms – we *cannot*.[21] At most we can pretend to be nihilistic, as nihilists do.

However, perhaps the least rational of all responses to the thesis that morality is a matter of emotion, and, therefore, a relative rather than absolute matter, is to be found among those writers who conclude their expositions of the subjective basis of morality by celebrating the moral benefits – in terms of increased tolerance for moral senses that differ from our own – to be accrued from recognizing the truth of moral relativism. This is yet another example of that extraordinary tendency to treat one's own moral feelings not only as *beliefs* but even beliefs that one is somehow responsible for. For, to *feel* one's own moral sense to be a relative matter would be to have no moral sense at all.

Nevertheless, while neither nihilism nor moral uplift is an appropriate response to the grounding of moral feeling in emotion proposed here, it should be clear by now that there are consequences for normative ethics that do follow from such a grounding. With many areas of philosophy, it matters very little that we should evermore come out by the same door as in we went. (In epistemology, for example, it would be alarming if we did not.) Ethics, however, is generally felt to be an area of philosophy where it is possible to achieve "results" in terms of establishing relative degrees of "wrongness" or "permissibility", or even in terms of establishing the relative consistency of ethical principles themselves; in short, to arrive at correct, generally applicable, solutions to moral dilemmas. That is, ethics is supposed to have a direct application to behaviour insofar as it helps us to discover what we *should* do. Indeed, it has often gone by the name of 'practical philosophy'. Thus, we have seen, particularly in Chapter 2, how central is the idea of moral debate (with the implication that solutions are possible) to many people's very concept of ethics.

It has already been conceded that reasoned moral debate is possible where those involved can appeal to a common criterion in the form of a general moral *judgement* that is not in question, that is, where the parties either tacitly agree on the existence of moral facts (they have responses in common) or tacitly agree to reason *as if* there were moral facts. As we saw in Chapter 1, with this type of "moral reasoning", reason works not to produce a moral response but rather to produce a further moral judgement, in the sense of a verdict on the wrongness of *x* on the basis of its being an instance of *y*, where the wrongness of *y* is *treated as a fact*.[22] Yet, *moral* judgements are such only insofar as they invoke the experience of moral responses, and any moral judgement ultimately must stand or fall before the individual's experience of such a response.

The moral response itself, in contrast to such judgements, defers to nothing (not even professed "moral beliefs") other than itself.

Moral feeling is an involuntary emotional response to tokens of harm, and what the individual takes as a token of harm depends entirely on the vividness of the connection between the relevant action/object and the individual's perception of what constitutes harm, which vividness and even the connections themselves are very much a matter of upbringing and experience. Moreover, I experience what are moral qualities *to me* as properties of my world: they are integral to my whole sense of what the world is/I am. We cannot, then, expect to achieve anything by arguing from principles, since principles are entirely beside the point. It is possible to "win" an argument about moral judgements, and what should, logically, follow from what, but principles and judgements are essentially artefacts of a feeling that is determined by quite other considerations than logic. Since philosophical ethics can never be exclusively a matter of judgements without losing its connection to life but must ultimately defer to that form of response that gives those judgements their identity as *moral* judgements, the perennial problems of ethics, which are also the constitutive elements of the discipline, must remain, like a flawed puzzle, forever insoluble.

Notes

Chapter 1

1. Gilbert and Sullivan, *The Pirates of Penzance*, Act 1, p. 197.
2. 'When a man denominates another his *enemy*, his *rival*, his *antagonist*, his *adversary*, he is understood to speak the language of self-love, and to express sentiments, peculiar to himself, and arising from his particular circumstances and situation. But when he bestows on any man the epithets of *vicious* or *odious* or *depraved*, he then speaks another language, and expresses sentiments, in which he expects all his audience are to concur with him. He must here, therefore, depart from his private and particular situation, and must choose a point of view, common to him with others; he must move some universal principle of the human frame, and touch a string to which all mankind have an accord and symphony.' Hume, *Enquiries Concerning Human Understanding and Concerning the Principles of Morals*, p. 272. Hume would have called moral responses 'moral sentiments'.
3. It is, of course, quite common to hear things like "That's wrong as far as I'm concerned", but the implication here is surely that if you could see the situation as the speaker does, you would also find it wrong, or if you had a moral sense (which you obviously don't), you would also find it wrong.
4. Hume, *A Treatise of Human Nature*, I, p. 303 (slightly modernized).
5. We shall come back to this phenomenon in Chapter 5.
6. We might argue, and it has been argued, that a response that could be shown to be definitely clear of self-interest would have to be more correct, more *really* moral. This is not warranted by the description of the moral response. It is, however, an argument that we shall encounter repeatedly throughout this book.
7. Since I am here describing moral responses rather than rationally justifying them, and given the "insolubility" of basic ethical questions, I take the very fact that this last formulation does not make sense as counting in favour of its accuracy.
8. As there would be in talk about "aesthetic beliefs" or "erotic beliefs".
9. We often do use "think" in this informal way, as we might say we "think" a comedian is funny, though we do not mean that we have arrived at this opinion in any way other than by laughing. "Think" here does not mean the same as it does in "I think my library card is in my wallet". Indeed, it is easy to imagine a language in which it would not be possible to use the same word in both contexts.
10. Shafer-Landau, *Moral Realism*, p. 4.
11. 2 Samuel 11. This example is used for a different purpose by Sharp in his *Ethics*, pp. 119–20.
12. 2 Samuel 12.
13. The anti-piracy trailer, usually known as 'You Wouldn't Steal a Car', made by the Motion Picture Association of America in 2004.

14 Think, for example, of the variety of responses possible to Kohlberg's 'Heinz dilemma'; 'The Development of Children's Orientations towards a Moral Order', p. 19.
15 Significantly, in law, the 'insanity defence' is not open to sociopaths: legal guilt depends not on the *feeling* that you were doing wrong but on the *knowledge* that you were doing wrong.
16 See, for example, Cudworth, *A Treatise Concerning Eternal and Immutable Morality*, pp. 16–19; Balguy, *The Foundation of Moral Goodness*, pp. 22; 28; Price, *A Review of the Principal Questions and Difficulties in Morals*, pp. 66; 73–5; Reid, *Essays on the Active Powers of Man*, p. 355.
17 Just as it would perhaps be possible to reach a conclusion about the relative strengths of the Hulk and the Thing given sufficient information regarding the properties of the fictional universes to which they belong.
18 Changes in customs are not as strong an indicator of consensus on moral responses as this argument makes them appear. What is permissible or impermissible within a society clearly depends at least as much upon the distribution of power within that society as it does upon the existence of any moral consensus. (Even twenty-first-century democracies do not, in reality, consistently represent the general will of the majority of the people they contain.) This is neither an argument for nor against the existence of common agreement or moral progress, only a caution against appealing to historical or cross-cultural data.
19 For example, the position Socrates attributes to Protagoras in Plato's *Theatetus*, 177d.
20 Hobbes, *Leviathan*, p. 39.
21 Ibid.
22 Hume, *A Treatise of Human Nature*, I, p. 301.
23 Ibid., p. 302.
24 Ibid. (slightly modernized).
25 Although Locke does not use sentimental language, his discussion of good and evil in terms of pleasure and pain entails, given that emotions are anticipations of pleasure or pain, that moral responses are emotional. Culverwell makes the feelings more aesthetic than sensational: 'there is such a Magnetical power in some good, as must needs allure and attract a Rational Being; there is such a native fairnesse, such an intrinsecal lovelinesse in some objects as does not depend upon an external command, but by its own worth must needs win upon the Soul: and there is such an inseparable deformity and malignity in some evil, as that Reason must needs loath it and abominate it'; *An Elegant and Learned Discourse of the Light of Nature*, p. 54. (Given, however, that we are created, such 'sentimentalism' does not at all contradict the idea of the objective reality of right and wrong: 'the Law of Nature is nothing but . . . the copying out of the eternal Law, and the imprinting of it upon the breast of a Rational being' (p. 35).) This appeal to our created nature allows such sentimentalism, in contrast perhaps to Hobbes' version, to be compatible with a form of realism. We find the same in Shaftesbury, Hutcheson, Butler, Hume and Smith, who famously refer to moral responses as matters of 'affection', 'passion', or 'sentiment' (Shaftesbury, *Characteristics of Men, Manners, Opinions, Times*, pp. 326–7; 413; Hutcheson, *An Essay on the Nature and Conduct of the Passions and Affections*, pp. 15–18; Butler, *Fifteen Sermons Preached at the Rolls Chapel*, pp. 6–13; Hume, *A Treatise of Human Nature*, I, pp. 301–2; Smith, *The Theory of Moral Sentiments*, pp. 11–52). Moreover, though emotional nomenclature gives way within ethics during the nineteenth century (for reasons discussed in the following note)

to moral 'ideas' or 'judgements', it continues within psychology. Cogan, for example, classifies what we might call 'positive judgements' (admiration) under 'passions and affections derived from the social principle', and such 'negative judgements' as indignation in both the preceding category and under 'passions and affections which owe their origin to the principle of self-love'; *A Philosophical Treatise on the Passions*, p. 46. Brown talks of the 'distinctive emotions of moral approbation or disapprobation' and of 'moral sentiment'; *Lectures on the Philosophy of the Mind*, III, pp. 483 (see also pp. 198–206). Ramsay not only refers to 'moral emotions' but also emphasizes their phenomenological contiguity with more obviously self-regarding emotions; *An Enquiry Into the Principles of Human Happiness and Human Duty*, pp. 397–8. Whewell describes approbation, disapprobation, indignation, and esteem as the 'moral sentiments'; *The Element of Morality, Including Polity*, I, pp. 27–8. He also speaks of a 'Sentiment of Rights' and a 'Sentiment of Wrongs' arising from the rights accorded to members of a particular society, which in turn give rise to a 'Sentiment of Obligation' (I, pp. 51–3). (His sentimentalism is unproblematic from a realist point of view, since he grounds the affections in general in the will of God: 'It was intended [by God] that Appetite should operate for the preservation of the individual; that the Affections should collect men into Families and Societies; that the Reason should direct and control both the Appetites and the Affections; that the Sentiments of Approbation and Disapprobation should aid the Reason in this office. It was intended, for instance, that Shame should prevent our doing shameful actions' (II, p. 5.)) Bailey consistently deals with morality under the title of 'moral sentiments'; *Letters on the Philosophy of the Human Mind*, pp. 193–258. Laurie talks of the 'sentiment of justice', alongside the 'sentiments' of the beautiful and the divine; *On the Philosophy of Ethics*, pp. 100–2. Bain refers to the 'moral sentiment', which he also calls 'conscience'; *Mental and Moral Science*, p. 448. Fowler refers, throughout his work, to the object of his study as 'the moral sentiment'; *Progressive Morality*, passim. Lotze places 'ethical feeling' alongside 'aesthetic feeling', on the grounds that approbation and disapprobation are nothing else but the expression of a value, or absence of value, which we perceive only as feeling: totally distinct from 'theoretical judgment concerning the truth or untruth of a proposition'; *Outlines of Psychology*, pp. 76–7. (See, however, his very different approach in Lotze, *Outlines of Practical Philosophy*.) Dewey refers to both moral 'feeling' and 'moral sentiment'; *Psychology*, pp. 335–7. James places 'moral, intellectual, and aesthetic feelings' together under the heading of the 'subtler emotions', though he there confines his discussion to the last of the three; *The Principles of Psychology*, II, pp. 468–72. Baldwin classifies 'ethical feeling' as an 'emotion of relation'; *Handbook of Psychology*, pp. 205–14. Stanley concerns himself exclusively with characterizing the precise nature of the 'ethical emotion' in contrast to the other emotions with which it might be confused; *Studies in the Evolutionary Psychology of Feeling*, pp. 332–44. Ribot classifies the 'moral sentiment' as one of the 'complex emotions'; *The Psychology of the Emotions*, pp. 275–6; 289.

26 Partly it is the result of an increased emphasis on the normative, in which context "judgement" is, as we have seen, a perfectly serviceable word. Partly, as a reaction against the Enlightenment, it is a desire to avoid the idea that morality is *just* a matter of emotion. There was, as we shall see, no problem with regarding moral feeling as a matter of emotion from a religious point of view, so long as it was accepted that God was responsible for our emotional composition. However, the practice becomes problematic where the internal consistency of the psychological account starts to

render a supernatural explanation *unnecessary*. It is this perceived lack of a need for God, rather than anything strictly irreligious in eighteenth-century philosophy that gives rise to a reaction against that philosophy. Conversely, it is also partly a desire to replace God-given emotion with reason. After a while, of course, the reason is simply because that is the accepted vocabulary within the discipline: one does as the others do.

27 The phrase is Sidgwick's; see *Methods of Ethics*, pp. xviii; 382; 420.
28 Ross, *The Right and the Good*, pp. 20; 20nI. 'The main moral convictions of the plain man seem to me to be, not opinions which it is for philosophy to prove or disprove, but knowledge from the start; and in my own case I seem to find little difficulty in distinguishing these essential convictions from other moral convictions which I also have, which are merely fallible opinions based on an imperfect study of the working for good or evil of certain institutions or types of action' (p. 20nI). (DePaul usefully defines 'intuition' as a belief not based on perception, introspection, memory, testimony or inference: a conviction that something is true simply because it 'seems true'; 'Intuitions in Moral Enquiry', p. 595.) The notion of moral feeling as intuition does not, of course, originate with Ross. It has been commonplace for centuries: 'Practical moral truths, when *simple* are discerned when the terms that express them are understood; not by reasoning, but instinctively by the moral sense, which, like other senses, is by nature implanted in us'; Kirwan, *Metaphysical Essays*, pp. 414–15. Moreover, although I here take Ross as exemplary, there are, as we shall see, contemporary philosophers who substantially align themselves with Ross in their belief in 'intuitive moral knowledge'. Shafer-Landau, for example, argues that having moral response is equivalent to discovering moral truth *a priori*, for moral properties are non-natural properties of natural substances: 'a moral fact supervenes on a particular concatenation of descriptive facts just because these facts *realize* the moral property in question. Moral facts [supervene on] descriptive ones because moral properties are always realized exclusively by descriptive ones'; *Moral Realism*, p. 77. (However, he believes that, since we discover moral truths *a priori*, ethics can never be a science (p. 64).) Audi is explicitly Rossian; see *The Good in the Right*, pp. 40–79. According to Audi, since there is 'moral perception' upon which 'some of our sound moral beliefs' rest, it is possible to say that there is 'moral knowledge'; *Moral Perception*, p. viii. 'Moral properties', he asserts, 'are anchored in the natural world in a way that makes possible moral knowledge and the ethical objectivity that goes with it' (p. 170). Although such 'moral properties' are not 'sensory', nevertheless 'there is a kind of perceptual experience that appropriately incorporates the properties that ground the moral property that we sense. Perceptibility is not exhausted by perceptuality' (pp. 40–1). The existence of such properties is guaranteed by the consensus of 'morally normal' people, though such people do not constitute a majority: 'many people *can* view a perceptible injustice without perceiving injustice', since 'the proportion of people who are morally percipient, or indeed even morally normal at all, is smaller than the proportion who are perceptually normal' (p. 43). Indeed, given that moral properties are properties of the world for Audi, consensus is not necessary at all: 'there could be such moral properties (and acts exhibiting them) even if there were no morally sound observers but only barbarous offenders' (p. 49).
29 Ross, *The Right and the Good*, p. 20nI.
30 Ibid., p. 21. I have added the sixth in accordance with what he says in the text, though he does not include it in his numbered list. I have used 'demonstrate' in (1) and (2) to reflect the fact that he emphasizes that we do not have a duty to have certain motives

but rather to do certain acts. This same conviction also explains Ross's choice of 'beneficence' and 'maleficence' over 'benevolent' and 'malevolent' (pp. 22–3). I have preferred Ross's examples over Huemer's, despite the fact that I address Huemer's version of intuitionism more closely in what follows, due to the shortcomings of his examples: 'Enjoyment is better than suffering' (does not contain a moral term), 'If *A* is better than *B* and *B* is better than C, then *A* is better than C' (is a necessary general truth arising from the use of any comparative), 'It is unjust to punish a person for a crime he did not commit' (describes an impossible circumstance, since it is not 'punishment' unless the person committed the crime), 'Courage, benevolence, and honesty are virtues' (is merely true of the meanings of the words and is not an assertion of the goodness of courage, benevolence, honesty, or virtue), 'If a person has a right to do something, then no person has a right to forcibly prevent him from doing that thing' (is a tautology), 'Suffering is bad' (is true by definition and not a moral proposition), 'If an action is wrong, then any qualitatively indistinguishable action (in identical circumstances) is also wrong' (holds true no matter what adjective takes the place of 'wrong'), 'No person is blameworthy for an action they did not perform' (is necessarily true, given the meaning of 'blameworthy'); *Ethical Intuitionism*, pp. 102; 231–2. In short, none of Huemer's explicit examples of moral intuitions qualify as the kind of specifically *moral* intuition that he is defending, though several genuine ones are embedded in his discussion.

31 Ross, *The Right and the Good*, p. 20nI.
32 Indeed Stratton-Lake makes this agreement between common sense and intuitionism an argument for intuitionism; 'Introduction', pp. 25–8. However, he is principally interested in a legislative function for ethics and thus sees intuitionism not as a contrast to an inquiry into the grounds of moral experience but rather as a contrast to theories that might systematize such experience into principles that feeling would then be obliged to defer to (p. 26). Nevertheless, since he is committed to a moral realism, he also believes that such systematization should be possible (p. 27).
33 Despite this difference, Huemer does appeal at one point to this informal use of "intuition". In describing how he arrived at an intuitionist standpoint, he relates how he 'noticed that there were *many* things I knew that I could never prove in any scientific, intersubjectively accessible way', such as the identity of a friend on the phone, or that someone was upset; Huemer, *Ethical Intuitionism*, p. 251. Indeed, he quotes Einstein on this kind of intuition – 'The only really valuable thing is intuition' – as the epigraph to his book (p. vi). However, Einstein's intuitions, the identity of the friend on the phone, and whether or not someone is upset, are all susceptible to falsification, and thus irrelevant to ethical intuitionism.
34 Huemer outlines his thesis as being that 'there are objective evaluative facts – facts such as that it is wrong to cause gratuitous suffering to others – over and above the natural, non-evaluative facts; that we have a kind of intellectual insight into some of these evaluative facts; and that they provide us with reasons for behaving in certain ways, irrespective of what we desire'; *Ethical Intuitionism*, p. xxiv.
35 Huemer, *Ethical Intuitionism*, p. 223.
36 Ibid., pp. 5; 201.
37 Huemer would evidently not be content with this conclusion, for he insists that moral intuitions are falsifiable: 'Not all intuitions are equal–some are more credible than others. . . . [One] reason for this is that some intuitions are simply stronger, or more clearly seem true, than others. Another reason is that some intuitions are more widely shared than others; other things being equal, an intuition that many

disagree with is more likely to be an error than is an intuition that nearly everyone shares. Another reason is that some intuitions have simpler contents than others, and are therefore less prone to error. And there are various reasons why some kinds of intuitions may be more open to bias [arising from self-interest, wishful thinking, group interests, interest in one's own self-image, culture, religion, or evolution] than others'; *Ethical Intuitionism*, p. 105. This, however, is to treat intuitions as beliefs based on other beliefs, which is precisely what he wishes to insist that intuitions are not (since they will otherwise be unable to adjudicate between our mere moral beliefs), and it necessarily involves him denying precisely that premise upon which intuitionism rests (pp. 106–7; 140–1; 219).

38 Huemer actually denies that moral intuitions are beliefs, appealing to the way in which 'when confronted with cases we have never previously considered, we often have moral intuitions that conflict with our moral theories'; *Ethical Intuitionism*, pp. 232–3. That intuition should be 'independent of belief' is important to his claim that intuition can help us to 'decide which moral beliefs are correct'; (pp. 102–4). However, I find his sense of 'moral beliefs' (like everyone else's) rather difficult to grasp. He seems to mean a kind of professed generalization, a provisional intuition like "All swans are white", that is then revised in the light of a more immediate intuition, like seeing a black swan. This fails, however, to show that the new intuition ("I am seeing a black swan") is not also a belief. In the cases he presents – such as professed utilitarians discovering that they would not be prepared to sacrifice the life of one healthy patient to save the life of five sick ones – what he is really describing are individuals who had not fully examined the contents of the beliefs they professed (see pp. 103–4). Indeed, despite positing intuitions as 'a sort of mental state or experience, distinct from and normally prior to belief' (p. 10), elsewhere he does, as he must, use the word "belief" to refer to the holding of a thing as a fact: 'Undoubtedly some moral beliefs are accounted for by inference from other moral beliefs. But since no moral belief can be derived from wholly non-moral premises, we must start with some moral beliefs that are not inferred from any other beliefs' (p. 103).

39 Though the appeal to the grammar of moral language is commonly made separately in this context, in fact it is not a separate argument. We clearly would not customarily describe something in terms that we did not feel accurately reflected how we felt about that thing. This, however, is a topic we shall return to in the next chapter.

40 In justice to Huemer, I should say that not only does he present his ethical intuitionism in precisely this way (p. 224) but also that I am in complete agreement with him as to the inadequacy of the other moral theories that he rejects, at least with regard to their conclusions if not with regard to their premises. He agrees, for example, with Hume that one cannot get from an "is" to an "ought": '(a) that we cannot know moral truths by observation, (b) that we cannot know (non-trivial) moral truths by deducing them from non-moral truths, (c) that we cannot know (non-trivial) moral truths by conceptual analysis, and (d) that we cannot know moral truths by scientific reasoning or inference to the best explanation'; *Ethical Intuitionism*, p. 74. True as all this is, it does not, however, follow that positing the existence of an "is" that is already an "ought", as moral intuitionism must, is actually less problematic than supposing any of these alternatives.

41 The negative formulation is what makes it possible for a seventeenth-century person to perceive a black swan, even if they hitherto did not believe that such a thing existed.

42 I take it that Mackie's 'argument from queerness' implies much of what I am here advancing; see Mackie, *Ethics*, pp. 38–9.
43 The question of how this non-human entity would itself *know* can be solved either by defining it as an entity that, by definition, knows what is really right and wrong, or by defining it as an entity that actually determines what is right and wrong. It might also be a combination of the two, so that its knowing and willing are identical, which, indeed, would make it experience moral responses much as we do. (This whole topic of non-natural realism is obviously closely related to the 'divine command theory' of moral knowledge, which posits what is right and wrong as what is either commanded or willed by God. It is not, however, the same topic.)
44 The expression comes from Stewart, *The Philosophy of the Active and Moral Powers of Man*, II, p. 459. Grotius, for example, affirms that 'even the Law of Nature itself, whether it be that which consists in the Maintenance of Society, or that which in a looser Sense is so called, though it flows from the internal Principles of Man, may notwithstanding be justly ascribed to God, because it was his Pleasure that these Principles should be in us'; *The Rights of War and Peace*, I, p. 91. More than 200 years later, McCosh vividly expresses a similar thought: 'The God who made us hath given us a nature which throws a halo and a radiance round certain kinds of everlasting verities and moral qualities, with the view of rendering them attractive, and gathering our affections about them'; *The Intuitions of the Mind*, p. 290.
45 Hume, *Enquiries Concerning Human Understanding and Concerning the Principles of Morals*, pp. 293–4.
46 Ibid., p. 294.
47 Kant, *Religion within the Boundaries of Mere Reason*, pp. 93–4. See also Chateaubriand, *The Genius of Christianity*, p. 190.
48 'Since there are practical laws that are absolutely necessary (the moral laws), then if these necessarily presuppose any existence as the condition of the possibility of their **binding** force, this existence has to be postulated, because the conditioned from which the inference to this determinate condition proceeds is itself cognized *a priori* as absolutely necessary'; Kant, *Critique of Pure Reason*, p. 585. In the *Critique of Practical Reason*, he asserts that the ideas of God and immortality gain their possibility from the fact that 'freedom is real, for this idea reveals itself through the moral law'; 'The ideas of *God* and *immortality*, however, are not conditions of the moral law but only conditions of the necessary object of a will determined by this law . . . hence with respect to those ideas we cannot affirm that we *cognize* and *have insight into* – I do not merely say the reality but even the possibility of them. But they are, nevertheless, conditions of applying the morally determined will to its object given to it a priori (the highest good)'; *Critique of Practical Reason*, pp. 139; 140. See also Kant, *Religion within the Boundaries of Mere Reason*, pp. 57–8.
49 Kant, *Religion within the Boundaries of Mere Reason*, p. 93.
50 See Kant, 'What Does It Mean to Orient Oneself in Thinking?', p. 12; *Critique of Practical Reason*, pp. 243–4; *Critique of the Power of Judgement*, pp. 316n; 320. For his assertion of 'moral theology' as the only rational version of theology, see *Critique of Pure Reason*, pp. 681–2; *Critique of Practical Reason*, pp. 251–2; *Critique of the Power of Judgement*, pp. 310–11. (For more on this question, see Beiser, 'Moral Faith and the Highest Good', *passim*.) I am, indeed, inclined to agree with Kant that the idea of God is implied by moral experience. However, I do not find that experience incomprehensible without the supposition of the existence of God.

51 Given this, there is obviously no point in discussing objectivity from Divine Command, since, even supposing the existence of the divine, this encounters precisely the same basic problem of verification. Incidentally, while the parallel between moral realism and religious faith is easy to draw, and has been, it falls down on the rather crucial point that religious faith is *consciously* faith.
52 Railton, 'Moral Realism', p. 5.
53 Ibid., p. 11.
54 Ibid., p. 12.
55 Ibid., p. 16.
56 Ibid., p. 21.
57 Ibid.
58 Ibid., p. 29. This notion of impartiality as the source of a universally valid moral standard is a cornerstone of the work of Sharp. A 'right volition', according to Sharp, is 'such a one as I desire should determine the action of everyone under the same conditions': 'no judgment can be correct, or valid, which turns upon the accidental relation of the action to my personal interests. For if the action is right here and now it must be equally right where I and my personal interests are absent, whether in China or Peru'; *Ethics*, p. 115; 120. In short, the judgement must be 'the outcome of an impersonal point of view' (p. 124). See also Firth's discussion of the 'ideal observer'; 'Ethical Absolutism and the Ideal Observer', pp. 333–45. Smith has also argued that 'If our concept of rightness is the concept of what we would desire ourselves to do if we were fully rational . . . then it does indeed follow that our moral judgements are expressions of our beliefs about an objective matter of fact'; *The Moral Problem*, p. 185. He claims that his argument is 'broadly naturalistic', since, even though 'rightness' may not itself appear be definable in naturalistic terms, insofar as a 'fully rational . . . psychology' can be determined naturalistically, the 'evaluating possible world is . . . naturalistic in the relevant respect' (p. 186). In a move that we shall see again when dealing with trivial realisms in the next chapter, Smith goes on to argue that this viewpoint, in conjunction with the empirical fact of moral convergence, leads him to believe that there may, indeed, be 'moral facts' (pp. 187–9).
59 Railton, 'Moral Realism', p. 22.
60 Ibid., pp. 29–30. Railton adds that this does not, however, yield any categorical moral imperatives, since 'what it would be morally right for me to do depends upon what is rational from a point of view that includes, but is not exhausted by, my own' (p. 30). Conversely, one might blow argument to the winds and argue that, since we know what well-being is, and since science shows us the best way to achieve this well-being, therefore, what is right (conducive to well-being) and what is wrong (the opposite) are 'matters of scientific fact'; see, for example, Harris, *The Moral Landscape*, passim.
61 Rousseau, for example, ascribes to humanity only one 'natural virtue': pity; *The Second Discourse*, pp. 106–8. This is also Darwin's position; *The Descent of Man*, I, pp. 71–2.
62 Stephen, for example, characterizes morality as 'the sum of the preservative instincts of a society, and presumably of those which imply a desire for the good of the society itself'; *The Science of Ethics*, p. 217 (see also pp. 91–2). Ellwood holds it to evident that 'morality, in an idealistic sense, seems from a sociological standpoint to be those forms of conduct which conduce to social harmony, to social efficiency, and so to the survival of the group'; *Sociology and Modern Social Problems*, p. 49. Huxley, too, gives to evolution, the role of an 'administrative authority' who best ensures

the survival of the colony that is humanity, though it is a ruthless one, insofar as it disposes of those who do not serve that end; *Evolution & Ethics*, p. 19; 21. However, he is anxious to establish that this is not the only standard of right, leading him to assert, to the outrage of some of his contemporaries, that 'ethical nature, while born of cosmic nature [the need for cooperation], is necessarily at enmity with its parent' (p. viii). 'Let us understand, once for all, that the ethical progress of society depends, not on imitating the cosmic process, still less in running away from it, but in combating it' (p. 83). It is almost needless to observe that Huxley's view has not prevailed. Wilson, for example, answers the question of whether or not autonomous ethical values can 'gain a direction and momentum' of their own in the negative: 'The genes hold culture on a leash. The leash is very long, but inevitably values will be constrained in accordance with their effects on the human gene pool. The brain is a product of evolution. Human behavior – like the deepest capacities for emotional response which drive and guide it – is the circuitous technique by which human genetic material has been and will be kept intact. Morality has no other demonstrable ultimate function'; *On Human Nature*, pp. 166-7. Richards simply 'supposes that a moral sense has evolved in the human group'; 'A Defense of Evolutionary Ethics', p. 272. Singer, who holds that it is 'now generally accepted that the roots of our ethics lie in patterns of behavior that evolved among our prehuman ancestors, the social mammals, and that we retain within our biological nature elements of these evolved responses', asserts that ethics probably began in 'pre-human patterns of behavior rather than in the deliberate choices of fully fledged, rational human beings'; *The Expanding Circle*, pp. xi; 4. Singer also believes that 'altruistic genes' are first selected for because the offspring of parents who look after them (because the parents possess such genes) are more likely to survive; moreover, helping relatives will ensure the survival of my own genes (pp. 12-13; 14-15).

63 Huxley, for example, traces the origins of rudimentary justice to 'a pack of men' hunting under the tacit or expressed understanding that they should not attack one another during the chase, just like wolves; *Evolution & Ethics*, pp. 56-7. Dewey, taking off from Huxley's treatment, observes that once an ethical society exists, this itself becomes part of the environment; 'Evolution and Ethics', p. 326. In consequence, he confesses it impossible to distinguish 'between this mediation of the acts of the individual by society and what is ordinarily called natural selection' (p. 337). Nevertheless, he feels that the ethical gets its 'surest and most ample guarantees when it is learned that the laws and conditions of righteousness are implicated in the working processes of the universe; when it is found that man in his conscious struggles, in his doubts, temptations, and defeats, in his aspirations and successes, is moved on and buoyed up by the forces which have developed nature; and that in this moral struggle he acts not as a mere individual but as an organ in maintaining and carrying forward the universal process' (p. 341). This is certainly the belief of Ferri, who sees the roots of socialism in the 'law of solidarity' (in balance with the 'law of the "struggle for life"'), according to which cooperation conveys a survival advantage; *Socialism and Positive Science*, pp. 34-7. This is, most famously, the argument of Kropotkin, who, in his *Mutual Aid*, moves from the advantages of cooperation among invertebrates up to a discussion of labour unions. The 'fittest' to survive, according to Kropotkin, are those who support one another; *Mutual Aid*, p. 6. According to Clodd, morality arises from the 'gregarious or social instinct', which in turn depends on the 'collective dependence' of social animals on one another, which 'demands an altruistic, rather than an egoistic, individual';

'Evolution (Ethical)', p. 624. According to Alexander, 'modern man has evolved socially around substitute advantages for predation-thwarting or food-obtaining benefits that are no longer present'; 'The Evolution of Social Behavior', p. 335. Nevertheless, he supposes that there might be 'genes for altruism', and that, even though 'such tendencies would consistently be selected out of human populations', they might persist where 'they may increase the reproduction of their bearer if they are viewed as true altruism by his fellows', since 'sincerity represents a valuable social asset' (p. 377). Axelrod, concentrating mainly on the findings of games theory, also emphasizes that cooperation has an evolutionary advantage but gets no further in explaining how this could arise (as opposed to how it would be advantageous) than the invocation of 'genes for cooperation'; *The Evolution of Cooperation*, p. 97. Stanley is one of the few who seems to recognize the gulf separating what is useful from moral feeling, that, indeed, there is a gulf separating either advantage, the regret arising from the 'baulking of the social instinct', or the 'desire to get even' and what is a distinctly moral emotion: that 'morality is not bound up necessarily with sociality'; *Studies in the Evolutionary Psychology of Feeling*, pp. 332–7. With regard to the philosophers we shall consider later, Gibbard seems to find it unproblematic to pass from the supposition of an evolutionary advantage to cooperation to an evolutionary advantage to us feeling guilt at what others are likely to resent, gratitude at favours done for us and so on: 'Systems of normative control in human beings . . . are adapted to achieve interpersonal coordination'; *Wise Choices, Apt Feelings*, p. 64. Joyce, holding that 'the tendency to employ the basic general categories of moral appraisal is innate', understands this to mean that 'we have a "hardwired" predilection to believe that moral obligations exist. A second, stronger, thesis is that we have a natural tendency to believe that certain types of action bear such moral properties – things such as caring for the young, looking out for family members, avoiding incest, not initiating hostility towards members of the community, repaying debts, playing fair, being antagonistic towards exploiters'; *The Myth of Morality*, p. 146.
64 See Ruse, *The Darwinian Paradigm*, pp. 230; 234; Joyce, *The Myth of Morality*, pp. 137; 140.
65 Darwin, as we have already noted, presupposes the existence of a sociable instinct. Stephen acknowledges that the mere usefulness of virtue to social welfare does not explain we can be capable of placing the social welfare before our own; *The Science of Ethics*, pp. 218–19. However, he bridges this gap, by identifying empathy (though he does not call it such) with sympathy: 'sympathy is not an additional instinct, a faculty which is added when the mind has reached a certain stage of development, a mere incident of intellectual growth, but [is] something implied from the first in the very structure of knowledge. I must be capable of representative ideas in order to think coherently or to draw the essential distinction between object and subject' (p. 262). He acknowledges the circularity: 'some power of altruistic feeling is presupposed in the very capacity to become moral' (p. 433). Carlile makes the pain we represent to ourselves as intending to inflict necessarily entailing the anger we have previously felt at being subject to pain into the reason we feel the contemplated action to be wrong, and our approval arise from the gratitude; 'The Conscience: Its Nature and Origin', pp. 71–3. This, too, presumes the existence of moral feeling (that our natures are not 'altogether base'). Westermarck, too, holds that it is 'sympathy' (by which he means empathy) 'aided by the altruistic sentiment', which humans, along with some other species, naturally possess (as an extension of the parental and conjugal affection that emerged as 'sociality, being an advantage to man, became his habit'), that produces

the 'disinterested retributive emotions', that is, the moral emotions; *The Origin and Development of the Moral Ideas*, I, pp. 111–13 (see also II, 186–228).
66 I shall leave aside, for the moment, the question of how a non-moral creature could possibly discern moral values in non-moral behaviour: the equivalent of a dog noticing that some spilled biscuits had accidentally spelled out its own name – in a world in which writing did not exist.
67 See Darwin, *The Descent of Man*, pp. 82; 100; Stephen, *The Science of Ethics*, pp. 101–10; 137. Mill's argument, in *Utilitarianism*, that happiness is the only end that all human beings desire, which we shall have cause to examine further in Chapter 3, seems to imply that something like a process of internalization is indeed how we acquire moral feeling (pp. 55–6). (Regarding his appeal to 'association', it is worth comparing Mill here with Hartley's more complete description of how morality might be acquired by the process now called internalization in his *Observations on Man*, I, pp. 494–7.) Elsewhere Mill asserts that sympathy is no less 'natural' than selfishness; indeed, were this not so, it would be impossible for 'goodness and nobleness' to ever be 'cultivated' in human beings; Mill, 'Nature', p. 49.
68 Spencer explicitly states that the origin of his ethics has shifted from the 'supernaturalistic interpretation' of his *Social Statics* (1851) to a 'naturalistic – that is, evolutionary' – one, though this has simply been a matter of making explicit the 'biological origin' of the same ethics; *The Principles of Ethics*, II, p. x. Kropotkin, too, discussed in note 63, writes of how 'Nature', that is, biology and anthropology, can provide the ideals that were once the province of 'superstition'; *Ethics*, p. 3. Kimball, an admirer of Spencer, combines evolution and God on the grounds that God created the universe and is thus responsible for evolution. Ethics, according to Kimball, is 'the outcome under evolution of the accumulated experiences of our race with regard to what is fittest in conduct, consolidated into intuitions and transmitted from generation to generation by heredity', but holds that the goal of this process is not the happiness of human beings but rather 'growth, fuller and finer life, an ever better state of things alike in the universe at large and in its individual parts'; *The Ethics of Evolution*, pp. 1; 3. See also Stewart, *The Philosophy of the Active and Moral Powers of Man*, I, p. 144.
69 Equally, of course, evolution does not help to establish emotivism either; see Joyce, 'Ethics After Darwin', p. 465.
70 This is not, of course, to say that it is impossible to entertain belief in what is unverifiable, nor that there might not be a survival advantage in so doing. Religious people are supposedly more consistently mentally content than non-religious people, and, for all I know, may, as a result, live longer too. This, however, is a matter of faith rather than genetic "programming". Moreover, the problem with drawing an analogy between faith and the belief implicit in moral experience is not only how belief can be selected for at all but also why such a belief would be selected for by evolution if the only reason this would happen is that there is genuinely an advantage to cooperation: something that, if true, could be believed without any epistemic sacrifice. It may be, of course, that an analogy can be drawn between the advantage of religious faith and the advantage of a belief in the objectivity of right and wrong, but evolution would be a redundant concept in such an analogy.
71 Ironically, the other way in which the idea of evolution enters into ethical debate is when it is invoked as the basis of a response in order to support the argument that the response in question is "mistaken". In this case the implication is that the response is merely an involuntary and now maladaptive reflex acquired during a

more primitive stage of ourselves: one that should, therefore, now be overcome by a more rational assessment. The contrary to the response thus surreptitiously becomes, by default, a matter of cognition.

72 Darwin himself points this out; *The Descent of Man*, I, p. 99.

73 Huxley points out that 'evolution may teach us how the good and the evil tendencies of man may have come about; but, in itself, it is incompetent to furnish any better reason why what we call good is preferable to what we call evil than we had before. Some day, I doubt not, we shall arrive at an understanding of the evolution of the aesthetic faculty; but all the understanding in the world will neither increase nor diminish the force of the intuition that this is beautiful and that is ugly'; *Evolution and Ethics*, p. 80. There is, nevertheless, no shortage of examples of those who, paradoxically, choose to be determined. We have seen Kropotkin in note 63, but he is arguably preceded by, for example, the Stoics and Ralph Waldo Emerson, and succeeded by many a host of contemporary figures enamoured of scientism. According to Spencer 'good' only takes on a meaning in terms of evolution (though it is moot whether he has biological evolution in mind); *The Principles of Ethics*, I, p. 25. Gibbard gestures towards a very weak form of this elected determinism when he writes that 'Our normative propensities constitute rough heuristics for promoting biological fitness, and our notion of benefit coincides roughly with biological fitness, through no accident. None of this guarantees an exact match between plausibility and advantage, but it makes a rough coincidence no surprise'; *Wise Choices, Apt Feelings*, pp. 229–30. However, Gibbard does ultimately reject the idea that a pragmatic accord in the acceptance of norms that serve the end of biological fitness either should, or even could, compel our assent to adopting those norms as morally right (pp. 225–7).

74 Significantly, all of these problems of connecting our responses to the authority of evolution have previously been rehearsed in connection with a supernatural grounding to those responses. We might, for example, claim that at least some responses are "correct" because they conform to what is in the mind of God, though this would still leave the problem of knowing which these were. (Appeal to scripture only works if I can trust myself to justifiably trust that source.) If we are to decide for ourselves, then the notion of the mind of God is superfluous (except as an explanation of why I have these feelings). God and evolution do differ fundamentally as sources of morality in that, while we could still question whether the ends of nature (our survival) are also our ends, whereas, since God is defined as omniscient, benevolent and omnipotent, however we may disagree with His ends, we could still have faith they would be ours if we only knew better. That is, while evolution is not *my* end – it is the easiest matter in the world to question whether humans should continue to exist – I might have faith, based on what I feel is a conformity of interests between God and I, that I could ultimately see the justification of His ends.

75 The aesthetic case – "That was exciting" – is a borderline one; it seems that here many people are capable of experiencing the object as, for example, objectively exciting, while at the same time remaining – up to a point – permissive towards alternative responses. Perhaps the difference here lies not in the quality of the response itself but rather in what it is a response to. The aesthetic response concerns only my own pleasure or displeasure and your agreement or dissent is not of crucial importance to those things (which is not to say that agreement, insofar as it appears to bolster the objectivity of the properties I like, is not pleasant). The moral response, on the other hand, concerns what I wish to be or not to be, and this involves everyone.

76 Hume, *A Treatise of Human Nature*, I, pp. 301–2.
77 The point is so simple that it is hard not to feel, as one does elsewhere in his work (particularly the *Dialogues Concerning Natural Religion*), that Hume may be teasing the reader. Consider, however, the arguments made regarding the common 'spring' and common goal of divergent moralities in 'A Dialogue' appended to his *Enquiries Concerning Human Understanding and Concerning the Principles of Morals*, pp. 324–43.
78 As we have seen, he says as much in *Enquiries Concerning Human Understanding and Concerning the Principles of Morals*, though one should also take into account Philo's argument in *Dialogues Concerning Natural Religion*.
79 Some of those mentioned earlier in dealing with straightforward realism were actually responding directly either to Hume or to Hutcheson's similar emphasis on feeling. Thus, Balguy feels that virtue is 'depreciated and dishonoured' by Hutcheson's claim that it is an 'instinct', that we have a 'moral sense': 'we must certainly think less highly and less honourably of it, then we should do if we looked upon it as *Rational*', since reason is 'the nobler principle'; *The Foundation of Moral Goodness*, pp. 20–1. Virtue, he claims, cannot derive 'merely from natural *Affection*' for, if it did, morality would be 'of an arbitrary and changeable Nature' (p. 25). Moreover, actions that flow from instincts are necessary rather than voluntary, and 'it seems utterly impossible to reconcile *Virtue* with any kind of *Necessity*' (p. 21). (We shall return to this question of free will.) Reid's target is Hume: 'There are . . . judgments, as well as feelings, that are excited by the particular structure and fabric of the mind. But there is this remarkable difference between them, That [*sic*] every judgment is, in its own nature, true or false; and though it depends upon the fabric of a mind, whether it have such a judgment or not, it depends not upon that fabric whether the judgment be true or not. A true judgment will be true, whatever be the fabric of the mind; but a particular structure and fabric is necessary, in order to our perceiving that truth. Nothing like this can be said of mere feelings, because the attributes of true or false do not belong to them'; *Essays on the Active Powers of Man*, p. 357.
80 Wittgenstein, 'Lecture on Ethics', pp. 6–10.
81 Ibid., pp. 9; 11. 'My whole tendency and I believe the tendency of all men who ever tried to write or talk Ethics or Religion was to run against the boundaries of language' (pp. 11–12).
82 Westermarck, *Ethical Relativity*, p. 60. (He had made the claim much earlier; *The Origin and Development of the Moral Ideas*, p. 17.) 'The belief that gives rise to an emotion, the cognitive basis of it, is either true or false; in the latter case the emotion may be said to be felt "by mistake" – as when a person is frightened by some object in the dark which he takes for a ghost, or is indignant with a person to whom he imputes a wrong that has been committed by somebody else; but this does not alter the nature of the emotion itself. We may call the emotion of another individual "unjustified", if we feel that we ourselves should not have experienced the same emotion had we been in his place, or, as in the case of moral approval or disapproval, if we cannot share his emotion. But to speak . . . of "right" and "wrong" emotions, springing from self-evident intuitions and having the same validity as truth and error, is only another futile attempt to objectivize our moral judgments . . . [. . .] If there are no moral truths it cannot be the object of a science of ethics to lay down rules for human conduct, since the aim of all science is the discovery of some truth. [. . .] It may, of course, be a subject for scientific inquiry to investigate the means which are conducive to human happiness or welfare, and the results of such a study may also be usefully applied by moralists, but it forms no more a part of ethics than

physics is a part of psychology. If the word "ethics" is to be used as the name for a science, the object of that science can only be to study the moral consciousness as a fact'; *Ethical Relativity*, pp. 60–1.

83 Barnes. 'A Suggestion about Value', p. 45. We see here already how a failure to distinguish between moral responses and moral judgements leaves Barnes's argument open to an easy rebuttal if interpreted in a certain way.

84 Barnes, 'A Suggestion about Value', p. 45. While many controversies arising out of value judgements (as, for example, with taste), he continues, can be settled by saying, "I like it and you don't, and that's the end of the matter", with morality it is a matter of possibly conflicting actions: 'If I maintain, "A is good" against the contention "A is bad", my attempt to prove the truth of my statement is not really what it pretends to be. I point out details in A which are the object of my approval. By so doing I hope that my opponent, when he becomes aware of these, will approve A: and so be ready to say "A is good". But what I have done is not really to gain his assent to a proposition but to change his attitude from one of disapproval to one of approval towards A. All attempts to persuade others of the truth of value judgement are thus really attempts to make others approve the things we approve' (p. 46).

85 Ayer, *Language, Truth and Logic*, p. 110.
86 Ibid., p. 112.
87 Ibid., pp. 116–17.
88 Stevenson, 'The Emotive Meaning of Ethical Terms' *passim*.
89 Ibid., p. 26.
90 Ibid., p. 30.
91 Ibid., p. 31. Anscombe, similarly, argues that our current moral language – "obligation", "duty", "right", "wrong", "ought" – is not intelligible without the widely rejected supposition of a legislator, and the moral philosophy 'should be laid aside ... until we have an adequate philosophy of psychology, in which we are conspicuously lacking'; 'Modern Moral Philosophy', pp. 29–31; 26. (I suspect the legislative cast of moral language derives not so much from theism as from the experience of childhood.) Stevenson suggests that, for the reasons he has given, ethics, at least as it has traditionally been pursued, is not a suitable topic for philosophy. 'I may add that if "X is good" is essentially a vehicle for suggestion, it is scarcely a statement which philosophers, any more than many other men, are called upon to make. To the extent that ethics predicates the ethical terms of anything, rather than explains their meaning, it ceases to be a reflective study. Ethical statements are social instruments. They are used in a cooperative enterprise in which we are mutually adjusting ourselves to the interests of others. Philosophers have a part in this, as do all men, but not the major part'; 'The Emotive Meaning of Ethical Terms', p. 31.
92 Russell, *Religion and Science*, pp. 230–1.
93 Ibid., p. 235.
94 Ibid., pp. 237–8.
95 Ibid., pp. 240–1.
96 Westermarck believed that the effect would be beneficial: 'I think that ethical writers are often inclined to overrate the influence or moral theory upon moral practice, but if there is any such influence at all, it seems to me that ethical subjectivism, instead of being a danger, is more likely to be an advantage to morality. Could it be brought home to people that there is no absolute standard in morality, they would perhaps be on the one hand more tolerant and on the other hand more critical in their judgments. Emotions depend on cognitions and are apt to vary according as the cognitions vary;

hence a theory which leads to an examination of the psychological and historical origin of people's moral opinions should be more useful than a theory which postulates moral truths enunciated by self-evident intuitions that are unchangeable. In every society the traditional notions as to what is good or bad, obligatory or indifferent, are commonly accepted by the majority of people without further reflection. By tracing them to their source it will be found that not a few of these notions have their origin in ignorance and superstition or in sentimental likes or dislikes, to which a scrutinizing judge can attach little importance; and, on the other hand, he must condemn many an act or omission which public opinion, out of thoughtlessness, treats with indifference. It will, moreover, appear that moral estimates often survive the causes from which they sprang. And what unprejudiced person can help changing his views if he be persuaded that they have no foundation in existing facts?'; *Ethical Relativity*, pp. 59–60. This is an argument that makes not the slightest sense, since, as we have seen, unless we suppose that certain responses are intuitions of what is really objectively good or that those intuitions could be replaced by something that is really objectively good, Westermarck has nothing to put in the place of those responses that he believes are the product of ignorance, superstition, sentiment, or thoughtlessness. He does not even have anything against which to measure what is, for example, *merely* sentiment. It should be noted, however, that, despite being nonsense, this same argument has been advanced by every recent subjectivist to address the question of effect.

97 Russell, *Religion and Science*, pp. 240–1. When Russell says that we have wishes that are 'not purely personal', such as the wish that the human race should be happy, it seems to be this kind of wish, rather than anything we experience as self-interest, that produces the morality. I would agree absolutely with this. However, I disagree with the implication that we can acknowledge our desire for the world to be happy as a purely personal desire, and therefore self-interested, and still experience that desire as the grounds of a morality. For it to be the grounds of a morality we would have to experience it without the reference to ourselves, that is, *as a fact that the world should be* a happy place.

98 In 1939, Ross described Ayer's work (taken as exemplary of positivism) as 'the latest attempt to discredit ethics'; *Foundations of Ethics*, p. 38. Both Westermarck and Wittgenstein should be exempted from such generalizations: 'What [Ethics] says does not add to our knowledge in any sense. But it is a document of a tendency in the human mind which I personally cannot help respecting deeply and I would not for my life ridicule it'; Wittgenstein, 'Lecture on Ethics', p. 12.

99 The 'Frege-Geach problem', so beloved by contemporary introductions to metaethics, surely deserves pride of place among these irrelevant responses.

100 Mackie, *Ethics*, p. 35.

101 We might, for example, concentrate on the problem of in what sense "Cruelty is wrong" is untrue, without even asking ourselves whether the original statement is closer in form to the verifiable "The bottle is under the table" or to the irrefutable "My ambition is to be a fireman".

Chapter 2

1 Kalderon, *Moral Fictionalism*, p. 155.
2 Ibid., pp. 148–9.

3 Ibid., p. viii.
4 Ibid., p. 139.
5 Ibid., p. viii.
6 Ibid., p. 95.
7 Ibid., pp. 28–32. See also pp. 147–8.
8 Ibid., p. 51. See also pp. 147–8.
9 Ibid., p. 130.
10 Ibid., pp. 131–2.
11 Ibid., pp. 95–6.
12 Ibid., pp. 119; 108.
13 Ibid., pp. 108; 112.
14 Ibid., p. 128.
15 Ibid., pp. 115–16.
16 Ibid., p. 150.
17 Ibid., p. 151.
18 Ibid.
19 Ibid., p. 152.
20 Ibid., p. 136.
21 Ibid., p. 154.
22 Ibid., pp. 154–5.
23 Ibid., pp. 155–6.
24 Ibid., p. 156.
25 Carnap, too, seems to take moral realism not as a general phenomenon but rather as a mistake peculiar to philosophers: 'The rule, "Do not kill", has grammatically the imperative form and will therefore not be regarded as an assertion. But the value statement, "Killing is evil", although, like the rule, it is merely an expression of a certain wish, has the grammatical form of an assertive proposition. Most philosophers have been deceived by this form into thinking that a value statement is really an assertive proposition, and must be either true or false'; *Philosophy and Logical Syntax*, p. 24.
26 Joyce, *The Myth of Morality*, p. 13. His list is drawn from Glassen and Geach: see Glassen, 'The Cognitivity of Moral Judgments' and Geach, 'Assertion'.
27 This is not to say that every aspect of a fiction can be represented another way; for example, Hemingway's narrative voice is visually reproducible in a way that Wodehouse's is not.
28 'As soon as we move [within fiction] from one word to an associated one, . . . then, unless their relationship is one of homonymity, we have moved through a portion of the real world'; Kirwan, *Literature, Rhetoric, Metaphysics*, p. 74.
29 Kalderon, *Moral Fictionalism*, pp. 131–2.
30 Kalderon's other examples of non-assertoric sentences – the discussion of the details of star signs by one who does not actually believe in astrology and figurative language – suffer from the same lack of parallelism with moral language. Knowingly talking as if astrology were true is very similar to describing a fictional universe; indeed, with regard to translatability, the fictional world of astrology could *conceivably* turn out to belong to the world of scientific fact. Figurative language is open to all the objections given above to fiction in general. According to Wittgenstein, moral language is full of similes, but 'as soon as we try to drop the simile and simply state the facts which stand behind it, we find there are no such facts. And so, what at first appeared to be a simile now seems to be mere nonsense'; 'Lecture on Ethics', p. 10.

31 Joyce, *The Myth of Morality*, pp. xi; 186.
32 Ibid., p. xi. That we cannot actually identify the current language with a fictionalist practice arises, for Joyce, from the way in which it embodies realist beliefs. He draws an analogy with what he refers to as 'witch discourse': '[The] whole point (one might say) of having a witch discourse was to refer to women with supernatural powers. To discover that no human has supernatural powers is to render the discourse pointless. Even if we were to learn that all and only the women who had been branded "witches" actually have some other distinctive property (say, playing a certain disruptive role in the patriarchal society), this would hardly show that they were all witches after all. By comparison, the point of having a "motion discourse" was to refer to the change in position of objects in space over time. There was never a particular need to refer specifically to absolute motion. The fact that people thought of the motion as absolute was not a vital aspect of the discourse; indeed, one doubts that they really thought much about that aspect of motion at all. So the question we must ask is: "Is moral discourse more like talk of witches or more like talk of motion?" – and the answer is that it is more like talk of witches. [. . .] Our ordinary use of the concept of motion is not much affected when we let go of absolutism; our ordinary use of the concept of moral rightness, by contrast, is completely undermined without absolutism. [. . .] [I] am certain that we most emphatically do speak of actions as wrong, period. Indeed, I have gone so far as to claim that it is "the whole point" of moral discourse that it allows us to speak of actions in such a manner' (pp. 96–7; 99).
33 Joyce, *The Myth of Morality*, p. 186.
34 Ibid., pp. 208–9; 213.
35 Ibid., p. 213.
36 Ibid., p. 206. Such a shift, he holds, is not only rationally requisite, but also practically advantageous, since 'no policy that encourages the belief in falsehoods, or the promulgation of false beliefs in others, will be practically stable in the long run' (p. 214). This obviously raises the question of how moral discourse has survived until now.
37 Joyce, *The Myth of Morality*, p. 215.
38 Ibid.
39 Ibid., p. 217. Joyce's preference for the word 'myth' does not overcome this problem (pp. 232–41). It may be that, as Malinowki claimed, myth can be defined in terms of the distinctive, practical role it plays in preserving a culture as it is, rather than in terms of its 'fabulous content', but this does not show that this content is taken both as false and 'as if' true.
40 Joyce, *The Myth of Morality*, pp. 218–19.
41 Ibid., pp. 186; 218.
42 Ibid., p. 218.
43 Ibid., p. 219.
44 Ibid., p. 169.
45 I take Horgan and Timmons' 'cognitivist expressivism' to suffer from all the theoretical shortcomings described here in connection with fictionalism. They, too, take an ostensibly irrealist stance, claiming that 'moral thought and discourse do not purport to be factualist in any robust way'; 'Morality Without Moral Facts', p. 231. However, they proceed to distinguish between '*descriptive* beliefs', which *are* in the business of representing facts and involve '*is-commitments*', and '*ought* beliefs', which are not, and which involve '*ought-commitments*' (p. 232). Horgan and Timmons believe that the latter qualify as beliefs insofar as they share 'certain generic features

that are characteristic of beliefs': they 'have the grammatical and logical trappings of genuine beliefs . . . they can figure as constituents in logically complex judgments . . . can figure in logical inferences . . . can combine with other beliefs to yield new beliefs that are appropriate given prior beliefs' (ibid.). (This is a good example of what we will meet again in dealing with trivial realisms later in this chapter, of the way in which the conflation of moral responses and moral judgements leads to the misrepresentation of the former.) Moreover, they continue, 'ought-commitments', like 'genuine beliefs' [*sic*], 'are experienced as psychologically involuntary (unlike voluntary commitments like intentions or promises), and as grounded in reasons. [. . .] So, ought-commitments are genuine beliefs whose primary role in human cognitive economy is reasoned action-guidance. Although they are indeed beliefs, they are not descriptive beliefs' (pp. 232–3). I have dealt with the distinction to be drawn between epistemic authority and moral-normative authority in Chapter 1. Clearly Horgan and Timmons are here mistaking the problem for the solution. (See also Timmons, *Morality Without Foundations*, Chapter 5, and Horgan and Timmons, 'Nondescriptivist Cognitivism: Framework for a New Metaethic' and 'Cognitivist expressivism', *passim*.)

46 Garner, 'A Plea for Moral Abolitionism', p. 78. He prefers the term 'amoralism' in his earlier *Beyond Morality*.
47 Garner, 'A Plea for Moral Abolitionism', pp. 78–9.
48 Ibid., p. 79.
49 Ibid.
50 Ibid., pp. 79–80.
51 Ibid., pp. 81; 87.
52 Garner, *Beyond Morality*, pp. 366–7.
53 Garner, 'A Plea for Moral Abolitionism', p. 92n10.
54 Ibid., p. 88.
55 Garner, *Beyond Morality*, p. 368; see also his discussion of 'hard questions', pp. 366–82.
56 See also Garner, 'Abolishing Morality', and a variety of approaches to the same question in the collection by Garner and Joyce containing his 'A Plea for Moral Abolitionism'.
57 As far as I can see, only the concept of fairness will yield such an obvious example. If I merely say something is bad and cite a personal interest to support my judgement, I might be using 'bad' with that personal meaning. On the other hand, if I cite a group interest, it may very well be that I am reporting a moral response – if my *sense* of right and wrong is actually constituted by the advancement or frustration of the interests of a particular group. (If it is not a group to which I belong, it becomes absolutely nonsensical; for example, "Homosexuality is wrong because it is illegal in X".) So, while some such instances would be examples of the misuse of moral terms, this would not be clear from the bare form of the statements themselves. That only fairness yields so unambiguous an example of misuse suggests that there may be something fundamental, morally, in the concept of fairness.
58 Russell, *Religion and Science*, p. 240.
59 Prinz, *The Emotional Construction of Morals*, p. 92.
60 Ibid., p. 167.
61 Ibid., p. 89.
62 Ibid., p. 107.
63 Ibid., p. 108. I have chosen Prinz to represent this particular argument in order to highlight how such an argument can emerge even in the most overtly subjectivist

contexts. However, it is by no means unique to Prinz. See, for example, Harman, *The Nature of Morality*, pp. 4–5, and Moore, 'Moral Reality Revisited'. p. 2517.
64 Prinz, *The Emotional Construction of Morals*, p. 167.
65 Ibid., pp. 168–9.
66 Ibid., p. 166.
67 Ibid., p. 167.
68 Ibid., p. 107. Indeed, the bald, probably incontrovertible statement commits us to neither realism nor subjectivism.
69 Prinz, *The Emotional Construction of Morals*, pp. 168–9.
70 Ibid. He asserts that the two – perception and projection – are 'hard to keep apart'.
71 Prinz, *The Emotional Construction of Morals*, pp. 168–9.
72 Ibid., p. 119.
73 Ibid., p. 128.
74 Nussbaum, *Upheavals of Thought*, p. 33. An emphasis on the cognitive aspects of emotion is perhaps most closely associated with the work of Solomon: 'An emotion is a *judgment* (or a set of judgments), something we *do*. An emotion is a (set of) judgment(s) which constitute our world, our surreality, and its "intentional objects". An emotion is a basic judgment about our Selves and our place in our world, the projection of the values and ideals, structures and mythologies, according to which we live and through which we experience our lives'; *The Passions*, p. 185.
75 Nussbaum, *Upheavals of Thought*, p. 27.
76 Ibid., pp. 27–8.
77 Ibid., pp. 28–30.
78 Ibid., pp. 30–3.
79 Ibid., p. 29.
80 Ibid., pp. 40–3.
81 Ibid., pp. 25–6.
82 Indeed, Roeser has made just this assumption with her 'affectual intuitionism', which supplements intuitionism with 'an epistemological role for emotions' that relies very much on the same emphasis on the cognitive role of the emotions that Nussbaum gives here; *Moral Emotions and Intuitions*, p. xii (see also pp. 149–79). According to Roeser, 'emotions are epistemological tools in our discovery of objective moral truths', since emotions are 'felt value judgments' (p. 139): 'A cognitive moral emotion is a complex state that is constituted by a moral judgment, positive or negative affection for the persons (or acts or states of affairs) who are the intentional object of that judgment, and of an agreeable or disagreeable feeling in ourselves' (p. 149). Examples of the kinds of emotions she has in mind are 'sympathy, empathy, compassion, shame, and guilt', which she believes, rather than registering the presence of moral feeling, are actually providing us with 'access to the moral value of a situation, action, or person' (p. 151). Later we shall see that Slote uses these emotions to attempt to establish an "objectivity" to moral feeling.
83 McDowell, 'Values and Secondary Qualities', pp. 132–3.
84 McDowell, 'Projection and Truth in Ethics', p. 157.
85 Ibid., pp. 151–2.
86 Ibid., p. 157.
87 Ibid.
88 Ibid., p. 158.
89 Ibid., pp. 158–9.
90 Ibid., p. 160.

91 Ibid., p. 160–2.
92 It might be, of course, that we mistake the nature of the object. So, for example, our disgust might completely disappear on discovering that what we took for a cockroach was just a toy. However, this caveat applies equally to the funny. Imagine, for example, a hilarious prat fall turning out to be the clown having a heart attack.
93 One can see, then, why McDowell should have chosen the comical rather than colour as his model. Seeing a thing as red hardly constitutes a "response" in the strong sense that laughing or seeking to rectify constitute responses. Moreover, humour does appear almost as inscrutable as morality. He gives his own reasons for rejecting an analogy between moral experience and the experience of colour in 'Values and Secondary Qualities', pp. 133–4; 143.
94 Wiggins, 'A Sensible Subjectivism?', pp. 209; 187).
95 There 'need not be any *dichotomy* between getting it right in matters of ethics, however distinctive that is, and getting it right in matters of fact'; Wiggins, *Ethics*, pp. 330–1. He refers to his position as 'moral objectivism' (p. 357).
96 Wiggins, 'A Sensible Subjectivism?', p. 195. He describes this position as 'subjectivist' (p. 190). This leads Wiggins to a fictionalist stance on moral language. While conceding that our shared linguistic practice does commit us strongly to the belief that we take *x* to be wrong precisely because *x is* wrong, he nevertheless holds that this practice can 'operate without any special or philosophical guarantee that truth and correctness *will* stay around in this way'. Indeed, he feels that our practice can 'continue to operate in full awareness of the flimsiness and contingency of the natural facts that it reposes upon' (p. 208).
97 Wiggins, 'A Sensible Subjectivism?', p. 190.
98 Ibid., p. 189.
99 Ibid.
100 Ibid., pp. 195–6. 'What is improbable in the extreme is that, either singly or even in concert, further explanations will ever add up to a *reduction* of the funny or serve to characterize it in purely natural terms (terms that pull their weight in our theoretical-cum-explanatory account of the mechanisms of the natural world' (pp. 195–6). On the contrary, it is not at all improbable that what makes things funny (what funniness consists in) may one day be explicable in naturalistic terms, though it does seem, given the complexities of the individual psyche, that it may never be possible to say why any particular individual finds a specific thing funny.
101 Wiggins, 'A Sensible Subjectivism?', p. 188.
102 Ibid., p. 202.
103 Ibid., p. 197.
104 Ibid., p. 206.
105 Ibid., pp. 204–5.
106 Wiggins, *Ethics*, p. 335.
107 Ibid., p. 336. It can be taken as a general rule that, in any discourse other than chemistry, as soon as things start emerging from crucibles, the argument is about to take a rhetorical turn.
108 Wiggins, 'A Sensible Subjectivism?', p. 210.
109 Ibid., pp. 190–2.
110 Wiggins, *Ethics*, p. 331. Wiggins rhetorically asks, 'If questions of value were not questions of real existence or matters of fact, then how could the criterion for being a good judge have that status?'; 'A Sensible Subjectivism?', p. 194. This notion of a 'good

judge' in moral questions, which harkens back to realist claims that moral properties must be objective because moral debate is possible, is, however, beside the point. One can be a good judge only within the context of a consensus, because it is only within a consensus that appeals to facts about feeling (rather than about the world) will carry any weight.

111 The criterion for a good judge, asserts Wiggins, 'is that he is apt to get things right'; Wiggins 'A Sensible Subjectivism?', p. 194. The only possible criterion for 'getting things right' in this context is that we find our own responses correspond to the judgement.

112 Wiggins, *Ethics*, p. 332. At this point in his exposition, Wiggins approvingly quotes Putnam: "'How could there be 'value facts'? After all, we have no sense organ for detecting them. We can say how we detect yellow since we have eyes, but what sense organ do we have for detecting value?" [...] But consider the parallel question: "How could we come to tell that people are elated? After all, we have no sense organ for detecting elation." The fact is that we can tell that other people are elated, and sometimes we can even see that other people are elated. But we can only do so after we have acquired the concept of elation. Perception is not innocent; it is an exercise of our concepts'; Putnam *The Collapse of the Fact Value Dichotomy and Other Essay*, p. 102. (I quote from the original; Wiggins's page numbers are incorrect.) Wiggins remarks: 'That which marks out or delimits or descries or discriminates the property of considerateness in acts or attitudes or human characters is an essentially ethical interest, in pursuit of which we can deploy any kind of perception or any mode of investigation or any associated concept that suits the case. The presence of *such* properties, that is of value properties, is ascertained by all the multifarious means that are called for by the exercise of our grasp of this or that ethical concept'; Wiggins, *Ethics*, p. 334. This is, clearly, going too far. The properties of actions that would lead us to designate those actions 'considerate' are not themselves 'value properties'. This is to confuse being able to perceive something with valuing it.

113 Wiggins, 'A Sensible Subjectivism?', p. 194.
114 Russell, 'Note on Philosophy', pp. 146-7.
115 Wiggins, 'A Sensible Subjectivism?', p. 210.
116 Ibid., pp. 210-11.
117 Gibbard, *Wise Choices, Apt Feelings*, pp. 9; 108.
118 Ibid., p. 187.
119 Ibid.
120 Ibid., p. 188.
121 Ibid., p. 6.
122 Ibid., pp. 6; 49.
123 Ibid., p. 7.
124 Ibid., p. 46.
125 Ibid., p. 47.
126 Ibid.
127 Ibid., pp. 51.
128 Ibid., pp. 51-2; 93.
129 Ibid., p. 72.
130 Ibid., pp. 72-3.
131 Ibid., p. 74.
132 Ibid., p. 75.
133 Ibid., p. 181.

134 Ibid., pp. 181–2.
135 Ibid., p. 183.
136 Ibid., p. 199.
137 Ibid., pp. 201; 203. Indeed, a large part of *Wise Choices, Apt Feelings* and Gibbard's subsequent work is devoted to this question of the conditions of debate.
138 Gibbard, *Wise Choices, Apt Feelings*, p. 152.
139 'Perhaps we understand evaluations only because we have the relevant emotions, and evaluations must be explained in terms of emotions – as I am proposing. [. . .] [My] own puzzle is not what an emotion is besides an evaluation, but what an evaluation is'; Gibbard, *Wise Choices, Apt Feelings*, p. 131.
140 Gibbard, *Wise Choices, Apt Feelings*, p. 189.
141 Gibbard makes a number of statements that indicate he considers moral discourse to be fictionalist; *Wise Choices, Apt Feelings*, pp. 218; 321; 327.
142 Blackburn, *Essays in Quasi-Realism*, p. 3. Gibbard, who makes several references to Blackburn's work in *Wise Choices, Apt Feelings*, also describes himself as a quasi-realist in *Thinking How to Live*, pp. xii.
143 Blackburn, 'Truth, Realism, and the Regulation of Theory', p. 15. According to Blackburn, quasi-realism is, in effect, 'the program begun by Hume in his treatment of both causal and moral belief'. (ibid.)
144 Blackburn, 'How To Be an Ethical Anti-Realist', p. 167. He describes projectivism as a modern version of Hume's theory of ethics (ibid).
145 Ibid. pp. 152–3.
146 Blackburn, 'Antirealist Expressivism and Quasi-Realism', p. 152.
147 Ibid., p. 153.
148 Ibid.
149 Ibid.
150 Blackburn, 'Errors and the Phenomenology of Value', pp. 152–3.
151 Ibid.
152 Blackburn, 'Antirealist Expressivism and Quasi-Realism', p. 154.
153 Ibid.
154 Ibid. He also points out that subjectivism is compatible with other aspects of moral discourse that might appear to commit us to moral realism, such as the idea that there is a truth to be discovered in moral matters, or that there might be one right answer to a moral issue (ibid. p. 155). With regard to the former, insofar as he makes this a matter of knowing the facts of the case before we judge, this falls under the topic of moral judgement rather than response and is thus not germane here. With regard to the second aspect – that there might be a right answer to moral dilemmas – he claims that '[a]ccepting such an attitude is not, however, the badge of realism, but simply the optimism that our best efforts can, in the end, close any issue, provided we keep at it long enough'. (ibid.) "There is a solution" is not, however, equivalent to "Let us behave as if there is a solution".
155 Blackburn, 'Truth, Realism, and the Regulation of Theory', pp. 19–20.
156 Blackburn, 'Errors and the Phenomenology of Value', p. 157. On one level this owning of one's own values *is* merely common sense. If, after I have delivered some evaluative judgement, my interlocutor is jejune enough to respond with "That's just your opinion", I will (and do) respond with "Of course it is. What else would it be?" However, that such a scenario should arise at all does suggest that there is a form of common sense – expressed by my interlocutor – that believes the personal nature of the judgement is an argument against its validity.

157 Blackburn, 'Errors and the Phenomenology of Value', p. 153.
158 Ibid., p. 154.
159 Ibid.
160 Ibid., p. 155.
161 Ibid.
162 Ibid., p. 156.
163 Ibid., p. 157.
164 Ibid., p. 155.
165 Blackburn, 'How To Be an Ethical Anti-Realist', p. 169.
166 Ibid., p. 176.
167 Ibid., p. 177.
168 Ibid., p. 176.
169 Ibid., pp. 176–7.
170 Ibid., p. 177.
171 Ibid., p. 179.
172 Ibid., p. 177.
173 Ibid., p. 178.
174 Ibid., pp. 178–9.
175 Ibid., p. 179.
176 Ibid. Elsewhere he writes that expressivism and quasi-realism are not 'morally conservative', since 'Attitudes vary with beliefs, and if relevant beliefs are shown to be false, the attitudes may have to change with them'; Blackburn, 'Quasi-Realism No Fictionalism', p. 330.
177 Blackburn, 'Quasi-Realism No Fictionalism', pp. 322–3.
178 Ibid.
179 Ibid., p. 326.
180 Ibid., p. 327.
181 Having said this, however, it should be remarked how much of Blackburn's work has been addressed to the *defence* of the (quasi-realistic) existence of moral values.
182 Blackburn, 'Errors and the Phenomenology of Value', p. 158.
183 Ibid., p. 157.
184 Ibid.
185 Ibid., p. 156.
186 It is a view, which seems to take the most literal interpretation of the most fundamentalist religious pronouncements as exemplary of the religious sense per se, that is, indeed, rather characteristic of his milieu.
187 (On this point, see Nucci, *Education in the Moral Domain*, pp. 20–51.) People do not have the moralities they have because they believe in God; rather they believe in God because they have the moralities they have. God is, as it were, the embodiment of their moral sense. A question like "Could God act immorally?" is thus strictly meaningless. The natural answer for a religious person would be simply "If God were immoral, He would not be God". I am not, of course, intending to defend this standpoint; I mention it only to point out that the notion that belief in God is what certain people, with 'defective sensibilities' have in the place of some other, more 'natural', moral sense is, frankly, asinine. Moreover, from a purely historical perspective, religion has been the externalization of the moral sense for so long that this identification of God and morality is second nature even today. (Try, for example, to paraphrase an expression like "the sanctity of human life", without producing something intolerably vapid.) Once you have posited God as an

omniscient, omnipotent being that means us well, it makes just as much sense to say that something is wrong "in God's eyes" as it does to say that something should not happen because it is, for example, a breach of human rights or an affront to human dignity – or even, in the last analysis, because "it is wrong".
188 Blackburn, 'Quasi-Realism No Fictionalism', p. 332.
189 As vice-president of the British Humanist Association, Blackburn subscribed to the bylaws of the International Humanist and Ethical Union. According to section 2.1 of the IHEU bylaws, adopted by the General Assembly in London in 2009, 'Humanism . . . affirms that human beings have the right and responsibility to give meaning and shape to their own lives.'
190 D'Arms and Jacobson, who discuss Blackburn, Gibbard, McDowell and Wiggins as 'neosentimentalists', identify the common thesis of neosentimentalism as 'to think that X has some evaluative property F is to think it appropriate to feel F in response to X', where 'to think a sentiment appropriate in the relevant sense is a normative judgment, of a type yet to be explicated, in favor of feeling it'; 'Sentiment and Value', p. 729. 'The trouble is that to call a response "appropriate" is vague praise. This is not merely a quibble about how well certain philosophers have chosen or defined their terms. Whatever one's preferred normative locution, the point remains that only certain good reasons for or against having a response bear on the associated evaluative judgment' (p. 731). D'Arms and Jacobson see the problem as being able to find a way to distinguish genuinely moral from prudential reasons for feeling a sentiment: 'The problem . . . is how to circumscribe the sense of "appropriate" such that the dictum "to think X is Φ is to think F an appropriate response to X" is true. Until this is done, talk of the truth or objectivity of evaluative judgments, or of such judgments manifesting knowledge, is still unearned' (pp. 731–2; 738). This, I take it, is what Slote, who is discussed later in the chapter, is trying to accomplish.
191 Slote, *Moral Sentimentalism*, pp. 81; vii.
192 Ibid., p. 54n13. Slote cites the work of Wiggins, McDowell, and Darwall, Gibbard, and Railton's, 'Toward Fin de Siècle Ethics: Some Trends' as precursors to his own sentimentalism and as agreeing with him that judgements can possess 'objective prescriptivity'; Slote, *Moral Sentimentalism*, p. 54n13. He does, however, fault both Wiggins and Darwall for treating 'moral judgments' as a posteriori, and, therefore, failing to give 'any definite account of the meaning of moral terms or claims' (p. 49). By contrast, his argument against Blackburn appears to be simply that he does not want Blackburn to be right: 'Simon Blackburn's projectivist error theory of moral judgment denies that moral utterances ever state moral truths or are objectively valid and does so with great panache and dexterity, and it isn't easy to see what is wrong with that view, except, perhaps, for the fact that it denies a *deep seated pretheoretical view of the nature of moral discourse*. I think most of us would prefer a theory that did justice to that intuitive, commonsense understanding of things but that could also do justice to the motivational (positive/negative) force of moral claims. [. . .] So until and unless it more clearly appears that such a way of proceeding is on the wrong track, I think we should leave projectivism to one side and continue with the present project' (p. 49).
193 Slote, *Moral Sentimentalism*, p. 71.
194 Ibid., pp. 57–8.
195 Ibid., p. 58.
196 Ibid., pp. 58–9.
197 Ibid., p. 59.

198 Ibid., pp. 59; 60.
199 Ibid., p. 60.
200 Ibid., p. 61.
201 Ibid., p. 75.
202 Ibid., p. 76.
203 Ibid.
204 Ibid., p. 77.
205 Ibid., p. 62.
206 Ibid. They are a mother who prefers to help someone else's child rather than her own because she can do somewhat more good for the other child, and the argument that, faced with miners trapped underground, whatever money is available should be spent on installing safety devices in the mine rather than rescuing them, since this will save a somewhat greater number of lives in the long run.
207 Slote, *Moral Sentimentalism*, p. 62.
208 Ibid.
209 Ibid., pp. 62–3.
210 Ibid., p. 63.
211 Ibid.
212 Ibid. (Slote's emphasis.)
213 Ibid., p. 64.
214 Ibid., p. 64n10.
215 Ibid., p. 67.
216 Slote, *The Ethics of Care and Empathy*, p. 31.
217 Slote, *Moral Sentimentalism*, p. 67.
218 Ibid., pp. 67–8.
219 Ibid., pp. 68; 70.
220 Ibid., p. 65.
221 Ibid., pp. 65–6.
222 Ibid., p. 66n13.
223 Ibid. 'Many people think that homosexuality, masturbation, or overindulgence in food is morally wrong or disgusting, apart from any ill effects on human lives. And it is difficult but not, I think, impossible to explain away all these (putative) opinions in the light of various philosophical views about moral concepts. But of course, Kantianism, Aristotelianism, and sentimentalism will all have different ways of working this out.'
224 Slote, *Moral Sentimentalism*, p. 71.
225 Ibid., p. 15.
226 Batson, *Altruism in Humans*, p. 11. Batson is also careful to distinguish his use of 'empathy' from seven other mental states that can go by the same name: knowing another person's internal state (including their thoughts and feelings), adopting the posture of an observed other, coming to feel as another feels, intuiting or projecting oneself into another's situation, imagining how another is thinking and feeling, imagining how one would think and feel in another's place and feeling distress at witnessing another suffering (pp. 12–19). Indeed, Slote's initial definition of 'empathy' corresponds to this last form, though, as Batson points out, feeling distressed *by* the state of the other is not the same thing as feeling distressed *for* the other, which is what he means by 'empathic concern' (p. 19).
227 Moreover, relieving someone's distress is obviously not the only way of ending the negative effect of that distress upon oneself.

228 If empathy were enough, it would hardly be the case that child abuse is so often passed from one generation to another.
229 Indeed, at some points Slote does gloss his 'empathy' as 'caring', which would seem to undermine his own argument. As we have seen, Batson also uses 'empathy' in a way similar to Slote, though he does make it clear how his use stands in relation to sympathy. However, 'empathy' has recently come to have this optimistic and misleading use (as equivalent to sympathy or compassion) even in some areas of psychology itself; see, for example, the way it is used throughout Haidt and Kesebir's, 'Morality'.
230 Slote, *Moral Sentimentalism*, p. 52.
231 Ibid., p. 53. The circularity is pronounced at this point in his exposition: 'We have argued that empathy enters into approval and disapproval, and since sentimentalism holds that our attitudes of approval and disapproval enter into the making of moral judgments, we can conclude that empathy enters into our understanding of moral claims . . . *because attitudes/feelings of approval/disapproval enter into the making of moral judgments*' (p. 53).
232 Russell, 'Note on Philosophy', pp. 146–7.

Chapter 3

1 I have argued elsewhere that this is also the case with aesthetic feeling, though I realize the point is controversial. The most significant parallel lies in the way in which, with both moral and aesthetic feeling, it is possible to experience the particular emotion, believe one can identify the event that precipitated it, yet still be unable to discover a causal connection between the two. The more complex emotional states mentioned earlier offer simpler examples of the same phenomenon on occasion, as do various neuroses.
2 Thus, as we have seen, the eighteenth century finds a "solution" in simply positing morality as an instinct – so that we desire the Good by nature – and many of our contemporaries use the idea of evolution to do the same.
3 It must be noted, however, that these are all questions that might require a more definite answer within a legal context: a context in which moral *judgements* are required.
4 Hutcheson, *An Inquiry into the Original of Our Ideas of Beauty and Virtue in Two Treatises*, p. 125.
5 Hence, its first appearance in the literature not as a hypothesis to be defended but rather as a statement of the obvious; see, for example, Beccaria, *On Crimes and Punishments*, p. 7.
6 Happiness, says Mill, is the one end that we can be sure is desired for itself: *Utilitarianism*, pp. 52–6. This is a sticking point for many in his account, which suggests that his argument in support of the claim is not particularly clear. I will, therefore, here give my own argument for the same claim.
7 Mill, as we saw in Chapter 1, includes the desire for the good in this category.
8 Undertaking the journey as self-punishment counts, of course, as using it as a means to an end.
9 As Mill says, once virtue has become, by 'association', an end in itself for someone, its pursuit becomes an *interest* for that person; *Utilitarianism*, pp. 54–5. '[Desiring] a thing

and finding it pleasant, aversion to it and thinking of it as painful, are phenomena entirely inseparable, or rather two parts of the same phenomenon; in strictness of language, two different modes of naming the same psychological fact: that to think of an object as desirable (unless for the sake of its consequences), and to think of it as pleasant, are one and the same thing; and that to desire anything, except in proportion as the idea of it is pleasant, is a physical and metaphysical impossibility' (p. 57).
10 Williams, 'A Critique of Utilitarianism', p. 105.
11 It is because these problems almost inevitably dog the word "happiness" that I have opted for "welfare" in other parts of the text. "Welfare" itself, however, has the problem of suggesting a concern only for what is necessary rather than what might be desired. A word that could capture both senses – without being as (currently) precious as "flourishing" – would be useful. I have given the sense in which 'welfare' is used throughout this work on page [235].
12 Williams, 'A Critique of Utilitarianism', pp. 99–100.
13 A more sophisticated understanding of 'alienation' than the one Williams employs might ask how we could be alienated from anything other than our own desire but, since it is clear enough from the context what he means by the word, we shall persist with his usage.
14 Williams, 'A Critique of Utilitarianism', p. 108.
15 Ibid., p. 94.
16 Ibid., pp. 98–9.
17 Ibid., p. 110.
18 Ibid., pp. 110–11.
19 Ibid., pp. 114–15.
20 Ibid., p. 112.
21 Elsewhere, as we shall see later, Williams does discuss the 'alienation' that may arise from a conflict between the verdicts of utilitarianism and moral feeling: the way in which a commitment to utilitarianism can run counter to our sense of right and wrong. His claim, in that context, that there are ends that lie outside our 'moral world' is actually more appropriate to the present question than it is there.
22 One readily sees here why Kant placed the desire implied by moral feeling *outside* nature.
23 Williams, 'A Critique of Utilitarianism', p. 116.
24 Ibid., pp. 116–17.
25 Ibid., pp. 117–18.
26 Railton, 'Alienation, Consequentialism, and the Demands of Morality', p. 147.
27 Ibid., p. 139.
28 Ibid., p. 140.
29 Ibid., p. 147.
30 Ibid.
31 Ibid., pp. 139–40.
32 Ibid., p. 148.
33 Ibid.
34 '[The] reduction of all goals to the purely abstract goal of happiness or pleasure, as in hedonistic utilitarianism, treats all other goals instrumentally. Knowledge or friendship may promote happiness, but is it a fair characterization of our commitment to these goals to say that this is the only sense in which they are ultimately valuable? Doesn't the insistence that there is an abstract and uniform goal lying behind all of our ends bespeak an alienation from these particular

ends?'; Railton 'Alienation, Consequentialism, and the Demands of Morality', p. 149.
35 Railton, 'Alienation, Consequentialism, and the Demands of Morality', pp. 148–9. Moreover, when he conjures up the reason we would refuse – 'our sense of loss in contemplating a life tied to an experience machine, quite literally alienated from the surrounding world' – he reveals precisely why some would not choose it: they fail to actually imagine it in the terms it is presented. This tendency to respond emotionally to the impossible ('To infinity and beyond!') dogs a multitude of thought experiments.
36 Railton, 'Alienation, Consequentialism, and the Demands of Morality', p. 149.
37 Ibid., p. 150.
38 Ibid., p. 152.
39 Ibid. We must, of course, understand this to mean acting with the intention of promoting the good. If I burn down an empty conference centre for fun on the day before a conference that was, unbeknownst to me, to have been the target of a terrorist attack on the following day, no one would want to claim that I had done the right thing. Objective consequentialism, as Railton defines it, can be nobody's conscious point of view.
40 Railton, 'Alienation, Consequentialism, and the Demands of Morality', p. 152.
41 Ibid., p. 153.
42 Ibid.
43 Ibid.
44 Ibid., pp. 154–5.
45 Ibid., p. 154.
46 Ibid., pp. 153–6.
47 One of the dangers of growing up in a culture that sets high store by the 'value of morality' is precisely this tendency to conflate what one *should* do with whatever one feels inclined to do. Nowell-Smith gives a much sounder account of what it would mean to have 'standing [moral] commitment' in discussing 'moral principles'; *Ethics*, pp. 307–9.
48 Foot, 'The Problem of Abortion and the Doctrine of Double Effect', p. 23. Moreover, as we shall see later, while we might wish to qualify this conclusion with "all things being equal", it usually rapidly emerges that the "equality" being invoked also contains a utilitarian appeal.
49 Foot, 'The Problem of Abortion and the Doctrine of Double Effect', p. 24.
50 Something like this reconciliation of the apparently contrasting intuitions of the two cases has been made by Schmidtz; *Elements of Justice*, p. 171. (I have already made the point that case-by-case utilitarian reasoning is not utilitarian reasoning.) Thomson's invocation of rights and 'distributive exemption' in her 'The Trolley Problem' perhaps represents a nascent form of a similar explanation.
51 Foot, 'The Problem of Abortion and the Doctrine of Double Effect', p. 23.
52 Moreover, we cannot even appeal, as with Foot's example of sacrificing one to create a serum or Williams's of the persecution of an unwelcome minority, to the effect of precedent on future total happiness. The instances are too singular and urgent.
53 Williams, 'A Critique of Utilitarianism', pp. 94–5.
54 Ibid., p. 93.
55 Perhaps because this point is mixed up with his other objection: that utilitarianism imposes too great an obligation from the point of view of our non-moral interests. Indeed, as we have seen, his point about the former derives a certain rhetorical force from its confusion with the current question of our moral interests.

56 Williams, 'A Critique of Utilitarianism', p. 92.
57 Ibid.
58 Ibid., pp. 103–4.
59 Ibid., p. 103.
60 This is the drama of the situation. If the captain presents Jim with the alternatives of shooting one Indian or letting them all go, the drama disappears.
61 Simpler souls that Williams tend to merely reach for the false antithesis of reason versus feeling, with utilitarianism representing the former and moral sense the latter.
62 Williams, 'A Critique of Utilitarianism', p. 150.
63 Brandt, 'Toward a Credible Form of Utilitarianism', pp. 109–110.
64 Ibid., p. 110.
65 Ibid., p. 109.
66 Ibid., p. 110.
67 Certainly, however, the existence of the rule, and the knowledge that the rule exists to ensure the greatest happiness for the greatest number, would be psychologically helpful, since it at least appears to add moral weight to a choice that filial affection might, in any case, make more attractive.
68 Brandt, 'Toward a Credible Form of Utilitarianism', p. 125.
69 Ibid., p. 139.
70 Ibid.
71 Ibid., pp. 130–1.
72 Ibid., p. 134.
73 This may be why people, in electing moral guides, generally opt either for those who feel as they do or, failing that, and even less justifiably, simply for the most confident.
74 Thomson, 'The Trolley Problem', p. 1402.
75 Ibid., pp. 1402–3.
76 Thomson, 'The Trolley Problem', p. 1403.
77 Ibid., p. 1409.
78 Ibid., p. 1415.
79 Ibid., pp. 1411–12.
80 Ibid., p. 1412.
81 Ibid., pp. 1414–15.
82 One study found that while around 85 per cent of respondents felt it was 'morally permissible' to redirect the train to the single person track in the basic tram dilemma, only 56 per cent felt the same about the Loop variant and a mere 12 per cent felt it would be 'morally permissible' to push the fat man off the footbridge; Hauser et al., 'A Dissociation Between Moral Judgments and Justifications', p. 6. (Though the source of these data is tainted, it is sufficiently in line with common sense to not entirely discount.) The research was intended to 'challenge the view that moral judgments are solely the product of conscious reasoning on the basis of explicitly understood moral principles', while showing that, though we may be unable to articulate principles, nevertheless 'operative, but not expressed principles, drive our moral judgments' (17–18). Obviously, I am sceptical that the idea of moral judgement as solely the product of conscious reasoning on the basis of explicitly understood principles is an idea that even requires challenging. I am more interested in the operative but unexpressed principles implicit in common patterns of judgement, though I feel the use of 'principles' here may be misleading.
83 Cushman et al., 'The Role of Conscious Reasoning and Intuition in Moral Judgment', p. 1086. The names of the principles belong to the authors.

84 Greene et al., 'Pushing Moral Buttons', pp. 365–6. They also discuss other variants (pp. 367–9).
85 Diderot, 'Letter on the Blind for the Use of Those Who See', pp. 81–2.
86 *The Third Man*, directed by Carol Reed, written by Graham Greene (1949). A possible precursor to this speech may be found in a conversation between Rastignac and Bianchon in Part III of Balzac's *Le Père Goriot*.
87 Chateaubriand, *The Genius of Christianity*, p. 188.
88 Singer, 'The Singer Solution to World Poverty', p. 44.
89 Smith, *The Theory of Moral Sentiments*, pp. 157–8.
90 See Blackstone, *Commentaries on the Laws of England*, IV, pp. 6–12. Blackstone's own view is that this is a 'melancholy fact'; 'Where the evil to be prevented is not adequate to the violence of the preventive, a sovereign that thinks seriously can never justify such a law to the dictates of conscience and humanity' (p. 7). Such 'sanguinary laws are a bad symptom of the distemper of any state, or at least of its weak constitution' (p. 11). Others obviously felt the same, since it apparently became common to falsely acquit prisoners of 'grand larceny' rather than be responsible for their deaths. There must, nevertheless, have been sufficient support for the idea that the security of one's linen was more important than another's life, at least among those with influence with the legislature, for such laws to have come into being.
91 Singer, 'Famine, Affluence, and Morality', pp. 5–6.
92 I take this to be the only objection to Singer's position that does not rely either on a logical fallacy or a misrepresentation of the facts. As an appeal to moral feeling, it is irrefutable.
93 Ord calls these the *Principle of Extreme Liberty* and the *Principle of Luxury* respectively; 'Global Poverty and the Demands of Morality', p. 190.
94 Singer, 'Famine, Affluence, and Morality', p. 32.
95 Ibid., p. 8.
96 Vividness is not, of course, always a matter of physical proximity. We must not forget the mind's eye here. Hence, the moral influence of art in all its manifestations: from Dickens to Nazi propaganda.
97 'The weeping of a Russian lady over the fictitious personages in the play, while her coachman is freezing to death on his seat outside, is the sort of thing that everywhere happens on a less glaring scale'; James, *The Principles of Psychology*, I, p. 125. James blames 'the habit of excessive novel-reading and theatre-going' for such apparent contradictions but, as we have seen earlier, either custom or a settled conviction as to one's own righteousness (such as is recommended by Railton) is all that is necessary. A combination of the two is, of course, even more effective.
98 Cushman et al., 'The Role of Conscious Reasoning and Intuition in Moral Judgment', p. 1087.
99 Ibid., p. 1086.
100 This inability to justify moral responses has been interestingly dealt with in Björklund et al., 'Moral Dumbfounding: When Intuition Finds No Reason'; Haidt, 'The Emotional Dog and Its Rational Tail', and Björklund, 'Intuition and Ex-post Facto Reasoning in Moral Judgment: Some Experimental Findings', which present experimental evidence of 'morally dumbfounded' responses to such scenarios as harmless incest. However, the position against which Haidt, for example, is arguing – that moral feeling is a matter of rational processes – hardly requires experimental evidence for its refutation.
101 Cushman et al., 'The Role of Conscious Reasoning and Intuition in Moral Judgment', pp. 1086–7.

102 We shall return to this in Chapter 6.
103 Foot, 'The Problem of Abortion and the Doctrine of Double Effect', p. 19.
104 Ibid., p. 30.
105 Thomson, for example, deduces from her own responses a set of hierarchies that she describes as 'a quite general moral truth'; 'If a person is faced with a choice between doing something *here and now* to five, by the doing of which he will kill them, and doing something else *here and now* to one, by the doing of which he will kill only the one, then (other things being equal) he ought to choose the second alternative rather than the first'; 'The Trolley Problem', p. 1415. However, in arriving at a rule she is also prepared to discount the more common response if her own differs from it; see pp. 1410–11. In contrast, the psychologists cited earlier are more likely to deduce principles solely from their subjects' responses rather than their own feelings or their desire for consistency. Thus Hauser et al. conclude from their research that the observed pattern of judgements was consistent with at least three possible moral distinctions: it is less 'permissible' to cause harm as an intended means to an end than as a foreseen consequence of an end; it is 'less permissible' to cause harm by introducing a new threat (e.g. pushing a man) than by redirecting an existing threat (e.g. turning an out-of-control train onto a man) and it is 'less permissible' to cause harm by direct physical contact than by an indirect means; 'A Dissociation Between Moral Judgments and Justifications', p. 15. If they were guilty of moral realism, it was only insofar as they took these results to be of more than local interest.
106 Thomson, 'Killing, Letting Die, and the Trolley Problem', p. 206. Thomson dissents from what she takes to be Foot's conclusion – that 'our "negative duties", such as the duty to refrain from killing, are more stringent than our "positive", duties, such as the duty to save lives' – on the grounds that this would oblige the tram driver to keep his tram on a line with five on it if he had to take positive steps to divert it to the one-man line (pp. 206–7). Once more it is visceral response that is appealed to. Indeed, the range of values Thompson here appeals to in order to show why, on occasion, killing may be more 'permissible' than letting die – providence, private-ownership, personal desert (the relative fecklessness of those involved) – will probably appear to some audiences as far more controversially a matter of emotion than Foot's solution. Incidentally, it is Thomson who rechristens Foot's tram dilemma 'the trolley problem'.
107 Thomson, 'Killing, Letting Die, and the Trolley Problem', p. 207.
108 Huemer, *Ethical Intuitionism*, pp. 224–53.
109 Ibid., pp. 103–5.
110 Indeed, the common response to a case like that of the magistrate faced with rioters is often advanced as a *refutation* of utilitarianism. As I have suggested, it may indeed be precisely the main function of systematic ethics to arbitrate in cases where no emotional response, or no unambiguous emotional response, is forthcoming.
111 Singer, 'Morality, Reason, and the Rights of Animals', p. 148. He refers to Greene and Haidt, 'How (and Where) Does Moral Judgment Work?'.
112 Singer, 'Morality, Reason, and the Rights of Animals', p. 148.
113 Ibid., p. 149. Extraordinary as this identification of reason and utilitarianism might seem, it is worth noting that the researchers themselves appear to have been working with a similar assumption. See note 82. Sometimes it feels as if the eighteenth century never happened.
114 Singer, 'Morality, Reason, and the Rights of Animals', p. 149.
115 Ibid., p. 150.
116 Ibid. (At the time of first drafting this chapter I did not know that Singer and Huemer had gone toe-to-toe on precisely this question of metaethical justification; see

Huemer, 'Singer's Unstable Meta-Ethics' and Singer, 'Reply to Michael Huemer'.) See Landy and Royzman, 'The Moral Myopia Model: Why and how reasoning matters in moral judgment', for the thesis that the greater the role of reason in a moral response/judgement, the more morally sound that response/judgement.
117 Sinnot-Armstrong, *Moral Skepticisms*, p. 203.
118 Ibid.
119 I am here borrowing from Williams: '"You can't kill that, it's a child" is more convincing as a reason than any reason which might be advanced for its being a reason'; 'Conflicts of Values', p. 81.
120 Hegel's *Phenomenology of Spirit* is a wonderful, if obscure, account of the many ways in which we can fool ourselves into believing that it is.
121 The possible utilitarian benefit of punishing whole families is considered in Boonin's, *The Problem of Punishment*, pp. 198–201. He feels that many would find this unacceptable even if it proved to be effective. He does not deal with the "they-should-not-be-allowed-to-get-away-with-it" types that I allude to here, that is, those who seem to be motivated almost by envy and who would probably approve such a policy even if it were shown to increase crime.

Chapter 4

1 This is not, of course, to say that merely positing such an "instinct" for others' welfare would solve our more general problem of the grounds of moral feeling itself, for the existence of such an instinct would still stand in need of explanation.
2 South avers that a distinction must be drawn between 'sins of infirmity' and 'sins of presumption', and that 'there is a vast difference between them; indeed, as vast as between *Inadvertency* and *Deliberation*, between *Surprize* and *Set purpose*'; South, *Twelve Sermons Preached Upon Several Occasions*, 2, pp. 207–8. Though he also concedes that 'to state exactly which are Sins of *Infirmity*, and which are not, is not so easy a Work' (p. 208).
3 We will come back to this distinction between perceiving a thing as morally preferable and perceiving it as more attractive, and the failure of the latter experience to evoke any reflexive moral response, in more detail later.
4 Gaut, 'The Ethical Criticism of Art', pp. 186; 198–9.
5 Gaut, *Art, Emotion and Ethics*, p. 236.
6 Gaut, 'The Ethical Criticism of Art', p. 187. That this is so, irrespective of whether it is also morally justifiable, is attested to by Nagel; 'Moral Luck', pp. 32–3. This must be distinguished from responding morally to a person's perceived disposition, even where that person is prevented by lack of opportunity and occasion from expressing that disposition in action; see Rescher, 'Luck', pp. 155–6.
7 I foresee a danger here of precisely the same problem occurring with my conclusion as with the original instance. So, yes, of course I realize it is hard to imagine an ongoing state of 'being satisfied' that would not in the end itself produce dissatisfaction. At this point, however, it is obviously no longer a state of being satisfied.
8 Devereaux, 'Beauty and Evil: The Case of Leni Riefenstahl's *Triumph of the Will*', p. 241 (my emphasis).
9 Ibid., pp. 241–2. This aspect of 'immoral art' is rarely acknowledged by aesthetics, which is mainly concerned either with proving that aesthetic value and edification

102 We shall return to this in Chapter 6.
103 Foot, 'The Problem of Abortion and the Doctrine of Double Effect', p. 19.
104 Ibid., p. 30.
105 Thomson, for example, deduces from her own responses a set of hierarchies that she describes as 'a quite general moral truth'; 'If a person is faced with a choice between doing something *here and now* to five, by the doing of which he will kill them, and doing something else *here and now* to one, by the doing of which he will kill only the one, then (other things being equal) he ought to choose the second alternative rather than the first'; 'The Trolley Problem', p. 1415. However, in arriving at a rule she is also prepared to discount the more common response if her own differs from it; see pp. 1410–11. In contrast, the psychologists cited earlier are more likely to deduce principles solely from their subjects' responses rather than their own feelings or their desire for consistency. Thus Hauser et al. conclude from their research that the observed pattern of judgements was consistent with at least three possible moral distinctions: it is less 'permissible' to cause harm as an intended means to an end than as a foreseen consequence of an end; it is 'less permissible' to cause harm by introducing a new threat (e.g. pushing a man) than by redirecting an existing threat (e.g. turning an out-of-control train onto a man) and it is 'less permissible' to cause harm by direct physical contact than by an indirect means; 'A Dissociation Between Moral Judgments and Justifications', p. 15. If they were guilty of moral realism, it was only insofar as they took these results to be of more than local interest.
106 Thomson, 'Killing, Letting Die, and the Trolley Problem', p. 206. Thomson dissents from what she takes to be Foot's conclusion – that 'our "negative duties", such as the duty to refrain from killing, are more stringent than our "positive", duties, such as the duty to save lives' – on the grounds that this would oblige the tram driver to keep his tram on a line with five on it if he had to take positive steps to divert it to the one-man line (pp. 206–7). Once more it is visceral response that is appealed to. Indeed, the range of values Thompson here appeals to in order to show why, on occasion, killing may be more 'permissible' than letting die – providence, private-ownership, personal desert (the relative fecklessness of those involved) – will probably appear to some audiences as far more controversially a matter of emotion than Foot's solution. Incidentally, it is Thomson who rechristens Foot's tram dilemma 'the trolley problem'.
107 Thomson, 'Killing, Letting Die, and the Trolley Problem', p. 207.
108 Huemer, *Ethical Intuitionism*, pp. 224–53.
109 Ibid., pp. 103–5.
110 Indeed, the common response to a case like that of the magistrate faced with rioters is often advanced as a *refutation* of utilitarianism. As I have suggested, it may indeed be precisely the main function of systematic ethics to arbitrate in cases where no emotional response, or no unambiguous emotional response, is forthcoming.
111 Singer, 'Morality, Reason, and the Rights of Animals', p. 148. He refers to Greene and Haidt, 'How (and Where) Does Moral Judgment Work?'.
112 Singer, 'Morality, Reason, and the Rights of Animals', p. 148.
113 Ibid., p. 149. Extraordinary as this identification of reason and utilitarianism might seem, it is worth noting that the researchers themselves appear to have been working with a similar assumption. See note 82. Sometimes it feels as if the eighteenth century never happened.
114 Singer, 'Morality, Reason, and the Rights of Animals', p. 149.
115 Ibid., p. 150.
116 Ibid. (At the time of first drafting this chapter I did not know that Singer and Huemer had gone toe-to-toe on precisely this question of metaethical justification; see

Huemer, 'Singer's Unstable Meta-Ethics' and Singer, 'Reply to Michael Huemer'.) See Landy and Royzman, 'The Moral Myopia Model: Why and how reasoning matters in moral judgment', for the thesis that the greater the role of reason in a moral response/judgement, the more morally sound that response/judgement.
117 Sinnot-Armstrong, *Moral Skepticisms*, p. 203.
118 Ibid.
119 I am here borrowing from Williams: '"You can't kill that, it's a child" is more convincing as a reason than any reason which might be advanced for its being a reason'; 'Conflicts of Values', p. 81.
120 Hegel's *Phenomenology of Spirit* is a wonderful, if obscure, account of the many ways in which we can fool ourselves into believing that it is.
121 The possible utilitarian benefit of punishing whole families is considered in Boonin's, *The Problem of Punishment*, pp. 198–201. He feels that many would find this unacceptable even if it proved to be effective. He does not deal with the "they-should-not-be-allowed-to-get-away-with-it" types that I allude to here, that is, those who seem to be motivated almost by envy and who would probably approve such a policy even if it were shown to increase crime.

Chapter 4

1 This is not, of course, to say that merely positing such an "instinct" for others' welfare would solve our more general problem of the grounds of moral feeling itself, for the existence of such an instinct would still stand in need of explanation.
2 South avers that a distinction must be drawn between 'sins of infirmity' and 'sins of presumption', and that 'there is a vast difference between them; indeed, as vast as between *Inadvertency* and *Deliberation*, between *Surprize* and *Set purpose*'; South, *Twelve Sermons Preached Upon Several Occasions*, 2, pp. 207–8. Though he also concedes that 'to state exactly which are Sins of *Infirmity*, and which are not, is not so easy a Work' (p. 208).
3 We will come back to this distinction between perceiving a thing as morally preferable and perceiving it as more attractive, and the failure of the latter experience to evoke any reflexive moral response, in more detail later.
4 Gaut, 'The Ethical Criticism of Art', pp. 186; 198–9.
5 Gaut, *Art, Emotion and Ethics*, p. 236.
6 Gaut, 'The Ethical Criticism of Art', p. 187. That this is so, irrespective of whether it is also morally justifiable, is attested to by Nagel; 'Moral Luck', pp. 32–3. This must be distinguished from responding morally to a person's perceived disposition, even where that person is prevented by lack of opportunity and occasion from expressing that disposition in action; see Rescher, 'Luck', pp. 155–6.
7 I foresee a danger here of precisely the same problem occurring with my conclusion as with the original instance. So, yes, of course I realize it is hard to imagine an ongoing state of 'being satisfied' that would not in the end itself produce dissatisfaction. At this point, however, it is obviously no longer a state of being satisfied.
8 Devereaux, 'Beauty and Evil: The Case of Leni Riefenstahl's *Triumph of the Will*', p. 241 (my emphasis).
9 Ibid., pp. 241–2. This aspect of 'immoral art' is rarely acknowledged by aesthetics, which is mainly concerned either with proving that aesthetic value and edification

can be linked, or with separating the sheep from the goats of aesthetic experience. Schellekens is an exception: '[Obscene] art can appeal to some of our morally prohibited desires – desires that one might find arousing in art but that one would not gain pleasure from in reality. [. . .] [Obscene] art may fulfil "meta-desires", for example, to break free from certain psychological or moral taboos: we may thus find delight in the idea of being someone who lacks some of the inhibitions that we actually do have'; *Aesthetics and Morality*, p. 80.

10 'The prayer, "Lead me not into temptation" means "Let me not see who I am"'; Schopenhauer, *The World as Will and Representation*, I, p. 367.

11 The fact that raping really does exist, while "consensual rape", which is what wishing to be raped implies, is a contradiction in terms, does not alter this point, though it might make it clear why enjoying the fantasy of the former *seems* more ominous than enjoying the fantasy of the latter.

12 MacKinnon uses the phrase 'fantasy expresses ideology' in positing a link between pornography and violence against women; *Feminism Unmodified*, p. 149.

13 This probably accounts for the disparity in most people's attitudes towards virtual murder within computer games and virtual paedophilia within computer games. For an excellent outline and discussion of the moral arguments involved in justifying the difference in our attitudes towards these two types of virtual entertainment, see Luck, 'The Gamer's Dilemma. An Analysis of the Arguments for the Moral Distinction Between Virtual Murder and Virtual Paedophilia'.

14 It is also sometimes used to refer to an agent who causes harm simply for the pleasure of causing harm, though even in this usage the harm must be perceived as substantial.

15 In this way, virtue ethics may seem to more directly reflect moral experience than do the more abstract concerns that dominated modern ethics; see, for example, Hursthouse, *On Virtue Ethics*, p. 6. However, from the point of view of metaethics, virtue ethics' combination of emphasis on the psychology of the moral experience and normativity, reminiscent of intuitionism, is not a strength.

16 I use the expression 'common good' here to mean any sense of obligation that is larger than the loyalty in question. This is not, then, an invocation of a universalist ethics: the sense of general obligation that constitutes this 'common good' might be merely the community in which one finds oneself rather than humanity or sentient life, or life, itself. One's ethical universe might be bounded by the limits of one's family, race, nationality, etc. When I say 'common good', I am not setting any bounds to how that "common" is to be defined but only pointing to the fact that every morality implies a concept of a "common good", no matter how restricted it might appear to one who does not share that morality.

17 As Keller points out, however, the sender and receiver of these signals may in fact be the same person. There are, as he says, 'rituals of loyalty' – saluting the flag in private, attending church out of loyalty to one's religious heritage, wearing a concealed love token – in which the veneration for the object of loyalty is not communicated to anyone else; *The Limits of Loyalty*, pp. 5–6. Moreover, the very tendency to identify with the object of loyalty – to feel, for example, pride in your team's success – expresses loyalty, even if the feeling is entirely private. 'Such reactions exist beyond any tendencies to want to advance the interests of the object of your loyalty, to serve as its advocate, or to venerate it through involvement in appropriate rituals' (p. 6). Keller's book is far and away the best treatment of loyalty that I am aware of. He defines "loyalty", in brief, as follows: 'Loyalty is the attitude and associated pattern of conduct that is constituted by an individual's taking something's side, and doing

so with a certain sort of motive: namely, a motive that is partly emotional in nature, involves a response to the thing itself, and makes essential reference to a special relationship that the individual takes to exist between herself and the thing to which she is loyal' (p. 21).

18 The only actual sacrifice that must be on show for us to identify this talk as evidence of loyalty is the sacrifice of the person's normal degree of epistemic integrity – the relationship between weight of evidence and formation or rejection of belief that is habitual to them – though this is not a form of 'self-sacrifice' that draws any admiration outside of the instance of loyalty itself. Patriotism, like authentic racism or sexism, is a willed stupidity. (By contrast, a genuine belief that one's country, race or sex possesses valuable characteristics that others do not is, as genuine belief, amenable to change in the face of contrary evidence.) It appears, however, to still be possible to respond positively to the spectacle of epistemic self-sacrifice where what principally strikes us in the particular instance is the way in which it evinces a strength of affection that we can either identify with (as affection per se) or pity (from the point of view of our identification with the motives that give rise to such sacrifice).

19 Bentham, of course, saw animals as both 'susceptible of happiness' and capable of suffering and, therefore, properly belonging within the moral domain, though not on the same footing as human beings; *An Introduction to the Principles of Morals and Legislation*, pp. 310; 310n. See also Mill, 'Whewell on Moral Philosophy', pp. 185–7.

20 Rorty, 'Justice as a Larger Loyalty', p. 44.

21 Hume, *A Treatise of Human Nature*, I, p. 359. Likewise, Price, though he describes the love of one's own country as 'a noble passion', nevertheless avers that, 'like all other passions, it requires regulation and direction'; Price, *A Discourse on the Love of Our Country*, p. 2 (see also pp. 3–6; 10).

22 Keller, *The Limits of Loyalty*, p. 22.

23 Dent, having noted that loyalty 'can be blind to or unmoved by' evidence of a lack of merit in its object, that it can be 'misguided, misplaced, or unquestioning', and that it 'need not be to universal or impartial causes', so that it can, potentially 'give rise to injustice' (in short, that loyalty is loyalty), gets round the difficulty of having discovered that there is nothing admirable in loyalty per se, despite its being 'normally regarded as admirable', by concluding that 'Only rarely has it been seen as a cardinal virtue' – a claim that is convenient, but not true; 'Loyalty', pp. 546–7.

24 Royce, *The Philosophy of Loyalty*, p. vii.

25 Ibid., pp. 9; 15–16.

26 Ibid., pp. 16–17; 18; 98; 194. I suspect it was Emerson who was responsible for popularizing the idea that using quasi-biblical syntax somehow guarantees the ethical soundness of what you are saying. He almost invariably resorts to the language of the King James' Bible when he is at his most unchristian.

27 Royce, *The Philosophy of Loyalty*, pp. 14–15. His definition of a 'worthy cause' does nothing to remove the problem (pp. 18–19).

28 Even if we interpret him (by disregarding much of what he says in the passage quoted) as having meant only that, having chosen the object of one's loyalty according to a certain set of moral criteria other than a concern for loyalty, henceforward the moral thing to do is to remain loyal to that object, this still would not solve the problem. For, having admitted the existence of other moral criteria, this would be as much as to say, persist in your initial choice even if it turns out to have been wrong (immoral). (And this is, in fact, precisely how we recognize and measure loyalty: the difference between a supporter and a loyal supporter is that the latter will continue to attend games even

after their team is relegated.) In this sense, his paean to loyalty does perfectly capture the self-admiring spirit of self-conscious loyalty.
29 Ladd, 'Loyalty', p. 595.
30 Ibid.
31 Ibid., p. 596.
32 Ibid.
33 Maistre, *Considerations on France*, p. 53.
34 Fletcher, *Loyalty*, pp. 18; 174.
35 Ibid., p. 77.
36 Ibid., pp. 16; 25.
37 Ibid., pp. 17–18.
38 Fletcher, indeed, acknowledges that he is establishing the moral goodness of loyalty by fiat – 'There comes a point at which logic runs dry and one must plant ones [*sic*] loyalty in the simple fact that it is *my* friend, *my* club, *my* alma mater, *my* nation'; ibid., p. 61. This does not, however, stop him from arguing on!
39 The most indulgent interpretation it is possible to give to this common piece of cant about *being yourself* is that it is an injunction to follow the impulses you admire in yourself rather than those you wish you did not have, coupled with an invitation to identify only with what the ego finds it comfortable to identify with. "Be yourself" is, necessarily, the rallying cry of bad faith.
40 Fletcher, *Loyalty*, p. 151.
41 Ibid., p. 164.
42 Ibid., p. 6.
43 Ibid., p. 35.
44 Ibid., pp. 163; 161.
45 This kind of simplistic contrast is one that many have erroneously, and approvingly, ascribed to Gilligan's work, though with small justification; see Chapter 3 of Gilligan's *In a Different Voice*.
46 Fletcher, *Loyalty*, p. 154. Sadly, this is not what Camus actually said in Stockholm in 1957. What he said, in response to a question about the unrest in Algeria, was, 'At this moment bombs are being thrown into the streetcars in Algiers. My mother might be in one of those streetcars. If that's justice, I prefer my mother'; quoted in Daniel, *Avec Camus*, p. 140, cited in King, *Camus*, p. 123. This leaves it open as to whether he thought throwing bombs into streetcars could be construed as justice and, therefore, whether the 'justice' he was referring to was his own sense of justice. Given, however, that, as we shall see, it is possible to make such a remark, I will continue as if "I prefer my mother to justice" is what he meant. Incidentally, in the same passage, Fletcher claims that Sartre made a similar remark – that he would always choose his mother over the Resistance – and refers to a passage in Sartre's *Existentialism Is a Humanism*. However, the whole thrust of the passage, in which Sartre makes no such assertion, is to establish precisely that there is no way to adjudicate between such choices, that is, that there are *not* loyalties arising from our historical selves that we are morally obliged to obey.
47 Fletcher, *Loyalty*, p. 154.
48 I may, however, be doing Camus a disservice here. As noted earlier, he never did actually say that he preferred his mother to justice per se. He may also have honestly (and perhaps with justification) believed that even if independence were desirable, the best thing for Algeria itself (regardless of his mother's safety) was not a victory by those, the FLN, who were currently fighting for it.

49 This is not to say that I am loyal to the idea of fatherhood – I have no feelings about how fathers in general *should* be regarded – but simply that I prefer *my* father to justice. Confucius, by contrast, offers another example of the championing of loyalty precisely in connection with fathers: 'The Duke of She said to Confucius, "Among my people there is one we call 'Upright Gong'. When his father stole a sheep, he reported him to the authorities." Confucius replied, "Among my people, those who we consider 'upright' are different from this: fathers cover up for their sons, and sons cover up for their fathers. 'Uprightness' is to be found in this"'.; *Analects*, 13.8, p. 147.

50 De Waal, 'The Tower of Morality', p. 165.

51 On the absurdity of deriving morality from nature, see Mill, 'Nature', pp. 28–32; 45–54.

52 At one point, in seeking to justify the moral nature of loyalty per se, Fletcher is driven to the most desperate throw. It may be, he says, that both logic and his own moral sense are against his thesis but, but what about the story of Abraham and Isaac?; *Loyalty*, pp. 39; 154. And Jephthah?

53 Royce does, indeed, make something like this claim; *The Philosophy of Loyalty*, p. 31. Except, of course, that if one had no ideal (inborn or not) present within oneself, one would have no criteria for choice of cause; neither would it be worth Royce's while trying to make you see the moral superiority of loyalty. It is as if Sartre's work, which much of this passage echoes (or anticipates, depending on which you read first), having brought the argument to the point of absolute freedom, should then recommend *mauvaise foi* as the next step.

54 Oddly enough, this motivation is particularly well described by Royce; *The Philosophy of Loyalty*, p. 19. (Royce's point here echoes Hegel's description of the self-alienation of the nobility under absolute monarchy; Hegel, *The Phenomenology of Spirit*, §§509–11, pp. 296–8. However, it would be strange if the echo were intentional, given the drift of Hegel's argument at this point.)

55 The objectification of the value is, of course, much more easily accomplished where it is a matter of shared loyalty – to nation, corporation and so on. Hence it is that, while a sudden perception that the object of loyalty is not as one has imagined can easily effect a sudden demise of loyalty, the same may also result from the sudden discovery that, despite what one previously assumed, one is alone in one's loyalty.

56 Kant, *Critique of Practical Reason*, p. 233. Though, of course, as Kant was well aware, we never can know if we have renounced our self-conceit.

57 Bryant, for example, makes her extended treatment of loyalty in Hasting's *Encyclopaedia of Religion and Ethics* purely positive by confining it exclusively to loyalty to objects that her readers can admire and by emphasizing the positive character traits it may entail; 'This ideal does, in fact, appear, both in pagan heroic story and in medieval romance, as characterizing bands of pre-Christian heroes and bands of Christian knights. The unwritten law – not mere personal law, but a pact of comradeship – that bound the Round Table knights to mutual loyalty, and to the king above all, is a notable case in point'; 'Loyalty', p. 184.

58 Royce, *The Philosophy of Loyalty*, p. 17.

59 Ibid., p. 18.

60 Hence the temptation to use "loyalty" to refer figuratively to any overcoming of self-interest. Thus Green, for example, speaks of the goodness of the individual being dependent upon that individual's 'loyalty' to moral standards; *Prolegomena to Ethics*, pp. 190; 284. It is 'disinterested loyalty to the moral law' that will allow us to overcome

not only obvious cases of our duty coming into conflict with self-interest but also the 'fictitious embarrassment' of 'cases of conscience' (p. 343).

61 For the same reason we might expect loyalty to be most often actually held up as a virtue in those cultures that place most emphasis on this self-restraining aspect of morality, on the omission of the bad rather than the commission of the good, together with an emphasis on self-improvement that might seem, to the outsider, to have become almost an autonomous ethical goal in itself – which does, indeed, appear to be the case.

62 However, disloyalty will only strike us as vicious where we can ourselves sympathize with the kind of tie that seemed implicit in the loyalty. So that what kind of object (family, company, nation, etc.) the person is disloyal to will be the index of how shocking we find that disloyalty. We have already seen, in a previous note, how Confucius identifies loyalty to one's father, even in defiance of the law, as exemplary of 'uprightness'. It must be noted in connection with the point made here that he explicitly states that 'filial piety and respect for elders constitute the root of Goodness'; *Analects*, 1.2, p. 1. Another more obvious motive for the immolation of logic in accounts claiming that loyalty is a moral duty is, of course, that those accounts emanate from within a context of self-consciously held particular loyalties. Regarding the sacrifice of epistemic integrity within loyalty, see Keller, *The Limits of Loyalty*, ch. 2 *passim*.

63 Writers on ethics are sometimes tempted to get around such apparent contradictions in feeling, where they cannot simply be attributed to a struggle between self-interest and morality, by attributing them to a conflict between moral and aesthetic feeling. The problem here is that different people would place different sides of the conflict into the aesthetic category. If we could point to what is "really" moral, we could tell which attributions were legitimate and which were not, but this is precisely what we cannot point to. Moreover, the boundaries of the aesthetic itself are not unproblematic. In sum, we cannot say what is constitutive of, or, therefore, what is an adulteration of, either moral or aesthetic feeling.

Chapter 5

1 For this and the following, see Kant, *Groundwork of the Metaphysics of Morals*, pp. 7–18. I take Kant's account here to be purely descriptive of the implicit meaning of the moral sense of 'good', and not in any way intended as prescriptive. Although I have used a formulation with obvious Kantian overtones, it is worth noting, particularly given that the contemporary discussion of blame has often taken this as a peculiarly Kantian position, that it is no such thing. See, for example, Augustine, *Of True Religion*, xiv, p. 238; *City of God*, I, 18, pp. 164–6; Aquinas, *On Evil*, pp. 89; 96–7; *Summa Theologica* II-IIae, Q. 64, art 8.

2 Regarding judging culpability not by the agent's intentions or even actions but by the consequences of those actions, see Walster, 'The Assignment of Responsibility for an Accident', pp. 73–9. According to Baron and Hershey, 'most subjects accept the irrelevance of outcomes; yet they show an outcome bias even though they think they should not, and some show an outcome bias even though they think they do not'; 'Outcome Bias in Decision Evaluation', p. 572. See also Van Der Keilen and Garg,

'Moral Realism in Adults' Judgment of Responsibility', and Young et al., 'Investigating the Neural and Cognitive Basis of Moral Luck'.
3 Rescher, 'Luck', pp. 152–3.
4 The Old Testament, for example, declares that the animal involved in bestiality should die along with the human, though it does not specify why: Exodus, xxi. 28 sq. Leviticus, xx. 15 sq.
5 See, for example, Cicero, 'To Brutus', in *The Letters to His Friends*, III, XXII (I. 12), pp. 696–801 (p. 699).
6 This is certainly how Sophocles' Jocasta and Oedipus, for example, see the matter.
7 Kames, by contrast, gives the 'punishment' of Ravilliac's house as an example of misplaced blame; *Sketches of the History of Man*, III, p. 769. The story of Xerxes may be found in Herodotus, *The Histories*, VII, 34–5, pp. 419–20. Apropos what has been said earlier, there is always the possibility that Xerxes did attribute agency to the Hellespont and genuinely believe he could intimidate it or had an audience that did. That is, there may be nothing morally or epistemologically anomalous in his response.
8 For the explicit prohibition of the "punishment" of the guiltless, see, for example, Richardson, *Hammurabi's Laws*, 130, p. 83; Deuteronomy xxiv, 16. Ezekiel xviii, 20; Plato, *Laws* IX, 855a; Seneca, *On Anger*, II, 34, p. 72. Of course, this is not to say that the 'guilty' and 'guiltless' intended by any of these texts would be recognized as such in another time or place. The laws of Hammurabi, for example, stipulate death for a builder whose inadequate workmanship leads to the collapse of a house and the consequent death of its owner. If, however, it leads to death of the son of the owner of the house, then the penalty is the death of the builder's son, and if it is a slave who is killed, then the builder must give a slave to the house owner; Richardson, *Hammurabi's Laws*, 229–31, p. 109.
9 Kames, *Sketches of the History of Man*, III, pp. 768–9.
10 The psychological literature on this phenomenon is usefully summarized in Young et al., 'Investigating the Neural and Cognitive Basis of Moral Luck', pp. 345–7. The only points where I would demur from their account would be (1) where they suggest that subjects 'initially make moral judgments based partially on outcomes, and then spontaneously seek to justify those judgments to themselves by appealing to differences along a dimension they rationally endorse', which seems to unjustifiably presume that the response is moral in nature *before* the subject gets down to changing reality to make it so, and, of course, (2) the authors' observation that the degree of influence the desire to blame exerts on subjects' judgements about agents' mental states is 'unexpected' (p. 346). (With regard to the first point, Knobe also observes that, contrary to the normal assessment of blame in terms of intentions, 'there are cases in which the process appears to be working in reverse – cases in which people's moral judgments seem to be serving as input to the process by which they arrive at theory-of-mind judgments. In cases of this latter type, it seems that people first arrive at a judgment as to whether the behavior itself was morally good or morally bad and then use this moral judgment as input to the process by which they arrive at judgments about the mind'; 'Theory of Mind and Moral Cognition', p. 358.)
11 Nagel, 'Moral Luck', p. 26. I begin with Nagel's paper rather than the paper by Williams – also called 'Moral Luck' – to which he was responding, since, although the two have often been subsequently cited together as statements of the same problem, Williams's paper has quite different concerns; see Williams, 'Moral Luck' *passim*, and 'Postscript', p. 255. The question of moral luck is also dealt with by Westermarck in *The Origin and Development of the Moral Ideas*, I, pp. 237–40.

12 Nagel, 'Moral Luck', pp. 25; 28.
13 Ibid., p. 28.
14 Ibid., p. 31.
15 Ibid., p. 33.
16 Ibid., p. 26.
17 Ibid., pp. 30–1.
18 Ibid., p. 30.
19 Ibid., p. 25.
20 Ibid., pp. 28; 31.
21 See Sverdlik, 'Crime and Moral Luck', p. 182; Rescher, 'Luck', pp. 158–9; 162; Statman, 'Moral Luck', p. 521; Proudfoot and Lacey, *The Routledge Dictionary of Philosophy*, p. 266; Jokic, 'Supererogation and Moral Luck', p. 223; Barceló, 'Semantic and Moral Luck', p. 210; Brogaard, 'Epistemological Contextualism and the Problem of Moral Luck', pp. 360–6; Enoch and Marmor, 'The Case Against Moral Luck', pp. 406–9; 418; Concepcion, 'Moral Luck, Control, and the Bases of Desert', pp. 456–7.
22 See, for example, Thomson, 'Morality and Bad Luck', p. 205; Jensen, 'Morality and Luck', pp. 138–9. Perhaps the oddest response to the conflict Nagel describes comes from Slote. He introduces the conflict to recommend that, since 'common-sense morality' can here be seen to be subscribing to a 'mutually contradictory set of assumptions' it reveals how we 'need to go beyond our ordinary thinking in this area of morality'; Slote, *From Morality to Virtue*, p. 36. A 'virtue ethics', he claims, will allow us to praise or blame depending on outcome rather than intention (pp. 117–24).
23 See, for example, Andre, 'Nagel, Williams and Moral Luck', p. 125; Royzman and Kumar, 'Is Consequential Luck Morally Inconsequential?', pp. 331–2; 341–3.
24 I refer to blaming where there is insufficient responsibility for blame as a matter of 'epistemic sacrifice' because, from the point of view of our natural moral realism, this is how it must appear to the subject.
25 Smith, *The Theory of Moral Sentiments*, pp. 108–27.
26 Ibid., p. 108.
27 Ibid., p. 109.
28 Ibid.
29 Ibid.
30 Ibid., pp. 109–10.
31 Ibid., p. 110.
32 Ibid.
33 Indeed, an absence of the sentiment might appear emotionally anomalous. Imagine, for example, a man whose family is murdered by a burglar with a carving knife he had found in the kitchen. Would it not be strange if, after the trial and conviction of the murderer, the bereaved man were to request the police to return the knife, on the grounds that he now had nothing to carve with? A modern treatment of this theme can be found in Richards, 'Luck and Desert', pp. 178–80.
34 Smith, *The Theory of Moral Sentiments*, pp. 110–11. See Gerard Manley Hopkins, 'Spring and Fall'.
35 Smith, *The Theory of Moral Sentiments*, p. 111.
36 Ibid., p. 114.
37 Ibid., pp. 116–17.
38 Ibid., p. 118.

39 I take it that this formula is abstract enough to capture, for example, both blaming someone for performing an honour killing and blaming someone for not performing an honour killing.
40 Lerner and Montada, 'An Overview: Advances in Belief in a Just World Theory and Methods', p. 1. The theory was first advanced under this name in Lerner and Simmons, 'The Observer's Reaction to the "innocent victim": Compassion or Rejection?'. See also, Lerner, *The Belief in a Just World*, and Furnham, 'Belief in a Just World: Research Progress over the Past Decade'. These references to experimental psychology are included here, as elsewhere, not because I feel that the contours of familiar human experience actually require experimental proof or statistical support but, rather, specifically for those readers who, as we saw with the response to Nagel, appear to find it difficult to allow "what happens" to exist as a separate category from "what is reasonable" or "what should happen".
41 Lerner and Montada, 'An Overview: Advances in Belief in a Just World Theory and Methods', p. 1. Blame is not the only possible response; 'rejecting, or avoiding the victim, or having faith that the victim will eventually be appropriately compensated' are also possible responses according to Lerner and Montada, but they do not concern us here. Likewise, the feeling that a punishment must have been deserved since it was administered that arises simply from our desire to identify with our group, though similar in appearance, is also not germane.
42 This apparent need to be reassured of the efficacy of our own agency giving rise to a demand that the universe be morally determined leads us back, of course, to the dual nature of moral experience – as affect and perception – that we observed in Chapter 1, though this is not the moment for such broader reflections.
43 Sidgwick, *The Methods of Ethics*, p. 217.
44 Ibid., p. 224.
45 Ibid., pp. 222–3.
46 Ibid., p. 223. Sidgwick's problems are only compounded if we take it that the 'settled resolution to abstain from unlawful lust' might better be designated 'continence', thus leaving chastity per se as the mere absence of sexual desire.
47 Sidgwick, *The Methods of Ethics*, p. 223.
48 Ibid., p. 225.
49 Ibid.
50 Sidgwick also includes those who have trained themselves into making good conduct habitual and therefore easier along with the naturally chaste as objects of a kind of moral admiration that is distinct from the apparently more morally consistent admiration of the 'energetic striving of the will to get nearer to ideal perfection'; *The Methods of Ethics*, p. 225. However, insofar as the results of this training do embody a history of intentionality, this seems a quite different object to natural chastity. We do not think less of a virtuoso's skill just because we reflect on the effort that has gone into its creation. ("Anyone could play like that if they practised six hours a day", when said dismissively, clearly misses the point.)
51 Often, with certain virtues that appear admirable simply by virtue of the willpower they exhibit (bravery, tenacity, etc.), it is simply enough to suffer harm through another's possession of them to bring one to a realization that they are not actually 'good in themselves'.
52 Hume, *A Treatise of Human Nature*, I, p. 364 (punctuation modernized).
53 Ibid.
54 Ibid., pp. 365–6.

55 Ibid., p. 366.
56 Ibid.
57 A modern subscriber to the theory would probably attribute the phenomenon to the "agency" of the 'selfish gene'. However, the appeal is strictly redundant, given our ineluctable tendency to interpret matter in terms of value: there seems nothing especially problematic about the idea of seeing a child as "one's own".
58 It should go without saying, though I fear it cannot, that I am not here appealing to biological determinism. While there may be physiological elements at work here, the unequal division of social power between the sexes and the way in which female sexuality has traditionally borne the character, within culture, of a currency are factors that are, in themselves, more than sufficient to account for the differences under discussion.
59 Of course, with regard to sexual desire per se (if there is such a thing), evidence of promiscuity may be a positive value, as suggesting accessibility. However, there is always the problem of the way in which this, as continuous in kind, may devalue 'the thing in itself'.
60 Where this 'chastity' is a class marker, a secondary interest in chastity will arise for women themselves: it becomes important to establish that one is "not that kind of woman". This is especially the case where the market is flooded with sexual provender, as in Victorian Britain or contemporary Thailand. On the other hand, in contemporary societies that have ostensibly rejected this notion of chastity, but where the feelings that produced the notion of it as a virtue are as alive as ever, life can be far more complicated.
61 Or, perhaps, where they feel, as with men, that their "conquest" has been undermined.
62 This same impeccable instinct will even lead a woman, more often I hope in romantic comedies than life, to seek to attract a man by making him jealous.
63 See Albert Camus's description of the 'desire for possession': *The Rebel*, pp. 261–2.
64 They may also reach for whatever plausible explanation will preserve their self-esteem, most effectively by the sacrifice of a less essential area of self-esteem; see, for example, Silent Bob's speech in *Chasing Amy* (1997, directed by Kevin Smith).
65 Mill, *Utilitarianism*, p. 76.
66 Ibid.
67 That the disparity between responses to female and male chastity should so precisely correspond to a historical disparity in relative power over rule making is, of course, no accident. This is not to say that there is no female vested interest in the status of chastity. In any given state of society there may be an advantage for (some) women in this value (consider the expression "sexual favours"), though, given their awareness of the speciousness of its origin, they are more likely to be conscious of it as a rule, rather than, as men do, experiencing it as a moral response, though the latter is still possible.
68 We are today more comfortable with the idea that feeling follows ideology than the idea that ideology expresses feeling; it is one way to avoid responsibility.
69 To some extent, the phenomenon of male jealousy examined here can appear overdetermined: it appears to involve sublimated revulsion at sexuality per se, sublimated interest in the extension of one's "existence" through offspring, sublimated envy at the sexual conquests of others, sublimated fear of sexual inadequacy (à la *Chasing Amy*), a hearty dose of *amour propre* and so on. It is not, however, necessary to determine precisely what the interest is; it is sufficient to note that the form the feeling takes, and the impossible demand on the world implicit in that feeling, marks

it out as sublimated interest in preserving what is instrumental to an untenable form of self-regard.
70 Indeed, as we shall see later in this chapter, even within our own moral consensus there can be ascriptions of culpability, senses of wrongdoing, that we cannot account for either in terms of concrete harm or the immoral intentions of the agent. We should recall here both how the breaking of a taboo is as culpable when it is done accidentally as when it is done deliberately, and that every society has its taboos.
71 Once more, the past fares better in this respect: see Hartley, *Observations on Man*, I, pp. 478–81, and Smith, *The Theory of Moral Sentiments*, pp. 79–83. Mill, whose father introduced him to Hartley's work, is still close to this tradition, despite his own ethical focus; see Mill, *Utilitarianism*, p. 76. See also Westermarck, *The Origin and Development of the Moral Ideas*, I, pp. 92–3. What distinguishes moral from non-moral resentment for Westermarck is that the former arises from sympathy in combination with 'altruistic sentiment or affection' (pp. 109–111). His theory is, in this respect, very similar to Slote's, examined in Chapter 2.
72 'Anger' in VandenBos, *A.P.A. Dictionary of Psychology*, p. 55.
73 Judging from trends within popular culture over the last couple of decades, a self-aware American might experience the same difficulty. Regarding this ancient taste for the pain of others, and the way in which it could even survive Christianization, see Tertullian, 'Spectacles', p. 106.
74 I borrow the hint for this expression from Chesterton's, 'On American Morals', p. 209. Other examples of materialist ethics can be inferred from moral responses aroused by less extreme forms of insecurity than that evinced by disgust – envy is an obvious common stimulus – but disgust is the most clear-cut example.
75 In fact, I remembered the final word as 'putrescence', but the point still stands. Kolnai declares the 'prototypical object of disgust' to be 'the range of phenomena associated with putrefaction'; *On Disgust*, pp. 53–4. See also Menninghaus, *Disgust*, p. 1; McGinn, *The Meaning of Disgust*, p. 14; 65.
76 McGinn, *The Meaning of Disgust*, p. 24.
77 Ibid., p. 47 (see also pp. 192–5). See also Smith, *The Theory of Moral Sentiments*, p. 34.
78 Miller, *The Anatomy of Disgust*, p. 51.
79 McGinn, *The Meaning of Disgust*, p. 37.
80 Ibid., p. 37.
81 See, for example, Rozin et al., 'The CAD Triad Hypothesis: A Mapping between Three Moral Emotions (Contempt, Anger, Disgust) and Three Moral Codes (Community, Autonomy, Divinity)'. Indeed, some authors actually hold contempt to be itself an admirable moral response; see Bell, *Hard Feelings*, p. 273.
82 Kolnai, *On Disgust*, p. 54. See also Augustine, 'Sermon: The Sacking of the City of Rome' (410/411) in *Political Writings*, pp. 205–14 (p. 208); McGinn, *The Meaning of Disgust*, pp. 91; 89–90.
83 The expression 'soul and form' is borrowed from Nietzsche, *The Gay Science*, p. 70.
84 Kass, 'The Wisdom of Repugnance', pp. 17–26.
85 Ibid., p. 20.
86 Ibid.
87 Ibid., p. 21.
88 Ibid., pp. 18; 21–2.
89 Nussbaum, *Hiding from Humanity*, p. 116.
90 Ibid., p. 117.
91 Ibid., p. 102.

92 Ibid.
93 McGinn, *The Meaning of Disgust*, p. 34.
94 Ibid.
95 Ibid., pp. 34–5.
96 Kelly, *Yuck! The Nature and Moral Significance of Disgust*, p. 140.
97 Ibid., p. 147.
98 Ibid., p. 148.
99 McGinn, *The Meaning of Disgust*, p. 34 (my emphasis).
100 Hauskeller, too, argues that disgust can 'qualify as moral' since, even when they cannot be justified in moral terms (by which he means in terms of how the action causes harm or otherwise violates someone's rights), it is no more or less ultimately justifiable than such moral feelings themselves; 'Moral Disgust', p. 572. 'In the absence of any good *moral* reasons *not* to trust our intuitions, we should take them seriously and act accordingly' (p. 600). Nevertheless, Hauskeller also seems committed to some form of realism, arguing that just because a feeling feels moral, this in itself does not commit us to accepting it 'as the expression of a *legitimate* moral concern' (p. 577). We can still ask, not if our feeling is rational but, rather, if it 'make[s] sense to us in the light of the complex of interrelated beliefs and feelings that define our specific way of living in, and looking at, the world' (p. 585). We should, he says, reflect on the grounds of our disgust and try to integrate any instance of it into 'the system of interconnected beliefs that make up our moral world' (p. 600). We must 'admit that there are some things that really *are* a horror, which simply should not happen, or be allowed to happen, which can never be justified, no matter whether we can rationally explain *why* they should not happen': things that 'we simply *know* or at least cannot *seriously doubt*' to be wrong (p. 586). 'It actually *is* an abomination to treat the dead as if they were a mere commodity to be used at our convenience', and to feel so is an 'essential part of our self-understanding as human beings' (pp. 592–3). The problem here, of course, is that another might easily substitute homosexuality for mistreatment of the dead, regretting perhaps the abridgement of sexual self-determination their position involves (i.e. acknowledging that there may be moral arguments on the other side), but nevertheless feeling that homosexuality is one of those things they simply *know* to be wrong. In short, there is, despite what Hauskeller says about the *legitimacy* of moral concerns, no alternative to feeling here.
101 Feinberg, *Offense to Others*, p. 5. Feinberg's nonpareil discussion of offence is the second volume of his *Moral Limits of the Criminal Law* (1984–1988).
102 Regarding the inanity of arguments against homosexual marriage from a consequentialist perspective, see Corvino, 'Homosexuality, Harm, and Moral Principles'. There are two general points that emerge from this debate: (1) The actual operative principle at work in the response of the majority of those who oppose homosexual marriage *is* disgust per se; (2) Those objectors, nevertheless, do not feel justified in appealing directly to that disgust for justification – at least when addressing those outside their own communion.

Chapter 6

1 See Hume, *Enquiries Concerning Human Understanding and Concerning the Principles of Morals*, pp. 293–4.

2 This is not a matter of the 'city of God' or Kant's 'moral world'; Kant, *Critique of Pure Reason*, pp. 677–80.
3 It is in this sense that such responses imply a 'disinterested' concern for the general welfare. Indeed, they are our concern for the general welfare. This is why so many have held that a positive concern for justice must somehow underlie and unite moral experience: that a concern with reciprocity is somehow the key to this area of our nature. However, the problem here is that such a concern is already a moral response, and thus itself stands in need of explanation. I will argue later in the chapter that the implicit concern for justice in our moral responses is not constitutive of them but merely artefactual.
4 Seen this way, it seems quite justifiable to speak of this disposition as a moral sense. It is worth remembering that, irrespective of his proposed grounding of morality, Hutcheson posits the existence of a 'moral sense' precisely because of the involuntary nature and sui generis character of what he calls our 'moral perceptions'.
5 It may be, of course, that I decide this desired world is too far out of reach and come instead to identify or compete with harm per se: defend myself by becoming a source of harm.
6 For reasons of space, I have been obliged to cut an account of moral development from this work. However, apropos the equation of morality and laws of nature, I would direct the reader to Piaget's account of childish *moral realism*: the child's initial conflation of the moral and physical laws of its universe, resulting from the way in which its spontaneous egocentric realism is complemented by adult moral constraint; *The Moral Judgement of the Child*, pp. 184–91; 250–61; 314. It is only natural, according to Piaget, that moral rules should retain something physical about them, as if they were necessary conditions of the universe (p. 187). The way in which Piaget describes the development from moral heteronomy to moral autonomy can make it seem as if, were the development to reach is logical conclusion, we should end with a situation in which, adult moral realism also having given way, all rules would be a matter of expediency (the kind of world we wished to live in) and there would be no such thing as a sui generis moral response: in effect, no morality. Thus, paradoxically, it seems that morality, understood as a feeling that certain things are good or bad *in themselves* (irrespective of my interests), is only possible because moral development is, in one sense, never complete. Of course, moral development is pragmatically complete when the individual arrives at a moral sense that does not conspicuously depart from the moral consensus of their community. (This does not preclude dissent from the moral consensus implicit in the practice of the community, providing this dissent is framed in terms of a moral conflict between elements of that practice, as, for example, with objections to the *cruelty* of meat production.) Nevertheless, from the point of view of the direction of moral development, any recognizable moral sense, since it must contain a foundational moral realism, might be viewed as an instance of arrested development. In this light we could consider the shortcoming of all systematic ethics as the inevitable results of their attempts to rationally work out the principles implied by moral development per se. Thus, we can say that it is only because at some point the moral view implied by the responses of those around us as we develop becomes internalized, that is, only because we come to experience qualities like fairness as values or ends in themselves, that morality exists at all. What is important here is that this internalization, while it takes place in the course of the rationalization of morality, appears to take place *despite* rationality – we "know" with a conviction that is more than knowing that x is wrong. In practice, the content of

the subject's moral sense – the particular configuration of stimuli that the subject will respond to morally – will vary according to the contents of the original childish *moral realism* and the, inevitably peculiar, process by which that subject has preserved, rejected and spontaneously extrapolated from ("interpreted") those original contents through the course of their experience. In this chapter, I have suggested a reason why the rationalization upon which this process depends does not actually result in the rationalization of the moral sense entirely out of existence.

7 See Bacon, *The New Organon*, pp. 44–5.
8 See Cudworth, *A Treatise of Freewill*, pp. 157; 209; Spinoza, *Ethics*, pp. 440; 483; 490; Vaihinger, *The Philosophy of 'As if'*, pp. 43–4; 49; Nagel, 'Moral Luck', pp. 26–8; 38. My account of the problem here closely follows Nagel's own, though from a point of view that takes the phenomenon to be a natural consequence of the grounds of moral experience and, thus, unproblematic.
9 Providing, of course, that we do not consider thrill-seeking as good in itself (which is possible), that we are not ourselves maliciously inclined towards the baker (also possible), or believe (like Emerson) that boys have rights that automatically override those of non-boys.
10 Where people appear hardest on themselves, this is generally not a matter of finding themselves more blameable for the same failings that others have but, rather, of believing that they are more prone to failings. It may also arise from the vividness of their experience of their own malice combined with a weak sense of that of other people. In some cases, of course, they may simply be right: they really are worse than most people.
11 See Schopenhauer, 'On the Freedom of the Will', pp. 45–8; 109; Nagel, 'Moral Luck', p. 37.
12 Sartre, *Existentialism and Humanism*, p. 28.
13 Ibid., pp. 44–5.
14 Pereboom, whose 'hard incompatibilism' holds that moral responsibility is incompatible with scepticism about free will, holds that 'living without a conception of our actions as freely willed in the sense required for moral responsibility in the basic desert sense', rather than undermining morality, 'holds out the promise of greater equanimity by reducing the expression of resentment and indignation that often impairs them'; *Free Will, Agency, and Meaning in Life*, p. 199. He eloquently explains his reasons for believing so, linking blame to anger and anger to actions that are themselves immoral in his *Living Without Free Will*, pp. 207–12. As will be clear from what follows in the present chapter, while I agree with his assessment of the morally deleterious effects of retribution, I do not believe that assent to hard incompatibilism, the relinquishing of 'our presumption of free will and moral responsibility', could ever be anything more than a pose (p. 213). I do so on precisely the same grounds that justify hard incompatibilism itself: we cannot choose what to believe any more than we can will what to will.
15 See Smith, *The Theory of Moral Sentiments*, pp. 112–13.
16 Indeed, the lack of symmetry between negative and positive moral responses is well attested to in the literature of ethics. Many writers begin with both and then quietly lay the positive aside, the implication being that positive responses/judgements will be self-explanatory once negative ones are understood.
17 The nearest thing to symmetry we discover between the positive and the negative is the way in which the perception of *excess* in the saintly is mirrored by the perception of *excess* in evil. Both perceptions are clearly aesthetic.

18 I would, then, divide Hume's category of 'taste' (see note 1) into three: the aesthetic (including positive moral approbation and disgust), the moral (in the form of blame) and prejudice. Although we are used to the idea that one of the characteristics of the aesthetic is that there is no relevant action implied in the response, in contrast to disgust (which prompts avoidance), moral feeling (which prompts help), the erotic (which prompts touch) and so on, we may think of the desire to prolong contemplation or imaginative involvement as a desire to act in a certain way. I will not here rehearse the other ways in which the aesthetic response may be elicited. See, instead, my *Beauty*, *passim*; *The Aesthetic in Kant*, pp. 108–18; 124–42; 149–54; *Sublimity*, pp. 160–5, and 'The Unconscious Grounds of Aesthetic Experience', *passim*.
19 The expression 'arrogance of consciousness' comes from Freud's *Five Lectures on Psycho-Analysis*, p. 39.
20 This is similar to the way we object to the idea of being dead in terms that imply a denial of the very loss of the capacity to experience anything that being dead would necessarily entail.
21 Though the grounding in the *desired world* might have the form of a neurosis, the possession of a moral sense is a human norm. Thus, it would be merely rhetorical to classify it in terms that suggested it was somehow a departure from mental health, somehow pathological.
22 Of course, moral argument is possible insofar as it is possible to elicit a moral response by laying out the facts of a case in such a way that the exposition causes a moral response to those facts. However, insofar as the desired response must already be potentially in place, this can only ever be a matter of showing a thing in a certain light, that is, a matter of rhetoric. This is, of course, hardly what normative ethics aspires to. For the connection between ethics and rhetoric, see Stevenson's 'The Emotive Meaning of Ethical Terms' and his extensive discussion of the 'persuasive' function of ethical language in *Ethics and Language*, though in neither work does he anywhere use the word 'rhetoric'.

Bibliography

Alexander, Richard, D. 'The Evolution of Social Behavior'. *Annual Review of Ecology & Systematics* 5 (1974): 325–83.
Andre, Judith. 'Nagel, Williams and Moral Luck' (1983). In *Moral Luck*, edited by Daniel Statman, 123–9. New York: State University of New York Press, 1993.
Anscombe, G. E. M. 'Modern Moral Philosophy' (1958). In G. E. M. Anscombe, *Ethics Religion and Politics: The Collected Philosophical Papers of G.E.M. Anscombe, Volume Three*, 26–42. Oxford: Blackwell, 1981.
Aquinas, Thomas. *Summa Theologica*, trans. the Fathers of the English Dominican Province, 22 volumes. London: Burns Oates & Washbourne, 1911–1925.
Aquinas, Thomas. *On Evil*, trans. Richard Regan, edited by Brian Davies. Oxford: Oxford University Press, 2003.
Audi, Robert. *The Good in the Right: A Theory of Intuition and Intrinsic Value*. Princeton: Princeton University Press, 2004.
Audi, Robert. *Moral Perception*. Princeton: Princeton University Press, 2013.
Augustine 'Of True Religion'. In Augustine *Earlier Writings*, edited by and trans. J. H. S. Burleigh, 225–83. Louisville: Westminster Press, 1953.
Augustine *City of God*, trans. Henry Bettenson. Harmondsworth: Penguin, 1984.
Augustine. 'Sermon: The Sacking of the City of Rome' (410/411). In *Political Writings*, edited by E. M. Atkins and R. J. Dodaro, pp. 205–14. Cambridge: Cambridge University Press, 2001.
Axelrod, Robert. *The Evolution of Cooperation*. New York: Basic Books, 1984.
Ayer, A. J. *Language, Truth and Logic* (1936/1946). Harmondsworth: Penguin, 1971.
Bacon, Francis. *The New Organon* (1620), edited by Lisa Jardine and Michael Silverthorne. Cambridge: Cambridge University Press, 2000.
Bailey, Samuel. *Letters on the Philosophy of the Human Mind: Third Series*. London: Longman, Green, Longman, Roberts, & Green, 1863.
Bain, Alexander. *Mental and Moral Science: A Compendium of Psychology and Ethics*. London: Longmans, Green, and Co., 1868.
Baldwin, James Mark. *Handbook of Psychology: Feeling and Will*. New York: Henry Holt, 1891.
[Balguy, John], *The Foundation of Moral Goodness: or A Further Inquiry into the Original of Our Idea of Virtue*. London: Printed for John Pemberton, 1728.
Barceló Aspeitia, Axel Arturo. 'Semantic and Moral Luck'. *Metaphilosophy* 43 (2012): 204–20.
Barnes, W. H. F. 'A Suggestion about Value'. *Analysis* 1 (1934): 45–6.
Baron, J. and J. C. Hershey. 'Outcome Bias in Decision Evaluation'. *Journal of Personality and Social Psychology* 54 (1988): 569–79.
Batson, C. Daniel. *Altruism in Humans*. Oxford: Oxford University Press, 2011.

Beccaria, Cesare. 'On Crimes and Punishments' (1764). In Cesare Beccaria *On Crimes and Punishments and Other Writings*, edited by Richard Bellamy, trans. Richard Davies, 1–113. Cambridge: Cambridge University Press, 1995.

Beiser, Frederick C. 'Moral Faith and the Highest Good'. In *The Cambridge Companion to Kant and Modern Philosophy*, edited by Paul Guyer, 588–629. Cambridge: Cambridge University Press, 2006.

Bell, Macalester. *Hard Feelings: The Moral Psychology of Contempt*. Oxford: Oxford University Press, 2013.

Bentham, Jeremy. *An Introduction to the Principles of Morals and Legislation* (1780/1823). Oxford: Clarendon Press, 1907.

Björklund, Fredrik, Jonathan Haidt, and Scott Murphy. 'Moral Dumbfounding: When Intuition Finds No Reason'. *Lund Psychological Reports* 1 (2000): 1–19.

Björklund, Fredrik. 'Intuition and Ex-post Facto Reasoning in Moral Judgment: Some Experimental Findings'. *Lund Philosophy Reports*, 2 (2004): 1–15.

Blackburn, Simon. 'Truth, Realism, and the Regulation of Theory' (1980). In Simon Blackburn *Essays in Quasi-Realism*, 15–34. Oxford: Oxford University Press, 1993.

Blackburn, Simon. 'Errors and the Phenomenology of Value' (1985). In Simon Blackburn *Essays in Quasi-Realism*, 149–65. Oxord: Oxford University Press, 1993

Blackburn, Simon 'How To Be an Ethical Anti-Realist' (1988). In Simon Blackburn *Essays in Quasi-Realism*, 166–81. Oxford: Oxford University Press, 1993.

Blackburn, Simon. *Essays in Quasi-Realism*. Oxford, 1993.

Blackburn, Simon. 'Quasi-Realism No Fictionalism'. In *Fictionalism in Metaphysics*, edited by Mark Eli Kalderon, 322–38. Oxford: Oxford University Press, 2005.

Blackburn, Simon. 'Antirealist Expressivism and Quasi-Realism'. In *The Oxford Handbook of Ethical Theory*, edited by David Copp, 146–62. Oxford: Oxford University Press, 2006.

Blackstone, William. *Commentaries on the Laws of England* (1765-1769/1783), edited by Wilfrid Prest, four volumes. Oxford: Oxford University Press, 2016.

Boonin, David. *The Problem of Punishment*. Cambridge: Cambridge University Press, 2008.

Brandt, Richard B. 'Toward a Credible Form of Utilitarianism'. In *Morality and the Language of Conduct*, edited by Hector-Neri Castaneda and George Nakhnikian, 107–43. Detroit: Wayne State University Press, 1963.

Brogaard, Berit 'Epistemological Contextualism and the Problem of Moral Luck'. *Pacific Philosophical Quarterly*, 84 (2003): 351–70.

Brown, Thomas. *Lectures on the Philosophy of the Mind* (1820), 'nineteenth edition', three volumes. Edinburgh: Adam & Charles Black, 1851.

Bryant, Sophie. 'Loyalty'. In *Encyclopaedia of Religion and Ethics*, edited by James Hastings, VIII, 183–8. Edinburgh: T. & T. Clark, 1916.

Butler, Joseph. *Fifteen Sermons Preached at the Rolls Chapel* (1726), 'fifth edition'. London: Printed for Robert Horsfield, 1765.

Camus, Albert. *The Rebel: An Essay on Man in Revolt* (1951), trans. Anthony Bower. New York: Vintage Books, 1956.

Carlile, William W. 'The Conscience: Its Nature and Origin'. *International Journal for Ethics* 6 (1895): 63–77.

Carnap, Rudolf. *Philosophy and Logical Syntax*. London: Kegan Paul, 1935.

Chateaubriand, [François-René] Viscount de. *The Genius of Christianity; or the Spirit and Beauty of the Christian Religion* (1802), trans. Charles I. White. Baltimore: John Murphy & Co., 1856.

Chesterton, G. K. 'On American Morals' (1927). In G. K. Chesterton *Generally Speaking*, 207–13. London: Methuen & Co., 1928.

Cicero. *The Letters to His Friends*, trans. W. Glynn Williams and M. Cary, three volumes. London: William Heinemann Ltd., 1943–1954.

Clodd, Edward. 'Evolution (Ethical)'. In *Encyclopaedia of Religion and Ethics*, edited by James Hastings, V, 623–8. Edinburgh: T. & T. Clark, 1912.

Cogan, T[homas]. *A Philosophical Treatise on the Passions*, third edition. London: Printed for T. Cadell and W. Davies, 1813.

Concepcion, David W. 'Moral Luck, Control, and the Bases of Desert'. *The Journal of Value Inquiry*, 36 (2002): 455–61.

Confucius *Analects: With Selections from Traditional Commentaries*, trans. Edward Slingerland. Indianapolis: Hackett Publishing Company, 2003.

Corvino, John. 'Homosexuality, Harm, and Moral Principles'. In *Contemporary Debates in Social Philosophy*, edited by Laurence Thomas, 79–93. Oxford: Blackwell, 2008.

Cudworth, Ralph. *A Treatise Concerning Eternal and Immutable Morality* (1731). In Ralph Cudworth *A Treatise Concerning Eternal and Immutable Morality with A Treatise of Freewill*, edited by Sarah Hutton, 1–152. Cambridge: Cambridge University Press, 1996.

Cudworth, Ralph. *A Treatise of Freewill* (1838). In Ralph Cudworth *A Treatise Concerning Eternal and Immutable Morality with A Treatise of Freewill*, edited by Sarah Hutton, 153–209. Cambridge: Cambridge University Press, 1996.

Culverwell, Nathaniel. *An Elegant and Learned Discourse of the Light of Nature* (1652), edited by Robert A. Greene and Hugh MacCallum. Indianapolis: Hackett Publishing Company, 2001.

Cushman, Fiery, Liane Young, and Marc Hauser. 'The Role of Conscious Reasoning and Intuition in Moral Judgment: Testing Three Principles of Harm'. *Psychological Science* 17 (2006): 1082–9.

D'Arms, Justin and Daniel Jacobson. 'Sentiment and Value'. *Ethics* 110 (2000): 722–48.

Darwall, Stephen, Allan Gibbard, and Peter Railton. 'Toward Fin de Siècle Ethics: Some Trends'. *The Philosophical Review* 101 (1992): 115–89.

Darwin, Charles. *The Descent of Man and Selection in Relation to Sex*, two volumes. London: John Murray, 1871.

Dent, Nicholas. 'Loyalty'. In *The Oxford Companion to Philosophy*, edited by Ted Honderich, 546–7. Oxford: Oxford University Press, 2005.

DePaul, Michael R. 'Intuitions in Moral Enquiry'. In *The Oxford Handbook of Ethical Theory*, edited by David Copp, 595–623. Oxford: Oxford University Press, 2006.

Devereaux, Mary. 'Beauty and Evil: The Case of Leni Riefenstahl's *Triumph of the Will*'. In *Aesthetics and Ethics: Essays at the Intersection*, edited by Jerrold Levinson, 227–56. Cambridge: Cambridge University Press, 1998.

De Waal, Frans. 'The Tower of Morality'. In *Primates and Philosophers: How Morality Evolved*, edited by Frans De Waal, Stephen Macedo and Josiah Ober, 161–81. Princeton: Princeton University Press, 2006.

Dewey, John. *Psychology*. New York: Harper & Brothers, 1887.

Diderot, Denis. 'Letter on the Blind for the Use of Those Who See' (1749). In Denis Diderot *Early Philosophical Works*, trans. and edited by Margaret Jourdain, 68–141. Chicago: The Open Court Publishing Company, 1916.

Ellwood, Charles A. *Sociology and Modern Social Problems*. New York: American Book Company, 1910.

Enoch, David. and Andrei Marmor. 'The Case Against Moral Luck'. *Law and Philosophy* 26 (2007): 405–36.

Evans, E. P. *The Criminal Prosecution and Capital Punishment of Animals*. London: William Heinemann, 1906.
Feinberg, Joel. *Offense to Others*. Oxford: Oxford University Press, 1985.
Ferri, Enrico. *Socialism and Positive Science (Darwin-Spencer-Marx)* (1894), trans. Edith C. Harvey. London: Independent Labour Party, 1905.
Firth, Roderick. 'Ethical Absolutism and the Ideal Observer'. *Philosophy and Phenomenological Research* 12 (1952): 317–45.
Fletcher, George P. *Loyalty: An Essay On the Morality of Relationships*. Oxford: Oxford University Press, 1993.
Foot, Philippa. 'The Problem of Abortion and the Doctrine of Double Effect' (1967). In Philippa Foot *Virtues and Vices and Other Essays in Moral Philosophy* (1978), 19–32. Oxford: Clarendon Press, 2002.
Fowler, Thomas. *Progressive Morality: An Essay in Ethics* (1884), 2nd edn. London: Macmillan and Co., 1895.
Freud, Sigmund. 'Five Lectures on Psycho-Analysis' (1910). In Sigmund Freud *The Standard Edition of the Complete Psychological Works of Sigmund Freud*, edited and trans. James Strachey in collaboration with Anna Freud, assisted by Alix Strachey and Alan Tyson, 24 volumes, XI, 3–55, (1957). London: The Hogarth Press, 1953–1974.
Furnham, Adrian. 'Belief in a Just World: Research Progress over the Past Decade'. *Personality and Individual Differences* 34 (2003): 795–817.
Garner, Richard. *Beyond Morality*. Philadelphia: Temple University Press, 1993.
Garner, Richard. 'Abolishing Morality'. In *A World Without Values: Essays on John Mackie's Moral Error Theory*, edited by Richard Joyce and Simon Kirchin, 217–33. Dordrecht: Springer, 2010.
Garner, Richard. 'A Plea for Moral Abolitionism'. In *The End of Morality: Taking Moral Abolitionism Seriously*, edited by Richard Garner and Richard Joyce, 77–93. New York: Routledge, 2019.
Gaut, Berys. 'The Ethical Criticism of Art'. In *Aesthetics and Ethics: Essays at the Intersection*, edited by Jerrold Levinson, 182–203. Cambridge: Cambridge University Press, 1988.
Gaut, Berys. *Art, Emotion and Ethics*. Oxford: Oxford University Press, 2007.
Geach, Peter. 'Assertion'. *Philosophical Review* 74 (1965): 449–65.
Gibbard, Allan. *Wise Choices, Apt Feelings*. Oxford: Clarendon Press, 1990.
Gibbard, Allan. *Thinking How to Live*. Cambridge, MA: Harvard University Press, 2003.
Gilbert, W. S. and Arthur Sullivan. 'The Pirates of Penzance' (1879). In W. S. Gilbert and Arthur Sullivan *The Complete Annotated Gilbert and Sullivan*, edited by Ian, Bradley, 193–263. Oxford: Oxford University Press, 1996.
Gilligan, Carol. *In a Different Voice: Psychological Theory and Women's Development*. Cambridge, MA: Harvard University Press, 1982.
Glassen, Peter. 'The Cognitivity of Moral Judgments'. *Mind*, 68 (1959): 57–72.
Green, Thomas Hill. *Prolegomena to Ethics* (1883), edited by A. C. Bradley, 3rd edn. Oxford: Clarendon Press, 1890.
Greene, Joshua and Jonathan Haidt. 'How (and Where) Does Moral Judgment Work?' *Trends in Cognitive Sciences* 6 (2002): 517–23.
Greene, Joshua D., Fiery A. Cushman, Lisa E. Stewart, Kelly Lowenberg, Leigh E. Nystrom, and Jonathan D. Cohen. 'Pushing Moral Buttons: The Interaction between Personal Force and Intention in Moral Judgment'. *Cognition* 111 (2009): 364–71.
Grotius, Hugo. *The Rights of War and Peace* (1625), edited by Richard Tuck, three volumes. Indianapolis: Liberty Fund, 2005.

Haidt, Jonathan. 'The Emotional Dog and Its Rational Tail'. *Psychological Review* 108 (2001): 814–34.
Haidt, Jonathan, and Selin Kesebir. 'Morality'. In *Handbook of Social Psychology*, edited by Susan T. Fiske, Daniel T. Gilbert, and Gardner Lidzey, 5th edn, two volumes, II, 797–832. Hobeken: John Wiley & Sons, 2010.
Harman, Gilbert. *The Nature of Morality: An Introduction to Ethics*. Oxford: Oxford University Press, 1977.
Harris, Sam. *The Moral Landscape: How Science Can Determine Human Values*. New York: Free Press, 2010.
Hartley, David. *Observations on Man, His Frame, His Duty, And His Expectations*, two volumes. London: Printed for James Leake and Wm. Frederick, 1749.
Hauser, Marc, Fiery Cushman, Liane Young, R. Kang-Xing, and John Mikhail. 'A Dissociation Between Moral Judgments and Justifications'. *Mind & Language* 22 (2007): 1–21.
Hauskeller, Michael. 'Moral Disgust'. *Ethical Perspectives: Journal of the European Ethics Network* 13 (2006): 571–602.
Hegel, Georg Wilhelm Friedrich. *The Phenomenology of Spirit* (1807), trans. and edited by Terry Pinkard. Cambridge: Cambridge University Press, 2018.
Herodotus *The Histories*, trans. Robin Waterfield. Oxford: Oxford University Press, 1998.
Hobbes, Thomas. *Leviathan* (1651), edited by Richard Tuck. Cambridge: Cambridge University Press, 1996.
Horgan, Terry and Mark Timmons. 'Nondescriptivist Cognitivism: Framework for a New Metaethic'. *Philosophical Papers* 29 (2000): 121–53.
Horgan, Terry and Mark Timmons. 'Cognitivist Expressivism'. In *Metaethics After Moore*, edited by Terry Horgan and Mark Timmons, 255–98. Oxford: Clarendon Press, 2006.
Horgan, Terry and Mark Timmons. 'Morality Without Moral Facts'. In *Contemporary Debates in Moral Theory*, edited by James Dreier, 220–38. Oxford: Blackwell, 2006.
Huemer, Michael. *Ethical Intuitionism*. Basingstoke: Palgrave Macmillan, 2005.
Huemer, Michael. 'Singer's Unstable Meta-Ethics'. In *Peter Singer Under Fire: The Moral Iconoclast Faces His Critics*, edited by Jeffrey A. Schaler, 359–79. Chicago: Open Court, 2009.
Hume, David. *A Treatise of Human Nature* (1739), edited by David Fate Norton and Mary J. Norton, two volumes. Oxford: Clarendon Press, 2007.
Hume, David. *Enquiries Concerning Human Understanding and Concerning the Principles of Morals* (1748, 1751), edited by L. A. Selby-Bigge, 3rd edn revised by P. H. Nidditch. Oxford: Clarendon Press, 1975.
Hume, David. 'Dialogues Concerning Natural Religion' (1779). In David Hume *Dialogues Concerning Natural Religion and Other Writings*, edited by Dorothy Coleman, 1–102. Cambridge: Cambridge University Press, 2007.
Hursthouse, Rosalind. *On Virtue Ethics*. Oxford: Oxford University Press, 1999.
Hutcheson, Francis. *An Inquiry into the Original of Our Ideas of Beauty and Virtue in Two Treatises* (1725/1726), edited by Wolfgang Leidhold. Indianapolis, 2004.
Hutcheson, Francis. *An Essay on the Nature and Conduct of the Passions and Affections, with Illustrations on the Moral Sense* (1728), edited by Aaron Garrett. Indianapolis: Liberty Fund, 2002.
Huxley, Thomas H. *Evolution & Ethics and Other Essays*. London: Macmillan and Co., 1894.
James, William. *The Principles of Psychology*, two volumes. New York: Henry Holt and Company, 1890.

Jensen, Henning. 'Morality and Luck' (1984). In *Moral Luck*, edited by Daniel Statman, 131–40. New York: State University of New York Press, 1993.

Jokic, Aleksandar. 'Supererogation and Moral Luck: Two Problems for Kant, One Solution'. *The Journal of Value Inquiry* 36 (2002): 221–33.

Joyce, Richard. *The Myth of Morality*. Cambridge: Cambridge University Press, 2001.

Joyce, Richard. 'Ethics After Darwin'. In *The Cambridge Encyclopedia of Darwin and Evolutionary Thought*, edited by Michael Ruse, 461–7. Cambridge: Cambridge University Press, 2013.

Kalderon, Mark Eli. *Moral Fictionalism*. Oxford: Clarendon Press, 2005.

Kames, Lord, Henry Home *Sketches of the History of Man, Considerably Enlarged by the Last Additions and Corrections of the Author* (1788), edited by James A. Harris, three volumes. Indianapolis: Liberty Fund, 2007.

Kant, Immanuel. *Critique of Pure Reason* (1781/1787), trans. and edited by Paul Guyer and Allen W. Wood. Cambridge: Cambridge University Press, 1998.

Kant, Immanuel. *Groundwork of the Metaphysics of Morals* (1785), trans. and edited by Mary Gregor. Cambridge: Cambridge University Press, 1998.

Kant, Immanuel. 'What Does It Mean to Orient Oneself in Thinking?' (1786). In Immanuel Kant *Religion and Rational Theology*, trans. and edited by Allen W. Wood and George Di Giovanni, 1–18. Cambridge: Cambridge University Press, 1996.

Kant, Immanuel. 'Critique of Practical Reason' (1788). In Immanuel Kant *Practical Philosophy*, trans. and edited by Mary J. Gregor, 133–271. Cambridge: Cambridge University Press, 1996.

Kant, Immanuel. *Critique of the Power of Judgement* (1790), edited by Paul Guyer, trans. Paul Guyer and Eric Matthews. Cambridge: Cambridge University Press, 2000.

Kant, Immanuel. 'Religion within the Boundaries of Mere Reason' (1793). In Immanuel Kant *Religion and Rational Theology*, trans. and edited by Allen W. Wood and George Di Giovanni, 39–215. Cambridge: Cambridge University Press, 1996.

Kass, Leon R. 'The Wisdom of Repugnance'. *The New Republic*, 2 June 1997, 17–26.

Keller, Simon. *The Limits of Loyalty*. Cambridge: Cambridge University Press, 2007.

Kelly, Daniel. *Yuck! The Nature and Moral Significance of Disgust*. Cambridge, MA: The MIT Press, 2011.

Kimball, John C. *The Ethics of Evolution, A Lecture given before The Cambridge Conferences and The Brooklyn Ethical Association*. New York: Chas. M. Higgins & Co., 1902.

King, Adele. *Camus*. London: Haus Publishing, 2010.

Kirwan, James. *Literature, Rhetoric, Metaphysics: Literary Theory and Literary Aesthetics*. London: Routledge, 1990.

Kirwan, James. *Beauty*. Manchester: Manchester University Press, 1999.

Kirwan, James. *The Aesthetic in Kant*. London: Continuum, 2004.

Kirwan, James. *Sublimity: The Non-rational and the Irrational in the History of Aesthetics*. London: Routledge, 2005.

Kirwan, James. 'The Unconscious Grounds of Aesthetic Experience'. *Journal of Aesthetics and Phenomenology* 6 (2019): 153–66.

Kirwan, Richard. *Metaphysical Essays: Containing the Principles and Fundamental Objects of that Science, 'Volume 1'*. London: Printed for Payne and Mackinlay, 1809.

Knobe, Joshua. 'Theory of Mind and Moral Cognition: Exploring the Connections'. *Trends in Cognitive Sciences* 9 (2005): 357–9.

Kohlberg, Lawrence. 'The Development of Children's Orientations Towards a Moral Order: I. Sequence in the Development of Moral Thought'. *Vita Humana* 6 (1963): 11–33.

Kolnai, Aurel. *On Disgust* (1929), edited by Barry Smith and Carolyn Korsmeyer. Chicago: Open Court, 2004.
Kropotkin, P. *Mutual Aid: A Factor of Evolution* (1902), revised edn. London: William Heinemann, 1904.
Kropotkin, P. *Ethics: Origin and Development* (1922), trans. Louis S. Friedland and Joseph R. Piroshnikoff. New York: The Dial Press, 1924.
Ladd, John. 'Loyalty' (1967). In *Encyclopedia of Philosophy*, edited by Donald M. Borchert, nine volumes, V, 595–6. Detroit: Thomson Gale, 2006.
Landy, Justin F. and Edward B. Royzman. 'The Moral Myopia Model: Why and How Reasoning Matters in Moral Judgment'. In *The New Reflectionism in Cognitive Psychology*, edited by Gordon Pennycook, 70–92. New York: Routledge, 2018.
Laurie, Simon S. *On the Philosophy of Ethics: An Analytical Essay*. Edinburgh: Edmonston and Douglas, 1866.
Lerner, Melvin J. *The Belief in a Just World: A Fundamental Delusion*. New York: Springer, 1980.
Lerner, Melvin J. and Leo Montada. 'An Overview: Advances in Belief in a Just World Theory and Methods'. In *Responses to Victimizations and Belief in a Just World*, edited by Leo Montada and Melvin J. Lerner, 1–7. New York: Springer, 1998.
Lerner, Melvin J. and C.H. Simmons. 'The Observer's Reaction to the "innocent victim": Compassion or Rejection?'. *Journal of Personality and Social Psychology* 4 (1966): 203–10.
Lotze, Hermann. *Outlines of Psychology* (1881), trans. and edited by George T. Ladd. Boston: Ginn & Company, 1886.
Lotze, Hermann. *Outlines of Practical Philosophy* (1884), trans. and edited by George T. Ladd. Boston: Ginn & Company, 1885.
Luck, Morgan. 'The Gamer's Dilemma: An Analysis of the Arguments for the Moral Distinction Between Virtual Murder and Virtual Paedophilia'. *Ethics and Information Technology* 11 (2009): 31–6.
Mackie, J. L. *Ethics: Inventing Right and Wrong* (1977). Harmondsworth: Penguin, 1991.
MacKinnon, Catharine. *Feminism Unmodified: Discourses on Life and Law*. Cambridge, MA: Harvard University Press, 1987.
Maistre, Joseph de. *Considerations on France* (1797), trans. Richard A. Lebrun. Cambridge: Cambridge University Press, 1994.
McCosh, James. *The Intuitions of the Mind Inductively Investigated*. London: John Murray, 1860.
McDowell, John. 'Values and Secondary Qualities' (1985). In John McDowell *Mind, Value, and Reality*, 131–50. Cambridge, MA: Harvard University Press, 1998.
McDowell, John. 'Projection and Truth in Ethics' (1987). In John McDowell *Mind, Value, and Reality*, 151–66. Cambridge, MA: Harvard University Press, 1998.
McGinn, Colin. *The Meaning of Disgust*. Oxford: Oxford University Press, 2011.
Menninghaus, Winfried. *Disgust: The Theory and History of a Strong Sensation* (1999), trans. Howard Eiland and Joel Golb. Albany: State University of New York Press, 2003.
Mill, John Stuart. 'Whewell on Moral Philosophy' (1852). In John Stuart Mill *Essays on Ethics, Religion and Society*, edited by J. M. Robson, 165–201. London: Routledge & Kegan Paul, 1969.
Mill, John Stuart. *Utilitarianism*. London: Parker, Son, and Bourn, 1863.
Mill, John Stuart. 'Nature'. In John Stuart Mill *Three Essays on Religion*, 3–65. London: Longmans, Green, Reader, and Dyer, 1874.

Miller, William Ian. *The Anatomy of Disgust*. Cambridge, MA: Harvard University Press, 1997.
Moore, Michael S. 'Moral Reality Revisited'. *Michigan Law Review* 90 (1992): 2424–533.
Nagel, Thomas. 'Moral Luck' (1976). In Thomas Nagel *Mortal Questions*, 24–38. Cambridge: Cambridge University Press, 1979.
Nietzsche, Friedrich. *The Gay Science: With a Prelude in German Rhymes and an Appendix of Songs* (1882/1887), edited by Bernard Williams, trans. Josefine Nauckhoff and Adrian Del Caro. Cambridge: Cambridge University Press, 2001.
Nowell-Smith, P. H. *Ethics*. Harmondsworth: Penguin, 1954.
Nucci, Larry P. *Education in the Moral Domain*. Cambridge: Cambridge University Press, 2001.
Nussbaum, Martha. *Upheavals of Thought: The Intelligence of Emotions*. Cambridge: Cambridge University Press, 2001.
Nussbaum, Martha. *Hiding from Humanity: Disgust, Shame, and the Law*. Princeton: Princeton University Press, 2004.
Ord, Toby. 'Global Poverty and the Demands of Morality'. In *God, the Good, and Utilitarianism: Perspectives on Peter Singer*, edited by John Perry, 177–91. Cambridge: Cambridge University Press, 2014.
Pereboom, Derk. *Living Without Free Will*. Cambridge: Cambridge University Press, 2001.
Piaget, Jean. *The Moral Judgement of the Child* (1932), trans. Marjorie Gabain. London: Kegan Paul, Trench, Trubner & Co., 1932.
Plato *Theatetus*, trans. Robin A. H. Waterfield. Harmondsworth: Penguin, 2004.
Price, Richard. *A Review of the Principal Questions and Difficulties in Morals* (1758), 2nd edn. London: Printed for T. Cadell, 1769.
Price, Richard. *A Discourse on the Love of Our Country*. London: Printed for T. Cadell, 1790.
Prinz, Jesse J. *The Emotional Construction of Morals*. Oxford: Oxford University Press, 2007.
Proudfoot, Michael. and A. R. Lacey. *The Routledge Dictionary of Philosophy*. London: Routledge, 2010.
Putnam, Hilary. *The Collapse of the Fact Value Dichotomy and Other Essays*. Cambridge, MA: Harvard University Press, 2004.
Railton, Peter. 'Alienation, Consequentialism, and the Demands of Morality'. *Philosophy and Public Affairs* 13 (1984): 134–71.
Railton, Peter. 'Moral Realism' (1986). In Peter Railton *Facts, Values, and Norms: Essays toward a Morality of Consequence*, 3–42. Cambridge: Cambridge University Press, 2003.
Ramsay, George. *An Enquiry Into the Principles of Human Happiness and Human Duty*. London: William Pickering, 1843.
Reid, Thomas. *Essays on the Active Powers of Man* (1788), edited by Knud Haakonssen and James A. Harris. Edinburgh: Edinburgh University Press, 2010.
Rescher, Nicholas. 'Luck' (1990). In *Moral Luck*, edited by Daniel Statman, 141–66. New York: State University of New York Press, 1993.
Ribot, Théodule-Armand. *The Psychology of the Emotions* (1896). London: The Walter Scott Publishing Co., 1897.
Richards, Norvin. 'Luck and Desert' (1986). In *Moral Luck*, edited by Daniel Statman, 167–80. New York: State University of New York Press, 1993
Richards, Robert J. 'A Defense of Evolutionary Ethics'. In *Biology and Philosophy* 1 (1986): 265–93.

Richardson, M. E. J. ed. *Hammurabi's Laws: Text, Translation and Glossary*. London: T & T Clark International, 2005.
Roeser, Sabine. *Moral Emotions and Intuitions*. New York: Palgrave Macmillan, 2011.
Rorty, Richard. 'Justice as a Larger Loyalty' (1997). In Richard Rorty *Philosophy as Cultural Politics: Philosophical Papers, Volume 4*, 42–55. Cambridge: Cambridge University Press, 2007.
Ross, W. D. *The Right and the Good* (1930), edited by Philip Stratton-Lake. Oxford: Clarendon Press, 2002.
Ross, W. David. *Foundations of Ethics: The Gifford Lectures Delivered in the University of Aberdeen, 1935–6*. Oxford: Clarendon Press, 1939.
Rousseau, Jean-Jacques. 'The Second Discourse: Discourse on the Origin and Foundations of Inequality Among Mankind' (1753). In Jean-Jacques Rousseau *The Social Contract and The First and Second Discourses*, edited by Susan Dunn, 69–148. New Haven: Yale University Press, 2002.
Royce, Josiah. *The Philosophy of Loyalty*. New York: The Macmillan Company, 1908.
Royzman, Edward, and Rahul Kumar. 'Is Consequential Luck Morally Inconsequential? Empirical Psychology and the Reassessment of Moral Luck'. *Ratio* 17 (2004): 329–44.
Rozin, Paul, Laura Lowery, Sumio Imada, and Jonathan Haidt. 'The CAD Triad Hypothesis: A Mapping Between Three Moral Emotions (Contempt, Anger, Disgust) and Three Moral Codes (Community, Autonomy, Divinity)'. *Journal of Personality and Social Psychology* 76 (1999): 574–86.
Ruse, Michael. *The Darwinian Paradigm: Essays on Its History, Philosophy, and Religious Implications*. London: Routledge, 1989.
Russell, Bertrand. *Religion and Science*. London: Thornton Butterworth, 1935.
Russell, Bertrand. 'Note on Philosophy'. *Philosophy* 35 (1960): 146–7.
Sartre, Jean-Paul. *Existentialism and Humanism* (1946), trans. Philip Mairet. London: Methuen & Co., 1948.
Schellekens, Elisabeth. *Aesthetics and Morality*. London: Continuum, 2007.
Schmidtz, David. *Elements of Justice*. Cambridge: Cambridge University Press, 2006.
Schopenhauer, Arthur. 'On the Freedom of the Will' (1839). In Arthur Schopenhauer *The Two Fundamental Problems of Ethics* (1841), trans. and edited by Christopher Janaway, 31–112. Cambridge: Cambridge University Press, 2009.
Schopenhauer, Arthur. *The World as Will and Representation* (1819–44), trans. E. F. J. Payne, two volumes. New York: Dover, 1969.
Seneca 'On Anger'. In Seneca *Moral and Political Essays*, edited and trans. John M. Cooper and J. F. Procopé, 1–116. Cambridge: Cambridge University Press, 1995.
Shafer-Landau, Russ. *Moral Realism: A Defence*. Oxford: Clarendon Press, 2003.
Shaftesbury, Anthony Ashley Cooper. Third Earl of *Characteristics of Men, Manners, Opinions, Times* (1711/1714), edited by Lawrence E. Klein. Cambridge: Cambridge University Press, 2000.
Sharp, Frank Chapman. *Ethics*. New York: The Century Co., 1928.
Sidgwick, Henry. *The Methods of Ethics* (1874), 7th edn. London: Macmillan & Co., 1907.
Singer, Peter. 'Famine, Affluence, and Morality' (1972). In Peter Singer *Famine, Affluence, and Morality*, 1–32. Oxford: Oxford University Press, 2015.
Singer, Peter. 'The Singer Solution to World Poverty' (2006). In Peter Singer *Famine, Affluence, and Morality*, 33–49. Oxford: Oxford University Press, 2015.
Singer, Peter. 'Morality, Reason, and the Rights of Animals'. In *Primates and Philosophers: How Morality Evolved*, edited by Frans De Waal, Stephen Macedo and Josiah Ober. 140–58. Princeton: Princeton University Press, 2006.

Singer, Peter. 'Reply to Michael Huemer'. In *Peter Singer Under Fire: The Moral Iconoclast Faces His Critics*, edited by Jeffrey A. Schaler, 380-94. Chicago: Open Court, 2009.
Singer, Peter. *The Expanding Circle: Ethics, Evolution, and Moral Progress* (1981). Princeton: Princeton University Press, 2011.
Slote, Michael. *From Morality to Virtue*. Oxford: Oxford University Press, 1995.
Slote, Michael. *The Ethics of Care and Empathy*. London: Routledge, 2007.
Slote, Michael. *Moral Sentimentalism*. Oxford: Oxford University Press, 2010.
Smith, Adam. *The Theory of Moral Sentiments* (1759/1790), edited by Knud Haakonssen. Cambridge: Cambridge University Press, 2004.
Smith, Michael. *The Moral Problem*. Oxford: Blackwell, 1994.
Solomon, Robert C. *The Passions*. New York: Doubleday, 1976.
South, Robert. *Twelve Sermons Preached Upon Several Occasions*, two volumes (1692-1694). London: Printed for Jonah Bowyer, 1727.
Spencer, Herbert. *The Principles of Ethics* (1879-1892), two volumes. New York: D. Appleton and Company, 1897.
Spinoza, Benedictus de 'Ethics' (1677). In Benedictus de Spinoza *The Collected Works of Spinoza*, edited and trans. Edwin Curley, I, 408-617. Princeton: Princeton University Press, 1985-2016.
Stanley, Hiram M. *Studies in the Evolutionary Psychology of Feeling*. London: Swan Sonnenschein & Co., 1895.
Statman, Daniel. 'Moral Luck'. In *Routledge Encyclopedia of Philosophy*, edited by Edward Craig, 10 volumes, VI, 520-2. London: Routledge, 1998.
Stephen, Leslie. *The Science of Ethics*. New York: G. P. Putnam's Sons, 1882.
Stevenson, Charles Leslie. 'The Emotive Meaning of Ethical Terms'. *Mind* 46 (1937): 14-31.
Stevenson, Charles L. *Ethics and Language*. New Haven: Yale University Press, 1944.
Stewart, Dugald. *The Philosophy of the Active and Moral Powers of Man*, two volumes. Edinburgh: Printed for Adam Black, 1828.
Stratton-Lake, Philip. 'Introduction'. In *Ethical Intuitionism: Re-evaluations*, edited by Philip Stratton-Lake, 1-28. Oxford: Clarendon Press, 2002.
Sverdlik, Steven. 'Crime and Moral Luck' (1988). In *Moral Luck*, edited by Daniel Statman, 181-94. New York: State University of New York Press, 1993.
Tertullian 'Spectacles'. In Tertullian *Christian and Pagan in the Roman Empire: The Witness of Tertullian*, edited by Robert D. Sider, 80-106. Washington: The Catholic University of America Press, 2001.
Thomson, Judith Jarvis. 'Killing, Letting Die, and the Trolley Problem'. *The Monist* 59 (1976): 204-17.
Thomson, Judith Jarvis. 'The Trolley Problem'. *Yale Law Journal* 94 (1985): 1395-415.
Thomson, Judith Jarvis. 'Morality and Bad Luck' (1989). In *Moral Luck*, edited by Daniel Statman, 195-215. New York: State University of New York Press,1993.
Timmons, Mark. *Morality without Foundations: A Defense of Ethical Contextualism*. Oxford: Oxford University Press, 1999.
Vaihinger, H. *The Philosophy of 'As if': A System of the Theoretical, Practical and Religious Fictions of Mankind* (1911), trans. C. K. Ogden, 2nd edn. London: Kegan Paul, Trench, Trubner & Co., 1935.
Van Der Keilen, Marguerite, and Rashmi Garg. 'Moral Realism in Adults' Judgment of Responsibility'. *The Journal of Psychology* 128 (1994): 149-56.
VandenBos, Gary R. ed. *A.P.A. Dictionary of Psychology* (2007), 2nd edn. Washington: American Psychological Association, 2015.

Walster, Elaine. 'The Assignment of Responsibility for an Accident'. *Journal of Personality and Social Psychology* 3 (1966): 73–9.
Westermarck, Edward. *The Origin and Development of the Moral Ideas* (1906), two volumes. London: Macmillan and Co., 1924.
Westermarck, Edward. *Ethical Relativity*. London: Kegan Paul, Trench, Trubner & Co., 1932.
Whewell, William. *The Element of Morality, Including Polity*, two volumes. London: John W. Parker, 1845.
Wiggins, David. 'A Sensible Subjectivism?' (1987). In David Wiggins, *Needs, Values, Truth: Essays in the Philosophy of Value*, 3rd edn, 185–214. Oxford: Clarendon Press, 2002.
Wiggins, David. *Ethics: Twelve Lectures on the Philosophy of Morality*. Harmondsworth: Penguin, 2006.
Williams, Bernard. 'A Critique of Utilitarianism'. In *Utilitarianism: For and Against*, edited by J. J. C. Smart and Bernard Williams, 75–150. Cambridge: Cambridge University Press, 1973.
Williams, Bernard. 'Moral Luck' (1976). In Bernard Williams, *Moral Luck: Philosophical Papers 1973–1980*, 20–39. Cambridge: Cambridge University Press, 1981.
Williams, Bernard. 'Conflicts of Values' (1979). In Bernard Williams, *Moral Luck: Philosophical Papers 1973–1980*, 71–82. Cambridge: Cambridge University Press, 1981.
Williams, Bernard. 'Postscript'. In *Moral Luck*, edited by Daniel Statman, 251–8. New York: State University of New York Press, 1993.
Wilson, Edward O. *On Human Nature*. Cambridge, MA: Harvard University Press, 1978.
Wittgenstein, Ludwig. 'Lecture on Ethics'. *Philosophical Review* 74 (1965): 3–12.
Young, Liane, Shaun Nichols, and Rebecca Saxe. 'Investigating the Neural and Cognitive Basis of Moral Luck: It's Not What You Do But What You Know'. *Review of Philosophy and Psychology* 1 (2010): 333–49.

Index

abolitionism   48–9
aesthetic   200, 218 n.75, 232 n.1, 238 n.9, 243 n.63, 252 n.18
Alexander, Richard D.   216 n.63
Andre, Judith   245 n.23
anger   167–71, 190–1, 192–3
Anscombe, G. E. M.   220 n.91
Aquinas   243 n.1
argument, *see* debate
Audi, Robert   210 n.28
Augustine   243 n.1, 248 n.82
Axelrod, Robert   216 n.63
Ayer, A. J.   37–8, 41, 221 n.98

Bacon, Francis   251 n.7
Bailey, Samuel   209 n.25
Bain, Alexander   209 n.25
Baldwin, James Mark   209 n.25
Balguy, John   208 n.16, 219 n.79
Barceló Aspeitia, Axel Arturo   245 n.21
Barnes, W. H. F.   36–7, 38
Baron, J.   243 n.2
Batson, C. Daniel   81, 231 n.226, 232 n.229
Beccaria, Cesare   232 n.5
Beiser, Frederick C.   213 n.50
belief, moral   11–12, 197–8, 223 n.45
Bell, Macalester   248 n.81
Bentham, Jeremy   240 n.19
Björklund, Fredrik   236 n.100
Blackburn, Simon   68–76, 82–4, 229 n.176, 229 n.181, 230 n.189, 230 n.192
Blackstone, William   236 n.90
Boonin, David   238 n.121
Brandt, Richard B.   108–10, 117
Brogaard, Berit   245 n.21
Brown, Thomas   209 n.25
Bryant, Sophie   242 n.57
Butler, Joseph   208 n.25

Camus, Albert   139–40, 142, 144, 241 n.46, 241 n.48, 247 n.63
Carlile, William W.   216 n.65
Carnap, Rudolf   222 n.25
chastity   162–7, 247 n.60, 247 n.67
Chateaubriand, [François-René] Viscount de   113, 213 n.47
Chesterton, G. K.   248 n.74
Cicero   244 n.5
Clodd, Edward   215 n.63
Cogan, Thomas   209 n.25
Cohen, Jonathan D.   111–12
colour   62, 77
comical   60–2, 226 n.92, 226 n.100
Concepcion, David W.   245 n.21
Confucius   242 n.49, 243 n.62
Conrad, Joseph   174
consensus   19, 62–4, 66–7, 208 n.18, 226 n.110
consequentialist admiration   141–2, 162–71
consequentialist blame   150–62, 165–71, 191, 243 n.2
Corvino, John   249 n.102
Cudworth, Ralph   208 n.16, 251 n.8
Culverwell, Nathaniel   208 n.25
Cushman, Fiery   111–12, 115–16, 235 n.82, 237 n.105

D'Arms, Justin   230 n.190
Darwall, Stephen   230 n.192
Darwin, Charles   214 n.61, 216 n.65, 217 n.67, 218 n.72
debate   14–17, 19, 23–4, 63–4, 66–8, 194, 204–5, 220 n.96, 228 n.154, 252 n.22
Dent, Nicholas   240 n.23
DePaul, Michael R.   210 n.28
desire   10–11, 87–8, 125, 168–9, 188, 190, 195–201, 232 n.9
development, moral   250 n.6
Devereaux, Mary   127–9
De Waal, Frans   140

Dewey, John   209 n.25, 215 n.63
Diderot, Denis   112
disgust   60–1, 129, 131, 172–82, 191–2, 226 n.92, 249 n.100

Ellwood, Charles A.   214 n.62
emotion   7, 20, 36–8, 56–9, 87, 118–20, 170–1, 185, 186–7, 192–3, 208 n.25, 209 n.26, 219 n.82, 225 n.74, 225 n.82, *see also* anger; desire; fear
empathy   32, 76–82, 231 n.226, 232 n.229
Enoch, David   245 n.21
Evans, E. P.   152
evil   130–1
evolution   30–5, 214 n.62, 215 n.63, 216 n.65, 217 n.68, 217 nn.70–1, 218 n.73, 232 n.2

fantasy   127–9, 239 n.11, 239 n.13
fear   147, 176, 188–9, 192, 196
Feinberg, Joel   181
Ferri, Enrico   215 n.63
fictionalism   41–51, 67, 73, 141, 186
Firth, Roderick   214 n.58
Fitzgerald, Edward   204
Fletcher, George P.   137–40, 142–3, 241 n.38, 241 n.46, 242 n.52
Foot, Philippa   104–5, 110–11, 117, 118, 237 n.106
Fowler, Thomas   209 n.25
free will   198–201, 251 n.14
Freud, Sigmund   252 n.19
Furnham, Adrian   246 n.40

Garg, R.   243 n.2
Garner, Richard   48–9
Gaut, Berys   126–9, 147
Geach, Peter   221 n.99, 222 n.26
Gibbard, Allan   64–8, 76, 82, 83, 216 n.63, 218 n.73, 228 n.137, 228 n.139, 228 n.141
Gilbert, W. S.   8
Gilligan, Carol   241 n.45
Glassen, Peter   222 n.26
Green, Thomas Hill   242 n.60
Greene, Graham   104–5
Greene, Joshua D.   111–12, 117, 118
Grotius, Hugo   213 n.44

Haidt, Jonathan   118, 232 n.229, 236 n.100, 243 n.111, 248 n.81
happiness   92–6, 233 n.11, 233 n.34, 240 n.19
harm   89–92, 121–2, 167–8, 178–9, 192, 193, 195–6, 198–9, 205
Harman, Gilbert   225 n.63
Harris, Sam   214 n.60
Hartley, David   217 n.67
Hauser, Marc   115–16, 235 n.82, 237 n.105
Hauskeller, Michael   249 n.100
Hegel, Georg Wilhelm Friedrich   238 n.120, 242 n.54
Herodotus   244 n.7
Hershey, J. C.   243 n.2
Hobbes, Thomas   20, 208 n.25
Hopkins, Gerard Manley   245 n.34
Horgan, Terry   223 n.45
Huemer, Michael   23, 118, 122, 211 n.30, 211 nn.33–4, 211 n.37, 212 n.38, 212 n.40, 237 n.116
Hume, David   9, 20, 28, 35–6, 70, 134, 163–4, 167, 200, 207 n.2, 208 n.25, 212 n.40, 219 n.77, 219 n.79, 228 n.143, 252 n.18
Hursthouse, Rosalind   239 n.15
Hutcheson, Francis   20, 90, 208 n.25, 219 n.79, 250 n.4
Huxley, Thomas H.   214 n.62, 215 n.63, 218 n.73
hypocrisy   126, 174

ideology   128–9, 247 n.68
Imada Sumio   248 n.81
imagination   126–8, 131, 149, 188–9, 234 n.35, *see also* vividness
intuitionism   20–7, 80, 185–6, 194, 210 n.28, 210 n.30, 211 nn.32–4, 211 n.37, 212 n.38, 212 n.40

Jacobson, Daniel   230 n.190
James, William   209 n.25, 236 n.97
Jensen, Henning   245 n.22
Jokic, Aleksandar   245 n.21
Joyce, Richard   43–4, 46–8, 216 nn.63–4, 217 n.69, 223 n.32
'just-world hypothesis'   161–2, 246 nn.40–1

Kalderon, Mark Eli 41–5, 48, 222 n.30
Kames, Lord, Henry Home 153, 244 n.7
Kang-Xing, R. 235 n.82, 237 n.105
Kant, Immanuel 28, 90, 143, 199,
 213 n.48, 213 n.50, 233 n.22, 242 n.56,
 243 n.1, 250 n.2
Kass, Leon R. 176–8
Keller, Simon 134, 239 n.17, 243 n.62
Kelly, Daniel 177–8
Kesebir, Selin 232 n.229
Kimball, John C. 217 n.68
King, Adele 241 n.46
Kirwan, James 222 n.28, 252 n.18
Kirwan, Richard 210 n.28
Knobe, Joshua 244 n.10
knowledge, *see* belief, moral
Kohlberg, Lawrence 15, 208 n.14
Kolnai, Aurel 176, 248 n.75
Kropotkin, P. 215 n.63, 217 n.68
Kumar, Rahul 245 n.23

Lacey, A. R. 245 n.21
Ladd, John 135–8, 145
Landy, Justin F. 238 n.116
language, moral 39, 41–5, 65–6,
 220 n.91, 222 n.25, 222 n.30, 223 n.32,
 224 n.57, 226 n.96
Laurie, Simon S. 209 n.25
Lerner, Melvin J. 161, 246 nn.40–1
Lotze, Hermann 209 n.25
Lowenberg, Kelly 111–12
Lowery, Laura 248 n.81
loyalty 132–48, 239 n.17,
 240 n.18, 240 n.23, 240 n.28, 241 n.38,
 242 n.49, 242 n.55, 242 n.57, 242 n.60,
 243 nn.61–2
luck, moral 154–62, 244 n.10
Luck, Morgan 239 n.13

McCosh, James 213 n.44
McDowell, John 59–61, 64, 68, 76, 82,
 83, 226 n.93
McGinn, Colin 173–4, 177, 178,
 248 n.82
Mackie, J. L. 39, 41, 48, 213 n.42
MacKinnon, Catharine 239 n.12
Maistre, Joseph de 136–7
Marmor, Andrei 245 n.21
Menninghaus, Winfried 248 n.75
Mikhail, John 235 n.82, 237 n.105

Mill, John Stuart 90, 92, 126–7, 167,
 217 n.67, 232 n.6, 232 n.9, 240 n.19,
 242 n.51, 248 n.71
Miller, William Ian 174
Montada, Leo 161, 246 n.41
Moore, Michael S. 225 n.63
moralism 11–12, 49, 54, 127–8, 142–3,
 234 n.47, *see also* belief, moral
moral judgement 12–18, 30, 39,
 48, 60, 66–8, 120, 170–1, 178, 193, 204–5
moral response, description of 8–12, 185
moral response, explanation of 195–202
Murphy, Scott 236 n.100

Nagel, Thomas 154–6, 157, 238 n.6,
 244 n.11, 251 n.8, 251 n.11
naturalism, ethical 29–35, 214 n.60
Nichols, Shaun 244 n.2, 244 n.10
Nietzsche, Friedrich 248 n.83
non-naturalism, ethical 27–8, 213 nn.43–4,
 213 n.48, 214 n.50, 218 n.74
Nowell-Smith, P. H. 234 n.47
Nucci, Larry P. 229 n.187
Nussbaum, Martha 56–9, 83, 116, 177–8, 179
Nystrom, Leigh E. 111–12

Ord, Toby 236 n.93

Pereboom, Derk 251 n.14
Piaget, Jean 250 n.6
Plato 208 n.19, 244 n.8
Poe, Edgar Allen 172–3
Price, Richard 208 n.16, 240 n.21
Prinz, Jesse J. 51–5, 68, 76, 83,
 224 n.63
projection 35, 53, 55–6, 59–61,
 69–73, 75, 83–4, 194–5, 196–7, 203–4
Proudfoot, Michael 245 n.21
Putnam, Hilary 227 n.112

quasi-realism 68–76

Railton, Peter 29–30, 99–104, 113, 114,
 121, 214 n.60, 234 n.39, 236 n.97
Ramsay, George 209 n.25
realism, moral 18–35, 118, 121, 122,
 185–6, 201, 219 n.79, *see also* debate;
 quasi-realism; reason; trivial realism
reductionism 202–5
Reid, Thomas 208 n.16, 219 n.79

religion   75–6, 198–9, 214 n.51,
   229 n.187, 242 n.52
Rescher, Nicholas   151, 238 n.6, 245 n.21
responsibility, *see* consequentialist
   admiration; consequentialist blaming
Ribot, Théodule-Armand   209 n.25
Richards, Norvin   245 n.33
Richards, Robert J.   215 n.62
Richardson, M. E. J.   244 n.8
Roeser, Sabine   225 n.82
Rorty, Richard   134
Ross, W. David   21, 210 n.28, 211 n.30,
   221 n.98
Rousseau, Jean-Jacques   214 n.61
Royce, Josiah   135–6, 140, 144–5, 146,
   242 n.54
Royzman, Edward   238 n.116, 245 n.23
Rozin, Paul   248 n.81
Ruse, Michael   216 n.64
Russell, Bertrand   37–8, 41, 50, 64, 83–4,
   221 n.97

Sartre, Jean-Paul   199–200, 241 n.46,
   242 n.53
Saxe, Rebecca   244 n.2, 244 n.10
Schellekens, Elisabeth   239 n.9
Schmidtz, David   234 n.50
Schopenhauer, Arthur   239 n.10,
   251 n.11
self-interest   142, 144–5, 150, 163–7,
   193, 195–6, 202–3
Seneca   244 n.8
Shafer-Landau, Russ   11, 210 n.28
Shaftesbury, Anthony Ashley Cooper,
   Third Earl of   20, 208 n.25
Sharp, Frank Chapman   207 n.11,
   214 n.58
Sidgwick, Henry   20, 162–7, 246 n.50
Simmons, C. H.   161, 246 n.40
Singer, Peter   113, 114–15, 118–19,
   215 n.62
Slote, Michael   76–82, 83, 225 n.82,
   230 n.192, 231 n.226, 232 n.229,
   245 n.22, 248 n.71
Smith, Adam   20, 113, 157–60, 208 n.25,
   214 n.58, 248 n.71, 248 n.77, 251 n.15
Smith, Kevin   247 n.64
Smith, Michael   214 n.58
Solomon, Robert C.   225 n.74
South, Robert   238 n.2

Spencer, Herbert   217 n.68, 218 n.73
Spinoza, Benedictus de   251 n.8
Stanley, Hiram M.   209 n.25, 216 n.63
Statman, Daniel   245 n.21
Stephen, Leslie   214 n.62, 216 n.65, 217 n.67
Stevenson, Charles Leslie   37–8, 41,
   220 n.91, 252 n.22
Stewart, Dugald   213 n.44, 217 n.68
Stewart, Lisa E.   111–12
Stratton-Lake, Philip   211 n.32
Sullivan, Arthur   8
Sverdlik, Steven   245 n.21

Tertullian   248 n.73
Thomson, Judith Jarvis   110–11, 118,
   234 n.50, 237 nn.105–6, 245 n.22
Timmons, Mark   223 n.45
tram problem   110–12, 115–18, 139–40,
   235 n.82, 237 nn.105–6
trivial realism   51–84, 88, 118, 149, 186,
   249 n.100
trolley problem, *see* tram problem

unconscious   149, 195–201, 203–4
universality   89–90, 133–4, 239 n.16
utilitarianism   78, 90–112, 122–3, 124,
   178, 187

Vaihinger, H.   251 n.8
Van Der Keilen, M.   243 n.2
vividness   103–4, 112–15, 144–6, 187,
   196, 205, 236 n.96

Walster, Elaine   243 n.2
Westermarck, Edward   36, 216 n.65,
   219 n.82, 220 n.96, 221 n.98, 244 n.11,
   248 n.71
Whewell, William   209 n.25
Wiggins, David   62–4, 66, 68, 76, 82, 83,
   226 nn.95–6, 226 n.100, 226 n.110,
   227 nn.111–12
will   148, 150, 162–3, 198–201, 246 n.50
Williams, Bernard   95–9, 101, 103, 106–8,
   119, 121, 233 n.21, 238 n.119, 244 n.11
Wilson, Edward O.   215 n.62
Wittgenstein, Ludwig   36, 39, 221 n.98,
   222 n.30

Young, Liane   111–12, 115–16, 235 n.82,
   237 n.105, 244 n.2, 244 n.10

www.ingramcontent.com/pod-product-compliance
Lightning Source LLC
Chambersburg PA
CBHW062125300426
44115CB00012BA/1811